Re ing

TERRORISM

A Humanistic Perspective

Re-Visioning

TERRORISM

A Humanistic Perspective

Edited by
Elena Coda and Ben Lawton

Purdue University Press, West Lafayette, Indiana

Cataloging-in-Publication data on file at the Library of Congress.

Paperback ISBN: 9781557537331
ePub ISBN: 9781612494456
ePDF ISBN: 9781612494449

Contents

Acknowledgments

This book consists of revised and expanded papers originally presented at the Re-Visioning Terrorism conference, held at Purdue University in September 2011 and attended by more than eighty scholars from all over the world. The event was funded by an Enhancing Research in the Humanities and the Arts Grant from the Office of the Vice President for Research and the College of Liberal Arts. We would like to thank Purdue University, the College of Liberal Arts, and the School of Languages and Cultures for their support. We are particularly grateful to Adrian Del Caro, former head of the School of Languages and Cultures, for his encouragement and assistance in the early stages of this work, and to the anonymous referees for their careful reading of the manuscript and their valuable comments and suggestions.

1

Re-Visioning Terrorism: The Rack Focus Response

ELENA CODA AND BEN LAWTON

The attacks against the World Trade Center (WTC) Twin Towers and the Pentagon on September 11, 2001, were tragic for their victims and traumatic for our nation. We Americans were sound asleep, comforted by the illusion that we were protected by two unsurmountable oceans when, suddenly, we were awakened by nightmarish visions of airplanes crashing into the Twin Towers over and over again, and then, again and again we watched these symbols of American might seemingly melt and collapse amidst billowing clouds of dust. We watched in horror as people leaped to their deaths; slack-jawed we admired the seemingly suicidal courage of the firefighters and other first responders; and we shared the shock, anguish, and confusion of the people at ground zero. Later we saw the images of the massive breach in the Pentagon and we heard about United Flight 93 and we wondered when and where the next attack would come. It all seemed like an inconceivable nightmare. How could this be happening? Who was attacking us and why? Who was responsible for killing 2,996 people and injuring some 6,000 more?[1] Who was responsible for this incalculable economic disaster, the first major attack against the United States since Pearl Harbor in 1941 and the first attack against the continental United States since the War of 1812?

It quickly became clear that these were terrorist attacks, but that confused us even more. Until that time, terrorism had been something that happened elsewhere, to other people. Now, suddenly, we, the United States, were no longer safe. And so, as the tenth anniversary of what has come to be known as 9/11 drew near,[2] like so many others, we began to reflect on those events, on the nature of terrorism, and on our individual and national response to the phenomenon.

What is terrorism?[3] To paraphrase Supreme Court Justice Potter Stewart on pornography in his opinion in Jacobellis v. Ohio (1964), "We can't define what terrorism is, but we know it when we see it."[4] After 9/11 we all knew what terrorism was. And we all knew what terrorists looked like. Or at least we thought we did. For a decade we watched the footage of the airplanes crashing into New York's Twin Towers and the pictures of Osama bin Laden and his Al Qaeda followers on countless TV shows and in newspapers and magazines. Terrorists, we came to understand, were dark-skinned, bearded "rag-heads," Islamic fundamentalists: irrational, fanatical, cowardly madmen who slaughtered innocent American civilians for absolutely no good reason.[5]

In the days immediately following 9/11, those were the images and concepts that were burned into our mind's eye. And the world seemed to share our feelings. We received messages of solidarity from around the world. The country came almost unanimously together in support of President George W. Bush's "crusade" and his Global War on Terror (GWOT).[6] At first we followed the American campaign against Al Qaeda and the Taliban in Afghanistan with feelings that approached jubilation. We read about and saw photographs of bearded United States Army Special Forces soldiers and Air Force Combat Controllers on horseback calling in air strikes in support of our Afghani allies.[7] The local population seemed to welcome enthusiastically its liberation from the almost inconceivably brutal and repressive Taliban regime. Our intervention, we were told, was not just motivated by a search for justice and retribution—we were liberating Afghan women from a condition of oppression unique, perhaps, in the modern world.[8]

All too soon, however, doubts began to surface. Were the attacks truly unexplainable?[9] Were the terrorists really irrational, cowardly madmen?[10] Did 9/11 really justify a war on terror that knew no geographical boundaries?[11]

Did it lead us to reject the international laws and conventions that had been laboriously constructed over time to bring order and humanity to the chaotic and inhuman nature of war?[12] Did 9/11 really justify jettisoning our civil liberties in the name of security?[13] Those very liberties which we had been told were the motivation for the 9/11 attacks in the first place?[14]

Individuals who expressed reservations openly or who challenged the dominant narratives were pilloried and ostracized.[15] But with the passing of time the stories that trickled out of Afghanistan told of "collateral damage," of innocent civilians killed and maimed "accidentally" in myriad different ways—stray bombs, wrong targets, bad intelligence.[16] And we began to see images that were more reminiscent of Vietnam than of the allegedly good war, World War II, when we were, we are told, welcomed as liberators. The callous brutalization of prisoners—the hoodings, the stress positions, the yelling and striking (perhaps the best known case is that of Dilawar of Yakubi)[17]—was so clearly pandemic that it seemed to be not an aberration, but the result of deliberate policy.[18] The hooding, and the sensory deprivation it implied, appeared to be a form of torture, even without the 1997 conclusion of the United Nations Committee against Torture, reconfirmed in 2004.[19]

And then came the invasion of Iraq, predicated on an ever-evolving set of narratives (find and remove Iraq's weapons of mass destruction, cut Saddam Hussein's links to Al Qaeda, end the regime of Saddam Hussein, deliver humanitarian support to Iraqi civilians, secure the oil fields, help Iraqis establish a representative government) that became increasingly ludicrous as they were debunked, one after the other. And we began to ask ourselves, why were we in Iraq?[20] Some even began to wonder why we had invaded Afghanistan in the first place. We had, we were assured, sent our armed forces into Afghanistan to eliminate Al Qaeda and kill or capture its putative leader, Osama bin Laden. But then, when he managed to slip away from us as a result of the Tora Bora debacle, we were told that he was no longer an important target.[21]

And from Iraq the horror stories multiplied. The images from Abu Ghraib shocked the world, and us,[22] and the so-called collateral damage reached incomprehensible numbers: 100 thousand Iraqi dead? Or perhaps 200 thousand? And hundreds of thousands more maimed or dispersed.[23]

After ten years of the Global War on Terror, what had we accomplished? Osama bin Laden had vanished. Al Qaeda presumably no longer exists as a terrorist organization, but it has metastasized into a worldwide terrorist rhizome. The Weapons of Mass Destruction (WMD) that had so threatened our nation as to justify the preventive invasion of Iraq were nowhere to be found. In fact, arguably, all we accomplished in Iraq was the deposition and execution of Saddam Hussein and the removal of his Ba'ath Party from power; and, of course, the killing of Osama bin Laden on May 2, 2011, an event which is rapidly joining the demolition of the World Trade Center (WTC) in the rank of the most popular conspiracy theories.[24]

By the time the last U.S. soldier left Iraq in 2012, 4,486 American military personnel had died, and tens of thousands had been physically and mentally maimed. When you add the 2,213 service members who died in Afghanistan as of January 6, 2015,[25] the total is well over twice the 2,996 people killed on 9/11. The eventual cost of an invasion that was supposed to pay for itself, in addition to the wars in Afghanistan and Pakistan, was estimated at between $3.7 trillion and $4.4 trillion.[26] As for Iraq, the damage was incalculable. The country was, arguably, in worse condition than it had been under the brutal and tyrannical rule of Saddam Hussein.[27]

What has the Global War on Terror accomplished? We are assured by the NSA and other government organizations that an undefined number of terrorist attacks have been foiled by the increased security measures at home and abroad. Regrettably, there is no way to verify these assertions since information related to these events is classified and so must remain among what former Secretary of Defense Donald Rumsfeld called "unknown unknowns . . . things we don't know we don't know."[28] That being the case, based on available information regarding terrorist events around the world (Rumsfeld's "known knowns . . . things we know we know"), it is fairly safe to say that the GWOT, or Overseas Contingency Operation, as it has come to be known by the Obama administration, is a failure or, at the very best, a stalemate.[29]

This, of course, is not the first occasion on which societal groups (tribes, cities, and states of varied political hues—cities, kingdoms, republics, empires, etc.) have endeavored to eliminate threats by parastate and nonstate actors of various sorts. Among the almost infinite targets for elimination it should suffice to mention:

- pirates (whom the Romans defined as *hostes humani generis*—enemies of the human race and thus beyond the protection of even the most draconian laws), from the Cilician pirates who captured Caesar as a youth and held him for ransom, to the pirates of the Caribbean, to the Barbary coast pirates referenced in the Marine hymn ("From the Halls of Montezuma to the Shores of Tripoli"), to the pirates now operating off the coast of Somalia);
- rebelling slaves (from Spartacus to Nat Turner);
- bandits (from the Indian thugs to Quantrill's raiders to the so-called brigands of Southern Italy);
- political assassins (from the Nizari Ismaili assassins, to the Hebrew Sicarii, to the Lashkar-i-Tayyaba, best known for the 2008 Mumbai terrorist attacks);
- ethnic rebels (from the Hebrew zealots, to the Jewish Haganah and Irgun, to the Palestinian Liberation Organization (PLO) to the Irish Republican Army (IRA) to the Basque Euskadi Ta Askatasuna (ETA) to the Ceylonese Tamil Tigers, to Nelson Mandela and the Umkhonto we Sizwe);
- religious heretics (from the Albigensians, to the Waldensians, to the Huguenots, the Lutherans, to the Sunni and Shia and Alawites and Sufi).

Seen from a different perspective, some might argue that most, if not all of these "outlaws" and "terrorists" were, presumably, fighting for their freedom from political, economic, or religious oppression—in short, defending themselves from state terrorism perpetrated by the following, among many others: The Roman Empire; the Catholic Inquisition; Cromwell, particularly in Ireland; the British Empire; Napoleon, particularly in Spain; the Union during the Civil War, and the Confederacy; King Leopold of Belgium in the Congo Free State; the Russian Czars; Adolph Hitler; Francisco Franco; Lenin; Stalin; Mao; Pol Pot; Israel; Africa—from European colonialism to tribal genocide; Bosnia, Croatia, Serbia; Saddam Hussein; the United States; and so forth.[30]

The victims of these states and leaders were, to use Giorgio Agamben's seminal concepts, almost invariably considered *homo sacer*, that is, essentially beyond the protection of all laws and reduced to a condition of "bare life," as a result of the establishment of a "state of exception."[31]

Given these realities, and starting from the understanding that the terrorist threat was and is real, and that there are individuals and organizations that wish us ill,[32] to put it mildly, the contributors to this volume have attempted to answer the following questions:

- Can terrorism be defined as only the actions of a relatively small group of irrational malcontents against the state?
- Can terrorism describe the deliberate actions taken by a state against individuals and minorities?
- Can actions taken against an enemy foreign state be considered terrorism?
- Can all political violence be classified as terrorism?
- Can one legitimately say that one person's terrorist really is another's freedom fighter?
- What are the objectives of terrorism?
- Who and what are the targets of terrorism?
- Does terrorism have to have a political objective?
- Are terrorists cowards or heroes?
- What motivates terrorists?
- How have societies dealt with terrorism over time?
- How are terrorist events represented in art, literature, theater, and cinema?
- What is the relationship between terrorism and the popular media?
- What is the American perception of terrorism post-9/11?
- How does this perception coincide or differ from that of peoples of other nations and other regions of the world?
- Is it possible to openly question American antiterrorism and counterterrorism post-9/11?
- What has the impact of 9/11 been on American laws and civil liberties?
- Does terrorism work in achieving its objectives?
- Can terrorism ever be ethically or morally justified?
- What should the role of the intellectual be vis-à-vis terrorism?

The attempt to answer the simplest of these questions confronts us with contradictory realities that have tended to be answered only from partisan perspectives. As Joseph Easson and Alex P. Schmid amply illustrate in their list of "250-plus Academic, Governmental and Intergovernmental Definitions of Terrorism" (99–157), there is no international agreement regarding terrorism.[33] Were the perpetrators of 9/11 terrorists or freedom fighters? Can actions that we describe as terrorism be ethically justified? These questions sound outrageous and yet, when he died, Nelson Mandela, who was on the U.S. terrorism watch list until 2008, was almost universally acclaimed and revered for his lifelong battle against apartheid in South Africa.[34]

Obviously, inevitably, every tentative answer we proposed, every attempt to "re-vision terrorism" inspired new questions and further discussion. As noted above, the GWOT has, to say the very least, not been a resounding success because, among other things, the U.S. and its allies have failed to understand what motivates terrorism. Outraged by the attack on our homeland on 9/11, we went searching for Al Qaeda with a baseball bat. Eventually, depending on whom you believe, we may have been able to squash Osama bin Laden and we may have chased Al Qaeda out of Afghanistan. But now new wasps' nests, large and small, have reconstituted around the globe. Do they constitute a serious danger to American civilians? Given that, "in the last five years, the odds of an American being killed in a terrorist attack have been about 1 in 20 million (that's including both domestic attacks and overseas attacks)," it seems hardly likely.[35] And yet, in our determination to exterminate terrorists wherever they may be found, we have created a national security state (NSS) comprised of a "labyrinthine structure of intelligence agencies morphing into war-fighting outfits, [of] the U.S. military (with its own secret military, the special operations forces, gestating inside it), and [of] the Department of Homeland Security, a monster conglomeration of agencies that is an actual 'defense department,' as well as a vast contingent of weapons makers, contractors, and profiteers bolstered by an army of lobbyists, has never stopped growing."[36]

One problem is that we have not identified our enemy's center of gravity.[37] More specifically, as Lorenzo Zambernardi notes in "Counterinsurgency's Impossible Trilemma," we have identified three main goals that cannot be achieved simultaneously: "1) force protection, 2) distinction between enemy combatants and noncombatants, and 3) the physical elimination of insurgents."[38] What may well be an even more fundamental problem in terrorism studies is summarized admirably by Lisa R. Stampnitzky: "'Terrorism' has proved to be a highly problematic concept for expert analysis: analysts have . . . routinely been criticized on both political grounds, with critiques from the left generally focusing on the exclusion of state violence from conceptualizations of terrorism, while critiques from the right have accused experts of 'sympathizing' with their research subjects" (457).[39]

RACK FOCUS RESPONSE

In trying to obviate this problem to the extent possible, we have come to realize that it isn't enough to look at terrorism again, or even with fresh eyes. Re-visioning terrorism requires what we have defined as a "rack focus response" (RFR). "Racking focus refers to the practice of changing the focus of a lens such that an element in one plane of the image goes out of focus and an element at another plane in the image comes into focus" (40). When the focal distance changes, the reality has not changed. Both items or events coexist, but given the nature of optics, we can only see clearly one or the other. This occurs, obviously, not just with lenses, but also with human eyes and with human perceptions, be they emotional or intellectual. A fixed camera lens will only be able to focus on a specific depth of field. What a nearsighted person can see clearly will be vastly different from what a farsighted person can see clearly. The response of a typical American to the events of 9/11 will be vastly different from that of a follower of bin Laden. We see each other reciprocally as "evil" and ourselves as "good." The reality, however, is that in this relationship, good and evil are completely imbricated, as Punya Mishra's ingenious ambigram suggests (Figure 1).

Between these two extremes there are myriad other possible responses, which can only be seen by shifting the focus of our gaze.

The first step in a RFR is a *reaction*. Inevitably, we focus initially only on one depth of field. When the events of 9/11 took place, all we could see was that we had been attacked—unexpectedly, inexplicably, outrageously,

Figure 1. Good Evil Ambigram (Punya Mishra).

unjustifiably, unforgivably. Eventually, as noted above, some people moved to the second step: *reflection*. Reflection requires that we try to focus on the depth of field that is absolutely clear to the "other." We don't necessarily have to arrive at the same conclusions. We certainly don't have to endorse the actions they took predicated on their limited vision of reality. But, if we don't, we will continue to be blindsided. Was the attack completely unexpected? Not really. Was it inexplicable? Clearly not. But these reflections caused individuals, whose ability to focus is limited to a very narrow depth of field, to go into what can only be described as a blind rage.

What would have happened if our national leaders had engaged in a programmatic process of RFR and had proceeded from reaction to reflection? That is, what would have happened if after the first outraged reaction, upon reflection, President Bush had said, "yes, the attacks were outrageous, unjustifiable, and unforgivable, but at the same time, they were not, or should not have been unexpected and inexplicable"? What if he had said, "we must capture and punish the perpetrators of this outrage," but then, rather than declaring the Global War on Terror, he had taken advantage of the worldwide outpouring of empathy for the United States and had proposed a Marshall Plan for Southwest Asia and at least attempted to initiate a dialog? While we have no way of knowing what the result would have been, it could not have been anything near the unmitigated disaster that our policies have been for the past 14 years.

The essays in this volume do not presume to offer a unitary or much less a comprehensive definition of or explanation for terrorism, and even less a solution to the problem. It would be preposterous for us to make such a claim. The field of terrorist studies is enormous and eclectic, when it is not internally contradictory (Schmid, 466–68). In his chapter, "The Literature on Terrorism," Schmid lists 38 examples of "shortcomings and gaps" among which the lack of understanding of the cultures[42] and languages[43] of the terrorists studied is prominent (468–70). Another major division in the field lies between so-called Orthodox Terrorism Studies (OTS) and Critical Terrorism Studies (CTS).[44] Interestingly, while both OTS and CTS[45] consider the somewhat symbiotic relationship between terrorism and the media, neither gives much shrift to the construction of terrorism and terrorists in the movies, even though they do contribute significantly to our mental image of the phenomena.[46]

What we do hope to accomplish by asking the most diverse and occasionally outrageous questions—questions that we felt could best be addressed by scholars in disparate humanistic fields of research—was to begin a discussion that would encourage a more flexible response to one of the more serious problems confronting the world today, one predicated on an RFR *forma mentis*. The papers collected here present recent directions in a wide range of academic fields.

One of the more difficult tasks, in a project that attempts to investigate existing terrorist violence, without the benefit of historical distance, is to find philosophical and theoretical approaches that can help us understand and respond to such acts. The three essays in the first section of this volume attempt to formulate new approaches that, escaping the facile rhetoric of good versus evil that still informs much literature and media, might help our understanding of political violence. Terrorism is not a sociopolitical problem that can be construed only through politicized agendas or ideology, or that can be easily solved through military intervention. As Kenneth Noe eloquently states in his essay (chapter 2), terrorism must be understood first and foremost as a philosophical problem—one that cannot be explained by traditional Platonic or post-Kantian approaches, because in order to find a coherent definition, they reduce it to a set of necessary or sufficient conditions that ignore its intrinsically variable nature. This does not mean that terrorism should be reduced to a meaningless concept just because it escapes any strong definition. The Deleuzian concept of the event, which emphasizes what is "properly *new* in every instance, that is, unprecedented, unpredictable, atypical, anomalous, singular, etc.," and thus "challenge[s] us to think differently and to consider things anew,"[47] might offer a useful approach to articulate the problem of terrorism without falling within preconceived notions. It is only by looking at the differences between instances of terrorism that we will be able to construct a creative response to the problem, one that ultimately will also challenge our ethical beliefs and assumptions.

Baudrillard's conception of symbolic violence becomes a useful notion to unveil the semiotic foundation of terrorism, where "violence becomes the act of the proliferation of the symbol." As Jonathan Beever explains (chapter 3), this is the *virulence* of simulacra, of empty signs, which have subsumed the real under a "mountain of misrepresentation[s]." Thus, our dealing and understanding of terrorism cannot escape this postmodern paradigm in which the image, the empty sign, takes precedence over the real. Following Baudrillard, Beever notes that a terrorist attack is effective only if it is able to enact a symbolic irruption against a given symbol (such as the attack on the Twin Towers). As a consequence, any response to terrorism should recognize the symbolic nature inherent to terrorism and act accordingly "with an appropriately symbolic response," which might prove to be a more effective strategy than traditional military and counterinsurgency actions have proven to be.

Turning to the suicide bomber as an object of philosophical inquiry, Akil, through a careful reading of Agamben notion of *der Muselmann* and *homo sacer*, points out that the suicide bomber, contrary to popular media, lies outside of the contingencies of religion and the promise of sex with 72 virgins (chapter 4). Instead, his or her motivation resides in bearing witness, to be witnessed, and to count as a person. Hatem Akil demonstrates the parallels between the suicide bomber's life as it crosses to death and the figure of the *Muselmann*, the Auschwitz prisoner who, "weeks and months before being snuffed out, . . . had already lost the ability to observe, to remember, to compare and express [himself],"[48] a man "reduced to a staggering corpse, a bundle of physical functions in its last convulsions."[49] Akil notes that both in the *Muselmann* and in the suicide bomber, it is possible to locate a commonality of suffering. Thus, the suicide bomber is viewed as an aberrant symptom of a human condition reduced to "bare life"[50] that is nevertheless an integral part of a network of violence in which the notions of victim and victimizer are violently welded together, and that can only be broken by a relinquishing of the very principle of terrorist violence of all kinds.

If philosophical approaches can shed new light on terrorism and challenge traditional political responses and our habitual perceptions of ethics, and also lead us to reflect on the complex motivations of the suicide bomber, a historical excursus on the development of terrorism from antiquity through the French *terror* allows us to provide a historical context to understand the ways in which concepts such as terror, insurgency, crusades, and freedom fighters have been used throughout the centuries. The second section of the volume examines the use of different linguistic and rhetorical strategies deployed in connection with acts of terror throughout the past, shedding new light on terms that might seem to refer only to our recent history. In so doing, these chapters offer a point of departure for an interdisciplinary and cross-cultural reading of terrorism that can deepen both our interpretation of the present and our understanding of the past. In chapter 5, Timothy Howe proposes a case study of ancient Athens to show how contemporary studies on insurgencies and counterinsurgencies (COIN) can become a useful tool to trace the development of Athenian opposition against Macedonian occupation. By focusing in particular on the ideological and rhetorical context of the early phases of the Athenian insurgency (reverence for the traditional practices of Athens, the ideal of patriotic self-sacrifice, a common religious ideology, the recruitment of youth in paramilitary training and their psychological indoctrination through the construction of common cultural and religious identities), he brings to the fore the similarities between "the ideology of ancient Athenian resistance and that of modern liberation insurgencies."

Departing from Livy's description of a "terrorist" incident in 460 BCE, when Appius Herdonius took over the Capitoline Hill and the citadel and demanded the freedom of slaves and the return of political exiles, Ricardo Apostol draws our attention to the ways in which Livy rhetorically constructs this minor event by using the same language that Sallust used to describe Catiline's conspiracy, thus conflating Herdonius's actions with those of a more famous conspirator, in order to both delegitimize him and, at the same time, emphasize his threat to the Roman state (chapter 6). In so doing, Livy "falsifies historical and cultural differences" and thus perverts "structures of knowledge . . . to serve state power." Apostol also analyzes the "counter-terrorist" response of the Roman ruling class that used this crisis to elevate artificially the threat level to the point of suspending citizens' rights on the ground of national security, and in this way prevented the vote on the Rex Terentilia, a law that sought to limit the power of the Roman oligarchy. For Apostol, an understanding of terrorist events must escape any essentialistic mold that gives the illusion of representing real, recurring threats. Ultimately, Livy's text shows modern historians the challenges "inherent in attempting to trace the workings of categories such as terror."

The analysis and contextualization of the term "crusade," famously used by George W. Bush on September 16, 2001 to define the war on terror, is the topic of Sarah-Grace Heller's essay (chapter 7) in which the author explores the Old French retelling of the first crusade. Following Pinker's definition of terrorist plots as "maximizing both unfathomability and dread," the author demonstrates how the Western crusaders used "terror-inspiring techniques" such as cannibalizing Muslim cadavers, raping, and catapulting cadavers over the wall of the besieged city in order to provoke fear, dread, and the final surrender of the Muslims. Here the texts, written for the entertainment of a Western audience, condone and promote the use of terrorist tactics that do not follow the conventions of traditional warfare. Moreover, the brutal episodes of cannibalism and desecration of bodies described in the Old French Crusade Cycle bring new insight into the rhetoric of the February 1998 fatwa, which proclaimed that the Western crusaders "are attacking Muslims like people fighting over a plate of food."

The inner logic of the reign of terror that took over France after the French revolution is explored by Guillaume Ansart in chapter 8. In his essay, the author explains the fictional construct of perfect harmony and equivalence between the people, perceived as a coherent, homogenous group, and the National Convention; as a result, anyone who in any way questioned or was perceived as undermining the will and authority of the National Convention was considered an enemy of the people, that is, of the state, and as such he or she lost his or her right as a "citizen to be judged" and became instead "an enemy to be destroyed" in the most expedient way possible. Moreover, for the terror to function and maintain "the fantasy of the unity of the people," it had to employ a language vague and indeterminate enough that on the one hand it would not undermine the fiction of equivalence between the will of the people as a whole and the will of its representatives, and on the other hand could conflate its enemies from the left or the right as a whole organic group, dismissing their intrinsic differences.

After a diachronic and cross-cultural reflection on terror, the next section of the volume considers the contemporary American Global War on Terror

(GWOT), in its political, strategic, rhetorical, and narrative constructions. The doctrine of counterinsurgency and its unfeasibility is the object of Louise Barnett's essay (chapter 9).[51] The author examines the disconnect between theory and practice in the American response to terrorism, primarily by comparing the policies advocated in the revised U.S. Army/Marine Corps *Counterinsurgency Field Manual* (2006) with actual military practice in Afghanistan and Iraq. As Barnett explains, these policies are in fact "fictions" because they can't be put into practice in any meaningful way: they create the illusion that military initiatives can effectively combat terrorism when their usual result is to breed more terrorism. The main dilemma with the counterinsurgency doctrine is that it requires troops at the same time to destroy the enemy and protect civilians, "to be—in the words of General Petraeus—nation builders as well as warriors." Moreover, "the deviation of language from reality into fiction performs an essential function in the military": it allows for a linear narrative where all contradictions and questions are easily dismissed and ignored.

Whereas Barnett unveils how the reality of counterinsurgency is turned into improbable fictions, Harold Williford, in the following article (chapter 10), exposes the ways in which fictional cultural narratives developed in the 90s, after the collapse of the Soviet Union, provided a clear blueprint for America's post-9/11 counterterrorist ideology and tactics. Departing from an analysis of Tom Clancy's bestseller *Rainbow Six* and Roland Emmeric's blockbuster *Independence Day*, Williford demonstrates that fictional representations of WMD-wielding terrorists functioned to establish and legitimize extralegal counterterrorist practices that anticipate controversial aspects of the War on Terror. As a result, the counterterrorists enter a "non-state environment where they wield rogue sovereign power." This analysis raises the possibility that 9/11 may have slipped into an already developing cultural narrative, been absorbed into its logic, and then been driven by its own independent compulsions.

The next two chapters consider the complex relationship between history and fiction in the representation of 9/11. Todd Kuchta reflects on our individual and collective ability to understand our present moment historically (chapter 11). Through a close reading of "first generation" post-9/11 novels by Jonathan Safran Foer, Ian McEwan, Don DeLillo, and Moshin Hamid, the author unveils their attempt to historicize the present as it unfolds, in order to create new and always renewable historical perspectives. Departing from the debate surrounding the historical efficacy of postmodern fiction, as articulated by Fredric Jameson and Linda Hutcheon, the author suggests that the concept of double death formulated by Žižek, where every initial trauma must be "retroactively reproduced through repetition" in order to "make possible a historical interpretation of the initial, hitherto unrepresentable trauma," and Michel Foucault's task to challenge "the historical forces that have made us" in order "to refuse what we are," offer viable keys to approach "the struggle for historicity in 9/11 fiction." The nature and relationship of history and fiction, of past trauma (as represented by the Holocaust) and present, is also explored in the next chapter (chapter 12), where Stella Setka proposes a reading of Philip Roth's *Plot Against America* and Art Spiegelman's *In the Shadow of No Towers* as critiques of the Bush Administration's reaction to 9/11, both in terms of its international and domestic policies, specifically with the ensuing deterioration of civil liberties. The true trauma of 9/11, Setka argues, is not what happened on that day, but "what happened in its wake." By directly linking images from the Holocaust to post-9/11 loss of civil liberties, Roth and Spiegelman's texts allow us to reflect on and question the internal terrorist practices of American politics.

The final section of the volume proposes a range of case studies in narrative, cinematic, and visual arts that analyzes the ways in which terrorism has been absorbed, constructed, and interpreted from a variety of perspectives by artists, film directors, and fiction writers. Fabian Winkler's essay (chapter 13) reflects on the ways in which contemporary art, moving away from facile sensationalism, can in fact provide the audience with the intellectual tools necessary to critique and reevaluate their responses to terrorism. Using as examples the controversial Royal Air Force Museum art exhibition in 2005, *Zur Vorstellung des Terrors*, which featured a number of artists who in different ways dealt with the terrorist acts of the Baader Meinhof Gang, along with Hans Haake 9/11 posters and his own work as an artist, Winkler argues that art does not necessarily glorify what it represents; on the contrary, it allows for ambiguity, complexity, and a "reflexive distance": "the artist creates a discourse, a tool for public debate that itself becomes part of the artwork."

The next two chapters, authored respectively by Jaume Martí-Olivella and Roland Vazquez, consider cinematic and narrative representations of Euskadi Ta Askatasuna (ETA), the Basque nationalist and separatist movement that has been responsible for terrorist actions in Spain and the Basque Country since it first appeared in the late 60s.[52] Similarly to Winkler, Martí-Olivella explores the reflexive distance between spectators and the cinematic representation of terrorism (chapter 14). Focusing on Jamie Rosales's *Bullet to the Head* (2008), the controversial and arguably the most unsettling film representing ETA terrorists in Spanish cinema, the author shows how the film forces the spectator into the uncomfortable role of voyeur of a faceless terrorist in his daily routine. However, the detailed view of the terrorist's banal behavior does not unveil his political motives or his views. The camera is always kept at a distance and never comes close enough for the viewer to hear what he might be saying. The true invisibility of the terrorist, Martì-Olivella argues, "is precisely the mask of his/her normalcy," a normalcy that, following Hannah Arendt famous dictum, underscores the "banality of evil." Moreover, for Martì-Olivella, the final sequence of the film, in which both perpetrator and victim of the terrorist act remain voiceless, can be interpreted as the challenge inherent in speaking about terrorism. While Rosales's *Bullet to the Head* brings to the fore the paradox of the invisibility and inscrutability of the terrorist, Vazquez notes the shift in recent Basque and Spanish "post-terrorist novels" from plots focusing mainly on terrorists motives and agendas to narratives that engage primarily with the psychological and interior lives of victims of terrorism (chapter 15). Through a detailed survey of recent literary works, some of which have been awarded prestigious literary prizes and recognitions, the author unveils the strong "ideological certainty" that informs such narratives, which, by being in service to a political agenda, ultimately negate any critical or complex interpretation of terrorism.

The popular media appropriation of terrorist plots, already analyzed in Williford's article, is also the topic of the final chapter of this collection (chapter 16). Through the analysis of *Code Geass*, an epic-length anime that features terrorists as heroic freedom fighters, Aaron Choo and Wilson Koh discuss how this internationally popular Japanese manga, praised by critics for its complex text and thought-provoking story line,[53] taps into the concerns and uncertainties of a post-9/11 audience in order to provide an escapist, reassuring, and oversimplified rendition of terrorism. The clever intertextual and historical references, although they provide a patina of sophistication to the series, are just a commercial ploy to attract a wide audience. In this series, as in typical Hollywood blockbuster movies, the complex problem of terrorism is reduced to an easily consumable and money-making entertainment.

The interdisciplinary approach of these chapters, with their diachronic and varied geopolitical concerns, aims to offer new readings and interpretations of terrorism and its multimediatic representations. These essays make no claim to being exhaustive; in fact, they cannot but be provisional interpretations of events that by their very nature are constantly evolving. We hope that the kaleidoscopic and antidogmatic approach will help us to shed critical suspicion on any fixed rhetorical construction that claims an absolute understanding of terrorism; at the same time we hope that this volume will encourage further research and criticism in the humanities about a phenomenon that affects all of us.

NOTES

1.   For a comprehensive tally of those killed and injured as direct and indirect result of the September 11 attacks see, CNN Library, "September 11th Fast Facts," *CNN.com*, updated September 7, 2015, http://www.cnn.com/2013/07/27/us/september-11-anniversary-fast-facts/.

2.   Henceforth we shall use the expression "9/11" as shorthand to refer to the terrorist attack perpetrated on September 11, 2001, since it has become as universally used as "Pearl Harbor" to refer to the Japanese attack on the Hawaiian port on December 7, 1941, or "Hiroshima and Nagasaki" to refer to the American bombing of those cities respectively on August 9 and August 15, 1945.

3.   Scholars and government officials from around the world have been endeavoring to find answers to this question for centuries. In his massive handbook, Alex P. Schmid lists 4600 titles dedicated to Terrorism Studies. Alex P. Schmid, "The Literature on Terrorism," *The Routledge Handbook of Terrorism Research* (Routledge: London, 2013), 457–74.

4.   The phrase "I know it when I see it" "is one of the most famous phrases in the entire history of Supreme Court Opinions." Paul Gewirtz, "On 'I Know It When I See It.'" *The Yale Law Journal* 105, no. 4 (1996): 1023.

5.   Josh Gerstein, "Terror Attacks Spark Cowardly Debate." *ABC News*, September 26, 2011, http://abcnews.go.com/Politics/story?id=121312. Both President Bush and the Congress described the hijackings as cowardly.

6.   George W. Bush, "Remarks by the President Upon Arrival," *The White House*, September 16, 2001, http://georgewbush-whitehouse.archives.gov/news /releases/2001/09/20010916-2.html. President Bush described the war as a "crusade" in this press release.

7.   At least one of the pilots was a woman, somewhat to the amusement of the allied Afghan warlord who broadcast to the Taliban, "Female up in this airplane is wreaking havoc on you." Alex Quade, "Commando Monument Near Ground Zero Unveiled on Veterans Day," *Washington Times*, October 27, 2011, http://www.washingtontimes.com /news/2011/oct/27/commando-monument-at-ground-zero-to-be-unveiled-on.

8.   *The New York Times* described the fact that "women in Afghanistan are uncovering their faces, looking for jobs, walking happily with female friends on the street and even hosting a news show on Afghan television" as a "collateral benefit" of the war in Afghanistan. See "Liberating the Women of Afghanistan," NYTimes. com, November 24, 2001, http://www.nytimes.com/2001/11/24/opinion/liberating-the -women-of-afghanistan.html.

9.   Osama bin Laden and others declared a holy war against the United States in 1998 and articulated its motivation in detail in a "Letter to America" in November of 2002. See Osama bin Laden, "Full Text: bin Laden's 'Letter to America,'" *The Guardian*, November 24, 2002, http://www.theguardian.com /world/2002/nov/24/theobserver.

10.   Bill Maher, host of the ABC late-night talk show *Politically Incorrect*, said, "We have been the cowards, lobbing cruise missiles from 2,000 miles away. That's cowardly. . . . Staying in the airplane when it hits the building, say what you want about it, it's not cowardly." Susan Sontag wrote in a *New Yorker* essay: "If the word "cowardly" is to be used, it might be more aptly applied to those who kill from beyond the range of retaliation, high in the sky, than to those willing to die themselves in order to kill others. In the matter of courage [a morally neutral virtue]: Whatever may be said of the perpetrators of Sept. 11's slaughter, they were not cowards." Maher and Sontag's remarks are cited in Gerstein, "Terror Attacks Spark Cowardly Debate."

11.   President Bush articulated what came to be considered his doctrine on terrorism in his address to a Joint Session of Congress on September 20, 2001: "We will pursue nations that provide aid or safe haven to terrorism. Every nation, in every region, now has a decision to make. Either you are with us, or you are with the terrorists. From this day forward, any nation that

continues to harbor or support terrorism will be regarded by the United States as a hostile regime." See George W. Bush, "Text: President Bush Addresses the Nation," *Washington Post*, September 20, 2001, http://www.washingtonpost.com/wp-srv/nation/specials/attacked/transcripts/bushaddress_092001.html.

12.   When asked whether Guantanamo Bay detainees would be protected by the Geneva or human rights conventions Supreme Court Justice Antonin Scalia replied: "If he was captured by my army on a battlefield, that is where he belongs. I had a son on that battlefield and they were shooting at my son, and I'm not about to give this man who was captured in a war a full jury trial. I mean it's crazy." Associated Press, "No Legal Rights for Enemy Combatants, Scalia Says," *Washington Post*, March 27, 2006, http://www.washingtonpost.com/wp-dyn/content/article/2006/03/26/AR2006032600819.html.

13.   The controversies surrounding the Patriot Act have only increased over time, particularly with the release of information concerning the massive collection of call records by the NSA. On June 6, 2013, Republican Congressman Jim Sensenbrenner wrote to Attorney General Eric Holder, "As the author of the Patriot Act, I am extremely disturbed by what appears to be an overbroad interpretation. . . . These reports are deeply concerning and raise questions about whether our constitutional rights are secure . . . . While I believe we found an appropriate balance, I have always worried about potential abuses of the Act. . . . How could the phone records of so many innocent Americans be relevant to an authorized investigation?" See F. James Sensenbrenner, "Letter to Attorney General Eric H. Holder, Jr.," *National Security Archive*, June 6, 2013, http://www2.gwu.edu/~nsarchiv/NSAEBB/NSAEBB436/docs/EBB-063.pdf.

14.   President Bush specifically addressed this issue in a September 16, 2001 news release: "I want to remind the American people that the prime suspect's organization is in a lot of countries - it's a widespread organization based upon one thing: terrorizing. They can't stand freedom; they hate what America stands for." See George W. Bush, "Remarks by the President Upon Arrival."

15.   In response to comments by Dinesh D'Souza on the September 17, 2001, Politically Incorrect TV show, Bill Maher said that the behavior of the 9/11 hijackers "took guts." Ari Fleischer, Bush White House spokesman asserted that it was "a terrible thing to say" and that all Americans "need to watch what they say, watch what they to." Maher was taken off the air, at first temporarily and the definitively on May 14, 2012. See Ari Fleisher, "Text: White House Briefing," *Washington Post*, September

26, 2001, http://www.washingtonpost.com/wp-srv/nation/specials/attacked /transcripts/fleischertext_092601.html. The University of Colorado fired professor Ward Churchill ostensibly for plagiarism and other academic misconduct but, more plausibly for his comments in an essay titled "Some People Push Back: On the Justice of Roosting Chickens," on the events of 9/11 in which he compared some of its victims to "little Eichmanns." See Dan Elliott, "Colorado Prof Fired After 9-11 Remarks," *Washington Post*, July 24, 2007, http://www.washingtonpost.com/wp-dyn/content /article/2007/07/24/AR2007072402000.html.

16.   For more details see "Costs of War," *Watson Institute of International & Public Affairs, Brown University*, March, 2015, http://costsofwar.org/article /afghan-civilians. Moreover, as Neta Crawford notes, "unlike Iraq, there is no long run tally, no 'Afghanistan Body Count' or similar independent public accounting of civilian injury and killing caused by all combatants since 2001. Uncertainty about the scale of the killing has been a problem since the start of fighting in October 2001." See Neta C. Crawford, "Civilian death and Injury in Afghanistan, 2001–2011," Cost of War, *Watson Institute of International & Public Affairs, Brown University*, June 13, 2011, http://costsofwar.org/sites/default/files /articles/14/attachments/CrawfordAfghanistanCasualties.pdf.

17.   For details on the death by torture of Dilwar at the hands of U.S. Army soldiers see, Tim Golden, "In U.S. Report, Brutal Details of 2 Afghan Inmates' Deaths," *NYTimes.com,* May 20, 2005, http://www.nytimes.com/2005/05/20/international /asia/20abuse.html. See also the documentary, *Taxi to the Dark Side,* directed by Alex Gibney, New York: Jigsaw Productions, 2007, which focuses on his brutalization and death.

18.   For confirmation, among many sources see, Jan Crawford Greenburg, Howard L. Rosenberg, and Ariane De Vogue, "Torture: Top Bush Advisors Approved 'Enhanced Interrogation," *ABC News*, April 9, 2008, http://abcnews.go.com/TheLaw /LawPolitics/story?id=4583256.

19.   For a description of "hooding," its effects, and the findings of the United Nations Committee Against Torture, see *Human Rights Watch* 17, no. 1(G) (2005): 34, http://www.hrw.org/reports/2005/us0405/us0405.pdf. The Senate Committee's Report on the C.I.A.'s use of torture describes in painful detail this and other forms of torture carried out by representatives of the United States government. See Dianne Feinstein, *Report of the Senate Select Committee on Intelligence Committee Study of the Central Intelligence Agency's*

Detention and Interrogation Program, Together with Foreword by Chairman Feinstein and Additional and Minority Views, 113th Congress, S. Rep. No. 113–288, 2014, http://alma.exlibrisgroup.com/view/action/uresolver.do;jsessionid =C4E431CC3BD4B85985B1642F375E360A.app1.prod.alma.exlibrisgroup .com:1801?operation=resolveService&package_service_id=11627111960001081 &institutionId=1081&customerId=1070.

20. Among the many who asked themselves if the invasion was worth it. See William Deresiewicz's "The New Greatest Rationalization: The Iraq War, 10 Years Later," *The American Scholar*, March 17, 2013, http://theamericanscholar.org/the-new -greatest-rationalization/#.UxI7GsuYZLO.

21. President Bush dismissed the importance of finding the person who justified the invasion of Afghanistan by saying, "Who knows if he's hiding in some cave or not. We haven't heard from him in a long time. The idea of focusing on one person really indicates to me people don't understand the scope of the mission. Terror is bigger than one person. He's just a person who's been marginalized. . . . I don't know where he is. I really just don't spend that much time on him, to be honest with you." See Alex Seitz-Wald, "Flashback: Bush On bin Laden: 'I Really Just Don't Spend That Much Time On Him,'" *ThinkProgress*, May 2, 2011, http://thinkprogress.org/security/2011/05/02/162774 /bush-bin-laden/.

22. U.S. military police personnel of the United States Army, members of the Central Intelligence Agency, and civilian contractors allegedly physically and sexually abused, tortured, raped, sodomized, and killed prisoners from late 2003 to early 2004 during the Iraq War. For some of the troubling images that emerged and broke the scandal, see "Torture Scandal: The Images That Shamed America," *The Guardian*, July 5, 2004, http://www.theguardian.com/gall/0,8542,1211872,00.html.

23. See the independent website *Iraq Body Count*, www.Iraqbodycount.org.

24. In addition to the tens of thousands of internet posts that allege that the killing of Osama bin Laden was a hoax and to the gruesome images of fake bin Laden's available online (for all, see Michael Rivero, "A Gallery of Fake Dead bin Ladens" *What Really Happened*, n.d., http://whatreallyhappened.com/WRHARTICLES /galleryoffakebinladens.php), Pulitzer Prize-winning journalist Seymour Hersh, best-known for having exposed the My Lai massacre during the Vietnam war and his reports on Abu Ghraib, also contends that it is all "one big lie" and that "not one word" of the story is true." See Lisa O'Carroll, "Seymour Hersh on Obama, NSA and the 'pathetic' American media," *The Guardian*, September 27, 2013,

http://www.theguardian.com/media/media-blog/2013/sep/27/seymour-hersh-obama
-nsa-american-media.

25. Associated Press, "US Military Deaths in Afghanistan at 2,213," *NYTimes. com*, December 30, 2014, http://www.nytimes.com/aponline/2014/12/30/us/ap-us -afghan-us-deaths.html.

26. Mark Thompson, "The $5 Trillion War on Terror," *Time,* June 29, 2011, http://nation.time.com/2011/06/29/the-5-trillion-war-on-terror/. Lawrence Lindsey, President Bush's economic advisor, stated that the invasion might cost $200 billion. Other administration officials rejected his figures out of hand. Secretary of Defense Donald Rumsfeld called his projections "baloney," Deputy Secretary of Defense Paul Wolfowitz said the war would pay for itself through increased oil revenues, and Office of Management and Budget Director Mitch Daniels estimated that it might cost between $50 and $60 billion. See Joseph E. Stiglitz and Linda J. Bilmes, "The $3 Trillion War," *Vanity Fair*, April 2008, http://www.vanityfair.com/politics /features/2008/04/stiglitz200804.

27. According to Nouri al-Maliki, the first post-Saddam Hussein Prime Minister, "Human rights abuses in Iraq are now as bad as they were under Saddam Hussein and are even in danger of eclipsing his record." See Peter Beaumont, "Abuse Worse Than Under Saddam, Says Iraqi Leader," *The Guardian*, November 26, 2005, http://www.theguardian .com/world/2005/nov/27/iraq.peterbeaumont.

28. In response to Edward Snowden's revelations about widespread government surveillance, President Obama stated, "We know of at least 50 threats that have been averted because of this information not just in the United States, but, in some cases, threats here in Germany. . . . So lives have been saved." However, Senator Patrick Leahy, Democrat of Vermont, told General Alexander that "We've heard over and over again the assertion that 54 terrorist plots were thwarted" by the two programs. . . . That's plainly wrong, but we still get it in letters to members of Congress, we get it in statements. These weren't all plots and they weren't all thwarted. The American people are getting left with the inaccurate impression of the effectiveness of NSA programs." See Justin Elliott and Theodoric Meyer, "Claim on 'Attacks Thwarted' by NSA Spreads Despite Lack of Evidence," *ProPublica*, December 17, 2013, http://www.propublica.org/article/claim-on-attacks-thwarted -by-nsa-spreads-despite-lack-of-evidence.

29. Admiral Bill McRaven, commander of the U.S. Special Operations Forces, in an interview on February 27, 2014, stated that "the threat posed by Al Qaeda is 'much

more broad today' and that it 'was metastasizing' with affiliate groups surging in Iraq, Syria, Yemen, and North Africa." See Washington Free Beacon Staff, "Special Ops Chief: Threat From al Qaeda is 'Much More Broad' Today," *Washington Free Beacon*, February 27, 2014, http://freebeacon.com/special-ops-chief-threat-from-al-qaeda-is-much -more-broad-today/.

30. One of the major criticism of "terrorologists" is that state terrorism tends to be neglected. See Alex P. Schmid, "The Literature on Terrorism," 462.

31. See Giorgio Agamben, *Homo Sacer: Sovereign Power and Bare Life*, translated by Daniel Heller-Roazen (Stanford: Stanford University Press, 1998); and Giorgio Agamben, *State of Exception*, translated by Kevin Attell (Chicago: University of Chicago Press, 2005).

32. Among the many books on the topic, Steve Coll's Pulitzer Prize-winning *Ghost Wars: The Secret History of the CIA, Afghanistan, and bin Laden, from the Soviet Invasion to September 10, 2001* (New York: Penguin, 2004) is particularly well researched and informative.

33. The result is that United Nations has been unable to reach an internation- ally agreed upon definition of terrorism because the Organization of the Islamic Conference (OIC), established in 1969 with the objective of liberating Jerusalem, insists that "peoples' struggle including armed struggle against foreign occu- pation . . . shall not be considered a terrorist crime." More specifically, in April 2002, as a reaction to the 9/11 attack, the OIC foreign ministers met in Malaysia and declared that they rejected "any attempt to link terrorism to the struggle of the Palestinian people in the exercise of their inalienable right to establish their independent state with al-Quds al-Sharif [Jerusalem] as its capital." See Patrick Goodenough, "Almost 10 Years After 9/11, U.N. Still Grappling to Define Terrorism," *CNSNews.com*, April 21, 2011, http://www.cnsnews.com/news /article/almost-10-years-after-911-un-still-grappling-define-terrorism.

34. Caitlin Dewey, "Why Nelson Mandela Was on a Terrorism Watch List in 2008," *Washington Post,* December 7, 2013, http://www.washingtonpost.com/blogs /the-fix/wp/2013/12/07/why-nelson-mandela-was-on-a-terrorism-watch-list-in-2008/.

35. Brad Plumer, "Nine Facts About Terrorism in the United States since 9/11," *Washington Post*, September 11, 2013, http://www.washingtonpost.com/blogs/wonkblog /wp/2013/09/11/nine-facts-about-terrorism-in-the-united-states-since-911/.

36. Tom Engelhardt, "Tomgram: Engelhardt, A Ripley's Believe It or Not National Security State—American Jihad 2014, The New Fundamentalists," *TomDispatch*

.com, January 5, 2014, http://www.tomdispatch.com/blog/175789/tomgram%3A
_engelhardt%2C_a_ripley%27s_believe_it_or_not_national_security_state/.

37.   The enemy "center of gravity" is a central object of study in all American War Colleges and strategic studies institutes. Its destruction is the sine qua non of any military operation. It has been defined as the "one element within a combatant's entire structure or system that has the necessary centripetal force to hold that structure together. This is why Clausewitz wrote that a blow directed against a center of gravity will have the greatest effect." See Douglas C. Lovelace, Jr., forward to *Clausewitz's Center of Gravity: Changing Our Warfighting Doctrine—Again!*, by Antulio J. Echevarria II, (*Strategic Studies Institute, U.S. Army War College*, 2002), iii, http://www.strategicstudiesinstitute.army.mil/Pubs/display.cfm?pubID=363.

38.   Zambernardi Lorenzo. "Counterinsurgency's Impossible Trilemma," *The Washington Quarterly* 33, no. 3 (2010): 21–34, http://dx.doi.org/10.1080/0163660X.2010.492722.

39.   Lisa R. Stampnitzky, "Disciplining an Unruly Field: Terrorism Studies and the State, 1972—2001," PhD diss, (University of California, Berkeley, 2008), cited in Schmid, "The Literature on Terrorism," 457.

40.   Yale University Film Studies Program, "Depth of Field," *Yale Film Studies Film Analysis Web Site 2.0*, August 27, 2002, http://classes.yale.edu/film-analysis/htmfiles/cinematography.htm.

41.   We are grateful to Punya Mishra, Professor of Educational Psychology and Educational Technology at Michigan State University for his kind permission to use his Good Evil ambigram. For more of his work, see punyamishra.com.

42.   Ironically, after 13 years of war and the expenditure of trillions of dollars, the U.S. military is just now beginning to address this question. According to the confidential minutes of a conference he called to address the issue of "What Makes the Islamic State so Dangerous?," Maj. Gen. Michael K. Nagata, commander of American Special Operations forces in the Middle East, stated: "We do not understand the movement, and until we do, we are not going to defeat it. . . . We have not defeated the idea. We do not even understand the idea." See Eric Schmitt, "In Battle to Defang ISIS, U.S. Targets Its Psychology," *NYTimes.com*, December 28, 2014, http://www.nytimes.com/2014/12/29/us/politics/in-battle-to-defang-isis-us-targets-its-psychology-.html.

43.   It is also ironic, to cite only one example, that in his brief bibliography on terrorism in Italy, Schmid only cites sources in English and German. See

Gillian Duncan and Alex P. Schmid, "Bibliography of Terrorism," *Routledge Handbook*, 486.

44. In particular see Richard Jackson, Lee Jarvis, Jeroen Gunning, and Marie Breen-Smyth, eds., *Terrorism: A Critical Introduction* (Basingstoke: Palgrave Macmillan, 2011), which approaches Terrorism Studies from a Critical Theory perspective and challenges the perceived weaknesses of OTS research predicated on its ties to the hegemonic establishments, the demonization of "terrorists," and the glorification of patriotism. CTS, however, is also not without critics. See, in particular, John Horgan and Micheal J. Boyle, "A Case Against 'Critical Terrorism Studies,'" *Critical Studies on Terrorism* 1, no.1 (2008): 51–64, which, while welcoming CTS, rebuffs them for creating an OTS "straw man" which they then knock down with facile generalizations.

45. Richard Jackson, *Writing the War on Terrorism: Language, Politics and Counter-Terrorism* (Manchester: Manchester University Press, 2005), 164–72.

46. For a partially annotated filmography and bibliography on the topic see, "Terrorism in the Movies," *Media Resource Center*, University of California, Berkley, January 13, 2013, http://www.lib.berkeley.edu/MRC/terrorismmovies.html.

47. Cliff Stagoll, "Event," in *The Deleuze Dictionary*, edited by Adrian Parr, 88–91 (New York: Columbia University Press, 2005), 88.

48. Primo Levi, *The Drowned and the Saved* (New York: Summit Books, 1988), 88.

49. Jean Améry, *At the Mind's Limits: Contemplations by a Survivor on Auschwitz and Its Realities* (Bloomington: Indiana University Press, 1980), quoted in Cavarero, *Horrorism: Naming Contemporary Violence* (New York: Columbia University Press, 2009), 34.

50. As Agamben explains, "The life caught in the sovereign ban is the life that is originarily sacred—that is, that may be killed but not sacrificed—and, in this sense, the production of bare life is the originary activity of sovereignty." *Homo Sacer, Sovereign Power and Bare Life* (Stanford: Stanford University Press, 1998), 53.

51. See also Zambernardi, 21.

52. Enric Martínez-Herrera, "Nationalist Extremism and Outcomes of State Policies in the Basque Country, 1979-2001," *International Journal on Multicultural Societies* 4, no. 1 (2002): 4.

53. Dani Cavallaro notes for instance that "*Code Geass* engages in some trenchant reflection on the vicissitudes of Realpolitik." See Cavallaro, *Clamp in Context: A Critical Study of the Manga and Anime* (Jefferson, NC: McFarland, 2012), 42.

WORKS CITED

Agamben, Giorgio. *Homo Sacer: Sovereign Power and Bare Life*. Translated by Daniel Heller-Roazen. Stanford: Stanford University Press, 1998.

———. *State of Exception*. Translated by Kevin Attell. Chicago: The University of Chicago Press, 2005.

Améry, Jean. *At the Mind's Limits: Contemplations by a Survivor on Auschwitz and Its Realities*. Bloomington: Indiana University Press, 1980.

Associated Press. "No Legal Rights for Enemy Combatants, Scalia Says." *Washington Post*. March 27, 2006. http://www.washingtonpost.com /wp-dyn/content/article/2006/03/26/AR2006032600819.html.

Associated Press. "US Military Deaths in Afghanistan at 2,213." *NYTimes. com*. December 30, 2014. http://www.nytimes.com/aponline/2014/12/30 /us/ap-us-afghan-us-deaths.html.

Beaumont, Peter. "Abuse Worse Than under Saddam, Says Iraqi Leader." *The Guardian*. November 26, 2005. http://www.theguardian.com/world/2005 /nov/27/iraq.peterbeaumont.

bin Laden, Osama. "Full Text: bin Laden's 'Letter to America.'" *The Guardian*. November 24, 2002. http://www.theguardian.com/world/2002/nov/24 /theobserver.

Bush, George, W. "Remarks by the President Upon Arrival." *The White House*. Press release. September 16, 2001. http://georgewbush-whitehouse .archives.gov/news/releases/2001/09/20010916-2.html.

Bush, George W. "Text: President Bush Addresses the Nation." *Washington Post*. September 20, 2001. http://www.washingtonpost.com/wp-srv /nation/specials/attacked/transcripts/bushaddress_092001.html

Cavallaro, Dani. *Clamp in Context: A Critical Study of the Manga and Anime*. Jefferson, North Carolina: McFarland, 2012.

Cavarero, Adriana. *Horrorism: Naming Contemporary Violence*. New York: Columbia University Press, 2009.

CNN Library. "September 11th Fast Facts." *CNN.com*. September 7, 2015. http://www.cnn.com/2013/07/27/us/september-11-anniversary -fast-facts.

Coll, Steve. *Ghost Wars: The Secret History of the CIA, Afghanistan, and bin Laden, from the Soviet Invasion to September 10, 2001*. New York: Penguin, 2004.

"Costs of War." *Watson Institute of International & Public Affairs, Brown University*. Last modified March 2015. http://costsofwar.org/article /afghan-civilians.

Crawford, Neta C. "Civilian Death and Injury in Afghanistan, 2001–2011." Costs of War. *Watson Institute of International & Public Affairs, Brown University*. June 13, 2011. http://costsofwar.org/sites/default/files /articles/14/attachments/CrawfordAfghanistanCasualties.pdf.

Deresiewicz, William. "The New Greatest Rationalization: The Iraq War, 10 Years Later." *The American Scholar*. March 17, 2013. http://theamericanscholar .org/the-new-greatest-rationalization/#.UxI7GsuYZLO.

Dewey, Caitlin. "Why Nelson Mandela Was on a Terrorism Watch List in 2008." *Washington Post*. December 7, 2013. http://www.washingtonpost .com/news/the-fix/wp/2013/12/07/why-nelson-mandela-was-on-a -terrorism-watch-list-in-2008/.

Duncan, Gillian, and Alex P. Schmid. "Bibliography of Terrorism." In *The Routledge Handbook of Terrorism Research*, edited by Alex P. Schmid, 475–97. London: Routledge, 2013.

Easson, Joseph, and Alex P. Schmid. "250-Plus Academic, Governmental and Intergovernmental Definitions of Terrorism." In *The Routledge Handbook of Terrorism Research*, edited by Alex P. Schmid, 99–157. London: Routledge, 2013.

Echevarria, Antulio J., II. "Clausewitz's Center of Gravity: Changing Our Warfighting Doctrine—Again!" *Strategic Studies Institute, U.S. Army War College*. September 1, 2002. http://www.strategicstudiesinstitute .army.mil/Pubs/display.cfm?pubID=363.

Elliott, Dan. "Colorado Prof Fired After 9-11 Remarks." *Washington Post*. July 24, 2007. http://www.washingtonpost.com/wp-dyn/content /article/2007/07/24/AR2007072402000.html.

Elliott, Justin, and Theodoric Meyer. "Claim on 'Attacks Thwarted' by NSA Spreads Despite Lack of Evidence." *ProPublica: Journalism in the Public Interest*. October 23, 2013. http://www.propublica.org/article/claim-on -attacks-thwarted-by-nsa-spreads-despite-lack-of-evidence.

Engelhardt, Tom. "Tomgram: Engelhardt, A Ripley's Believe It or Not National Security State—American Jihad 2014: The New Fundamentalists." *TomDispatch.com*. January 5, 2014. http://www.tomdispatch.com

/blog/175789/tomgram%3A_engelhardt%2C_a_ripley%27s_believe_it
_or_not_national_security_state/.

Feinstein, Dianne. *Report of the Senate Select Committee on Intelligence Committee Study of the Central Intelligence Agency's Detention and Interrogation Program, Together with Foreword by Chairman Feinstein and Additional and Minority Views.* 113th Congress. S. Rep. No. 113–288. Washington, DC: Government Printing Office, 2014. http://alma.exlibrisgroup.com/view/action/uresolver.do;jsessionid =C4E431CC3BD4B85985B1642F375E360A.app1.prod.alma .exlibrisgroup.com:1801?operation=resolveService&package_service _id=1162711960001081&institutionId=1081&customerId=1070.

Fleisher, Ari. "Text: White House Briefing." *Washington Post*. September 26, 2001. http://www.washingtonpost.com/wp-srv/nation/specials/attacked /transcripts/fleischertext_092601.html.

Gerstein, Josh. "Terror Attacks Spark Cowardly Debate." *ABC News*. September 26, 2014. http://abcnews.go.com/Politics/story?id=121312.

Gewirtz, Paul. "On 'I Know It When I See It.'" *The Yale Law Journal* 105, no. 4 (1996): 1023–47.

Golden, Tim. "In U.S. Report, Brutal Details of 2 Afghan Inmates' Deaths." *NYTimes.com*. May 20, 2005. http://www.nytimes.com/2005/05/20 /world/asia/in-us-report-brutal-details-of-2-afghan-inmates-deaths.html.

Goodenough, Patrick. "Almost 10 Years After 9/11, U.N. Still Grappling to Define Terrorism." *CNSNews.com*. April 21, 2011. http://www .cnsnews.com/news/article/almost-10-years-after-911-un-still-grappling -define-terrorism.

Greenburg Crawford, Jan, Howard L. Rosenberg, and Ariane De Vogue. "Torture: Top Bush Advisors Approved 'Enhanced Interrogation.'" *ABC News*. April 9, 2008. http://abcnews.go.com/TheLaw/LawPolitics/story ?id=4583256.

Horgan, John, and Michael J. Boyle. "A Case Against 'Critical Terrorism Studies.'" *Critical Studies on Terrorism* 1, no. 1 (2008): 51–64.

Human Rights Watch. *Getting Away with Torture? Command Responsibility for the U.S. Abuse of Detainees*. Vol. 17, no. 1(G) April 2005. http://www .hrw.org/reports/2005/us0405/us0405.pdf.

Iraq Body Count. n.d. www.Iraqbodycount.org.

Jackson, Richard. *Writing the War on Terrorism: Language, Politics and Counter-Terrorism*. Manchester: Manchester University Press, 2005.

Jackson, Richard, Jeroen Gunning, Lee Jarvis, and Marie Breen-Smyth, eds. *Terrorism: A Critical Introduction*. Basingstoke: Palgrave Macmillan, 2011.

Levi, Primo. *The Drowned and the Saved*. New York: Summit Books, 1988.

"Liberating the Women of Afghanistan." *NYTimes.com*. November 24, 2001. http://www.nytimes.com/2001/11/24/opinion/liberating-the-women-of-afghanistan.html.

Lovelace, Douglas C., Jr. Forward to *Clausewitz's Center of Gravity: Changing Our Warfighting Doctrine—Again!*, by Antulio J. Echevarria II, iii. *Strategic Studies Institute, U.S. Army War College*, 2002. http://www.strategicstudiesinstitute.army.mil/Pubs/display.cfm?pubID=363.

Martínez-Herrera, Enric. "Nationalist Extremism and Outcomes of State Policies in the Basque Country, 1979-2001." *International Journal on Multicultural Societies* 4, no. 1 (2002): 17–41.

Mishra, Punya. "Good Evil Ambigram." 2002. *Punya Mishra's Web*. http://punyamishra.com.

O'Carroll, Lisa. "Seymour Hersh on Obama, NSA and the 'Pathetic' American Media." *The Guardian*. September 27, 2013. http://www.theguardian.com/media/media-blog/2013/sep/27/seymour-hersh-obama-nsa-american-media.

Plumer, Brad. "Nine Facts about Terrorism in the United States since 9/11." *Washington Post*. September 11, 2013. http://www.washingtonpost.com/blogs/wonkblog/wp/2013/09/11/nine-facts-about-terrorism-in-the-united-states-since-911.

Quade, Alex. "Commando Monument Near Ground Zero Unveiled on Veterans Day." *Washington Times*. October 27, 2011. http://www.washingtontimes.com/news/2011/oct/27/commando-monument-at-ground-zero-to-be-unveiled-on.

Rivero, Michael. "A Gallery of Fake Dead bin Ladens." *What Really Happened*. http://whatreallyhappened.com/WRHARTICLES/galleryof fakebinladens.php.

Schmid, Alex P. "The Literature on Terrorism." In *The Routledge Handbook of Terrorism Research*, edited by Alex P. Schmid, 457–74. London: Routledge, 2013.

Schmid, Alex P., ed. *The Routledge Handbook of Terrorism Research*. London: Routledge, 2013.

Schmitt, Eric. "In Battle to Defang ISIS, U.S. Targets Its Psychology." *NYTimes.com*. December 28, 2014. http://www.nytimes.com/2014/12/29 /us/politics/in-battle-to-defang-isis-us-targets-its-psychology-.html.

Seitz-Wald, Alex. "Flashback: Bush On bin Laden: 'I Really Just Don't Spend That Much Time On Him.'" *ThinkProgress*. May 2, 2011. http:// thinkprogress.org/security/2011/05/02/162774/bush-bin-laden/.

Sensenbrenner, Jim. "Letter to Attorney General Eric Holder." *National Security Archive*. June 6, 2013. http://www2.gwu.edu/~nsarchiv /NSAEBB/NSAEBB436/docs/EBB-063.pdf.

Stagoll, Cliff. "Event." In *The Deleuze Dictionary*, edited by Adrian Parr, 88–91. New York: Columbia University Press, 2005.

Stampnitzky, Lisa R. "Disciplining an Unruly Field: Terrorism Studies and the State, 1972—2001." PhD diss., University of California, Berkeley, 2008.

Stiglitz, Joseph E., and Linda J. Bilmes. "The $3 Trillion War." *Vanity Fair*. April 2008. http://www.vanityfair.com/politics/features/2008/04 /stiglitz200804.

Taxi to the Dark Side. Directed by Alex Gibney. New York: Jigsaw Productions, 2007. DVD.

"Terrorism in the Movies." *Media Resource Center*. University of California, Berkley. January 13, 2013. http://www.lib.berkeley.edu/MRC /terrorismmovies.html.

Thompson, Mark. "The $5 Trillion War on Terror." *Time*. 29 June 29, 2011. http://nation.time.com/2011/06/29/the-5-trillion-war-on-terror/.

"Torture Scandal: The Images That Shamed America." *The Guardian*. July 5, 2004. http://www.theguardian.com/gall/0,8542,1211872,00.html.

Washington Free Beacon Staff. "Special Ops Chief: Threat from al Qaeda is 'Much More Broad' Today." *Washington Free Beacon*. February 27, 2014. http://freebeacon.com/national-security/special-ops-chief-threat -from-al-qaeda-is-much-more-broad-today/.

Yale University Film Studies Program. "Depth of Field." *Yale Film Studies Film Analysis Web Site 2.0*. August 27, 2002. http://classes.yale.edu /film-analysis/htmfiles/cinematography.htm.

Zambernardi, Lorenzo. "Counterinsurgency's Impossible Trilemma." *The Washington Quarterly* 33, no. 3 (2010): 21–34. http://dx.doi.org/10.1080 /0163660X.2010.492722.

PART I

Approaches to Understanding Terrorism

2

Deleuze, the Event, and the Problem of Terrorism

KENNETH E. NOE

INTRODUCTION

This article argues that Deleuze's discussion of events as encounters with the novelty of difference presents a challenge to predominant methodologies in the philosophy of terrorism. I argue that the novelty exhibited by terroristic events invites philosophical reflection on the difference or singularity of terroristic events, a feature often overlooked in the philosophy of terrorism. Specifically, my argument seeks to undermine a widespread methodological assumption in the philosophy of terrorism, namely, that the concept of terrorism is of a kind with traditional identity-based concepts, an assumption which takes for granted epistemic norms that selectively privilege stable, shared features among a series of instances. The article thereby addresses the limits of definitional methodologies in the philosophy of terrorism by challenging the epistemic norms governing both contextualist descriptions of terrorist acts as well as universalizing methodologies that abstract similarities from received historical instances of terrorism.

I claim that such definitional methodologies are highly problematic in the context of the philosophy of terrorism, since terroristic events are illegitimately presumed to be determinate events whose explanation can be exhausted by sets of necessary or sufficient conditions (whether empirically or conceptually attributed). By contrast, my aim is to problematize terrorism as an event that is already involved in relational processes of becoming other. I argue that what is needed in the philosophy of terrorism is a revised conceptual pragmatics, one which recognizes and accepts that any enacted definition of the nature of terrorist activity inevitably creates new conditions for future instances of terroristic events. Such conditions are inevitably implicated in further unforeseen terrorist acts since, paradoxically, to define terrorism is also to create a space of vulnerability to future events. In light of this problematic dynamic, I claim that the disclosure of terrorism's processual architecture can not only structurally ground the actual terror experienced in terroristic events, but can also readily tether our determinate descriptions of terrorist events, and the subsequent definitions of "terrorism" that follow upon them, to such processes of becoming other, thereby securing a structural space for the active problematization and possible critique of such descriptions. With the conceptual resources of Deleuze's philosophy of difference, then, I argue that terrorism ought to be analyzed as a differential rather than a stable or otherwise self-identical concept. Finally, I conclude by offering some brief reflections on the relationship between the idea of terrorism as an event and Deleuze's ethics of "becoming worthy" of events.

Why enlist Deleuze into the philosophy of terrorism? Throughout his work, Deleuze directs most of his attention to concepts and ideas that seem to be involved in processes of becoming other (concepts that, by their very nature, seem to exhibit a quality of intrinsic variation that renders them elusive of a single definite description), such as the concept of difference, the concept of the new, the concept of the singular (as opposed to the traditional philosophical concept of the "particular"), or the concept of creativity. The connection of Deleuze's interest in differential concepts with the concept of "event" becomes explicit in a 1988 interview, where Deleuze comprehensively remarks that, "I've tried in all my books to discover the nature of events; it's a philosophical concept, the only one capable of ousting the verb 'to be' and attributes" (*Negotiations*, 141).[1] The intrinsically variable nature of such concepts, then, finds a unifying foundation in the problem of the nature of events. The unifying function of "event" in Deleuze's philosophy is intended to replace, or in the very least to considerably loosen, our habitual tendency to philosophize about concepts in a strictly categorical manner. "The event" in Deleuze thereby functions as a grounding concept that unifies a project for reconceiving the nature of concepts as primarily relational, differential, and productive, rather than as categorical, self-identical, or otherwise representational.

However, the nature of "the event" in the Deleuzian sense must be pieced together from the various, and sometimes conflicting, references Deleuze makes to it throughout his works. Indeed, "the event" is treated rather ambiguously by Deleuze, and as such lacks the kind of rigorous discursive clarity necessary for constructing possible methodological alternatives in the philosophy of terrorism. It is far from obvious what Deleuze has in mind when he speaks of events as productive encounters with difference, or beyond that, how such a claim might serve as a ground from which predominant definitional methodologies in the philosophy of terrorism might be challenged. It should be recognized from the start, then, that to introduce Deleuzian philosophy into the philosophy of terrorism is to face a host of issues, including that of getting clear on Deleuze's notoriously difficult terminology, that of the proper translation of Deleuze's concepts in the philosophy of terrorism, and that of the charitable critique of established views in the philosophy of terrorism on Deleuzian grounds.

With these considerations in mind, it will be useful first to discuss two exemplary philosophical approaches in the philosophy of terrorism in order to reveal by way of contrast the distinctiveness of Deleuzian methodological pragmatics. I will therefore proceed as follows. First, I will offer two brief sketches of what we might, rather loosely, call (1) the Platonic approach to understanding terrorism, which seeks a properly objective definition of terrorism; and (2) the post-Kantian approach to the problem of terrorism, which assumes the empirical fact of particular instances of terrorism, and then from such instances attempts to map out the very conditions under which terroristic activity becomes a possibility. As we shall see, both of these methods assume that terrorism is a phenomenon that is adequately addressed in terms of necessary or sufficient conditions. Second, I will offer a brief reconstruction of Deleuze's concept of events, outlining the event's double or problematic structure as the site of the interaction between the intensive immediacy of what Deleuze calls "real experience" and descriptive practices that promote determinate understandings of such experiences. I will refer briefly to the events of September 11 as a case study that exhibits the ways in which events become inscribed with determinate content and meaning. Finally, I will conclude by arguing that the structure of terrorism should be described as objectively problematic, since the actual experience the notion of "terrorism" evokes is one of variability and indeterminability. As such, it is at the level of the very concept of terrorism itself that we find the kind of intrinsic variability shared with concepts such as difference, the new, or the singular.

DEFINITIONS, EPISTEMIC NORMS, AND TRADITIONAL PHILOSOPHIES OF TERRORISM

The Platonic philosophy of terrorism seeks the proper definition of terrorism and is motivated by the notion that terrorism has a determinate objective structure that can be specified in a definition. Traditionally, defining concepts lies at the heart of philosophical inquiry;[2] it is a central preoccupation since Plato (*Meno, Republic, Theaetetus*) and continues into the present. In modernity, the view has been similar: concepts are understood as sets of features that are jointly necessary for any thing to be an instance of that concept. For example, in his seminal "On Sense and Reference," Gottlob Frege argues that truth not only depends on a proposition having a reference to something in the world, but also requires that the proposition have a *sense*, which he defines as an "objective content, which is capable of being the common property of several thinkers," regardless of language or whatever beliefs and desires are tied to the thought (28). A necessary condition for the truth of a proposition is that it has a sense. But, Frege argues, this is by no means a sufficient condition for truth. A proposition can "make sense" without actually referring to a determinate object or state of affairs in the world, as instanced in the proposition, "The Queen of Mars wears argyle socks." It is because we can conceive of a logically possible world in which the statement would be true that it achieves its sense (though Frege does not use this more contemporary language of "possible worlds"). Because it has no referent, such a statement cannot be true. However, as in cases of poetry or works of art, Frege observes that a lack of reference has no bearing on the sense of the proposition as a whole. The proposition "Odysseus was set ashore at Ithaca while sound asleep" (28), for instance, has a sense but not a referent. Yet it is only in works of art that we are content with the dimension of sense. As Frege says, "It is the striving for truth that drives us always to advance from the sense to the reference" (29). On Frege's view, then, it is the individually necessary and jointly sufficient components of sense and reference that define the concept of truth.

More recently, post-Gettier epistemology has been devoted to debates surrounding the necessary conditions for a concept of "knowledge." In his landmark 1963 paper, "Is Justified True Belief Knowledge?," Edmund Gettier challenged the notion that knowledge consists of three joint components of justification, truth, and belief, known traditionally as the JTB analysis of knowledge. Gettier argues by example: if Smith, who unknowingly happens to have ten coins in his pocket, has good evidence to believe the false proposition that "Jones, who has ten coins in his pocket, is the man who will get the job," then it follows that (*i*) "The man who will get the job has ten coins in his pocket." Smith sees this inference and believes the latter on the basis of the former. But if in truth, unbeknownst to Smith, it is actually Smith himself who will get the job, then Smith is justified in believing the true proposition (*i*), while it remains equally clear that he does not in fact possess knowledge of that claim since it does not reference the same individual as originally conceived by Smith. In the wake of Gettier's paper, a deluge of criticism flooded the epistemological landscape. Indeed, most epistemologists have accepted "the Gettier problem," taking it as having demonstrating that the traditional conjunction of justified true belief is not a jointly sufficient condition for knowledge (Jenkins).

It should not be surprising, then, that this tendency follows us into the literature on philosophy and terrorism. Michael Baur, for instance, writes, "Plato tells us that there must be some intrinsic characteristic about pious activity that makes it pious, apart from the further question of whether or why that activity is pleasing to the gods. In a similar vein, I want to suggest that there is some intrinsic characteristic about terrorism that makes it terroristic, apart from the further question of whether or why that activity is immoral or unjustified" (9). Granting this assumption, the debate turns on isolating these distinctive features: Is terrorism a certain kind of violence? A certain kind of war? Is it perpetrated only against noncombatants? Only against states? Is it morally neutral or intrinsically unjustified? Does terrorism require an agenda and a target audience? My point is not to downplay the importance of such questions; at the very least, they are crucial for understanding the nature of the problem. But the search for definitions that are neither over- nor underinclusive, nor merely question begging (e.g., is terrorism simply the activity of terrorists?), is apparently endless—especially given the various subcategories of terroristic phenomena such as cyberterrorism, industrial terrorism, and even ecoterrorism, which would all have to be accounted for under a comprehensive definition. Such proliferations of categorization, however, should be taken as reflecting the very nature of terrorism, that is, as indicative of the fact that terrorism itself is structured such that the necessity of increasing specification is a function of the essential variability of terrorism. Rather than invoking subjective limitations or relegating variable features to contingent material factors, as argued below, terrorism should be conceived as intrinsically mutable.

The next step, it seems, would be to qualify our many definitions of terrorism by grounding them within the contexts to which they are applicable. The insight here is that while some definitions of terrorism work in some contexts, other definitions prove more useful in other contexts. This might be the advantage of the post-Kantian approach, which abandons the search for strong definitions by making definitions function within certain points of view. Kant argued that before we can make genuine knowledge claims that pertain to either empirical objects or metaphysical objects (such as God, the soul, or the cosmos), we must first examine our subjective capacities for making such claims, that is, we must examine our point of view as rational agents and ask if such questions make sense for us in the first place, so that our claims to knowledge can be legitimately grounded. Kant grants the fact of cognition or knowledge and traces the conditions under which that knowledge is possible in the first place, in order to generalize the conditions for the possibility of knowledge as such. In a similar way, the post-Kantian approach to the problem of terrorism grants the empirical fact of terroristic acts and examines conditions under which such events obtain, in order to generalize the conditions under which terroristic acts can be predicted as a possibility.

The post-Kantian approach is applied in sociological, political, or socioeconomic theorizations of terroristic activity, in which the empirical evidence of terroristic acts is said to reflect the sorts of empirical conditions that are conducive to producing terrorist activity. Certain conditions of social, political, or economic injustice—specifically where the citizens of a particular social body see no way out of an unjust or oppressive situation—are often placed under such descriptions. Similarly, if the beliefs of a group of radicals include the notion that violence or its threat can effectively and productively usher in social change, and it is believed that an agenda (ideological or otherwise) can be so leveraged to influence an audience through the means of violence, it becomes clear that such conditions might be conducive to producing terroristic activities. Rather than gathering up many instances and debating about which are the essential features, the post-Kantian approach looks to specific instances of terrorism and interrogates the conditions under which such events take place, drawing qualified generalizations about those conditions in order to construct tentative definitions of terrorism sufficient enough to predict future events.

The post-Kantian approach seems recognize a key aspect of the problem of terrorism that is missed by its Platonic precursor, namely, that terrorism does not appear to have a unified essence, but rather exhibits—to use an oft-cited phrase from Wittgenstein—"family resemblances," which we can roughly sketch when we compare various instances of activities described as terroristic acts. Still, one might resign to skepticism since the various terroristic events appear to have nothing in common that would serve to unite them under a single, all-encompassing, unitary concept (the dream of the traditional Platonic essentialist). I would argue, however, that we should rather take this as a clue to the differential nature of terrorism, and not, in the extreme, become nominalists or relativists. Likewise, it should not be claimed that terrorism is ultimately a meaningless concept, or that the elusiveness of its true nature should lead us to describe its use in discourses as solely a function of politicized agendas or ideology. As we shall see, in turning to Deleuze, the function of the activity of problematization, whose basis lies in the event, is to break open the received descriptions that frame the solutions to problems in order to disclose the forces that structure the relationships between problems and solutions more generally. Such forces (what Deleuze polemically describe as, e.g., "common sense" or "good sense") preclude the movement of thought in new directions (*Difference and Repetition*, 129–67). Deleuze and Guattari define philosophy as the creation of concepts, where the latter serves not to represent a given state of affairs or to remain limited to exhaustive sets of either necessary or sufficient conditions, but rather to "extract" an event in order to formulate a problem in a new manner and push how we think about given problems in new directions.

From a Deleuzian perspective, then, the limits of these predominant methodologies stem from a shared practice of constructing determinate concepts of terrorism from received notions of what terrorism is, thereby precluding a differential methodology in the philosophy of terrorism. On the one hand, the Platonic view holds that the objective formal structure of terrorism must be constructed by discovering those essential features of terrorism that are jointly necessary for legitimating a claim that attributes an event's participation in that concept. Similarly, the post-Kantian approach looks to instances of terrorism in order to outline the conditions under which terroristic acts become a possibility. Here, for instance, cyber-terrorism and ecoterrorism share a fluid border rather than a robust participation in an overarching concept.

At a superficial level, the traditional philosophical charge would be that such methods are inherently circular—that is, in asking what it is that constitutes terrorism, such methods look to received instances of it, thereby presupposing the very concept in question. Yet are we not to look to instances of terrorism in order to discover what it is? How else could we possibly proceed? From a Deleuzian perspective, however, the issue lies elsewhere. It is not that such methods should be outright abandoned. Rather, the issue lies in the presupposition that such methods exhaust the issue, as if philosophy were concerned only with the discovery of the universal, and not, in addition, with its responsible employment. To a certain degree, the discovery of the universal features of terrorism is a useful and necessary enterprise; yet, over time, that which at one point is a necessary prolegomena to the creation of concepts—namely, the activity of selecting universals—risks becoming an end in itself, such that, to take the example of terrorism, differences among terrorist events fall by the wayside in favor of similarities that serve a purported universal concept. Such methods, in short, exhibit an indifference to the genuinely variable features of terroristic activity, where it is presupposed that only similar features play an active role in the construction of concepts, and where singular or variable features of particular instances of terrorism figure only minimally in discussions of its actual nature. The problem, then, is not that such methods are circular; it is rather that such methods bracket contingent features that might break up that circularity. Moreover, one might ask, would not such variability be an essential part of an understanding of terrorism, since the enactment of policy based on circularity in one's reasoning might leave one vulnerable to future instances? Indeed, if terrorists are interested in striking precisely where we are not looking, then it is downright dangerous to allow for a single-standing universal definition (à la Platonism) or a even a multiplicity of context-dependent definitions (à la post-Kantianism).

In short, the problem with such predominant methodologies in the philosophy of terrorism lies in a basic presupposition of the activity of most philosophizing more generally, namely, the presupposition that variable differences are themselves unproductive of concept construction, and that it is only by tracing similarities between instances that useful concepts can be produced. Therefore, while it is true that in both cases a received view of terrorism is already either consciously or unconsciously in place from the beginning—which risks a situation in which the outcome of the inquiry is already set up in advance, a situation that risks exploitation—such a presupposition is only possible, in the first instance, if we deny that positive concepts can be constructed out of the variable features between series of instances. In his early work, Deleuze will question the notion that a series or repetition of instances is adequately represented with reference only to the similarities among serial elements. As he argues, it must in fact be *difference* that allows an actual series to be constituted, where the condition of the actuality of repetition is difference, and sameness is an epiphenomenon resulting from selective mechanisms (*Difference and Repetition*). A Deleuzian approach to terrorism thus suggests that each event of terrorism is the birth of a potential series of determinate similar instances, rather than an instance of a predetermined concept. So, while the search for similar instances of terrorism is useful, a philosophical methodology that makes such a selective inquiry the basis for understanding the nature of terroristic events risks masking the variable features that render such events unpredictable, and hence in part terroristic, in the first place. Accordingly, it is variability rather than sameness that constitutes (at least in part) the essence of terrorism—an admittedly paradoxical conclusion, to be sure, but one which at least accounts for the unpredictability and senselessness associated with experiences of terroristic events.

So the problem comes into sharper relief when we observe that, in a specifically Deleuzian idiom, part of what it means for an event to be described as genuinely terroristic in nature is that it be properly new in every instance—that is, unprecedented, unpredictable, atypical, anomalous, singular, and so forth. Indeed, that the very experience of "terror"[3] is invoked to describe such events indicates that there is something about terrorism that exceeds our interpretations, representations, determinate descriptions, or even stipulative definitions. It seems, then, that terrorism is something that fits the description of properly Deleuzian concepts that exhibit the intrinsic variability that is grounded in events rather than in states of affairs or otherwise determinate conditions. As such, it is imperative that we come to an understanding of terrorism that grounds its concept in the experience of an event (i.e., in a concept that takes seriously what Deleuze refers to as temporal and "differential" conditions).

THE STRUCTURE AND ACTUALIZATION OF EVENTS IN DELEUZE

In order to understand terrorism as a kind of "event" in the Deleuzian sense, it is helpful to examine what Deleuze means when he says that events have a double or "problematic" structure. Deleuze does not have in mind our ordinary way of thinking about events, in which events either confirm or disconfirm a particular theory or notion already operative within a scientific, cultural, or sociopolitical imaginary. Such a description of events renders them a function of received terms and conditions that are already pre-understood. Deleuze seeks to invert this description by arguing that, far beyond any act of mere confirmation or refutation, events provide a resource for constructing and reconstructing our understandings of problems in new ways.

As such, events are neither simply given "facts" about the world, nor are they completely determined by either linguistic or otherwise ideal structures imposed by various forms of consciousness. Events exhibit a rich interplay of both realist and idealist structures of meaning. They are only minimally endowed with sense and meaning as given to consciousness, and as such, occupy a fluid border between the familiarity of meaning-endowed experience and the incomprehensibility of what is other or different—that is, phenomenologically, the unfamiliarity of exteriority. As Deleuze says, events are "virtual," that is, "real without being actual, ideal without being abstract" (Deleuze and Guattari, *What Is Philosophy?*, 156). Moreover, most events are typically not consciously present to our minds. Most events occur in our perceptual field at a relatively low degree of *intensity*, as Deleuze might say. Walking along the beach, for instance, I do not necessarily notice the grains of sand under my feet, the gradual tanning of my skin, or the sound of seagulls in the distance. Rather, such events are a confluence of these differential elements, which when taken individually in themselves are constituted by further events in their own right (e.g., the gradual erosion producing grains of sand under foot, or the multiplicity of factors producing the speed and direction of the wind at any particular moment). As such, events are multiplicities of differential elements that shape singular, unrepeatable experiences. Events occur in the here and now, and never twice; in short, they are essentially *indexical* in nature. To be sure, such experiences can be categorized under particular determinate contents and meanings, but this is how neither the form nor the matter of experience is initially given. In the first instance, experience is always already new, in at least some minimal sense. Therefore, as Deleuze argues, because events are given as only minimally determinate in this way, they are the closest approximation to the real itself, exhibited in consciousness as the "real experience" of raw and unfiltered novelty in its immediacy (Deleuze, "Bergson's Conception," 46; *Difference and Repetition*, 68–69, 154, 285; 1990, 260).

One of the more concrete ways in which we can establish what "event" means is by turning to the social and political sphere. Consider what takes place when agents stage a genuine challenge to received social and political institutions. The abolition of apartheid, the movement for women's equality, and the civil rights movement can all be characterized as attempts to extract a historical event in its immediacy, an event which could have gone one way but went another—the goal of which is to create a practical awareness of social and political forces that agents might desire to either oppose or advance. In doing so, individuals or groups must break prevalent habits of thought and action, in order to allow new or "minor" possibilities to emerge, wresting new possibilities from the determinate descriptions that would otherwise exclude such possibilities. Such are attempts to specify or "unmediate" an event in order to generate resources for experimental thought and action.

Consider, for instance, Martin Luther King's "dream," which envisioned the equality of races as the equality of human beings as beings who bear rights, an idea which escapes and disrupts the determinate conditions of King's historical situation (understood as the totality of facts of that particular moment in history). In Deleuze's language, King's dream follows a "line of flight" or creates a "war machine" that opposes the well-defined rules laid out by prevailing social matrices of the day (Deleuze and Guattari, *A Thousand Plateaus*, 422–23). From Deleuze's point of view, however, it is crucial that such acts of resistance are neither voluntary nor wholly autonomous, but rather fall upon the agents involved. It must be experienced that the situation truly necessitates a fundamental change and that the group has no choice but to engage experimental practices in the interests of effecting change. Indeed, Deleuze rejects autonomous voluntarism for the reason that, quite plainly on his view, no one truly changes his or her problematic habits unless something happens that truly necessitates it. While King's dream upsets the role that the dominant discourse maintains, it is as if the vision is *forced* into consciousness like a sublime inspiration, rather than being wholly voluntary. It is an event of the highest intensity, as Deleuze might say. It is in this sense that, by denaturalizing social and political institutions, in order to critically survey a multiplicity of indeterminate possibilities for constructing novel responses to the present, King's vision discloses the very possibility of reconstructing experience in genuinely new and meaningful ways—under the weight of the idea-event that necessitates that thought and action reconsider raced habits of exclusion.

Hence Deleuze's description of the double nature of events. While it is obvious that empirical events do in fact take place (their corporeal dimension), and such events are readily categorized and inscribed with a familiar meaning, it is also the case that events so often exhibit a potentiality for taking on new meanings—that is, events exhibit, however minimally, an inherent potentiality for reconstructing present experience (their ideal or incorporeal dimension [Deleuze 1990, 151]). To be sure, there is little at stake in average everyday events such as boiling water or tuning up a car (although while brushing one's teeth one might suddenly notice oneself in the mirror and experience an existential crisis). Yet with events like terrorism, or more specifically 9/11, by contrast, the stakes are obviously very high. The question concerning how these major events should be described is critical, given that bare events, in themselves, have no meaning until they are either consciously or unconsciously attributed a meaning by a collective body. Moreover, given this intrinsic variability within the structure of the event itself, we can observe with Paul Patton that this is precisely the reason why so much time and energy in politics is spent struggling over the appropriate description of events, since it is little more than the description, that is, the meaning attribution, that is going to guide our thought and action in responding to events. In addition, then, there is important performative dimension involved in the description of events, since it is this or that particular discourse that shapes the meaning of events, channeling events in particular selective ways, and effectively creating conditions of which certain responses to events become necessitated.

The immediate aftermath of 9/11 provides us with a useful case study of the ways in which such major events become actualized. As an event, 9/11 exhibits the double structure that we have briefly outlined above. On the one hand, there is the actualized terrorist act that 9/11 has come to signify, namely, the "turning point" in America's sociopolitical self-understanding (though the actual positive effects of that transformation remain debatable) and, on the other hand, the "moment" that took place on September 11, 2001, the "instant," the pure event, or brute happening prior to its taking on a particular content and meaning, where chaos reigned amid attempts to stabilize precisely what was happening. This latter dimension can usually be described only in negative terms: we know that something is happening, but we cannot be sure what it is; its singularity escapes our familiar structures of meaning. Whatever it is, it is utterly and painfully new.

One process by which the event is "actualized," that is, inscribed with a determinate content and meaning, is found in the social functioning of language. Various discrete happenings—such as planes crashing into buildings, people running aimlessly through the streets, and firefighters heroically facing the chaos—are unified through determinate description. In making sense of the event, words and phrases such as "terrorism," "act of war," "freedom is under attack," and "enemies of freedom" simultaneously produce and reproduce the actualized event, through jointly present words and images that provide it with a determinate narrative.[4] In this way, the prepersonal and singular event is transformed, taking on a unified meaning that compels us to understand the event in particular ways, not only as individuals, but as a collective social body—we as "the American people" are no longer the same. Through the endless repetition of words and images, the meaning of the event becomes naturalized in shared consciousness, where agents are compelled to understand the event in certain ways.

It should be noted that I do not mean to imply that our collective understanding of 9/11 is a mere fiction. I am not interested in arguing such absurd claims, nor am I interested in melodramatic statements such as "9/11 never happened." I am furthermore not interested in some form of "media critique," in which we decry the media for politicizing and distorting the flow of information of events. The point is simply to draw our attention to the manner in which an event becomes actualized through competing discourses that represent the event in particular ways, veritably creating the experience and recall of events, both individually and collectively. It is by paying close attention to such selective mechanisms—as non-value-neutral tactics and strategies that govern naturalized representations—that we come to see most explicitly the double structure of events, processes of the actualization of events, and the productive and reproductive social function of language in the creation and naturalization of particular narratives of events.

TERRORISM AS AN OBJECTIVELY PROBLEMATIC STRUCTURE

Deleuze's analysis of the event seeks to show that the event and its description are not innately coextensive phenomena, but rather that there remains in the empirical or actualized event a pure or incorporeal dimension that not only resists our attempts to ground it categorically, but more importantly, implicates our descriptions in processes of variation and mutability. The possibility of thinking the nature of events, then, brings us to a level of a pure variability, which throughout his work Deleuze seeks to access by creating concepts like the virtual, the new, the creative, or the singular. Yet to describe terrorism as new in each case still does not accurately capture what actually happens in a terroristic event; it does, however, get us relatively closer to the objectively problematic structure of terrorism itself. To describe terrorism as objectively problematic is to invoke an order of problems that are never fully captured by the subjective conditions for possible experience that understand the world through interpretations or description. Therefore, such problems are not fully resolvable through an examination of the structures that produce the order of experience, but are rather presented to us at the very limit between what is familiar to us and what in principle remains foreign to us—not only given relative subjective finitude, but also given that, objectively, events seem to be imbricated within and among one another in an infinite continuity.

More positively, however, the problematic nature of terrorism opens up the experimental character of thought and action. What, then, would a properly Deleuzian answer to the question "what is terrorism?" look like? First, it should be clear that, realistically, terrorism is not a problem that can be resolved once and for all; since it is a properly objective problem, it can only be dealt with pragmatically and temporarily. As John Protevi ("Case Studies") suggests, such problems can be resolved only relatively well or poorly, since our actions now at resolving the problem have consequences that introduce differences into the conditions of future instances of the problem. A Deleuzian position mandates a substantial degree of realist or Stoic acceptance of, for instance, the sorts of global and economic hegemony associated with the production of terrorist activity. At the same time, however, a Deleuzian position mandates a perhaps higher degree of idealist optimism that such associated issues can be mitigated, as I will suggest in more detail below, by activities involving social consciousness, nonviolent resistance, and conscientious objection.

In posing the question of terrorism on Deleuzian terms, then, we are not simply looking for a set of universal and necessary conditions that define terrorism. More deeply, we are looking for those differences that make terrorism terroristic in the first place in order to disclose possibilities for not only combating terrorism through familiar means, but also through activities of resistance that seek to change cultural patterns of thought and behavior, which contribute to the production of the very conditions that make terrorism possible (such as perceived global and economic inequality and systematized injustice). Deleuze himself supports such a position when, echoing the sentiments of a genuinely experimental and creative approach to concept construction, he says that "it's not a matter of bringing all sorts of things together under a single concept but rather of relating each concept to variables that explain its mutations" (*Negotiations*, 31). This means that when we philosophize about terrorism we should not only draw out similarities in the direction of constructing a universal concept, but also take equally seriously the genuine differences between situations, treating such differences as opportunities for reconceiving the values that our categories possess. This is for two reasons: (1) it is going to be those differences that are constitutive of the singularity of the event itself, and (2) those differences are going to allow us to construct a creative response to the problem, since they will be new features of the problem that are revealed by its particular relation to the given situation.

In other words, to paraphrase Protevi ("An Approach") once more, the problematic is not just about recognizing "terrorism," as if we could produce a finite set of necessary and sufficient conditions so that we can judge something as falling within the category of "terrorism"; the problem lies rather in the conditions for the creative transformation of terrorism, that is, the ways in which terrorism exhibits an internal potential for mutation along its differential or singular turning points. It follows that the transformation of our concept of terrorism is also a critical transformation of ourselves. It should be clear, then, that the Deleuzian approach differs from either the Platonic or post-Kantian methods in at least one crucial aspect, namely, that the latter look to instances of terrorism, but, in bracketing what makes individual instances different, merely reaffirm received views; while the Deleuzian approach looks to instances of terrorism with an eye to the differences or mutations that indicate terrorism's variable nature, those features which would render necessary our thinking the concept in new ways by forcing our habits of philosophizing out of traditional normative-epistemic molds. As Deleuze says, concepts as historically conceived "lack the claws of absolute necessity—in other words, of an original violence inflicted upon thought," where *necessity* has less to do with the laws of logic and is more deeply founded in experiences where thought is truly awakened and forced into action through problematic encounters, as in our example of King above (*Difference and Repetition*, 139). This more originary sense of "necessity," I would argue, is an important part of philosophizing about the nature of terrorism, as bearing a nonlinear and differential structure, since the event of a terrorist act is also a symptom of the necessity of a transformation of our own collective habits of thought. It is therefore part of the very meaning of "terrorism" for it to be problematic, since its most important consequence—philosophically, as well as socially and politically—mandates an experimental comportment of thought and action, one which takes seriously the shifting relations within globalized communities, and necessitates an equally variable approach to philosophizing about global issues.

In line with the foregoing argument, I would like to conclude by emphasizing one basic takeaway point. In *What Is Philosophy?*, Deleuze and Guattari announce that the sole task of philosophy is to ask what it means to become "worthy" of events (160). Naturally, this is a nebulous question on its own, especially given the difficulty of discerning just what is actually meant by the phrase "becoming worthy." Now it is well known that the idea of becoming worthy shows up in the ethical reflections of Kant, in the context of uniting the ends that seek to promote our individual happiness with the unconditional obligations that are dictated by the moral laws of pure practical reason (the conjunction of which Kant calls the highest good). However, perhaps closer to what Deleuze has in mind is actually Nietzsche's description of those he calls "noble ones" that is, those who face the events of life with an affirmative posture, aiming in the direction of creative and productive self-transformation. I take this to mean that any transformation that carries with it a robust challenge to received patterns of thought and action calls for an openness to the general problematization of such patterns, where to "become worthy of the event" requires that we take seriously the challenge to put our received views into question, allowing encounters with the new to present themselves as a real experience of the possibility of positive transformation, rather than a mere acknowledgment of different points of view while for the most part remaining faithful to our own problematic behaviors.

Placing this notion of transformation into the core of ethical reflection is complex, but it relates first of all to Deleuze's challenge to modern ethical concepts, which tend to centralize agency and autonomy. Deleuze's deeply Spinozist-Nietzschean ethics, by contrast, is radically relational, emphasizing the composition of the ethical subject as a complex body of flows, forces, intensities, and most importantly, constitutive relations to others—where "other" is extended beyond the Levinasian-Derridean intersubjective sense to include organic and nonorganic material processes, sociopolitical institutions, and cultural norms. As Rosi Braidotti summarizes (195), Deleuze poses a threefold challenge to contemporary ethics. First, the object of ethical inquiry is found in the material conditions under which the transformation of the individual and the collective becomes a live option, rather than the application of universal rules to variable conditions. Second, this challenge shifts the focus away from subjectivity and moral agency toward a vision of ethical life generated primarily by affects and relations. Third, it rejects theories of subject constitution that emphasize historical development via negation, or psychological development via conditioning in favor of constitutive relations of alterity not limited to (inter)subjectivity. This in turn reflects a threefold pragmatic ideal in Deleuzian ethics. First, there is the ideal of a politically resistant notion freedom as self-determination or self-styling, which opposes juridical conceptions of freedom in terms of universal rights or entitlements. Second, this notion of freedom ideally resists forms of governmentality conceived as regimes of knowledge and disciplinary matrices that produce desired forms of subjectivity. Third, it conceives of an ideal of emancipatory practices as a "micropolitics" wherein localized and concrete ethical acts are valued over grand overarching visions. As Braidotti maintains, all of this is geared toward concrete practices of actualizing *sustainable* modes of transformation, where openness to the new, the different, and the singular constitutes the core of ethical reflection.

Ethical worth therefore lies in the degree to which one is able to engage a Spinozist-Nietzschean depersonalizing of whatever injustice has been suffered, truly "the ultimate ethical challenge," as Braidotti (182) suggests. On this view, ethics is not about avoiding pain in the interest of pleasure, nor about justifying retributive acts for injustices inflicted; nor is it about the application of universal principles that confer moral worth on particular actions. Deleuze's is an *affirmative* ethics of positive transformation, wherein the moral strength of an individual or social body is determined by the degree to which one is able to sustain negative and reactive affects and transform them into positive and productive values, themselves open to transformation. In short, ethics concerns collective and individual *moral health*, where the latter is achieved to the degree that an individual or social body is open to new modes of thought and action—without, on the one hand, merely reacting to the forces that necessitate moral/political transformation by clinging to static principles removed from the affective nexus of problems that gave rise to them, and without, on the other hand, falling into forms of relativism that also in principle isolate individuals and collectives from the affective forces conducive to positive transformation.

What I would like to suggest, then, is that becoming worthy of the event of terrorism should include, in the very least, responses to the event that do not issue in further reactive violence, but rather allow the question of our self-reflection to genuinely and concretely pose itself both privately and publicly. Of course, there really is no question that the perpetrators of 9/11 acted in unspeakably reprehensible manner. Dominant discourses, however, typically emphasize victimization and retribution, and it is clear that the responses that follow depend upon such descriptions of the event that conceal the need for a new social and political transformation, for which terrorism is almost always a symptom. In the case of 9/11, descriptions that treat the event as an "act of war," or descriptions that continue to contextualize the event in terms of the "enemies of freedom," actively create and recreate a political imaginary in which a "war on terrorism" is necessary. Indeed, such responses play an active role in reinforcing received views of the problem, rather than letting the problem present itself as an event that challenges us to question our implicit biases concerning the nature of social and political relations in a globalized context. From a Deleuzian perspective, and in contrast to such reactive mechanisms, it is rather by letting events usher in creative responses for thinking in new ways that we become worthy.

NOTES

1.   By "attributes" of being, I take Deleuze to mean traditional concepts of, for example, essence, form, substance, or identity.

2.   Here I borrow from Timothy Shanahan's opening remarks in his lucid paper, "Betraying a Certain Corruption of Mind: How (and How Not) to Define Terrorism" (2010).

3.   As a phenomenological point of interest, one might argue that terror is distinct from both anxiety and fear, where the latter is typically experienced only in the presence of some fearful object. While terror certainly takes place in the present,

it seems to spread beyond present experience, drawing on one's memories of being fearful or anxious, as well as projecting into future anxieties of what is to come that might possibly produce further fear or anxiety. In this sense, terror plays on a more complex and integrated temporal structure than does fear, which is, again, typically grounded only in the present experience of something fearful. What's more, while terror shares with anxiety this complex temporal structure, it could be argued that its distinction from anxiety lies in its taking place on a collective social and political level rather than on an individual or existential level. Finally, it should be borne in mind that terror is not simply the result of a collection of anxious individuals, since it is terror that in fact characterizes the situation in which the individuals are involved, rather than obtaining solely on a psychological level. Phenomenologically, then, the terror that characterizes individuals obtains collectively, that is, jointly with its obtaining in any single individual, unlike anxiety, which can obtain solely within an individual.

4.   By contrast, recall Jeremiah Wright, whose claim that 9/11 represents "America's chickens coming home to roost," effectively implicating the United States for the attacks on a national scale, was treated as a scandal and immediately politicized, especially given President Obama's ties to that church.

WORKS CITED

Baur, Michael. "What Is Distinctive About Terrorism, and What Are the Philosophical Implications?" In *Philosophy 9/11: Thinking About the War on Terrorism*. Edited by Timothy Shanahan. Chicago: Open Court, 2005. 3–21.

Braidotti, Rosi. "Nomadic Ethics" In *The Cambridge Companion to Deleuze*, edited by Daniel W. Smith and Henry-Somers Hall, 170–97. New York: Cambridge University Press, 2012.

Deleuze, Gilles. "Bergson's Conception of Difference." In *The New Bergson*, edited by John Mullarkey, translated by Melissa McMahon, 42–65. New York: Manchester University Press, 1999.

———. *Difference and Repetition*. Translated by Paul Patton. New York: Columbia University Press, 1994.

———. *The Logic of Sense*. Edited by Mark Lester with Charles Stivale. Translated by Constantin Boundas. New York: Columbia University Press, 1990.

———. *Negotiations 1972–1990*. Translated by by Martin Joughin. New York: Columbia University Press, 1997.

Deleuze, Gilles and Felix Guattari. *A Thousand Plateaus*. Translated by Brian Massumi. Minneapolis: University of Minnesota Press, 1987.

———. *What Is Philosophy?* Translated by Hugh Tomlinson and Graham Burchell. New York: Columbia University Press, 1994.

Frege, Gottlob. "On Sense and Reference." In *Meaning and Reference*, edited by A. W. Moore, 23–42. New York: Oxford University Press, 1993.

Gettier, Edmund. "Is Justified True Belief Knowledge?" *Analysis* 23, no. 6 (1963): 121–23. http://dx.doi.org/10.1093/analys/23.6.121.

Ichikawa, Jonathan Jenkins and Steup, Matthias. "The Analysis of Knowledge." *The Stanford Encyclopedia of Philosophy* (Spring 2014 ed.). Edited by Edward N. Zalta. Last updated November 15, 2012. http://plato.stanford.edu/entries/knowledge-analysis/.

Patton, Paul. "The World Seen From Within: Deleuze and the Philosophy of Events." *Theory & Event* 1, no. 1 (1997). http://dx.doi.org/10.1353/tae.1991.0006.

Protevi, John. "An Approach to *Difference and Repetition*." *Journal of Philosophy: A Cross-Disciplinary Inquiry* 5, no. 11 (2010). http://dx.doi.org/10.5840/jphilnepal20105115.

———. "Case Studies: Beyond Thought Experiments and Experimental Philosophy." *NewAPPS: Art, Politics, Philosophy, Science*. September 24, 2010. http://www.newappsblog.com/2010/09/case-studies.html.

Shanahan, Timothy. "Betraying a Certain Corruption of Mind: How (and How Not) to Define Terrorism." *Critical Studies on Terrorism* 3, no. 2 (2010): 173–90. http://dx.doi.org/10.1080/17539150903306139.

3

Symbolic Violence as Subtle Virulence: A Philosophy of Terrorism

JONATHAN BEEVER

The analysis of terrorism by contemporary French philosopher and cultural theorist Jean Baudrillard presents terrorism as the violence of empty representation—from symbolic representation to simulation. While there has been a significant amount written on Baudrillard's work on terrorism (see Staples), few scholars have focused on his analysis as not merely cultural but more specifically and interestingly semiotic. This focus gives us a way to better understand Baudrillard's analysis and its implications post-9/11. In this essay, I employ a semiotic framework to explore the contemporary problem of terrorism, outline three levels of violence, and distinguish these from terrorism. The goal of this analysis is to reenvision a not only political but also symbolic response to terror.[1]

THE PROBLEM OF TERRORISM

The relationship between modernity and postmodernity is a useful conceptual heuristic for analysis of modes of cultural thinking. Neither modernity

nor postmodernity ought to be considered descriptions of particular historical moments, but rather markers of modes of thought characterized by their
relationship to the so-called grand narratives of society—nature, the good,
the state, and so forth. One marker of modernist thought is the assumption
that we can take such concepts as baseline epistemic markers against which
to evaluate knowledge and value claims. Postmodernity, problematizing the
stability of these concepts, likewise problematizes the ways in which we justify claims about truth and goodness. We can evaluate terrorism within this
structure of modernity and postmodernity.

Terrorism as the violence of modernity can be understood as any reaction against the structure of the institution—broadly construed, a reaction of
good against evil. The United States Department of Defense defines terrorism
as "the calculated use of unlawful violence or threat of unlawful violence to
inculcate fear; intended to coerce or to intimidate governments or societies
in the pursuit of goals that are generally political, religious, or ideological"
(Defense Technical Information Center). The political democratic state represents terrorism as intentionally violent threats to the system and our political ideology. Here, terrorism is a specifically political form of violence—one
threatening civil ideologies, cultural norms, or systemic infrastructures. As a
result of this definition, the United States has seen the rise of entire economic
and political machinery in response to terrorism. Much effort has been spent
in definition of, defense against, and response to real and imagined terrorist threats during the United States' notorious Global War on Terror. But we
must not accept this cultural definition tout court. The Department of Defense
offers, as a function of its specific purpose, a narrow definition of a multi-
faceted and deeply complex concept. This model provides dangerous space
for the labeling of an incredibly broad group of anti-institutionalists as terrorists: foreign nationals, local militias, the prolific independent radio host,
the local author, the anarchistic philosophy professor, the Iranian-American
neighbor. By shifting the modes of representation through reinterpretation and
the manipulation of signs, arbitrary but definitive representations of differences between "us" and "them" can be made in response to real or imagined
threats. But setting apart the other through the manipulation of signs leaves
no space to distinguish political violence from acts of terrorism. Whether
violence is politically justified or an unjustified act of terror is a normative

question. The conditions that dictate the answer, in this case, are not political but semiotic. Whereas political violence may be justifiable in conditions of political oppression, terrorism, on this model, may be justifiable in conditions of symbolic oppression. So to hold up this definition—and, by extension, this way of thinking—as normative or ethically binding is to deliver a coup on behalf of the state: as long as there is a monopoly of control over representation, the definition of the enemy—the other—becomes merely a tool of power and of control, on this modernist reading.

Baudrillard offers an alternative anti- or postmodernist view. His analysis foreshadowed the possibilities of a postmodern landscape and remained critical of the structures of modernity. As an antimodern response, Baudrillard's analysis is grounded in an understanding of the implications of semiotic or sign-based representation as a means of decentralizing the grand narratives of modernity. Here we find a delineation of the boundaries and implications of terrorism quite unlike the political structures of modernity; this postmodern analysis offers a cynical celebration of the virulence of signification. We must here ask: what do we mean by signification, and furthermore, virulent signification? Signification is the action of signs forming these basic relationships between signified and signifier that are the foundations of meaning.[2] This dyadic relationship between the real object and its representation stands as the basic ontological foundation for Baudrillard's analysis of antimodern violence. Virulent signification, however, as we will see, is uniquely related to violence divorced from this dyadic exchange—it is linked to the production of what Baudrillard calls simulacra, signs divorced from their real referents.

THE FORMS OF VIOLENCE

Baudrillard's semiotic analysis leads us through three forms of violence. In one form, violence is aggressive. Aggression is the most basic form of violence—the violence of brute strength, be it physical, economic, or political. This is not the violence of Odyssean slyness, but rather that of Achillean brutality: the simple and efficient violence of the schoolyard bully, the corporate takeover, or political campaign maneuvering. Baudrillard, in "The Violence of the Image," describes this form simply as "the unilateral violence of the most powerful." This violence may manifest as the seat of class struggle or as interpersonal and ideological clashes.

In another form, violence is historical: the political (r)evolutions of the right over the wrong, and of moral good over moral evil. This historical form of violence is the revolutionary reaction to aggression. It is the political overthrow, the critical, negative reaction to the oppression endemic to aggressive violence. Baudrillard also calls this form "the violence of analysis and interpretation," suggesting that historical violence signifies or stands for the very event to which it responds ("The Violence"). Baudrillard notes, "in the name of Good, people try to give shape to Evil, for example in the terrorism they see everywhere" (*The Agony*, 112). These first and second forms of violence offer descriptions of modes of modernist political violence.

But in a third and perhaps more fundamental form, violence becomes the act of the proliferation of the symbol. While Baudrillard wrote in 1976 that "symbolic violence in itself has no more to do with signs than it has to do with the relationship between forces" (*Symbolic Exchange*, 242), he intended to uphold the distinction between signs and simulacra. However, simulacra are signs, albeit ones divorced from real objects. Thus, I claim that symbolic violence is indeed semiotic in nature. The act of representation, the giving of meaning to a symbol, takes on a life of its own in an act of semiotic self-replication. The further removed from the real object of representation this replication gets, the more transient the sign becomes, the further it is removed from its original meaning, in a movement reminiscent of the telephone game of whispers from our childhood. Such proliferation creates a subtle and violent virulence of simulacra: the symbolic becomes a viral simulation that threatens to subsume the real under a mountain of misrepresentation. For Baudrillard, this third form of violence is the exploitation and eventual disintegration of the signified real through the proliferation of what he calls the "murderous image." Violence in this form is endemic to terrorism. "We are witnessing the rise," Baudrillard wrote in 1993, "of terrorism as a transpolitical form . . . these forms are viral—fascinating, indiscriminate—and their virulence is reinforced by their images" *(The Transparency,* 36). If the first two forms of violence are characteristic of modernity, the third symbolic form—the virulence of empty signs, or simulacra—is characteristic of the semiotic postmodernity described above.

Understanding the historic conflation of these types of violence offers us a context by which to understand the ultimate failure of militaristic responses to "terror"; a symbolic challenge cannot be mitigated by an aggressive response or by ideological assertions from the political machine. This third form of violence is different in kind, not merely in scope or by degree. The semiotic nature of symbolic violence pushes beyond the boundaries of what I have defined as the violence of modernity, not merely by representing violence through the image, but also by proliferating a virulent strain of empty signs, or simulacra.

Under the modernist paradigm, the sign represents the real, the objective; the sign becomes an image of the real. The rapid and continued development of technological information systems has done something inherently violent to the real through the viral proliferation of the image. The image begins to take precedence: reality shows and advertising campaigns, political slander and ideological newscasts, stand up in place of the real. The relation to the real offered by the sign becomes one of suggestion or manipulation. We wonder why the number of Americans who believe that President Obama is a Muslim had grown to one in five by 2010 (The Pew Forum), or why a single book-burning by an ultra-conservative Florida pastor that same year seemed to be considered a legitimate threat to the fastest-growing and second largest religion in the world (Cave and Barnard). For Baudrillard, the answer lies in the virulent rise of the simulacra: "Finally, the real world becomes a useless function, a collection of phantom shapes and ghost events. We are not far from the silhouettes on the walls of the cave of Plato" ("The Violence"). This restatement of the theoretical point Baudrillard had made as early as 1976 marks violence as transposed from the interaction of real substance to the interplay among images in such a way that we are left actually unaffected.[3] It is as if the referent disappears and is lost among the virulence of signification.

This explosion of viral signification became, for Baudrillard, a marker of our cultural condition, and gave structure to his analysis of terrorism. In 1985, Brussels' Heysel Stadium erupted in violence when Liverpool soccer fans broke through a barricade and rushed Juventus fans. The latter retreated, killing several in a stampede that ended in the collapse of a concrete retaining wall and further death. Baudrillard's account of this event was a reiteration of a social theoretical point: such violence is the direct result of the political and social disaffection society suffers as a result of the virulence of the image. Explanations "by political, sociological, or psychological approaches are simply not capable of accounting for such events" (*The Transparency*, 75–76). A richer account is offered by Baudrillard's analysis of the proliferation of signs replacing real events. This same analysis places the Heysel Stadium event in the same category of terror: the viral symbol running rampant over the real event as an impetus for violence.

When signs begin to simulate rather than reference, the objects of those signs—be they physical or ideological—lose their footings. Political reactions, aggression against oppression, and even basic assertions to truth claims become tenuous if not impossible to uphold. The intentional aspect of violence toward the state from our modernist definition of terrorism—good versus evil—here loses its centrality, and terrorism becomes tied instead to the collapse of the symbol.

THE SYMBOLIC FORM OF TERRORISM

The events of the 1980s that influenced this early analysis of symbolic violence were, for Baudrillard, heightened by the actions of and reactions to the events of September 11, 2001. The symbolic importance of 9/11 extends his analysis from violence to terrorism. The historical violence that existed as a response to oppression by the state is replaced by violence that exists in response to the virulence of simulated representation—the violence of terrorism. The strikes against and eventual collapse of the Twin Towers can be classified a terrorist attack within both frameworks we have outlined. For the Department of Defense, the event was a terrorist attack because it was an intentional aggressive-violent movement against the state. For Baudrillard, the event was a terrorist attack because it was a symbolic irruption against the simulacra of the United States as the modernist state. If a handful of men had detonated explosives with no other effect than their own deaths and some collateral damage, 9/11 would not hold the significance that it does. If the towers had not fallen, the event would be insignificant.[4] Consider, as another example, the earthquake on August 24, 2011 that cracked the Washington Monument. "Sure we're disappointed the monument is closed," a woman was reported to have said, "but it would be really upsetting if it had fallen over." Another proclaimed, "People say that the monument is broken like our political system. But the fact is, it's still standing and so are we" (Thompson, A16). Imagine if the monument had collapsed in sympathy with the Twin Towers. Given slightly different circumstances, the August 24 earthquake could have easily been read as a terrorist event—the collapse of yet another symbol of the state, the earthquake as the terrorist other. Imagine, on the other hand, if the Twin Towers had not collapsed.

The spirit of terrorism is semiotic in nature; it is grounded in the symbolic representation of violence. The strike against the Twin Towers was a symbolic one, even if the twin collapse was not the intention of the agents involved: "Neither politically nor economically did the abolition of the Twin Towers put the global system in check. Something else is at issue here: the stunning impact of the attack, the insolence of its success and, as a result, the loss of credibility, the collapse of image" (Baudrillard, "The Spirit," 82). An act of violent aggression became an act of terrorism through the symbolic collapse of the towers-as-symbol. Beyond the immense physical damage, the terrible loss of human life, and the temporary interruption of financial and social information transfer, the stability, security, and power that the Twin Towers symbolized was threatened. A hole was stabbed through that empty signifier, and at least for a moment, the world saw through to the fragile and raw signified object underneath the pile of empty signs.

The attacks of 9/11 were unlike political violence, civil unrest, or even international acts of war in that the terrorists managed, through the resulting collapse of the image for which the Twin Towers stood, to snub the rules of violent engagement with which the state is attuned. Pearl Harbor, the Cold War standoff, and the resulting Cuban Missile Crisis were instances of violence or potential violence that fell within the framework of the political, social, and economic system of which they were a part. These were not, or would not have been, acts of terrorism because their primary target was political, not symbolic. The violence of the 9/11 attacks, however, can be classified as terrorism; the results of the bombers' actions were symbolic in nature as well as and even to a greater degree than they were political. It was as if they had followed Baudrillard's own "advice" when he wrote:

Never attack the system in terms of relations of force. That is the (revolutionary) imagination the system itself forces upon you—the system which survives only by constantly drawing those attacking it into fighting on the ground of reality, which is always its own. But shift the struggle into the symbolic sphere, where the rule is that of challenge, reversion, and outbidding. *So that death can be met only by equal or greater death.* Defy the system by a gift to which it cannot respond except by its own death and its own collapse. ("Hypotheses," 17)

Symbolic violence is terrorism in that it perpetuates events that thrust the ontological emptiness of simulacra up against the representations of the real. This form of terrorism frames the collapse of image around the ontological fragility of whatever the foundations of this representation might have been. In this way, symbolic violence is the violence of terrorism.

RESPONSES TO TERROR

Violence is never terrorism unless it exists first as a symbolic action. This is the contribution Baudrillard offers to the ongoing international discussion seeking to define this concept. Terrorism is understood as a symbolic act—specifically the virulent proliferation of the image—as a function of systemic political antagonism, but also as a function of the condition of semiotic simulation under which this paradigm functions. The lucid moment that the terrorist action brings to light is the recognition that the good is not absolute or unchanging, but is itself a semiotic concept held up by the play of simulacra. This is the fundamental point that contemporary responses to terror have failed to comprehend.

The Department of Defense and other political, militarized organizations often respond to symbolic terrorist acts as if they were a form of aggression against the sociopolitical machinery of the state: they mobilize forces, exert power, seek revenge against the other. Baudrillard's insightful analysis claims that this political power "plays at the real, plays at crisis, plays at remanufacturing artificial, social, economic, and political stakes" in the face of the "play of signs" (*Simulacra*, 22). This "play of signs"—the viral symbolic nature of terror—is something that, from within a modernist framework, the state has failed to recognize. It remains unable to comprehend its own weakness regarding symbolic representation and the possibility of simulation. Instead, it offers an inappropriate response to such an inherently symbolic event.

Indeed, what is the appropriate response to terror if our access is only to the precession of models, of possible symbolic representations, of simulacra? "We are in a logic of simulation," Baudrillard writes, "which no longer has anything to do with a logic of facts and an order of reason. Simulation is characterized by a *precession of the model*, of all the models based on the merest fact. . . . These facts no longer have a specific trajectory, they are born at the intersection of models, a single fact can be engendered by all the models at once" (*Simulacra*, 16). Responses to terror must themselves "play the game," so to speak. To avoid falling into an abyss of terror—to effectively respond to viral representation and reproduction of the symbolic event of terror—they must differentiate terrorism from political violence by its symbolic nature.

This viral semiotic form of violence is a challenge to our political order of power that takes into account the symbolic nature of terror and the modes of simulation and finds space between political violence and terrorist acts. Only in these terms can the state respond to that symbolic challenge with an appropriately symbolic response. And yet perhaps we see the first recognition of Baudrillard's challenge in the killing of Osama Bin Laden in May 2011 (Phillips). His assassination and the burial of his body at sea set up one symbol and denied another: the political symbol destroyed and the martyr denied. The killing of Osama Bin Laden (Phillips) was, arguably, the destruction of a simulacrum, a symbolic response. It was not centrally a political move or a moment of "frontier justice," as was the trial and execution of Saddam Hussein in 2006, but rather a primarily and importantly symbolic action—an image for an image, the reciprocal justice of Hammurabi done in the name of the symbol, the simulation of the good and the right.

Baudrillard wrote of the Gulf War, "Saddam Hussein, for his part, bargains his war by overbidding in order to fall back, attempting to force the hand by pressure and blackmail, like a hustler trying to sell his goods. The Americans understand nothing in this whole psychodrama of bargaining, they are had every time until, with the wounded pride of the Westerner, they stiffen and impose their conditions. . . . The Americans . . . have much to learn about symbolic exchange" (*The Gulf War*, 54–55). While we had "much to learn about symbolic exchange" in 2006, perhaps May 2011 indicated our ability to learn. As such, it should be recognized as indicating impressive conceptual acuity. On the view offered here, the objective of terrorism is rightly defined as the manipulation of the viral simulacrum. As such, it is rightly owed a symbolic response.

NOTES

1.   A version of this essay has been previously published in the International Journal of Baudrillard Studies. This version appears here with permission.

2.   While I describe Baudrillard's approach to signification in his dyadic terms (Saussure's signifier and signified), the virulence of simulacra may be better explained in triadic terms (Peirce's interpretant, representamen, and object). That is, *meaning* by way of the *interpretant* plays an active role distinct from the *representamen* and the *object* on a triadic reading. This triadic understanding likewise offers better support for Baudrillard's insistence on the symbolic as an *exchange* rather than a concept or category (see "Toward a Critique," 113).

3.   "Simulation, in the sense that, from now on, signs are just exchanged against each other rather than against the real. . . . The emancipation of the sign: remove this 'archaic' obligation to designate something and it finally becomes free, indifferent and totally indeterminate, in the structural or combinatory play which succeeds the previous rule of determinate equivalence" (Baudrillard, *Symbolic Exchange and Death,* 7).

4.   Baudrillard foreshadows the symbolic importance of the Twin Towers even in his 1976 *Symbolic Exchange and Death*: "The fact that there are two identical towers *signifies* the end of all competition, the end of every original reference. . . . This new architecture no longer embodies a competitive system, but a countable one where competition has disappeared in favour of correlation" (69).

WORKS CITED

Baudrillard, Jean. *The Agony of Power.* Translated by Ames Hodges. Los Angeles: Semiotext(e), 2010.

———. *The Gulf War Did Not Take Place*. Translated by Paul Patton. Bloomington: Indiana University Press, 1995.

————. "Hypotheses on Terrorism." In *The Spirit of Terrorism*, by Jean Baudrillard, translated by Chris Turner, 49–84. New York: Verso, 2002.

————. *Simulacra and Simulation*. Translated by Sheila Faria Glaser. Ann Arbor: The University of Michigan Press, 1994.

————. "The Spirit of Terrorism." In *The Spirit of Terrorism*, translated by Chris Turner, 3–34. New York: Verso, 2002.

————. *Symbolic Exchange and Death*. Translated by Iain Hamilton Grant. 1976. London: Sage, 1993.

————. "Toward a Critique of the Political Economy of the Sign." Translated by Carl R. Lovitt and Denise Klopsch. *SubStance* 5, no. 15 (1976): 111–16. http://dx.doi.org/10.2307/3684064.

————. *The Transparency of Evil*. Translated by James Benedict. London: Verso, 1993.

————. "The Violence of the Image." Lecture. *The European Graduate School,* Saas-Fee, Switzerland, 2004. Video, 1:26:48. http://www.egs.edu/faculty/jean-baudrillard/videos/violence-of-the-image/.

Cave, Damien, and Anne Barnard. "Minister Wavers on Plan to Burn Koran." *NYTimes.com*. September 10, 2010. http://www.nytimes.com/2010/09/10/us/10obama.html.

Defense Technical Information Center. "Terrorism." *DOD Dictionary of Military Terms*. http://www.dtic.mil/doctrine/dod_dictionary/data/t/7591.html.

The Pew Forum on Religion and Public Life and Pew Research Center for the People and the Press. "Growing Number of Americans Say Obama is a Muslim." *Pew Research Center.* August 18, 2010, http://pewforum.org/Politics-and-Elections/Growing-Number-of-Americans-Say-Obama-is-a-Muslim.aspx.

Phillips, Macon. "Osama Bin Laden Dead." *The White House Blog*, May 2, 2011, http://www.whitehouse.gov/blog/2011/05/02/osama-bin-laden-dead.

Staples, Sacha. "Incarcerated by a Discourse of Binaries: America's Mediated Culture of Terror." *International Journal of Baudrillard Studies* 6, no. 2 (2009).

Thompson, Ginger. "Quake Leaves Cracks in Washington Monument, Closing It for Now." *The New York Times*, August 24, 2011, A16.

4

The Martyr's Vision: Why the Suicide Bomber's Eye Is Cast Not to the Sky—But to the Other

HATEM N. AKIL

TERRORISM: BODY AND VISION

Suicide bombers lie outside the contingencies of religion and the promise of sex with 72 virgins. Instead, their desire may be viewed as a quest for inclusion in the field of vision and to count as human beings. This paper proposes an alternative critical discourse to the question of identity-based suffering and culpability. It aims to raise doubts about certain established notions concerning historical trauma that are thought to be unique, incomparable, and the result of fixed dichotomies. Instead, it traces the inconsistencies in the "official narrative" in order to challenge current distributions of victimhood and culpability. As such, this paper calls for a rejection of the notion of competitive suffering and of culpability as limited to the group perpetrating the last act of violence.

I draw upon Agamben's notions of *der Muselmann* and *homo sacer* in order to locate a commonality of suffering in which the human body is foregrounded as "bare life," a zero point of humanity. I also deploy Judith Butler's notion of precarity to the splicing of life between identity-based frames that the suicide bomber intends to violently suture back together.

THE MUSLIM AT AUSCHWITZ

The *Muselmann* was described by Holocaust survivors as the Auschwitz "prisoner who was giving up and was given up by his comrades, who no longer had room in his consciousness for the contrasts of good or bad, noble or base, intellectual or unintellectual. He was a staggering corpse, a bundle of physical functions in its last convulsions."[1]

In *Remnants of Auschwitz*, Giorgio Agamben characterizes the *Muselmann* as the stage that Auschwitz inmates reached when they arrived at such a state of physical decrepitude that other inmates would look at them almost as if they were already dead. Agamben quotes Holocaust survivor and writer Primo Levi's description of the *Muselmann*: "One hesitates to call them living: one hesitates to call their death death."[2]

The *Muselmann* becomes the threshold between the states of life and death, but more importantly between the categories of human and inhuman. Deprived of all of dignity and moral composition as human, there still remains a faint biological connection between the *Muselmann* and our species. Not a "living being" anymore, he is a "walking corpse," "non-human," "living dead," and "mummy-man."[3] To Agamben, the *Muselmann* "is the guard on the threshold of a new ethics, an ethics of a form of life that begins where dignity ends."[4] He is cast outside the gaze; no one bears to look at him. In other words, he becomes a counter-Medusa who gazes at no one, but one who cannot be gazed at either. He is "unbearable to the human eye."[5] This inability to look at the *Muselmann* is not predicated on sympathy or abundance of compassion, but rather because he is unworthy of being looked at.[6]

But where did the term *Muselmann* come from? How was it that someone who was transformed into a *Muselmann* became a separate being from his former self, a Jewish inmate at Auschwitz? Agamben states that the word *Muselmann* means Muslim, literally, and he uses the two terms interchangeably.[7] However, Agamben also explains that although there is little certainty about the origin of the term, it may have been that the word *Muselmann* was used at Auschwitz as a reference to the image of a Muslim prostrating himself in prayer—all curled up with his face touching the ground.[8] The term *Muselmann* may also be referring to the Muslims' belief in submitting to the will of God, and as such are seen as losing their individual will to fate.

Agamben mentions that there were other terms that were used at the various concentration camps as synonyms for the *Muselmann*: "In Majdanek, the word *Muselmann* was unknown. The living dead there were termed 'donkeys'; in Dachau they were 'cretins,' in Stutthof 'cripples,' in Mauthausen 'swimmers,' in Neuengamme 'camels,' in Buchenwald 'tired sheikhs,' and in the Ravensbruk women's camp, Muselweiber (female Muslims) or 'trinkets.'"[9]

One may imagine that Jewish Auschwitz inmates had to invent a new category for their Jewish identity as it began to descend into a nonhuman state, an identity that did not resemble their original self, but one that was categorically different. Agamben notes, "it is certain, that with a kind of ferocious irony, the Jews knew that they would not die at Auschwitz as Jews."[10] In other words, the Jews who were targeted solely for their religious/ethnic identity, in order to affirm the solidity of their identity as they descended into a nonhuman state, needed to invent an Other (The Muslim) to whom they could ascribe their own degeneration.

The Jew, in that state, became the Muslim. The Jew was stripped down to the final remnants of his biological existence, to the physical body as "bare life"; thus, he became no longer a Jew, but a *Muselmann*. One may wonder why the Muslim became the Other of the Jewish inmate at Auschwitz. Has the Muslim, a descendant of Ishmael, not been the Jew's brother all along? Both sons of Abraham, the father of all?

Could one consider this division of Semitic identity to be the product of a "Western" perspective that has been obsessed by a fantasy of Otherness—one as perceived in the Jew, and a further Otherness as perceived in the Muslim? It is as if Othello were Shylock's tormentor in the European fantasies of Otherness. Was Othello, a paranoid and violent man of war, meant to be the tragic counterpoint to Shylock's tale of greed?

JEWISH KEBAB IN BAGHDAD

Where else do the Jew and the Arab meet? Don't they meet in the person of the Arab Jew? Israeli scholar Ella Shohat, in "Reflections of an Arab Jew,"[11] excavates the figure of the Arab Jew, a term that to many in the West is seen more like a paradox. Shohat argues, however, that until the establishment of the state of Israel, the Arab Jew has been a fundamental part of the socioeconomic, cultural, and even political life in many communities throughout the Middle East, and along with Arab Muslims and Arab Christians, developed through the centuries a common cultural identity that is imprinted with the sounds, sites, and aromas of the region.

The life of the Jew as an Arab was richly, albeit romantically, described in *Memories of Eden: A Journey through Jewish Baghdad*, by Violette Shamash.[12] She speaks tenderly of the fascinating life she experienced as a young person within the vibrant Jewish community of Baghdadi Jews in Iraq before 1945. Shamash paints a loving, idyllic portrait of the city as seen from her family mansion on the banks of the Tigris, characterized by the fragrance of walnut and apricot trees in the garden with kebabs being grilled on a tanoor oven. Shamash traces her Jewish community in Iraq back to Babylonian times as the home of "our patriarch Abraham," and the birthplace of the Talmud.

In *Baghdad, Yesterday: The Making of an Arab Jew*,[13] Sasson Somekh writes of his youth in Baghdad, describing details of the education he received in Arabic from a Shia cleric, and how it started his interest in writing Arabic poetry as a teenager. Somekh's memoir recounts his life as a writer involved in the political and cultural life of Baghdad, meeting other writers in cafés on al-Rashid Street and sharing in the city's lively cultural scene.

In "Reflections by an Arab Jew," Ella Shohat points out Israel's systematic discrimination against Mizrahis (and Sephardic Jews in general) through state "institutions that deployed their energies and material to the consistent advantage of European Jews and to the consistent disadvantage of Oriental Jews."[14]

According to Shohat, Oriental Jews constitute 50% of Israel's Jews, and when you add the indigenous Palestinian residents, Israelis who do not come from a European past total more than 70% of the whole population. Nevertheless, Shohat notes that much of the cultural and educational systems in Israel were established without any consideration of the Oriental Jews' identity and with only European Jews in mind:

> Stripped of our history, we have been forced by our no-exit situation to repress our collective nostalgia, at least within the public sphere. The pervasive notion of "one people" reunited in their ancient homeland actively disauthorizes any affectionate memory of life before Israel. We have never

been allowed to mourn a trauma that the images of Iraq's destruction only intensified and crystallized for some of us.[15]

Arab Jews in Israel were made to learn a whole new history (of the European Jews) that was not necessarily their experience. Further, betrayed by their language (they spoke Arabic at home) and their own physiognomy, they were often mistaken for Palestinians, and subsequently profiled as such. Shoat explains that the misidentification of the Jew as Arab (as a result of their appearance and language) at times led to incidents where Arab Jews were physically assaulted or arrested under the suspicion of being Arab.

Biopolitics works its perverted way into the Jewish imagination one more time. As the European Jew, interned at Auschwitz and subjected to unthinkable trauma, began to degenerate physically into the *Muselmann*, in Israel, the Oriental Jew, likewise, lends his body to the Muslim, deprived of freedom, reduced, by a visual profiling regime, to the status of an inmate. Here, too, the Jew's body is visually indistinguishable from that of an Arab. The eye that accuses the Palestinian also accuses his mimesis in the Oriental Jew.

In her earlier work, *Sephardim in Israel: Zionism from the Standpoint of Its Jewish Victims* (1988), Shohat explores in postcolonial terms the ways in which Oriental Jews have been treated with prejudice by European Jews in Israel in a manner reminiscent of the same colonialist and Orientalist treatment that Europeans used with colonized nations: as undercivilized, barbaric, and even subhuman. She contrasts the cultural and historical backgrounds of Arab Jews with those of European Jews, as representative of separate and uneven cultural domains. European Jews are the ones who imagined Zionism in order to solve the European problem of anti-Semitism and built the state of Israel in their own image. As such, they came to dominate the cultural, educational, and political discourse in the new state of Israel, and therefore, exercised toward Arab Jews the same Orientalist approach of Europeans toward Orientals in general.[16]

THE UNTESTIFIABLE MARTYRDOM OF THICKLIPS

In the *Merchant of Venice*, when Shylock had the opportunity to defend his outlandish ransom for a pound of flesh, his defense was to adduce the humanity of the Jew as manifested in his corporeality, his biological composition:

I am a Jew. Hath

not a Jew eyes? hath not a Jew hands, organs,

dimensions, senses, affections, passions? fed with

the same food, hurt with the same weapons, subject

to the same diseases, healed by the same means,

warmed and cooled by the same winter and summer, as

a Christian is? If you prick us, do we not bleed?

if you tickle us, do we not laugh? if you poison

us, do we not die? (3.1, 57–64)[17]

Along the same lines, and contrary to Shylock's reasoning, the physical attributes of Othello (the other outsider in Venice) were repeatedly foregrounded as signifiers not of resemblance but of alterity. In the play, Othello is described as "a Barbary horse" and "an old black ram." He is referenced as "thicklips" and as having "the gross clasps of a lascivious Moor" (all in 1.1).[18] Notwithstanding caricatured, theatrical depictions of Shylock, there is no suggestion in the play that he is distinguishable from Europeans because of his physiognomy.

Othello's Otherness, instead, is all too visible. Therefore, Othello had to be cast outside of the field of vision—he had to become the abject. In that sense, Othello's role as a soldier on behalf of the Venetian state is emphasized as the person whose place is to die for others. Othello the Moor, like the *Muselmann*, is viewed as nonhuman, closer to an animal, or worse, totally invisible, as one who is implicated in his own death through his own self-sacrifice. By analogy, might one argue that in Western society, even when the Arab and the Jew reach high levels of power (Othello) and wealth (Shylock), they are still subject to deportation, internment, and the burden of proving their ideological citizenship and loyalty to state systems?

At the concentration camp, the *Muselmann* was visibly invisible. He was not dead, but perceived as such. When he became *Muselmann*, the inmate crossed over to a condition where he would not be counted as human any longer, but only as "bare life." Agamben describes the *Muselmann* as the "untestifiable, that to which no one has borne witness."[19]

In *Remnants of Auschwitz*, Agamben quotes many survivors who wanted to stay alive specifically because they wanted to be witnesses to the atrocities committed at the camp. What they have seen, although unsayable, must be told. In fact, survivors, like Primo Levi, felt a constant compulsion to tell their story. But who testifies for whom no one is able or willing to testify for?

Indeed, at the beginning of the chapter on "The Witness," Agamben quotes an Auschwitz prisoner, asserting that he would not take his own life because he "did not want to suppress the witness that I could become."[20] Witness in this sense should probably be understood in the narrow sense of witnessing and the functional sense of testifying. But we already know that there are parallels between the act of witnessing and the act of martyrdom. The martyr as witness exists in a state that intertwines the act of seeing with that of the witness's certain death.

The semantic meanings of the word martyr in Greek (*martis*) and Arabic (*shaheed*) are similar. Both words originally refer to a person who had witnessed and who had died for a certain cause. Also, implied in witnessing is the imperative of testifying to what was seen. So, how can witnesses testify when they are destined to be killed? Can one say that the act of dying is itself the testament? To the martyr, the act of martyrdom is a violent, desperate testimony of the "truth" that others are unable or unwilling to hear by other nonviolent means.

Here I would like to emphasize the apparent opposition that one may find along the continuum of the states of living, witnessing, and martyrdom. These states seem to resolve around a fourth state, which we might call that of "action"—since which state a person ends up in is a crucial consequence of the action (or nonaction) chosen. I argue that there is an inherent split in the notion of martyrdom between testifying and sacrifice, and that at the core of this split we find the question of action.

A martyr's testimony is delivered not in the narrow sense of a verbal witness, but in the corporeal sense of delivering one's body as evidence. As such, the *Muselmann*'s position in the concentration camp, emptied of all human dignity, and pushed to the threshold of the nonliving could be mirrored by the other Arab/Muslim at that other camp, the Palestinian refugee camp. The Arabs in the Palestinian refugee camps in Gaza and the West Bank, likewise robbed of all dignity, cast a different kind of gaze on their own predicament, and locate their own bodies as a site of action and resistance.

This connection of suffering to the predicament of bare life as an expression of biopolitics has been noted by Hannah Arendt in her work on the commonality of life in concentration camps ("The Concentration Camps"). Arendt finds any comparison between concentration camps and other forms of imprisonment and banishment, even slavery, to be futile. However, she does find parallels among the types of concentration camps, which she likens to the Western conceptions of life after death. She categorizes these types as Hades, Purgatory, and Hell. Hades corresponds to refugee camps, concentration camps for stateless persons, and the like. Purgatory is represented in labor camps found in the Soviet Union. And Hell, she posits, "is embodied by those types of camp perfected by the Nazis, in which the whole of life was thoroughly and systematically organized with a view to the greatest possible torment."[21]

Arendt finds that the commonality among these camps lies in the fact that "the human masses sealed off in them are treated as if they no longer existed, as if what happened to them were no longer of any interest to anybody, as if they were already dead and some evil spirit gone mad were amusing itself by stopping them for a while between life and death before admitting them to eternal peace."[22]

Arendt clearly exposes the link between life in the concentration camp (which is lived as a form of death in life) and the state of being unseen and considered as unworthy of living. The state of nonliving is particularly a result of the refugee/intern/inmate being invisible to others, untestifiable, unintelligible. In a certain way, Arendt frees the Auschwitz prisoners from the singularity of their suffering: Auschwitz is perceived as a unique, unrepeatable, unspeakable event beyond history.

BUT WHOSE BLOOD IS IT, ANYWAY?

Primo Levi, the Auschwitz witness par excellence, about 40 years after his release found himself confronted by the moral obligation to speak in support of residents of another camp: the Palestinian refugee camps. Commenting on the aftermath of the massacres of civilians in the Palestinian refugee camps of Sabra and Shatila in 1982, following the Israeli invasion of Lebanon, Levi located the Jew in the Arab, once more. He wrote: "Everybody is somebody's Jew. And today the Palestinians are the Jews of the Israelis."[23]

In her biography of Levi entitled *Primo Levi: Bridges of Knowledge* (1995), Mirna Cicioni underlines Levi's moral obligation as a witness to Auschwitz in making such a clear and direct connection between the plight of the Jews at Auschwitz and the Palestinians in their refugee camps. Cicioni explains that Levi "implicitly acknowledged that he was being asked to speak as an Auschwitz survivor as well as an internationally famous writer, and agreed to do so to counteract the ideological use of the Holocaust by the Israeli ruling class as a justification of its attempt to wipe out the Palestinian people."[24]

Judith Butler, in "Primo Levi for the Present" (2006), also notes Levi's clear and unequivocal moral objection to the instrumentalization of the Shoah to legitimize violence against the Palestinian people. Butler quotes Levi's answer to an interviewer's question whether his position accusing the Israelis of violence could be seen as an affront to the Jewish blood spilled during the Holocaust: "I reply that the [Jewish] blood spilled pains me just as much as the blood spilled by all other human beings."[25]

The extreme violence perpetrated against the *Muselmann* at Auschwitz is echoed in the indignity and nonliving state of the Palestinian refugee, who remains, much like the Holocaust intern, without a home, without a country. Both are positioned as the objects of a horrific attempt at the destruction of human life and dignity. As Arendt noted, life is the threat of death at any time.

In the refugee camp, however, a new form of *homo sacer* is born, one who recognizes her or his own bio-power and who turns her or his own body— already a biological bare life, a zero level of humanity—into a resurrection of the notion of sacrifice. Whereas Auschwitz survivors described the *Muselmann* as a walking corpse, the new refugee as *homo sacer* understands such a state too well, and becomes intent on threatening death itself instead of (and because of) being the object of the threat of death by others.

The suicide bomber inhabits the same "extreme threshold between life and death, the human and the inhuman,"[26] and draws upon the same explicit political meaning, "the anthropological meaning of absolute power in an especially radical form," of the *Muselmann*.[27] Suicide bombers are "martyrs" who have witnessed their own inescapable state as *homo sacer*, and who have become convinced that their lack of dignified life is specifically so because it lies outside the field of vision, that they are invisible to others. Unable to

sustain a life that does not view them as human, equal to other humans, suicide bombers seem committed to validating Shylock's fundamental questions:

> Hath not a Palestinian eyes? Hath not a Palestinian hands, organs, dimen-
> sions, senses, affections, passions; fed with the same food, hurt with the
> same weapons, subject to the same diseases, heal'd by the same means,
> warm'd and cool'd by the same winter and summer as a Jew is? If you
> prick us, do we not bleed? If you tickle us, do we not laugh? If you poison
> us, do we not die?

By foregrounding the body as a zero-point of equalization, the suicide bomber
violently and relentlessly attempts to suture the unnatural slit between the
humanity of Jews and Arabs.

It is evidently naïve to fantasize about the suicide bomber as merely a
religious fanatic duped with the promise of sex with 72 virgins. How can
one not notice that the wave of suicide bombers in the Middle East started in
1985 when an attractive 18-year-old Lebanese sales clerk, who worked at a
video store and was a member of the secular Syrian Nationalist Party, drove a
white Peugeot laden with explosives into an Israeli army convoy in Southern
Lebanon. She had recorded a video message in which she appeared in military
uniform and introduced herself by saying: "I am martyr Sana Mhaidali, I am
18 years old," and then went on to address her family and her countrymen
to explain the patriotic reasoning that drove her to become a human bomb.
The specificity of video as the medium of her last testimony was meant as an
eye-opener, a realignment of vision to the plight of a people who have been
invisible for years while under foreign occupation.

Initial news reports, unable to comprehend Mhaidali's motivation, claimed
that she was pregnant and wanted to hide her shame, or that she was severely
depressed. Both claims were meant to empty Mhaidali's action of any political
motivations. Neither was true. Others who studied female suicide bombers have
looked for uniquely female contingencies that would drive women to die (too
young, psychologically disturbed, under male influence, revenge seeking, etc.),
only to find no single consistent explanation. According to Lindsey O'Rourke,
who conducted an extended study of female suicide bombers, "There is precious
little evidence of uniquely feminine motivations driving women's attacks."[28]

The suicide bomber has no illusions of coming home. Instead, she, or he, has only the certainty of death. By turning the body into a weapon, the suicide bomber is clearly deploying the ultimate form of bio-power. As *homo sacer*, the suicide bomber is beyond the threat of death and has already passed through the threshold of destruction of human life. And, as the suicide bomber aims at the destruction of the lives of others, by destroying her life first and foremost, she is confirming the commonality of suffering, and that one can never speak of one's suffering as deeper as or more painful than another's. By physically and violently blending her/his own blood with that of those he thought were not able to see him as a person, the suicide bomber is confirming Levi's statement that spilled blood anywhere, by anyone, should cause the same pain for all of us.

In *Cutting the Fuse: The Explosion of Global Suicide Terrorism and How to Stop It* (2010), Robert Pape and James Feldman present the outcome of their work at the University of Chicago's Project on Security and Terrorism. The report studies over 2,200 suicide attacks across the world for a period of about 30 years. Its findings categorically reject religious fundamentalism as the key motivator of suicide bombers. The researchers find that 95% of suicide attacks were carried out in response to foreign occupation. Their evidence indicates that 90% of worldwide attacks are anti-American in areas occupied by the U.S., and that there was a 90% drop in suicide bombing in Israel after Israel's withdrawal from Gaza and large parts of the West Bank.

Pape and Feldman explain that the suicide bomber phenomenon is determined by two factors: "perceived cultural difference between occupier and occupied" and the existence of "prior rebellion."[29] In that sense, suicide bombing becomes a weapon of last resort, when other attempts at resistance have failed.

When Pape and Feldman look at the environment after the September 11 attacks, they note the emergence of an American grand narrative on terror that surfaced after the terrorist attacks. Since the 9/11 hijackers were all Muslims, it was convenient to construct Islamic fundamentalism as the central motivating force driving the 19 hijackers to kill themselves in order to kill Americans. Within weeks after the attack, surveys of American attitudes showed that this presumption was quickly congealing into a hard reality in the public mind. Americans immediately wondered, "Why do they hate us?"

and many quickly came to the conclusion that it was because of who we are and not what we do.[30]

The media generally followed with a concerted representation of "Fundamentalist Islam" as a staunch adversary of "Western" culture and supporter of terrorism against the American "way of life." The goal of forcible, or at best, interventionist transformation of Arab societies into Western-style democracies was advocated by political strategists such as Richard Perle, David Frum,[31] and writers like Fareed Zakaria, who wrote in Newsweek that "the United States must help Islam enter the modern world."[32] It should be noted that Zakaria, who did not explicitly call for the use of military force, still refers to "Islam," a religion, as the target of U.S. intervention.

As a result of this narrative, few felt able to seriously question the terrorists' motivations. Therefore, it became "understandable" that America needed to strike back at Al Qaeda and the Taliban in Afghanistan; as it is currently "understandable" to place the entire Muslim American community on trial through the Congressional Commission on Radical Islam, chaired by Representative Peter King. The commission's aim is to have the American Muslim communities "prove" that U.S. Muslims are not radicalized and that they're willing to cooperate with security forces. The underlying assumption clearly is that a defense is necessary because American Muslims are radicalized and uncooperative.

Western narcissism appears to have caused many to believe that Western civilization is not only the sole target of terrorism, but that terrorism did not materially exist before September 11. Somehow U.S. media started coupling and conflating the terms "Islamic" and "terrorism." Such disconnect from history fails to note, as anyone who follows current events knows, that many "liberation movements" in the world as early as the 1970s had adopted violence as the means to effect social change. These groups had similar ideological agendas but nonetheless operated with a local focus. They included the Baader-Meinhof gang in Germany, the Red Brigades in Italy, ETA in Spain, the IRA in Ireland, the PLO in Palestine, the Japanese Red Army, and others.

Slavoj Žižek, in *Welcome to the Desert of the Real* (2002), relates the birth of such groups to the failure of European student movements of the late 1960s that demonstrated "that the masses were so deeply immersed in their apolitical consumerist stance that it was not possible to awaken them through standard political education and consciousness-raising—a more violent intervention was needed to shake them out of their ideological numbness, their hypnotic consumerist state, and only direct violent interventions like bombing supermarkets would do the job." Žižek questions if "the same holds, on a different level, for today's fundamentalist terror?" He goes on to ask, "Is not its goal also to awaken us, Western citizens, from our numbness, from immersion in our everyday ideological universe?"[33]

Žižek finds violence, delivered by so-called "fundamentalist terrorists," to be a revelatory act that aims at penetrating through the spectacularity of everyday social reality to reveal a "passion for the Real," which we are not supposed to experience directly. He posits that what we experience in our everyday life is a virtual reality. It is a reality without its substance.

Žižek notes the surprising lack, in TV images, of actual carnage at the WTC collapse: "no dismembered bodies, no blood, no desperate faces of dying people." He contrasts these images with "reporting on Third World catastrophes, where the whole point is to produce a scoop of some gruesome detail: Somalis dying of hunger, raped Bosnian women, men with their throats cut."[34]

This repackaging of reality, Žižek contends, is intended to control the piercing of the Real that was done by the terrorist attacks. This kind of representation, he argues, is proof that even in this moment of trauma, there exists a distance between us and them, that "the real horror happens THERE not HERE." He says, "Again, the ultimate truth of the capitalist utilitarian despiritualized universe is the dematerialization of 'real life' itself, its reversal into a spectral show."[35] The insistence on distanciation between the contemporary Western citizen and the experience of historical trauma is felt clearly in the aftermath of Hurricane Katrina, when the use of the word "refugees" to describe the displaced population of New Orleans was seen as an insult. President Bush was quoted as saying, "The people we're talking about are not refugees. They're Americans." Jesse Jackson went even further: "It is racist to call American citizens refugees."[36]

Žižek takes this concept to its extreme opposite by locating the WTC events in "the twisted logic of dreams." He says that these attacks were not "the intrusion of the Real which shattered our illusory Sphere: quite the reverse—it was before the WTC collapse that we lived in our reality, perceiving Third World horrors as something which was not actually part of our social reality, as something which existed (for us) as a spectral apparition on the (TV) screen—and what happened on September 11 was that this fantas-matic screen apparition entered our reality. It is not that reality entered our image: the image entered and shattered our reality."[37]

Žižek tells a story in "The Smell of Love" about a famous Jewish bal-lerina who was asked by concentration camp officers to dance "as a gesture of special humiliation." As she started to dance and was able to capture the officers' attention, Žižek says "she quickly grabbed the machine-gun from one of the distracted guards, and before being shot down herself, succeeded in killing more than a dozen officers."[38]

The above story, even if accurate, certainly belongs in the realm of fantasy and dreams. Žižek uses it as an illustration of an "action" that undermines the "servicing of the goods," one that interrupts the "reign of the pleasure-reality principle," He finds another example of such an action by the passengers of the hijacked UA Flight 93 over Pennsylvania who took over the plane to prevent another major catastrophe, even though this act cost them their lives and those of everyone on the plane. This act, like the ballerina's act, may be viewed as part of a network of relations in which both the passengers and hijackers are participants: an act of violence that will lead to their own sacri-fice, and a nightmarish state of total destruction and mutual collapse.

What is evident is that the confirmation of life has to be based on the recognition that life, all life, is precarious, and as such, precious, as posited by Judith Butler in *Precarious Life* (2004) and *Frames of War* (2009). If the killing of any person is tantamount to the killing of all mankind, as the Quran tells us, and if spilled blood, any person's blood, pains all of us, as stated by Primo Levi, it becomes necessary then to acknowledge that violence, any violence, when it threatens life, is egregious and a source of terror.

Butler suggests that "specific lives cannot be apprehended as injured or lost if they are not first apprehended as living. If certain lives do not qualify as lives or are, from the start, not conceivable as lives within certain epis-temological frames, these lives are never lived nor lost in the full sense."[39]

This intelligibility of life may be seen in the *Muselmann* and in the refugee, in the news story that allocates half a front page for a white man kidnapped in Colombia and a small third-page column for thousands of Africans killed by civil war or by a natural disaster. To understand how these differentiations function, Butler asks us to understand how meaning is constructed as the result of epistemological frames. She says "frames of war are selective in carving up experiences that are essential to the war."[40] But by extending this notion to the questions of violence and the apprehension of life, one is confronted by the frame itself being extended to include all kinds of modes and manifestations of violence and counterviolence.

It is necessary that one be aware of the essentialist and abbreviated nature of terms like terrorist, Muslim, Arab, and Westerner, since it is impossible to encompass all those who are referenced by these terms. The concept of violence, although multimodal, must be viewed as a universal notion—the poison that kills the Jew, kills the Arab just the same. Butler emphasizes: "Precarity cuts across identity categories as well as multicultural maps, thus forming the basis for an alliance focused on opposition to state violence and its capacity to produce, exploit, and distribute precarity for the purposes of profit and territorial defense."[41] Butler, here, calls for a perspective that is capable of seeing that the application of (political) violence leads to the same results regardless of the ethnic, cultural, or national identity of its victim. The same could also be said about the identity of the perpetrator.

As shown in the fieldwork of Pape and Feldman, Lindsey O'Rourke, and others, it is not only problematic to theorize the suicide bomber, it is also difficult to categorize her or him. The temptation to find a unitary explanation that would cover all possible motivations is blatantly naïve and clearly futile. Terrorists could be motivated by a desire to sacrifice themselves so that others might benefit (at times even monetarily), or it could be that their motivation lies in hatred, fanaticism, ignorance, poverty, vengeance, idealism, and so forth.

Attempts to categorize "terrorists" or "suicide bombers" under one classification or another could, therefore, merely function as a self-defeating generalization. As one theorizes the concept of suicide bombing, one should not ignore the fact that the instrument of terrorism, specular violence, is itself universal in its effect and in its experience, which is, in some ways, both the irony and the genius of the suicide bomber.

There are commonalities between suffering and aggression. Far beyond the intricacies of identity, one is called to acknowledge the precarity of life and the mutuality of culpability. The notions of victim and executioner are essential links in a Hegelian "long chain of conjunction" where "victim and executioner are equally ignoble."[42] These notions are imbedded in the public imagination and, as part of the official narrative, do not negate the possibility of subversion. When Derrida received the Theodor Adorno award on September 22, 2001, he commented on the attacks of September 11 by saying, "My unconditional compassion, addressed at the victims of September 11, does not prevent me from saying aloud: with regard to this crime, I do not believe that anyone is politically guiltless."[43] It is not only that Žižek's observation that "ultimately, we are all *homo sacer*,"[44] rings true, but one needs, most decidedly, to keep in mind the constant complexity discovered at Auschwitz that "no group was more human than any other . . . the lesson of the camps is brotherhood in abjection."[45]

Once one realizes that suffering is universal, it becomes clear that any sort of instrumentalization intended to exploit the misery of a group is actually a disavowal of the meaning of suffering. A still viable alternative to the endless cycle of terrorist violence is the form of resistance relentlessly and successfully advanced by Mahatma Gandhi in the 1930s. Gandhi's foregrounding of his own frail and almost naked body as a site of both sacrifice and political threat (to British imperialism) stands in contrast to an endless chain of victims and violators, who both deploy and assail the human body. In the same spirit, one notes that the current movements for freedom and democracy in the Middle East and elsewhere have initially moved away from violent resistance, while at the same time doing so by being physically present in public at the peril of being subjected to state violence. The apparent degeneration of these movements into a spiral of violence and counterviolence is a symptom of the tension between victim-creation and voluntary victimization that will continue to breed new generations of martyrs who will be willing to deploy their suffering against those who are perceived to have not suffered or not suffered as much.

NOTES

1.   Giorgio Agamben, *Remnants of Auschwitz: The Witness and the Archive* (New York: Zone Books, 1999), 41.

2.   Ibid., 44.

3.   Ibid., 54.

4.   Ibid., 69.

5.   Ibid., 50.

6.   Ibid., 43.

7.   Ibid., 41.

8.   Ibid.

9.   Ibid., 44.

10.   Ibid., 45.

11.   Ella Habiba Shohat, "Reflections of an Arab Jew," *Solidarity*, May–June 2003, http://www.solidarity-us.org/node/626.

12.   Violette Shamash, *Memories of Eden: A Journey through Jewish Baghdad*, edited by Mira Rocca and Tony Rocca (Surrey, UK: Forum Books, 2008).

13.   Sasson Somekh, *Baghdad, Yesterday: The Making of an Arab Jew* (Jerusalem, Israel: Ibis Editions, 2007).

14.   Shohat, "Reflections of an Arab Jew."

15.   Ibid.

16.   Ella Shohat, "Sephardim in Israel: Zionism from the Standpoint of Its Jewish Victims," *Social Text* no. 19/20 (Autumn, 1988): 7.

17.   William Shakespeare, *The Illustrated Stratford Shakespeare* (San Francisco: AbeBooks, 1982), 201.

18.   Ibid., 864–865.

19.   Agamben, *Remnants of Auschwitz*, 41.

20.   Ibid.

21.   Hannah Arendt, "The Concentration Camps," *Holocaust Reflections, Modern American Poetry*, n.d., http://www.english.illinois.edu/maps/holocaust/reflections.htm.

22.   Ibid.

23.   Judith Butler, "Jews and the Bi-National Vision," *Logos Journal* 3, no. 1 (2004), http://www.logosjournal.com/butler.htm.

24.   Mirna Cicioni, *Primo Levi: Bridges of Knowledge* (Oxford: Berg, 1995), 129.

25.   Judith Butler, "Primo Levi for the Present," lecture, *The European Graduate School*, Saas-Fee, Switzerland, 2006, video, 1:30:23, http://www.egs.edu/faculty/judith-butler/videos/primo-levi-for-the-present/.

26.   Agamben. *Remnants of Auschwitz*, 47.

27.   Wolfgang Sofsky, *The Order of Terror, The Concentration Camps* (1997), qtd. in Giorgio Agamben, *Remnants of Auschwitz: The Witness and the Archive* (New York: Zone Books, 1999), 47–48.

28. Lindsey O'Rourke, "Behind the Woman Behind the Bomb," *NYTimes.com*, August 2, 2008, http://www.nytimes.com/2008/08/02/opinion/02orourke.html.

29. Robert K. Pape and James A. Feldman, *Cutting the Fuse: The Explosion of Global Suicide Terrorism and How to Stop It* (Chicago: University of Chicago Press, 2010), 100.

30. Ibid., 320.

31. David Frum and Richard Perle, *An End to Evil* (New York: Random House, 2003).

32. Fareed Zakaria, "The Politics of Rage: Why Do They Hate Us?" *Newsweek .com*, October 15, 2001, http://www.newsweek.com/politics-rage-why-do-they -hate-us-154345.

33. Slavoj Žižek, *Welcome to the Desert of the Real* (London: Verso. 2002), 5–6.

34. Ibid., 9.

35. Ibid., 11.

36. Associated Press, "Calling Katrina Survivors 'Refugees' Stirs Debate," *NBCNews.com*, September 7, 2005, http://www.msnbc.msn.com/id/9232071/ns/us _news-katrina_the_long_road_back/.

38. Žižek, *Welcome to the Desert of the Real*, 11.

39. Ibid., 142–43.

40. Judith Butler, *Frames of War* (London: Verso, 2009), 1.

41. Ibid., 26.

42. Ibid., 32.

43. Wolfgang Sofsky, *The Order of Terror, The Concentration Camps* (1997), qtd. in Agamben, *Remnants of Auschwitz*, 17.

44. Žižek, *Welcome to the Desert* of the Real, 57.

45. Ibid., 100.

47. Wolfgang Sofsky, *The Order of Terror, The Concentration Camps* (1997), qtd. in Agmben, *Remnants of Auschwitz*, 17.

WORKS CITED

Agamben, Giorgio. *Remnants of Auschwitz: The Witness and the Archive*. New York: Zone Books, 1999.

Arendt, Hannah. "The Concentration Camps." *Holocaust Reflections*. *Modern American Poetry*. n.d. http://www.english.illinois.edu/maps/holocaust/reflections.htm.

Associated Press, "Calling Katrina Survivors 'Refugees' Stirs Debate." *NBCNews.com*. September 7, 2005. http://www.msnbc.msn.com/id/9232071/ns/us_news-katrina_the_long_road_back/.

Baudrillard, Jean. "Violence of the Image." Lecture. *The European Graduate School*. Saas-Fee, Switzerland, 2007. Video, 9:57. http://www.youtube.com/watch?v=9QF-eThkBOg.

Bhabha, Homi K. "Interrogating Identity." In *The Location of Culture*, 57–93. New York: Routledge, 2004.

Butler, Judith. *Frames of War*. London: Verso, 2009.

———. "Jews and the Bi-National Vision." *Logos Journal* 3 no. 1 (2004). http://www.logosjournal.com/butler.htm.

———. "Primo Levi for the Present." Lecture. *The European Graduate School*. Saas-Fee, Switzerland, 2006. Video, 1:30:23. http://www.egs.edu/faculty/judith-butler/videos/primo-levi-for-the-present/.

Cicioni, Mirna. *Primo Levi: Bridges of Knowledge*. Oxford: Berg, 1995.

Frum, David, and Richard Perle. *An End to Evil*. New York: Random House, 2003.

O'Rourke, Lindsey. "Behind the Woman behind the Bomb." *NYTimes.com*. August 2, 2008. http://www.nytimes.com/2008/08/02/opinion/02orourke.html.

Pape, Robert K., and James A. Feldman. *Cutting the Fuse: The Explosion of Global Suicide Terrorism and How to Stop It*. Chicago: University of Chicago Press, 2010.

Shakespeare, William. *The Merchant of Venice*. *William Shakespeare: The Complete Works by Linda Alchin*. n.d. http://www.william-shakespeare.info/act3-script-text-merchant-of-venice.htm.

———. *Othello*. *William Shakespeare: The Complete Works by Linda Alchin*. n.d. http://www.william-shakespeare.info/act1-script-text-othello.htm.

———. *The Illustrated Stratford Shakespeare*. San Francisco: AbeBooks, 1982.

Shamash, Violette. *Memories of Eden: A Journey through Jewish Baghdad*. Edited by Mira Rocca and Tony Rocca. Surrey, UK: Forum Books, 2008.

Shohat, Ella. "Reflections of an Arab Jew." *Solidarity* (May–June 2003). http://www.solidarity-us.org/node/626.

———. "Sephardim in Israel: Zionism from the Standpoint of Its Jewish Victims." *Social Text* no. 19/20 (Autumn 1988): 1–35. http://dx.doi.org/10.2307/466176.

Somekh, Sasson. *Baghdad, Yesterday: The Making of an Arab Jew*. Jerusalem, Israel: Ibis Editions, 2007.

Zakaria, Fareed. "The Politics of Rage: Why Do They Hate Us?" *Newsweek.com*. October 15, 2001. http://www.newsweek.com/politics-rage-why-do-they-hate-us-154345.

Žižek, Slavoj. *Welcome to the Desert of the Real*. London: Verso, 2002.

PART 2

Perspectives on Terrorism Through the Ages

5

Resisting Alexander: Insurgency and Terrorism in Ancient Athens

TIMOTHY HOWE

Given the level of attention in media and foreign policy, an outside observer might be forgiven for thinking insurgency and terrorism are historically recent developments. They are not. By offering a few key incidents from ancient Athenian history as a case study, this paper aims to: (1) provide historical context for understanding resistance as an analytic tool, (2) demonstrate the usefulness of insurgency and terrorism as concepts for understanding historical behavior, and (3) offer a methodological foundation and point of departure for future scholarly research and conversation about subversion and resistance among scholars of many periods, regions, and disciplines.

METHOD: UNDERSTANDING RESISTANCE

Before we can begin to contextualize Athenian resistance, it is useful to establish some methodological ground rules and define terms. "Terrorism" and "insurgency" have become emotionally charged words, and because of their centrality in other fields of scholarship (e.g., international studies, political science, and contemporary history), ancient Mediterranean historians have begun to sprinkle them here and there with little attention to method.[1] For the most part, this has been problematic and consequently yielded uneven results.[2] And yet, although one must be both skeptical and cautious to avoid anachronism, a careful examination of resistance scholarship reveals that "insurgency," "terrorism," and their derivatives can be used appropriately, so long as the methodology is clearly defined.[3] For example, the most widely recognized definition of insurgency as a revolt or rebellious movement "intended to overturn or eliminate a *recognized* government or authority by subversion and military force,"[4] seems sufficiently broad to fit situations in the ancient world. The addition of language acknowledging either military force or active subversion allows the ancient Mediterranean historian to make a distinction between ideological, subversive violence (or the threat of violence), what many scholars today label terrorism,[5] and outright combat, and thus describe a spectrum of behavior that might not otherwise fit within the parameters of "declared wars," but, as Jonathan Roth has cogently argued, fit within recognized political activity:

> [political] factionalism plays an especially important role in insurgency and counterinsurgency and deserves more study. Insurgent forces are generally made up of a more or less loose alliance of forces, representing different clans, tribes, religions and ideologies, *mutatis mutandis*. It has been said that all rebellions are, in a sense, civil wars, and in addition to the factions of the insurgents, there will be elements of the group associated with it that remain loyal to the government. (Roth, 361)

But I should be clear, in this context insurgency is not simply a rebellion, nor must it involve combat; insurgency is an ideological movement that is, at least in its early stages, more psychological than physical.[6]

Scholars of insurgency and counterinsurgency (COIN) often group insurgent movements into two distinct types, "national" and "liberation," which is relevant and useful to historians of antiquity. National insurgencies align the primary antagonists, the "insurgents," against a recognized government. The guerilla actions against the recognized, governmental forces in El Salvador during the 1980s, for example, are classified as a national insurgency (Hoffman, 5). For the most part, the language of national insurgency is inappropriate for the ancient Mediterranean, largely because we are dealing with nation-like states, rather than true, modern nation states (Hansen "Polis, Civitas," 19–22, "Polis," 9–15, "Was the Polis a State," 17–47). Liberation insurgencies, on the other hand, fit Mediterranean situations well, since they "pit insurgents against a ruling group that is seen as outside occupiers (even though they might not actually be) by virtue of race, ethnicity, or culture. "The goal of the insurgents is to 'liberate' their nation from alien occupation" (Metz and Millen, 2–3). Palestine, Afghanistan, and Assam have all witnessed liberation insurgencies against outside occupiers (Israel, USSR, and India, respectively) during the twentieth and now twenty-first centuries (Hoffman, 6–7; Prabhakara, 777; Baruah, 951–74).

Although insurgency scholarship has recognized that the history of a particular region has a significant influence on the nature and evolution of any given insurgency, scholars have found that there were certain basic components common to all liberation insurgent movements: (1) strong leadership, (2) common ideology, and (3) clear objectives.[7] Of these, leadership is the most critical component. Without effective and charismatic leaders, a liberation insurgency cannot last and can never succeed. In addition, without a clear and appealing ideology that provides a vision of societal improvements, the leadership of an insurgency is unable to create an alternative to the existing sociopolitical structure. As Alex Schmid and Bradley McAllister show ("Theories of Terrorism," 219), group differentiation results, first, from social categorization and ideology-construction, which emphasizes the similarities among members of the in-group and the distinctions between the in- and out-groups. The second mechanism that facilitates this process of differentiation is social comparison, which entails the creation of positive images for the in-group and negative perceptions of the out-group and its goals. A liberation insurgency, then, is not simply random action, but instead a directed and focused movement by those too weak (or too cautious) to engage in full-scale, regular combat that launches both rhetoric and violence against occupation forces.

In addition to tracking the general categories of insurgency, scholars have also identified five phases through which liberation insurgencies in particular tend to progress, which, since they are general in scope, apply well to the ancient Mediterranean world: (1) preinsurgency, (2) organization,

(3) subversive action (usually terrorism and guerilla warfare), (4) conventional warfare, and (5) postinsurgency (U.S. Department of the Army, D–5). In phase 1, preinsurgency, all of the characteristics of insurgency are present in nascent form; most importantly, the leadership has begun to articulate both an ideology and objectives, to distinguish between in-group and out-group population. At this point, a catalyst is required to spur the insurgent movement to action. During phase 2, organization, the insurgency establishes and expands its influence and develops its ideology beyond the core supporters to the general populace. In this phase, the leadership begins to exert control and test its authority through small-scale subversive and terrorist actions against the occupiers. As Metz and Millen put it, insurgents "avoid battlespaces where they are weakest—often the conventional military sphere—and focus on those where they can operate on more equal footing, particularly the psychological and the political" (2). Phase 3, subversive action, consists of increased guerilla warfare and greater use of sabotage and terrorism. Again, Metz and Millen frame the situation well, "Insurgents try to postpone decisive action, avoid defeat, sustain themselves, expand their support, and hope that, over time, the power balance changes in their favor" (2). In phase 4, conventional warfare, the insurgency has developed militarily, in terms of resources and manpower, and is finally able and willing to challenge the establishment forces openly and directly in combat. Insurgencies progress rapidly from phase 3 to phase 4 because of military and political success, often as the result of some game-changing event (or series of events) that shifts the balance of power in the insurgents' favor. Phase 5, postinsurgency, sees the final result where the occupation government is either overthrown, has satisfied the insurgents' demands, or the insurgency has been soundly defeated.

In what follows, I will trace the development of Athenian resistance against Macedonian occupation through each of these phases of insurgency, paying particular attention to phases 1 through 3. I use these general phases in particular because of their rich ideological context as well as their familiarity to insurgency and terrorism scholars, so as to lay the groundwork for new, cross-disciplinary conversations. Indeed, using the same toolkit allows for greater analysis between the ideology of ancient resistance and that of modern liberation insurgencies.[8]

THE TEST CASE: ATHENS UNDER MACEDONIAN HEGEMONY

Ancient Athens had a long history of resistance to outside occupation. For example, when the Persians invaded in 490 and again in 481 BCE, the Athenians praised themselves for leading the Greeks in defending the homeland at the battles of Marathon, Salamis, and Plataea (Cawkwell). And when Spartan hegemony, backed by Persian gold, threatened Greek self-rule in the 370s BCE, Athens again organized her fellow Greeks to resist, through both guerilla action and open combat (Buckler). It is in this historical context, then, that we must place the Athenian resistance against Macedon in the 330s and 320s BCE. In 338, at the pass of Chaeronea, just south of Thermopylae in central Greece, Athens led all of the southern Greek powers except the Spartans in an effort to block the expanding empire of Philip II and his son Alexander. Athens failed: Philip won at Chaeronea and ordered all combatants to assemble at the city of Corinth to hear his terms. At Corinth, in the spring of 337, Philip forced an occupation government on the Greeks that allowed Athens and her fellows no autonomous foreign policy. As Ian Worthington puts it, the Macedonian system differed from others of the past in that "it was an enforced peace (thanks to Macedonia's military power). . . . Hence, behind the façade of the Greeks seemingly making their own decisions in an allied *synhedrion* without Macedonian involvement, it was the Macedonian king who was pulling all of the strings" (*Philip II*, 161). According to the League of Corinth settlement, then, Athens could no longer be openly autonomous, but rather controlled by a new system imposed by the conqueror, Philip of Macedon. This paper will show in what follows that because of this systematized occupation by Philip, Athens sought to reassert her freedom by creating a general ideology of resistance that evolved through the five main phases of insurgency discussed above. Yet because Athens was relatively weak militarily with respect to Macedon, and had just been forced to surrender her sovereignty at Chaeronea, the Athenians had to resist Macedonian hegemony in a subtle manner, by engaging in subversion and liberation rhetoric. If such rhetoric were used by an occupied state today, many analysts would identify it as a preinsurgency.[9]

Initially, the anti-Macedonian insurgency was fueled by a strong ideological theme: a combination of independence rhetoric, what the ancient

Greeks called *autarchia* (Will), or what Schmid and McAllister ("Theories of Terrorism") would call the process of identity formation, in which the in-group draws distinctions between themselves and others, highlighting the positive attributes of the in-group while simultaneously denoting the inferiority of the out-group population. After Philip imposed the League of Corinth, this in-group/out-group identity formation began in Athens with an intense commemoration of the city's past defense of her *autarchia*, in such battles as Marathon, Salamis, and Plataea, and the religious festivals that these victories inspired (Kellogg, 355–76; Rhodes and Osborne, 447–49). To sharpen the point further and thus focus public attention on how different Athens was from the Macedonians, and emphasize how much Athens had lost under Macedonian occupation, the Athenians created new military oaths, the Ephebic Oath and the Oath of Plataea, that required that all to demonstrate their loyalty to the "ancient traditions" of independent, self-ruled Athens.[10] Tradition was also invoked through public works. Immediately after Chaeronea, for example, Athens engaged in the largest-scale building project since the Parthenon (Hurwit, 255). This construction focused on symbolic public spaces such as the Athenian Assembly's official meeting space on the Pnyx, the Theatre of Dionysos, and the Panathenaic Stadium, which resonated with Athenian traditional values, Athenian cultural greatness, and Athenian independence.[11]

In addition, the public rhetoric of the time, such as the public speeches of Demosthenes and Lykourgos, underscored the in-group's reverence for the cults and traditional practices of Athens, as well as the importance of patriotic self-sacrifice, while at the same time crying out against the out-group's (and those who collaborated with it, such as pro-Macedonians like Leokrates) denigration of those same traditions (e.g., Lykourgos, *Leoc.*, 75–95). This rhetoric, or "consensus of religious ideology,"[12] allowed the Athenian insurgency to take on a liberation identity that would resonate deeply with every Athenian citizen (Schmid, 23–27). In short, Athenian demagogues such as Lykourgos employed liberation rhetoric to differentiate Athens from the occupiers and at the same time reassert Athens's former role as cultural and political leader of the free Greeks.[13] For Lykourgos and his followers, Athens could now defeat the out-group, barbarian Macedonians because she had once defeated the barbarian Persians.[14]

This Lykourgos, son of Lykophron, was well placed to lead the Athenian insurgency through phases 1, 2, 3, and 4. As a member of the ancient Eteoboutad aristocratic clan, student of both Plato and Isokrates, he had both the education and connections to claim the first place in Athenian public opinion and thereby frame Athenian in-group identity.[15] To put it another way: in the person of Lykourgos, the Athenian insurgency had that all-important charismatic leader. After the defeat at Chaeronea, because of his abilities and anti-Macedonian stance, Lykourgos was given authority by the Athenian democracy to run the finances of Athens for a four-year period (Mitchel, "Athens in the Age of Alexander"). His authority was renewed twice more, with the result that from 338 to 326 BCE, Lykourgos controlled the Athenian purse. Over the 12 years of his supervision, he managed between 14,000 and 18,650 talents, or between 504 million and 671 million days of a skilled laborer's services ([Plut.], *Moralia,* 841b). But in addition to being Athens' paymaster, Lykourgos also held the superintendence (*phylake*) of the city's morals and public order (Markianos, 325–31). He took his job so seriously that he even fined his own wife for public indecency ([Plut.], *Moralia,* 841e).[16]

Lykourgos broadcast his anti-Macedonian ideology early on, when he prosecuted the general Lysikles, commander of the Athenian forces at Chaeronea, for being a Macedonian sympathizer who lost the battle on purpose because he secretly supported Philip and Alexander (Diod. 16.88). This and other anti-Macedonian rhetoric mere days after the Macedonian victory over Athens, which could only have been intended as provocative, spurred Alexander to demand that Lykourgos be handed over for punishment ([Plut.], *Moralia,* 841e). The Athenians refused. The fact that they refused to hand over Lykourgos shows just how appealing his anti-Macedonian rhetoric was to his fellow citizens—and how far Athens had moved in creating its own identity in opposition to the Macedonian occupation. Indeed, Lykourgos was building a textbook insurgency; one of the first steps of any insurgent leader is to remove his potential rivals by tying them to the occupiers (Metz and Millen, 2). In this case, Lykourgos attacked the Chaeronea generals Lysikles and Leokrates for being stooges to Macedon (Lykourgos, *Leoc.*, 75–130).

The second step for an insurgent leader is to focus on the youth (Metz and Millen, 2; McAllister and Schmid, 217–60). Soon after Chaeronea, Lykourgos instituted a new system of military training, the so-called ephebic reforms, which involved two years of paramilitary service from all 18-year-old young men (Reinmuth). J. L. Friend is undoubtedly correct that the Athenians "probably created the ephebeia after Alexander's destruction of Thebes in September 335 B.C. because they needed a standing army to defend Attica against Boeotian raiders."[17] By focusing on Boeotian renegades, some of whom were surely survivors of the destruction of Thebes, the Athenian ephebeia would serve as a pretext for paramilitary training and would consequently not raise any negative attention from Alexander, after he had taken over control of Macedon and Greece after his father's death in 336. After all, Athens had every right under the League of Corinth to defend herself from neighborly aggression (Ryder; Jehne). Nevertheless, the ephebeia was not wholly physical. Part of the training these 18- and 19-year-old Athenians underwent was, as Fordyce Mitchel called it, "intensive indoctrination in patriotism" ("Athens in the Age of Alexander," 198).

The ephebes were organized by tribal "eating companies" that recalled the famous Spartan education system, the *agoge*.[18] The young men would eat in a common mess, bunk in common barracks, and train in common units. They would also swear a daily oath to liberate Athens against outsiders— classic in-group/out-group ideology (McAllister and Schmid). The ephebes' first year was spent close to the city and the naval center of Piraeus, so that they might be inculcated in the rituals of Athenian democracy and Athenian sea power. The second year required service along the border, so the young men might understand both the extent and vulnerability of the Athenian polis. But before training commenced, and seemingly at regular intervals, such as important national holidays like the anniversary of the Battle of Marathon, the ephebes would swear an oath to protect the sovereignty of the Athenian gods and land against outside occupation (Rhodes and Osborne, 447–49). They would also repeat the oath the united Greeks supposedly swore before the battle against the Persians at Plataea in 479 B.C. This construction of a common identity among newly enrolled fighters (including the swearing of an oath of allegiance) has much in common with the recruiting tactics of certain modern insurgent groups currently operating throughout the Middle East (Marsden and Schmid, 180–82).

It is not my purpose here to address the questions of whether the Lykourgan ephebic oath was the actual "ancestral oath" sworn by all Athenian soldiers from the beginning of the polis, or whether the Lykourgan oath of Plataea is the actual version sworn before the battle of Plataea in 479.[19] But it might be useful to view both of these oaths as what Eric Hobsbawm called "invented traditions." Hobsbawm argued that groups manipulate, or purposely fabricate, certain traditions in order to justify current actions or ideologies. Symbolic repetition, such as the public oath ceremony and daily training rituals of the ephebes, serve to fix the traditions and construct a sense of continuity with the past (1). Michael Flower has documented this phenomenon in Athens's fellow polis, Sparta, arguing that after particularly humiliating military defeats such as the Battles of Leuktra (371 BCE) and Sellasia (222 BCE), Sparta manipulated the "ancestral" constitution and other important "national" institutions such as the youth training system of the *agoge*, in order to rearticulate Spartan political identity and reassert Spartan independence and power against outside occupation. It is significant that in these times of defeat, the Spartans specifically targeted the education system of young Spartan citizens. Viewed in this light, the ephebic oath and the Oath of Plataea make sense as a way for fourth-century Athenians to engage the defensive anti-outsider, autonomy rhetoric of the Persian Wars and appropriate it against the current Macedonian occupation in a way that polarized in-group and out-group relations (Lawton).

Just as the Plataean and Ephebic oaths served to recall and underscore among the impressionable youth Athens's great history in leading the Greeks to resist invasion and occupation, so too did Lykourgos's public rhetoric against Macedon. Indeed, engaging past heroes and their successful liberation movements certainly seems behind Lykourgos's comparison between the cowardice of the Athenian general Leokrates during and after Chaeronea and the heroic acts of Athenian greats such as Miltiades, the commander of Marathon in 490 (Lykourgos, *Leoc.*, 75–130). As Rhodes and Osborne (447–49) argue in their commentary on the Acharnai inscription, which records both the Ephebic and Plataean oaths, there is a well-documented tendency among Athenians of this period to elaborate and view such "ancient" stories around current historical circumstances, and alternatively, to elaborate current historical circumstances so that they explain and contextualize "ancient" stories.

So, after their defeat at Chaeronea, Lykourgos organized a paramilitary movement that included psychological indoctrination for the Athenian youth. In order to assure that they trained well and bought into the ideology of the movement, Lykourgos gave out public honors at the end of training to the best and most patriotic young fighters in a grand public ceremony. At the same time, he had the names of these young heroes inscribed on large monuments placed in prominent religious venues such as the Athenian Akropolis (*IG* II² 1156; Rhodes and Osborne, 448–56; Schwenk). By engaging the age-old dynamic of *philotimia*, competition for honors, and by making that competition public and religiously meaningful, Lykourgos guaranteed good results and good recruit "buy-in" (Whitehead; Howe, 99–123). All of these strategies, but especially the religious recruiting of paramilitaries, are typical strategies of modern insurgent groups (McAllister and Schmid, 217–60).

Lykourgos's paramilitary reforms allowed the insurgency to move to phase 2, to take hold and build for 12 full years before Athens ever engaged in full-scale combat. Reflect on this: a decade of 18- and 19-year-olds passed through the ephebic program, swore their oaths, chafed at the Macedonian occupation, and killed those outsiders who crossed Athenian boundaries. All the while their families cheered them on. As J. L. Friend put it, the Lykourgan ephebeia, by instilling "piety and patriotic fervor in the ephebes, sought to make them virtuous citizens both dedicated to preserving the democracy and deeply motivated to freeing Athens from Macedonian domination. This devotion to the state explains why the institution was abolished by the pro-Macedonian oligarchy (321/0–319/8 B.C.) established after Athens' defeat in the Lamian War in 322 B.C." (vii).

Now that Athens had a strong leadership, a clear ideology, and a devoted base, she was ready to progress to phase 3, subversive action and terrorism. Alexander's invasion of Asia in 334 B.C., and the vacuum he left in Greece when he took his army east, provided the necessary catalyst for the insurgency to evolve to this next phase. Since Lykourgos had firmly established a patriotic narrative at home and had a ready supply of paramilitaries, the Athenians were ready to strike out against Alexander's supply lines, thereby lessening his overall military effectiveness with terror and guerilla action. At the same time, the Athenians could use these raids on Alexander's shipping to secure their own food supply.

At this point in the resistance, securing a food supply was essential for Athens—for the past 100 years, since the middle of the fifth century, Athens had no longer produced enough grain locally to support its population, and had thus become dependent on imports from the Black Sea and other regions (Garnsey, *Famine and the Food Supply, Food and Society*; Oliver). As the Great Peloponnesian War had shown, Athens was only as strong as her food supply; the war only came to an end in 404 because Sparta successfully cut off the grain fleets coming through the Bosporus and Dardanelles. Since Philip's siege of Byzantium and subsequent control over the Bosporus and Dardanelles (340 B.C.), Macedon could cut off Athens's grain supply at will. Indeed, Philip had often done so (Worthington *Philip II*, 132–35). In the end, so long as Macedon controlled Athens's food, Athens could not act independently, and consequently would be unable to resist the Macedonian occupation in the long term. Athens had to subvert Alexander's supply lines for her own use, but since Lykourgos did not have the military strength to engage Alexander's forces in open combat, he would have to use piracy and terrorism to seize control of the all-important grain supply.[20]

In 334/3, once Alexander was occupied fighting the Persians in Asia, the Athenians launched a search-and-seize expedition consisting of two ships of the line (triremes) under the command of one Diotimos. Diotimos's goal was to secure grain shipments coming through the Bosporus and Dardanelles. Unfortunately, we do not know any details of this mission other than the fact that Diotimos was honored for having completed his task successfully (*IG* II^2 1623.276–308; [Plut.], *Moralia,* 844a; Schwenk, no. 25). We can infer, however, that Diotimos was not assisting Alexander's invasion, or any Macedonian interests, since he had been a member of the anti-Macedonian faction in Athens that Alexander demanded surrender to Macedonian custody after the rebellion of Thebes (Arr. *Anab.* 1.10). Moreover, Diotimos was not conducting a regular patrol but rather a defined mission, to a specific location, the Bosporus (de Souza, 41). Given Athens's dependence on Black Sea grain at the time, it seems most likely that taking grain ships from the northern Aegean fits the context. Regardless, after the success of Diotimos's naval action, and the lack of any Macedonian reaction, the Athenians were encouraged to act more boldly and try to take greater control over the Black Sea grain. In 332/1, the Athenians sent out 100 triremes under a certain Menestheus to steal the grain fleet Alexander had assembled near the island of Tenedos ([Dem.], 17.20). They seem to have succeeded, though this seems to have been a one-time success and Athens never was able to ensure a permanent control over Alexander's grain fleets.[21]

With the guerilla raids of 334/3 and 332/1 behind her, the Athenian insurgency was ready to broadcast an ideological message to an outside audience. In 327/6, Athens honored Memnon of Rhodes, nephew of Alexander's opponent, also named Memnon, during the sieges of Miletos and Halikarnassos in 334 (*IG* II² 356). While Memnon-the-nephew had not actively campaigned against Alexander, all of his family had, and were closely connected with high-ranking Persians who were currently fighting against Alexander in what is now Iran and Afghanistan. Athenian honors for the Memnon family sent a signal that Athens was not wholly Alexander's creature, and that other enemies of Alexander might find a home, or at least support, in Athens.

The main audience for this message seems to have been other Greeks in the Peloponnese and Aitolia. It is significant that in the next year, 326/5, Athens established a military base in the Adriatic, on land adjacent to the Aitolians. This Adriatic foundation seems undoubtedly to have been placed here to assist the Aitolians in their raids on Alexander's allies, the Epirotes and Illyrians.[22] An Athenian military base in that region, too, would allow the ephebe paramilitaries to see some action; a base would also provide unfettered access to the shipbuilding timber of the Dalmatian coast and Southern Italy (Meiggs).

And ships were the key to taking the insurgency to phase 4, conventional war. But for now, Athens could build up her "pirate" fleet and continue to terrorize Alexander's supply lines and friends. *IG* II² 1629 is an extract from the accounts of the curators for the Piraeus dockyards for the year 325/4. This and other documents attest to a massive buildup of naval capacity after 330, a time when Athens was technically at peace, legally barred by the League of Corinth accords from engaging in regular combat, and not required by Alexander to supply him with ships—in short, Athens had no legitimate reason to build up a navy. And yet, by 325/4, Athens had built 50 quadriremes, 7 quinquerimes, and 392 triremes. To give some idea of what this means in terms of manpower, I offer some figures:[23] triremes had three banks of oars, each pulled by one man, with a total of 170 rowers; quadriremes had two banks of oars, each pulled by two men, with 176 rowers; quinqueremes had three banks of oars, two banks pulled by two men each, with a third pulled by one man, and a total of 264 rowers. If all of these ships were put to sea at once—and I should stress that this was not policy—the fleet would require 77,288 men. A contemporary decree proposed by one Stratokles commends Lykourgos for managing all of this. It also honors him for stockpiling weapons on the Akropolis ([Plut.], *Moralia,* 852c). Because of its success on sea and land, as well as Alexander's preoccupation with Afghanistan and India, the Athenian insurgency was emboldened into preparing for violence on a large scale.

Included in the report of the curators of the Piraeus is a status update about the Athenian military base in the Adriatic. Here, we see that the Adriatic colony was clearly a priority for Lykourgos, since he has offered incentives as well as punishments to ensure the fleet was prepared in time. All of this military action was led by one Miltiades, a descendant of the famous Miltiades, hero of the Battle of Marathon; that was no accident. Throughout the Lykourgan period, Persian War rhetoric was used to the utmost—Persian occupation will become a cypher for Macedonian. Indeed, as Rhodes and Osborne (512–27) observe, the phrasing of the Adriatic decree employs the imperialistic, military language of the fifth century and the early Delian League, which is unusual for the entire fourth century, except, of course, the Lykourgan period.

While Mitiades assembled his fleet, another war hero, Leosthenes, was given 50 talents (almost 3,000 pounds of silver) and a consignment of weapons to raise a southern force of paramilitaries from the mercenary recruiting center at Tainarum, a fortified base in Spartan territory, guarding the passage to the Ionian and Adriatic Seas (Diod. 18.9.4). At the same time, Leosthenes was ordered to engage in secret negotiations with the anti-Macedonian Aitolians to step up the raids on Macedon and her allies, Epiros and Illyria (Diod. 17.108.7; Justin 13.5.2.). To add insult to injury, while Alexander was busy fighting in what is now Afghanistan, Athens invited Persian governors and military commanders who had survived Alexander's purges to meet at Tainaron and assist in the raids against Macedonian territory and materiel (Bosworth, 199). Even old Greek heroes, such as Epikrates, who had fought against Philip at Chaeronea, joined the gathering at Tainaron. The beauty of Tainaron was that it was not in Athenian territory. By placing the insurgent training camp in neutral but friendly territory, and by manning a naval base in the Adriatic, near the Aitolians, Athens distanced herself from the anti-Macedonian movement.[24]

The training campus at Tainaron and in the Adriatic, coupled with the naval build-up in the Piraeus, allowed the Athenian insurgency to develop militarily, in terms of resources and manpower. Each new success built the Athenians' confidence and honed their skills. Indeed, only one year after the Athenians began to supply Tainaron, Athens was ready and willing to challenge Alexander openly and directly, she only needed a catalyst to move from subversion and terrorism to open combat. But insurgencies do need a catalyst to progress from phase 3 to phase 4, and Athens was no exception. Like many insurgent groups, the Athenians were waiting for a game-changing event (or series of events) that would make them abandon the so far extremely successful subversive tactics (U.S. Department of the Army, D–5). The game-changing event for Athens was the Exiles Decree of 324.

In 324 B.C., Alexander ordered all of the Greek cities to reintegrate all exiled citizens, regardless of the original rationale for exile, and to restore to those exiles their original lands and properties (Bosworth, 220–28; see also Blackwell, 146). This especially affected Athens, who had exiled many Samians from the island of Samos and replaced them with Athenian colonists. Alexander's Exiles Decree forced the Athenians to return to the Samian exiles land that Athens had held since occupying the island in 365, eleven years before Alexander the Great had even been born. Such interference in issues of local citizenship is especially dangerous for occupation governments dealing with insurgencies. For example, Baruah observes that when the Indian government retrospectively legalized the status of undocumented immigrants from Bangladesh in the Assam region of modern India, and thereby recognized their rights to own property, the native Assam residents repudiated the authority of the government and stepped up their independence movement (954). First, the local authorities refused to recognize as citizens the migrants whom they considered foreigners and interlopers, and then the native population as a whole engaged in combat against the Indian government forces. Being forced to give up Samos seemed to have had a similar effect on the Athenians. Fortunately, Alexander died before the decree could be fully implemented, but the damage had been done. Emboldened by years of successful terror and guerilla war, her huge naval reserves, and upset by what they perceived as Macedonian oppression (not to mention the sudden and unexpected death of Alexander), the Athenians advanced their insurgency against the Macedonians to phase 4, conventional warfare, in what we now call the Lamian War.

The Lamian War of 323/2 pitted a coalition of Greek cities, led by Athens and the Aitolians, against Macedonia (Walsh). Athens had long prepared for this moment, and at first the Athenians were victorious, but the defeat of their navy in one massive engagement led Athens and her allies to surrender to Alexander's regent, Antipater. The end result of the Lamian War was phase 5 of the Athenian insurgency, renewed Macedonian occupation. Unfortunately for Athens, the days of glory and victory over the occupiers were over. Macedonian forces once and for all crushed all hopes of Athenian *autarchia* (Hammond and Walbank, 107–17).

CONCLUSIONS

This paper has attempted to offer a new context to both ancient history and counterinsurgency by exploring the underpinnings and wider ideological context of Athenian resistance to Alexander the Great. I have attempted to demonstrate that under Lykourgos, son of Lykophron, Athens created a liberation insurgency that would, after the death of Alexander, throw Athens against the Macedonian kingdom in a conventional war. By viewing both the anti-Macedonian rhetoric of Lykourgos and Demosthenes and the *autarchia* ideology visible in honorary decrees,[25] the Plataian Oath and Ephebic reforms, I have sought a wider context for the Lamian War of 322/2. It is hoped that we can view the conventional military action of the Lamian War in a new light, as a culminating event of Athenian liberation rhetoric, rather than an opportunistic war, brought about by nothing more than the power vacuum created by Alexander's sudden death (Walsh), and that this wider perspective will shift scholarly attention away from Great Men like Alexander, Demonsthenes, and Lykourgos toward the wider context of resistance rhetoric and ideology. In the end, I hope this paper will provide a deeper methodological foundation and point of departure for future scholarly conversation about subversion and resistance.

NOTES

1.   For example, Angelos Chaniotis and Pierre Ducrey, eds., *Army and Power in the Ancient World* (Stuttgart: Franz Steiner Verlag, 2002); Susan Mattern,

"Counterinsurgency and the Enemies of Rome," in *Makers of Ancient Strategy, from the Persian Wars to the Fall of Rome*, edited by V. D. Hanson (Princeton: Princeton University Press, 2010), 163–84; Seth F. C. Richardson, ed., *Rebellions and Peripheries in the Cuneiform World*, American Oriental Society 91 (Chicago: American Oriental Society, 2010); Gregory Bolich, "Terrorism in the Ancient Roman World," *MHQ: Military History Quarterly* 18, no. 3 (2006): 52–59; Richard A. Horsley, "The *Sicarii*: Ancient Jewish 'Terrorists,'" *Journal of Religion* 59, no. 4 (1979), 435–58; Adrienne Mayor, *The Poison King* (Princeton: Princeton University Press, 2010); T. Ñaco del Hoyo et al., "The 'Ultimate Frontier': War, Terror and the Greek *Poleis* Between Mithridates and Rome," in *Frontiers in the Roman World: Proceedings of the Ninth Workshop of the International Network Impact of Empire (Durham, 16–19 April 2009)*, edited by O. Hekster and T. Kaizer (Leiden: Brill, 2011), 291–304; Gianpaolo Urso, ed., *Terror et Pavor: Violenza, intimidazione, clandestina nel mondo antico. Atti del convegno internazionale Cividale del Friuli, 22–24 settembre 2005* (Pisa: Edizioni ETS, 2006).

2.   Bolich ("Terrorism in the Ancient Roman World"), in particular, exemplifies the need for a methodologically grounded approach. He uncritically equates the crime of piracy in the Roman Empire and the September 11, 2001 hijacking. In this he demonstrates both an incomplete understanding of how both policy analysts and scholars define modern terrorism *and* insensitivity to historical and cultural differences.

3.   So argues Lee L. Brice, "Insurgency and Terrorism in the Ancient World, Grounding the Discussion," in *Brill's Companion to Insurgency and Terrorism in the Ancient Mediterranean*, edited by Timothy Howe and Lee L. Brice (Leiden: Brill, 2015), 3–27. For a discussion of the dangers of anachronism and ways to avoid it, see J. Roth, "Epilogue: Looking Ahead," in *Brill's Companion to Insurgency and Terrorism in the Ancient Mediterranean,* edited by Timothy Howe and Lee L. Brice (Leiden: Brill, 2015), 344–364. For treatments of method see, e.g., Ian F. W. Beckett, *Modern Insurgencies and Counter-Insurgencies: Guerrillas and Their Opponents Since 1750* (New York: Routledge, 2001); Bard E. O'Neill, *Insurgency and Terrorism: From Revolution to Apocalypse*, 2nd ed. (Dulles, VA: Potomac, 2005); William R. Polk, *Violent Politics: A History of Insurgency, Terrorism, and Guerrilla War, From the American Revolution to Iraq* (New York: Harper, 2007); Russell Howard, Reid Sawyer, and Natasha Bajema, *Terrorism and Counterterrorism: Understanding the New Security Environment, Readings and Interpretations* (New York: McGraw Hill, 2008); Elleke Boehmer and Stephen Morton, *Terror and the Postcolonial: A*

Concise Companion (Malden, MA: Wiley-Blackwell, 2009); Alex Schmid, *Routledge Handbook on Terrorism Research* (New York: Routledge, 2011). See also S. Metz, "Psychology of Participation in Insurgency," *Small Wars Journal*, January 27, 2012, http://smallwarsjournal.com/print/12195.

    4.   NATO Standardization Agency, *AAP-6(2010): NATO Glossary of Terms and Definitions* (Brussels: North Atlantic Treaty Organization, 2010); www.nato.int /docu/stanag/aap006/aap-6-2010.pdf (emphasis added). Not only do modern government agencies worldwide use this definition, which appears in the current official NATO glossary, but it has now appeared in common English dictionaries including Webster's New International dictionary, an indication that it has entered popular usage simultaneously. While both the NATO and the U.S. Army definitions in FM 3–24 (2008) exclude the participation of state institutions, such organizations frequently participate in uprisings. This definition reflects the U.S. military's theoretical debates over the use of counterinsurgency, informed by the United States' experiences with, and perceptions of, guerilla war in Southeast Asia and the Middle East. Used in this sense, insurgency excludes political insurgencies, which is what we are dealing with in Athens's resistance against the Macedonian Occupation. Thus, in the case of Athens, which swore an oath to recognize Philip and Alexander's hegemony over Greece, the recognized federal government is the monarchy of Macedon and the collaborator federation, the League of Corinth. See Ian Worthington, *Philip II of Macedonia* (New Haven: Yale University Press, 2008), 161–63. See also Lee. L. Brice, "Insurgency and Terrorism," 8–12 for a recent update to this definition and a discussion of its application to ancient world realities.

    5.   Pre-9/11 there was intense interest in terrorism as a result of the numerous postcolonial insurgencies occurring after World War II (Harry Eckstein, *Internal War* [New York: Free Press, 1964]). Analysts of insurgent movements recognized a need to define terrorism in more concrete, social-psychological terms. By 1964, the definition common in international literature was, "terror is a symbolic act designed to influence political behavior by extra-normal means, entailing the use or threat of violence" (T. P. Thornton, "Terror as a Weapon of Political Agitation," in *Internal War*, edited by Harry Eckstein [New York: Free Press, 1964], 73). Researchers working in the following fifteen years refined the definition somewhat, but made little meaningful adjustment (M. Hutchinson, "The Concept of Revolutionary Terrorism," *Journal of Conflict Resolution* 16, no. 3 (1971): 393–95; H. E. Price, "The Strategy and Tactics of Revolutionary Terrorism," *Comparative Studies in Society and History* 19, no. 1 (1977):

52–66). During the mid-1980s scholars crafted a statement that more fully covers the historical experience: terrorism is "the purposeful act or threat of violence to create fear and/or compliant behavior in a victim and/or audience of the act or threat" (M. Stohl and George A. Lopez, eds., *The State as Terrorist: The Dynamics of Governmental Violence and Repression* [Westport, CT: Greenwood, 1984], 7). I will use this definition throughout. For further discussion on the suitability of Stohl and Lopez's definition to ancient contexts, see S. Richardson, "Insurgency and Terror in Mesopotamia," in *Brill's Companion to Insurgency and Terrorism in the Ancient Mediterranean*, edited by Timothy Howe and Lee L. Brice (Leiden: Brill, 2015), 47–55).

   6.   S. Metz and R. Millen, *Insurgency and Counterinsurgency in the 21st Century: Reconceptualizing Threat and Response* (Carlisle, PA: Strategic Studies Institute, U.S. Army War College, 2004), 2, argue that insurgency is "a strategy adopted by groups which cannot attain their political objectives through conventional means or by a quick seizure of power. It is used by those too weak to do otherwise." See also B. Hoffman, *Insurgency and Counterinsurgency in Iraq* (Santa Monica, CA: RAND Coparation, 2004); R. Shulz and A. Drew, *Insurgents, Terrorists, and Militias: The Warriors of Contemporary Combat* (New York: Columbia University Press, 2006); S. Metz, "Rethinking Insurgency," *Strategic Studies Institute*, 2007, http://www.strategicstudiesinstitute .army.mil/pubs/display.cfm?pubID=790; cf. D. Porch ("The Dangerous Myths and Dubious Promise of COIN," *Small Wars and Insurgencies* 22, no. 2 (2011): 239–57), who cautions against such a narrow perspective.

   7.   U.S. Department of the Army, *Field Manual 3-07*, D-1; cf. the warning of Porch, "The Dangerous Myths and Dubious Promise of COIN," 239–44, and Brice, "Insurgency and Terrorism," 5–6, against too narrowly defining insurgency.

   8.   Since the time of Philip II we see Athenian politicians engaging a combination of liberation and independence rhetoric, what the ancient Greeks called *autarchia* (Wolfgang Will, *Athen und Alexander: Untersuchungen zur Geschichte der Stadt von 338 bis 322 v. Chr* [Munich: Beck, 1983]; P. Hunt, *Demosthenes' Athens* [Cambridge: Cambridge University Press, 2010], 134–53); this is not dissimilar to that of any modern liberation insurgency (Metz and Millen, "Reconceptualizing Threat and Response").

   9.   E. Badian, "Harpalus," *Journal of Hellenic Studies* 81 (1961): 14–43; C. Blackwell, *In the Absence of Alexander: Harpalus and the Failure of Macedonian Authority* (New York: Peter Lang, 1999); P. Green, *Alexander of Macedon 356–323 BC: A Historical Biography*, 2nd. ed. (Berkeley: University of California Press, 1991);

R. Lane Fox, *Alexander the Great* (London: Penguin, 1973). See I. Worthington, "Harpalus and the Macedonian Envoys," *Liverpool Classical Monthly* 9 (1984): 47–48; "The First Flight of Harpalus Reconsidered," *Greece and Rome* 31 (1984): 161–69; "The Chronology of the Harpalus Affair," *Symbolae Osloenses* 61 (1986): 63–76; "The Harpalus Affair and the Greek Response to the Macedonian Hegemony," in *Ventures Into Greek History. Essays in Honour of N. G. L. Hammond*, edited by I. Worthington, 307–30 (Oxford: Oxford University Press, 1994); "Alexander and Athens in 324/3: On the Greek Attitude to the Macedonian Hegemony," *Mediterranean Archaeology* 7 (1994): 45–51; *Demosthenes: Statesman and Orator* (New York: Routledge, 2000); "Alexander's Destruction of Thebes," in *Crossroads of History: The Age of Alexander*, edited by Waldemar Heckel and Lawrence A. Tritle (Claremont, CA: Regina Books, 2003), 65–86. Because of the impact of Alexander the Great's conquests in Asia, the general scholarly focus on the actions and policies of Alexander himself, and the desire to see late fourth-century Athens in the light of its fifth-century imperial glory, this Athenian resistance to the Macedonian occupation during the decade or so between Chaeronea and Alexander's deaths has received little focused scholarly attention. For the most part, work has centered on the tensions between two great men—Demosthenes and Alexander—and the strange actions of renegades such as Alexander's friend and erstwhile treasurer Harpalos.

10. *SEG* 21.519; F. Mitchel, "Athens in the Age of Alexander," *Greece and Rome* 12, no. 2 (1965): 189–204; P. Siewert, "The Ephebic Oath in Fifth-Century Athens," Journal of Hellenic Studies 97 (1977): 102–11; Carol Lawton, "Athenian Anti-Macedonian Sentiment and Democratic Ideology in Attic Document Reliefs in the Second Half of the Fourth Century B.C.," in *The Macedonians in Athens, 322–229 B.C.*, edited by O. Palagia and S. V. Tracy, 117–27 (Oxford: Oxford University Press, 2003); G. Oliver, *War, Food, and Politics in Early Hellenistic Athens* (Oxford: Oxford University Press, 2007), 175–76; J. Friend, *The Athenian Ephebeia in the Lycurgan Period: 334/3–322/1 B.C.* (Austin: University of Texas, 2009) . For a discussion of Athenian self-rule, ancestor reverence and the place of the ephebes in this wider context, see Hunt, *Demosthenes' Athens*, 123–32.

11. Andrew Stewart, *Classical Greece and the Birth of Western Art* (Cambridge: Cambridge University Press, 2008). The Pnyx was the main meeting place for the Athenian government through the fifth and fourth centuries. The Theatre of Dionsyos hosted the main dramatic festivals of Athens, the City Dionysia and the Lenaia, where comic and tragic playwrights used drama to critique and contextualize contemporary

politics. The Panthathenaic Stadium held the All-Athenian games, a celebration of Athenian identity and athleticism.

12. Metz and Millen, *Reconceptualizing Threat and Response*, 2. For further discussion see M. Ranstorp, "Terrorism in the Name of Religion," *Journal of International Affairs* 50, no. 1 (1996): 41–62; A. Cronin, "Behind the Curve: Globalization and International Terrorism," *International Security* 27, no. 3 (2003): 30–58; V. I. Vasilenko, "The Concept and Typology of Terrorism," *Statues and Decisions: The Laws of the USSR and Its Successor States* 40, no. 5 (2004): 46–56; Sarah V. Marsden and Alex P. Schmid, "Typologies of Terrorism and Political Violence," in *The Routledge Handbook on Terrorism Research*, edited by A. P. Schmid (New York: Routledge, 2011): 180–82.

13. Cf. Isokrates, *Panegyricus* 133–34; 172–89; *Philipus* 8–9; 16; 30–31; 68; 83; 115; 120–23; 127; 154–55.

14. See Stewart, *Classical Greece*, who argues that the artwork from both the post-Persian war period and the latter fourth century celebrates Athenian victory and Athenian power over the Barbarian; cf. Hunt, *Demosthenes' Athens*, 135–53.

15. Michele Faraguna, *Atene nell'età di Alessandro: problemi politici, economici, finanziari* (Rome: G. Bardi, 1992): 280–85; Will, *Athen und Alexander*; Humphreys, "Lycurgus of Butadae," in *The Craft of the Ancient Historian: Essays in Honor of C. G. Starr*, edited by J. W. Eadie and J. Ober (Lanham, MD: University Press of America, 1985), 199–252; Fordyce Mitchel, "Lykourgan Athens 338–22," in *Lectures in Memory of Louise Taft Semple*, Second Series, 1966–1970, edited by C. G. Boulter, D. W. Bradeen, and A. Cameron (Cincinnati: University of Cincinnati Press, 1973), 163–214; Friend, *The Athenian Ephebeia*.

16. The connection between enforcing morality and leading an insurgency is not uncommon. See Marsden and Schmid, "Typologies of Terrorism and Political Violence," 158–200.

17. Friend, *The Athenian Ephebeia*, vi. See also Andrzej S. Chankowski, *L'Éphébie hellénistique: Étude d'une institution civique dans les cités grecques des îles de la Mer Égée et de l'Asie Mineure. Culture et cité, 4* (Paris: De Boccard, 2010), 45–233, in particular, who deconstructs the commonly accepted idea that "ephebe" represented a primeval age designation that survived into the Classical period; cf. Oliver, *Early Hellenistic Athens*, 174–76.

18. See Oliver, *Early Hellenistic Athens*, 213–23, for a discussion of the interplay between training the ephebes, defense, and the food supply.

19. See Danielle Kellogg, "οὐκ ἐλάττω παραδώσω τὴν πατρίδα: The Ephebic Oath and the Oath of Plataea in Fourth Century Athens," *Mouseion*, Series III, 8 (2008): 355–76, for further discussion of the debate surrounding the historicity of the Oath.

20. Hoffman, *Insurgency and Counterinsurgency in Iraq*; Metz and Millen, *Reconceptualizing Threat and Response*. Piracy and guerilla raids on the occupiers' supply lines are common actions during liberation insurgencies.

21. In 330/29, and again in 328/7, Athens suffered major grain shortages. These were alleviated by gifts from friendly, non-Macedonian controlled regions—Salamis on Cyprus and Cyrene in North Africa (*IG* II² 360; *SEG* 9.2). See P. J. Rhodes and Robin Osborne, *Greek Historical Inscriptions 404–323 BC* (Oxford: Oxford University Press, 2003), 478–93 for discussion, particularly their observation that Kyrene was not operating under Macedonian orders. A few years later, in 325/4, the Athenians established a colony in the Adriatic, one of whose purposes was to protect Italian and Sicilian grain ships on their way to Athens (*IG* II² 1629.2157–223; cf. Diod 16.5.3). That grain was a concern of the Adriatic colony is clear. As Rhodes and Osborne (*Greek Historical Inscriptions*, 525) note, both in this inscription (line 859ff.) and the naval list for the previous year (*IG* II² 1628.339-95), "the fines imposed on trierarchs are reduced if they or their close associates have been responsible for gifts of grain in 328/7." The Athenian Insurgency could not advance until Athens had secured a stable food supply. Seemingly, only after 325, and the establishment of the Adriatic colony, was this finally achieved.

22. Jack Cargill, *Athenian Settlements of the Fourth Century B.C.*, Mnemosyne, Supplements 145 (Leiden: Brill, 1995), 33 suggests that anti-Macedonian sentiment at Athens underpinned the timing of this colony.

23. See Lionel Casson, *Ships and Seamanship in the Ancient World* (Princeton: Princeton University Press, 1971), and William M. Murray, *The Age of Titans: The Rise and Fall of the Great Hellenistic Navies* (Oxford: Oxford University Press, 2012), for a full discussion of the fighting contingents and capabilities of these warships.

24. One need only recall Al Qaeda training camps in friendly Afghanistan, before 9/11, or Taliban training campus in Pakistan after the US-led invasion of Afghanistan, to see how useful such a friendly, but neutral, training center could be to an insurgency (Metz and Millen, *Reconceptualizing Threat and Response*).

25. Lawton, "Athenian Anti-Macedonian Sentiment and Democratic Ideology," 117–27.

WORKS CITED

Badian, Ernst. "Harpalus." *Journal of Hellenic Studies* 81 (1961): 14–43.

Baruah, Sarah. "Separatist Militants and Contentious Politics in Assam, India. The Limits of Counterinsurgency." *Asian Survey* 49, no. 6 (2009): 951–74. http://dx.doi.org/10.1525/as.2009.49.6.951.

Beckett, Ian. F. W. *Modern Insurgencies and Counter-Insurgencies: Guerrillas and Their Opponents Since 1750.* New York: Routledge, 2001.

Blackwell, Christopher W. *In the Absence of Alexander: Harpalus and the Failure of Macedonian Authority.* New York: Peter Lang, 1999.

Boehmer, Elleke and Stephen Morton. *Terror and the Postcolonial: A Concise Companion.* Malden, MA: Wiley-Blackwell, 2009.

Bolich, Gregory. "Terrorism in the Ancient Roman World." *MHQ: Military History Quarterly* 18, no. 3 (2006): 52–59.

Bosworth, A. B. *Conquest and Empire: The Reign of Alexander the Great.* Cambridge: Cambridge University Press, 1988.

Brice, Lee L. "Insurgency and Terrorism in the Ancient World, Grounding the Discussion." In *Brill's Companion to Insurgency and Terrorism in the Ancient Mediterranean*, edited by Timothy Howe and Lee L. Brice, 3–27. Leiden: Brill, 2015.

Buckler, John. *Central Greece and the Politics of Power in the Fourth Century BC*. Cambridge: Cambridge University Press, 2008.

Cargill, Jack. *Athenian Settlements of the Fourth Century B.C.* Mnemosyne, Supplements 145. Leiden: Brill, 1995.

Casson, Lionel. *Ships and Seamanship in the Ancient World*. Princeton: Princeton University Press, 1971.

Cawkwell, George. *The Greek Wars: The Failure of Persia*. Oxford: Oxford University Press, 2006.

Chaniotis, Angelos and Pierre Ducrey, eds. *Army and Power in the Ancient World*. Stuttgart: Franz Steiner Verlag, 2002.

Chankowski, Andrzej S. *L'Éphébie hellénistique: Étude d'une institution civique dans les cités grecques des îles de la Mer Égée et de l'Asie Mineure.* Culture et cité, 4. Paris: De Boccard, 2010.

Cronin, Audrey K. 2003. "Behind the Curve: Globalization and International Terrorism." *International Security* 27, no. 3 (2003): 30–58.

de Souza, Philip. *Piracy in the Graeco-Roman World*. Cambridge: Cambridge University Press, 2000.

Eckstein, Harry. *Internal War*. New York: Free Press, 1964.

Faraguna, Michele. *Atene nell' età di Alessandro: Problemi politici, economici, finanziari*. Rome: G. Bardi, 1992.

Flower, Michael. "The Invention of Tradition in Classical and Hellenistic Sparta." In *Sparta: Beyond the Mirage*, edited by A. Powell and S. Hodkinson, 193–219. London: Classical Press of Wales/Duckworth, 2002.

Friend, John L. "The Athenian Ephebeia in the Lycurgan Period: 334/3–322/1 B.C." PhD Diss., University of Texas, 2009.

Gabrielsen, Vincent. *Financing the Athenian Fleet: Public Taxation and Social Relations*. Baltimore: Johns Hopkins University Press, 1994.

Garnsey, Peter. *Famine and the Food Supply in the Graeco-Roman World*. Cambridge: Cambridge University Press, 1988.

———. *Food and Society in Classical Antiquity*. Cambridge: Cambridge University Press, 1999.

Green, Peter. *Alexander of Macedon, 356–323 BC: A Historical Biography*. 2nd ed. Berkeley: University of California Press, 1991.

Hammond, N. G. L., and F. W. Walbank. *A History of Macedonia, Volume III: 336–167 BC*. Oxford: The Clarendon Press.

Hansen, M. H. "Polis as the Generic Term for State." In *Yet More Studies in the Ancient Greek Polis. Papers from the Copenhagen Polis Centre 4*. Historia Enzelschriften 117, edited by Thomas Heine Nielsen Neilsen, 9–15. Stuttgart: Franz Steiner, 1997.

———. "Polis, Civitas, Stadtstaat and City-State." In *From Political Architecture to Stephanus Byzantius. Papers from the Copenhagen Polis Centre 1*. Historia Enzelschriften 87, edited by D. Whitehead, 19–22. Stuttgart: Franz Steiner, 1994.

———. "Was the Polis a State or a Stateless Society?" In *Even More Studies in the Ancient Greek Polis. Papers from the Copenhagen Polis Centre, 6*. Historia Einzelschriften 162, edited by Thomas Heine Nielsen, 17–47. Stuttgart: Franz Steiner, 2002.

Hobsbawm, Eric. "Introduction: Inventing Traditions." In *The Invention of Tradition*, edited by E. Hobsbawm and T. Ranger, 1–14. Cambridge: Cambridge University Press, 1983.

Hoffman, Bruce. *Insurgency and Counterinsurgency in Iraq*. Santa Monica, CA: RAND Corporation, 2004.

Horsley, Richard A. "The *Sicarii*: Ancient Jewish 'Terrorists.'" *Journal of Religion* 59, no. 4 (1979): 435–58.

Howard, Russell, Reid Sawyer, and Natasha Bajema. *Terrorism and Counterterrorism: Understanding the New Security Environment, Readings and Interpretations*. 3rd ed. New York: McGraw Hill, 2008.

Howe, Timothy. *Pastoral Politics. Animals Agriculture and Society in Ancient Greece*. Claremont, CA: Regina Books, 2008.

Howe, Timothy, and Lee L. Brice, eds. *Brill's Companion to Insurgency and Terrorism in the Ancient Mediterranean*. Leiden: Brill, 2015.

Humphreys, S. C. "Lycurgus of Butadae." In *The Craft of the Ancient Historian: Essays in Honor of C. G. Starr*, edited by J. W. Eadie and J. Ober, 199–252. Lanham, MD: University Press of America, 1985.

Hunt, Peter. *War, Peace, and Alliance in Demosthenes' Athens*. Cambridge: Cambridge University Press, 2010.

Hurwit, Jeffrey M. *The Athenian Acropolis: History, Mythology, and Archaeology from the Neolithic Period to the Present*. Cambridge: Cambridge University Press, 1997.

Hutchinson, Martha C. "The Concept of Revolutionary Terrorism." *Journal of Conflict Resolution* 16, no. 3 (1971): 393–95.

Jehne, Martin. *Koine Eirene: Untersuchungen zu den Befriedungs-und Stabilisierungsbemühungen in der griechischen Poliswelt des 4. Jahrhunderts v. Chr.* Stuttgart: Franz Steiner Verlag, 1994.

Kellogg, Danielle. "οὐκ ἐλάττω παραδώσω τὴν πατρίδα: The Ephebic Oath and the Oath of Plataea in Fourth Century Athens." *Mouseion*, Series III, 8 (2008): 355–76.

Lane Fox, Robin. *Alexander the Great*. London: Penguin, 1973.

Lawton, Carol L. "Athenian Anti-Macedonian Sentiment and Democratic Ideology in Attic Document Reliefs in the Second Half of the Fourth Century B.C." In *The Macedonians in Athens, 322–229 B.C.*, edited by O. Palagia and S. V. Tracy, 117–27. Oxford: Oxford University Press, 2003.

Markianos, Sophocles S. "A Note on the Administration of Lycurgus." *Greek, Roman, and Byzantine Studies* 10, no. 4 (1969): 325–31.

Marsden, Sarah V. and Alex P. Schmid. "Typologies of Terrorism and Political Violence." In *The Routledge Handbook on Terrorism Research*, edited by A. P. Schmid, 158–200. New York: Routledge, 2011.

Mattern, Susan. "Counterinsurgency and the Enemies of Rome." In *Makers of Ancient Strategy, from the Persian Wars to the Fall of Rome*, edited by V. D. Hanson, 163–84. Princeton: Princeton University Press, 2010.

Mayor, Adrienne. *The Poison King*. Princeton: Princeton University Press, 2010.

McAllister, B., and A. P. Schmid. "Theories of Terrorism." In *Routledge Handbook on Terrorism Research*, edited by Alex P. Schmid, 201–71. New York: Routledge, 2011.

Metz, Steven. "Rethinking Insurgency." Carlisle, PA: Strategic Studies Institute, U.S. Army War College, 2007. http://www.strategicstudies institute.army.mil/pubs/display.cfm?pubID=790.

———. "Psychology of Participation in Insurgency." *Small Wars Journal*. January 27, 2012. http://smallwarsjournal.com/print/12195.

Metz, Steven and Raymond Millen. *Insurgency and Counterinsurgency in the 21st Century: Reconceptualizing Threat and Response*. Carlisle, PA: Strategic Studies Institute, U.S. Army War College, 2004.

Meiggs, Russell. *Trees and Timber in the Ancient World*. Oxford: Clarendon Press, 1982.

Mitchel, Fordyce. "A Note on *IG* II² 370." *Phoenix* 18, no. 1 (1964): 13–17.

———. "Athens in the Age of Alexander." *Greece and Rome* 12, no. 2 (1965): 189–204.

———. "Lykourgan Athens 338–22." In *Lectures in Memory of Louise Taft Semple*. Second Series, 1966–1970, edited by C. G. Boulter, D. W. Bradeen, and A. Cameron, 163–214. Cincinnati: University of Cincinnati Press, 1973.

Murray, William M. *The Age of Titans: The Rise and Fall of the Great Hellenistic Navies*. Oxford: Oxford University Press, 2012.

Ñaco del Hoyo, T., B. Antela-Bernárdez, I. Arrayás-Morales, and S. Busquets-Artigas. "The 'Ultimate Frontier': War, Terror and the Greek *Poleis* Between Mithridates and Rome." In *Frontiers in the Roman World: Proceedings of the Ninth Workshop of the International Network Impact of Empire (Durham, 16–19 April 2009)*, edited by O. Hekster and T. Kaizer, 291–304. Leiden: Brill, 2011.

Oliver, Graham J. *War, Food, and Politics in Early Hellenistic Athens*. Oxford: Oxford University Press, 2007.

O'Neill, Bard E. *Insurgency and Terrorism: From Revolution to Apocalypse*. 2nd ed. Dulles, VA: Potomac, 2005.

Polk, William R. *Violent Politics: A History of Insurgency, Terrorism, and Guerrilla War, From the American Revolution to Iraq*. New York: Harper, 2007.

Porch, Douglas. "The Dangerous Myths and Dubious Promise of COIN." *Small Wars and Insurgencies* 22, no. 2 (2011): 239–57.

Prabhakara, M. S. "Assam: 'Talking about Talks.'" *Economic and Political Weekly* 41, no. 9 (2006): 777.

Price, H. E., Jr. "The Strategy and Tactics of Revolutionary Terrorism." *Comparative Studies in Society and History* 19, no. 1 (1977): 52–66. http://dx.doi.org/10.1017/S0010417500008495.

Ranstorp, M. "Terrorism in the Name of Religion." *Journal of International Affairs* 50, no. 1 (1996): 41–62.

Reinmuth, Oscar W. *The Ephebic Inscriptions of the Fourth Century B.C.* Mnemosyne, Supplements 14. Leiden: Brill, 1971.

Rhodes, P. J. and Robin Osborne, eds. *Greek Historical Inscriptions 404–323 BC*. Oxford: Oxford University Press, 2003.

Richardson, Seth F. C., ed. *Rebellions and Peripheries in the Cuneiform World*. American Oriental Series 91. Chicago: American Oriental Society, 2010.

———. "Insurgency and Terror in Mesopotamia." In *Brill's Companion to Insurgency and Terrorism in the Ancient Mediterranean*, edited by Timothy Howe and Lee L. Brice, 31–61. Leiden: Brill, 2015

Roth, J. J. "Epilogue: Looking Ahead." In *Brill's Companion to Insurgency and Terrorism in the Ancient Mediterranean*, edited by Timothy Howe and Lee L. Brice, 344–64. Leiden: Brill, 2015.

Ryder, T. T. B. *Koine Eirene: General Peace and Local Independence in Ancient Greece*. Oxford: Oxford University Press, 1965.

Schmid, Alex. P. Introduction to *Routledge Handbook on Terrorism Research*, edited by Alex P. Schmid, 1–38. New York: Routledge, 2011.

Schmid, Alex, ed. *Routledge Handbook on Terrorism Research*. New York: Routledge, 2011.

Schwenk, Cynthia J. *Athens in the Age of Alexander: The Dated Laws and Decrees of the "Lykourgan Era" 338–322 B.C.* Chicago: Ares, 1985.

Shulz, Richard H., Jr., and Andrea J. Drew. *Insurgents, Terrorists, and Militias: The Warriors of Contemporary Combat.* New York: Columbia University Press, 2006.

Siewert, P. "The Ephebic Oath in Fifth-Century Athens." *Journal of Hellenic Studies* 97 (1977): 102–11. http://dx.doi.org/10.2307/631025.

Stewart, Andrew. *Classical Greece and the Birth of Western Art.* Cambridge: Cambridge University Press, 2008.

Stohl, Michael, and George A. Lopez, eds. *The State as Terrorist: The Dynamics of Governmental Violence and Repression.* Westport, CT: Greenwood, 1984.

Thornton, T. P. "Terror as a Weapon of Political Agitation." In *Internal War*, edited by Harry Eckstein, 71–99. New York: Free Press, 1964.

Urso, Gianpaolo, ed. *Terror et Pavor: Violenza, intimidazione, clandestina nel mondo antico. Atti del convegno internazionale Cividale del Friuli, 22–24 settembre 2005.* Pisa: Edizioni ETS, 2006.

U.S. Department of the Army. *Field Manual 3-07 Stability Operations and Support Operations.* Washington, DC: Government Printing Office, 2008.

Vasilenko, V. I. "The Concept and Typology of Terrorism." *Statutes and Decisions: The Laws of the USSR and Its Successor States* 40, no. 5 (2004): 46–56. http://dx.doi.org/10.1080/10610014.2004.11059722.

Walsh, John. "The *Lamiaka* of Choerilus of Iasos and the Genesis of the Term 'Lamian War.'" *Classical Quarterly* 61, no. 2 (2011): 538–44.

Whitehead, D. "Competitive Outlay and Community Profit: Filotimia in Classical Athens." *Classica et Mediaevalia* 34, no. 5 (1983): 55–74.

Will, Wolfgang. *Athen und Alexander: Untersuchungen zur Geschichte der Stadt von 338 bis 322 v. Chr.* Munich: Beck, 1983.

Worthington, Ian. "Alexander and Athens in 324/3: On the Greek Attitude to the Macedonian Hegemony." *Mediterranean Archaeology* 7 (1994): 45–51.

———. "Alexander's Destruction of Thebes." In *Crossroads of History: The Age of Alexander*, edited by Waldemar Heckel and Lawrence A. Tritle, 65–86. Claremont, CA: Regina Books, 2003.

———. *Alexander the Great: Man and God.* London: Pearson, 2003.

———. "The Chronology of the Harpalus Affair." *Symbolae Osloensis* 61 (1986): 63–76.

————. *Demosthenes: Statesman and Orator*. New York: Routledge, 2000.

————. "The Harpalus Affair and the Greek Response to the Macedonian Hegemony." In *Ventures Into Greek History. Essays in Honour of N. G. L. Hammond*, edited by I. Worthington, 307–30. Oxford: Oxford University Press, 1994.

————. "Harpalus and the Macedonian Envoys." *Liverpool Classical Monthly* 9 (1984): 47–48.

————. *A Historical Commentary on Dinarchus. Rhetoric and Conspiracy in Later Fourth-Century Athens.* Ann Arbor: University of Michigan Press, 1992.

————. *Philip II of Macedonia*. New Haven: Yale University Press, 2008.

————. "The First Flight of Harpalus Reconsidered." *Greece and Rome* 31 (1984): 161–69.

6

State Counterterrorism in Ancient Rome: Toward a New Basis for the Diachronic Study of Terror

RICARDO APOSTOL

In book 3 of *Ab Urbe Condita*, his monumental history of the city from its foundation, the Roman historian Livy writes in great detail about a "terrorist" incident in fifth-century BCE Rome and the official state response to that threat. His method of narrating said incident is of the greatest interest, since it seems paradoxical to both tell of the recurring and immanent threat of such violent acts, and thus valorize the continuing need for preparedness and swift and ready response; and simultaneously to marginalize, and even minimize, the reality of the threat, instead treating it as an artificial construct of various state apparatuses. This intricate and seemingly contradictory web of competing discourses precisely enacts the tensions inherent in any attempt to follow a category such as "terrorism" diachronically, and it is no surprise that the text of such an eminent and thoughtful historian (and one more attuned to the narrative aspects of his history than many other, more "reliable" sources) should provide deep insights into the inherent challenges of historiography. Yet what might be more surprising to the contemporary reader is how little the essential problems of historical narrative have changed over the past two thousand years, and thus how much can be gleaned for the diachronic study of an analogous modern category such as terror from the work of this ancient master.

It would perhaps be simplest to begin by briefly recounting the event with which Livy's narrative is concerned, and then to turn to a consideration of how that content is packaged within the larger structure of book 3. The incident itself, namely the terrorist attack, comprises book 3.15.4–7 and 9, a matter of but a few lines. According to Livy, in 460 BCE, a Sabine by the name of Appius Herdonius unexpectedly seized the Capitoline hill and citadel in a night attack with a force of 4,500 political exiles and slaves (Capozza I.37ff; Cornell, "Rome and Latium," 286). They indiscriminately slaughtered all those present whom they could capture and who refused to join their cause. The following morning they made their plea and demands: Appius Herdonius claims to represent the disenfranchised of the state, and offers freedom to the slaves and the opportunity of return to political exiles. He emphasizes that he wishes for the Romans to accede to his demands willingly, but is willing to call in neighboring powers (the Aequi and Volsci, traditional enemies of Rome at this time) if they refuse. 3.15.9, which reports the terrorists' agenda, is almost twice as many lines as the description of the attack itself.

The bulk of Livy's account of the year 460 BCE, which runs from 3.15 to 3.21, is occupied with the attendant circumstances for, the reaction to, and the fallout from this incident (thus, incidentally, dwarfing it in length). It is worth noting here how much of sections 3.15–18 deal with the manifold fears of various factions within the Roman population, some of them even in direct reaction to Herdonius's attack (most of them not, though we shall take that matter up again later). In terms of properly categorizing the incident, the fear directly springing from the terrorists' violence and threat of further violence is of crucial importance. Of the survivors of the night attack, it is said that *praecipites pavore in forum devolant*, "in their panic they flew headlong into the forum" (3.15.6);[1] the consuls *timebant*, feared (3.15.7), to arm the populace in response to the crisis, due to the deep social divisions Livy everywhere represents in his book. The consuls are described as *incerti*, hesitant or irresolute, on two occasions (3.15.7, 8), the second time paired with *solliciti*, alarmed or agitated, thus revealing their anxious state of indecision, which makes them completely ineffective. They try calming the population, but their attempt does as much harm as good;[2] for the *pavida et consternata multitudo*, "the cowed and worried multitude," was impossible to control (3.15.8).

The next day, after the list of demands is released, the *patres*[3] and consuls find new aspects of the situation terrifying. They are afraid lest neighboring states take the opportunity to attack Rome. Furthermore, the call to slave insurrection is particularly terrifying; as Livy tells us, *multi et varii timores; inter ceteros eminebat terror servilis*, "There was a great variety of causes for fear; among them all, the terror of slaves loomed large" (3.16.3). Their own slaves form a potential fifth column in their midst, and could become the source of new "terrorist" attacks.

That this event meets the usual criteria for terrorist activity is scarcely debatable. Without adopting any single definition of the many that have been proposed for the term "terrorism,"[4] one can still make the claim that Appius Herdonius's night attack possesses all the major traits usually proposed as part of such definitions. It is the action of a nongovernment group;[5] it inflicts violence indiscriminately (on whomever happened to be on the Capitol at the time); this violence is intended to draw popular attention,[6] especially in view of Herdonius's proclamation; there is a call for political changes (return of exiles, freedom for slaves); and the object is to use fear to cause the Romans to relent (Herdonius prefers for the Romans to make the changes themselves, rather than to be invaded; the latter threat is meant to provoke the former course of action). Furthermore, the fear caused by the attack clearly reaches far beyond the victims of the attack, and into every corner of Roman society.

This may convince the reader that Appius Herdonius and company were terrorists by our definition; but how did the Romans think of them? Certainly there was no term or concept precisely the equivalent of "terrorism" or "terrorist" in ancient Rome. Yet simply because there is no single word or category that fulfills this function does not mean that the Romans did not have other ways of doing the same, or similar, work. For instance, it would have been clear to Livy's educated contemporary readers that Herdonius and his fellows were being labeled to their disadvantage through an allusion and word choices such as *coniurare/coniurati*, "to conspire/conspirators." The allusion is, of course, to the conspirator Lucius Sergius Catilina, more familiar to the English-speaking world as Catiline, who in 63 BCE attempted to oust the Roman senate.[7] He offered debt relief, caused a slave revolt in Capua, ranked many political outcasts among his followers, and approached foreign forces (the Allobroges) to secure aid against the Roman state, which he eventually fought openly. More specifically, the allusion is to Sallust's depiction of Catiline in his famous *Bellum Catilinae*, a fact that is blatantly obvious since Livy often borrows Sallust's language almost verbatim. One notable instance is Livy's description of Herdonius as claiming that *se miserrimi cuiusque suscepisse causam*, "he had taken up the cause of the wretched" (3.15.9), which reproduces Sallust's *publicam miserorum causam pro mea consuetudine suscepi*, "I [Catiline] publically took up the cause of the wretched according to my custom" (35.3), even to the point of attributing the claim directly to his villain. The same section of Livy also has Herdonius claiming that *se . . . omnia extrema temptaturum*, "he would essay the very utmost means" (3.15.9), which alludes to Sallust's description of Catiline as determined *extrema omnia experiri*, "to try the very utmost means" (26.5). A third example, the echo of Sallust 36.2 *ab armis discedere*, "to leave off arms", in Livy's *arma poni et discedere*, "to set aside arms and leave off" at 3.17.1, is particularly interesting because it uses the same language that Sallust employed to describe Catiline's (largely plebeian) coconspirators in a passage wherein the general population of Rome lays down its arms in order to vote on new laws during the crisis. To further drive the allusion home, later in the same sentence (3.17.1) Livy describes the consul Publius Valerius Publicola as *se ex curia proripit*, "he hurried himself from the senate house," where Sallust at 32.1 describes Catiline himself as *se ex curia domum proripit*, "he hurried himself home from the senate house" after he is denounced by Cicero.

By repeatedly alluding to Sallust's hostile description of Catiline and his coconspirators, both in specific language and by making Herdonius's demands and program basically the same as Catiline's (freedom for slaves, return of exiles, threat of armed intervention from abroad, etc.), Livy essentially states that they are members of the same category and class of criminal.[8] Categorization can, of course, be accomplished by establishing a profile that matches the category (e.g., describing actions and attitudes) as well as by the more concise use of accepted terminology (e.g., directly designating someone a conspirator or terrorist). Livy does both, combining his description of Herdonius as a Catilinarian "type" with use of the term *coniurare*, as

in Livy's phrase *coniurare et simul capere arma*, "to conspire/join the con-
spiracy/swear allegiance (to the conspiracy) and take up arms together," at
3.15.6. *Coniurati*, literally meaning "those having been sworn together," is
a common term of abuse for "conspirators" of any sort, and thus has a delegitimizing function in its own right. Of course, just as in the English phrase
"the Catilinarian conspiracy," forms of *coniurare/coniurati* are commonly
used in Latin to describe Catiline and his companions.[9] Other marginaliz-
ing characteristics of both Appius Herdonius and Catiline are their alliances
with exiles/outcasts; their association with slaves; their readiness to side
with outsiders; and, in Herdonius's case, his Sabine provenance. All of these
traits call into question the legitimacy of their "Roman-ness," a big issue in a
society that not only considered its people and culture *ipso facto* superior,[10] but
also determined appropriate treatment and legal rights based on citizenship.

We thus seem to have ample reason to proceed with our analysis of this
incident without fear of falling short of modern standards of the definition
of terrorism, nor yet of reading ancient history in an anachronistic manner.
Yet, having dealt thus summarily (as Livy does) with the mere event and its
content, we are now forced to confront the strangeness of the Roman state's
response to and contextualization of the attack as we move into an examination of the titular ancient Roman state's counterterrorism. For, as was discussed earlier, not only were the conspirators successful in raising a variety
of fears among the Roman elites, but it seemed that the senate was actually
paralyzed by indecision regarding who or what the biggest threat might be,
and how to deal with it. It is instead the plebs and their representatives, the
tribunes of the people, who for better or worse take a stance and act decisively. Livy writes that amidst the chaos *tantus enim tribunos furor tenuit ut
non bellum, sed vanam imaginem belli ad avertendos ab legis cura plebis
animos Capitolium insedisse contenderent*, "such madness seized the tribunes that they claimed that it was not war, but the mere mirage of war that
had seized the Capitol, in order to divert the people's attention from considering the Law" (3.16.5). They thus call on the people to lay down their arms
and go vote on the aforesaid measure; the consuls call the senate together,
since *alio se maiore ab tribunis metu ostendente quam quem nocturnus hostis
intulerat*, "a greater fear was now apparent, due to the tribunes' actions, than
that which the night attack had called forth in them" (3.16.6).

The law in question is the Lex Terentilia, which was introduced by Gaius Terentilius Harsa in 462 BCE as described in Livy 3.9. This law sought to rein in the power of the ruling oligarchy by establishing a code of written and publicly accessible laws that would apply to everybody equally. The bulk of Livy's third book is occupied with the attempted introduction of the law and its fallout: the *patres* spend most of book 3.9–32 fighting the law by any means at their disposal, while the tribunes try desperately to have it ratified. Eventually, after an embassy is sent to Athens to study their laws in 454, a board of ten men (the *decemviri legibus scribundis*) is appointed in 451 BCE. Livy devotes book 3.33–54 to this board, and the remainder of the book (3.55–72) to the aftermath. I bring up the book and section numbers merely to show that, in the years with which we are concerned, the struggle over the Lex Terentilia was the true crisis of Rome (at least according to Livy's narrative); and that Appius Herdonius and his attack are a mere blip on the radar compared to that issue, both in terms of the narrative and of the aforementioned dismissal of his threat by the Senators upon hearing of the plebs' actions.

It is now possible to approach the first instance of the formal construction of the terrorist event occurring within the narrative. P. Valerius Publicola makes a speech to the tribunes and citizenry in which he implies that the tribunes are in league with Appius Herdonius, and ironically (and unfavorably) compares them to slaves, for although Herdonius's appeal failed to cause a slave uprising, it has been effective in winning over the tribunes (3.17.2). He then turns to the people and accuses them of impiety for failing to free the temples on the Capitol from enemies (3.17.3–6). Finally, and most strikingly, he makes a fearsome threat: he would issue the call to arms, and if any should obstruct it, *iam se consularis imperii, iam tribuniciae potestatis sacratarumque legume oblitum, quisquis ille sit, ubicumque sit, in Capitolio, in foro, pro hoste habiturum*, "he would ignore the limits of his consular authority, the power of the tribunes, and the sacred laws, and treat them, whosoever and wheresoever they might be, whether in the Capitol or forum, as enemies" (3.17.7)—an extreme position for a man who has just used traditional religion as the basis for his appeal to the populace. Throwing another rhetorical twist into the mix, the consul adds that *ausurum se in tribunis, quod princeps familiae suae ausus in regibus esset*, "he would dare to do to the tribunes what the founder of his family had done to the kings" (3.17.8); this is a reference to his ancestor of the same name, who led the antimonarchical revolution of 509 BCE along with Lucius Junius Brutus and helped drive the Tarquin kings from Rome. The direct threats drive off the tribunes as night begins to fall: they are *timentes consulum arma*, "in fear of the consuls' arms" (3.17.9), while the people, bereft of their leaders, are then plied by the *patres* with arguments as to how they are putting the city in danger (3.17.10).

The method of state counterterrorism in Rome, then, is to return terror for terror, and to ensure unity through fear. All, even the most sacred and time-honored protections due to Roman citizens, are potentially suspended before the supposed threat from the capitol. The person of the tribunes, for example, was supposed to be completely inviolable under any circumstances; the consular *imperium* did not extend to the slaughter or execution of Roman citizens. Yet the threat level is elevated to such a pitch that the argument could be made that any lack of cooperation constituted an immediate and over-whelming danger to the state, and thus was tantamount to terrorist activity in its own right. Valerius Publicola is quite direct in his conflation of the tribunes with Herdonius's conspiracy. At the same time, he further delegitimizes the tribunes through comparisons to rebellious slaves (who have no protections under Roman law and are usually tortured, punished, and executed in various horrible ways, of which crucifixion is the most infamous); and to the tyran-nical kings of early Roman legend, who could also be treated harshly with impunity, as being, by nature, enemies of the Republic.

Furthermore, it might easily be argued, this is an artificial elevation of the threat Herdonius poses, since it has been shown that nobody is really very concerned about it at all: while the senate dawdles, holds a meeting, and then scarcely arms the plebs lest they rise up against them, the plebs decide to vote on laws. There is something strange in the logic of the *patres'* posi-tion, whereby they experience, in Livy's words, a "greater fear" of the plebs' decision to vote on the laws (supposedly an ancillary development in the grand scheme of the terrorist crisis) than of Herdonius's attack itself; and yet go on to justify their disruption of that vote precisely on the grounds that all orders of Roman society must unite against a greater threat. Either the vote is the greater threat, or Herdonius is; and it is crystal clear that, in spite of the rhet-oric, the *patres* know very well which one is which. Thus the event, whatever its "true" nature might be, is constructed by the *patres* in such a way that it becomes a powerful weapon in their arsenal against constitutional reform.

This construction of Herdonius's attack as a major threat with which people can be dangerously complicit in a variety of direct and indirect ways endows it with a flexible and devastating delegitimizing function, much like the label "terrorism." Yet what is fascinating about this function in the Roman context is that it is not primarily utilized against Herdonius and his crew, who are already entirely illegitimate in the eyes of all concerned, *patres* and plebs, well before Valerius deploys his consular propaganda machine (Valerius's public speech, the groups of sympathetic *patres* who make the rounds among the common folk once the tribunes have been frightened off, etc.). The actual offenders, as active enemies within the city, are simply considered fair game. An obvious truth that these facts expose is that delegitimizing functions are by definition only effective when they are deployed against "legitimate" targets; they exist for no other reason. The conventional wisdom that misrecognizes labels such as, and analogous to, "terrorism" as generally intended to delegitimize their objects is quite simply wrong. Rather, the dynamics of the situation flow precisely in the opposite direction: the already tarnished group, properly labeled, becomes a source of illegitimacy which can be channeled against legitimate targets "back home" through aggressive media branding and campaigns of redefinition.

This process can be unpacked as follows: first, the application of the label. In order for society to readily and unthinkingly accept the label "terrorist," it has to be applied to an already tarnished and unsympathetic target. There was no need to tarnish the 9/11 attackers in the United States, for instance, any more than there was need to do so in the case of Herdonius in 460 BCE. Instead, the particular application of the label "terrorist," along with the counterterrorist methods proposed to accompany it, gain in traction by being associated with a heinous target. Since the label only "sticks" because it reflects existing popular prejudice, it is clear that its delegitimizing power must spring from the terrorist group, rather than from the label "terrorist." Likewise, as has been previously argued, the only potential target for delegitimization is one that is considered legitimate. Now that we know the starting point and end point of the delegitimizing process, it also becomes clear that the function of the label is to channel this flow of taint by association according to the needs of the labeling agency. This process is a truly powerful tool in the hands of whichever state force is able to control the discourse, hence the efforts of consul and *patres* to get their version of events out as quickly and as broadly as possible.

In this case, the targets are those two inviolable boundaries: the body of the male Roman citizen in general;[11] and in particular the traditionally sacrosanct bodies of the threatening tribunes. Under the new senatorial construction of the situation in Rome, these bodies are now available for slaughter. This counterterrorist counterthreat is so serious that it drives the tribunes from the political field. Meanwhile, there is an attempt, as was previously mentioned, to frighten the population into setting aside their vote to deal with the present threat. Thus, fear and violence are no less tools of the counterterrorist state than of the terrorists themselves, at least in Livy's portrait of ancient Rome. Yet, in order to understand the full extent and effectiveness of the Roman state's ideological manipulations, it is illuminating to consider how the Herdonius episode ends. The actual battle is dealt with summarily: Tusculum, a Roman ally, sends troops, which join the Romans, who have been convinced to take arms by P. Valerius's promise to allow a vote. This promise, it should be noted, is mentioned almost as an afterthought in section 3.18, between the arrival of the men of Tusculum and the battle itself, rather than being included in the consul's speech in 3.17. The wording of the promise is strange, too; Livy describes it thus: *auctoritas viri moverat, adfirmantis Capitolio reciperato et urbe pacata si se edoceri sissent quae fraus ab tribunis occulta in lege ferretur . . . concilium plebis non impediturum,* "the man's authority had persuaded them when he affirmed that, after the Capitol had been retaken and the city pacified, and so long as they would first allow him to reveal the trickery that the tribunes had concealed within the law . . . he would not impede the assembly of the plebs" (3.18.6). The parallel but slightly different account of the historian Dionysios of Halicarnassus makes no bones about it: the plebs had to be promised the chance to vote on the law before they would agree to fight (Dion. Hal. 10.15.3–7). Livy's text thus constitutes a strange evasion of the facts. Events culminate with a series of short, sharp clauses: *multi exsulum caede sua foedavere templum, multi vivi capti, Herdonius interfectus. Ita Capitolium reciperatum,* "many exiles polluted the temple with their blood; many were taken alive; Herdonius was killed.

Thus was the Capitol retaken" (3.18.10). It is perhaps no coincidence that the longest scene in the account of the fighting is that in which P. Valerius is killed, 3.18.8–9. Livy writes that the consul is killed in the first assault on the temple's vestibule; that his fellow consul, P. Volumnius, sees him fall, tells his men to cover up the body, and then takes his place in battle; and that the soldiers are so fixated on the fighting that they fail to notice they have lost their commander until after their victory. Valerius's death is particularly significant because it results in further power struggles that remain indissolubly tied to the chain of events surrounding Herdonius's short-lived insurrection; yet Livy's account of the consul's death is only comparatively long, and it remains a noteworthy fact that the entire battle narrative is primarily distinguished by its brevity. In fact, it might be argued that Livy's narrative again places the emphasis on the political consequences of the terrorist episode by dealing with the actual "event" in such a cursory, almost dismissive manner. The text performs the fading of the historical event in the face of its ideological reconstruction: just as Livy's account of Herdonius on the Capitol is dwarfed by his account of the political context in the narrative, so is the actual event co-opted and obscured by the *patres*' propaganda; and in the aftermath of the attack, it is the state's agenda that looms largest. To what, then, does this agenda, this construction, amount?

Rather than accede to the demands of the plebs that P. Valerius's promise be honored, the *patres* replace him with the man least likely to do so, L. Quinctius Cincinnatus, whose son had been forced into exile by the tribunes and plebs, and who had lost his wealth as a result of the forfeit of a kind of bail on his behalf.[12] Furthermore, it was because his son had been so violent in his opposition to the new law that he had been charged with a capital crime (Lintott, 56–60). Cincinnatus begins his term in office (3.19) by haranguing the tribunes, again conflating them with the conspirators: *"Aulus" inquit "ille Verginius, quia in Capitolio non fuit, minus supplicii quam Appius Herdonius meruit? Plus hercule aliquanto,"* "Did Aulus Verginius there [one of the tribunes] deserve a lesser punishment than Appius Herdonius just because he wasn't in the Capitol? No, by Hercules, he even deserved more" (3.19.6); Cincinnatus goes on to promise that it will be a terrible thing for the state if the law is passed (3.19.11); and ends by declaring his intention to march against the neighboring Volsci and Aequi: *"quantum periculum ab illis populis fuerit si Capitolium ab exsulibus obsessum scissent*," "How great a danger those peoples would have presented if they had known the Capitol to be occupied by exiles" (3.19.12). War, of course, would preclude a vote, and in his speech Cincinnatus makes it clear that this is the real reason for the attack, all the while couching it in justifications on grounds of state security and fear of recurrent attack. But that is not all; a legalistic wrangle ensues when the tribunes say they will refuse to allow a levy. Cincinnatus responds that the plebs took an oath to muster until released from duty during Herdonius's insurrection, and that, since they have not yet been released from that muster, he does not need to make a new levy (3.20.3–4). He adds that he would have them assemble near Lake Regillus, where he would have the augurs ritually prepare a spot for assembly business. Due to Roman traditions of *imperium*,[13] since the location was more than a mile outside the city, the consul could do whatever he wanted without possibility of legal appeal, even on the part of the tribunes, and so the "assembly" would have to vote whichever way he wished. Again, as a direct result of the terrorist act of Appius Herdonius, the state is able to suspend citizen rights on the grounds of military expediency and national security, and its tool, Livy tells us, is terror.[14] If, then, the vanishing terrorist "event" is more conspicuous for smoke than fire, and if the state employs that smoke as screen, then what it does behind that screen under the guise of counterterrorist policy is not just fighting fire with fire (that is again a pretext, and a rhetorical turn); rather, it unilaterally brings the heat.

Terrebant haec; sed ille maximus terror animos agitabat, quod saepius Quinctius dictitabat se consulum comitia non habiturum . . . dictatore opus esse rei publicae, "These things were terrifying; but the greatest terror before their [the tribunes and plebs[15]] minds was that Cincinnatus continually stated that he would have no fellow consul . . . the republic had need of a dictator" (3.20.8). In order to avoid this, the tribunes and plebs have to surrender to the authority of the senate, which decrees that in exchange for not continuing the levy, the people and their representatives must not bring the law up for vote that year, and the tribunes must not stand for re-election (3.21.1–2). Except for his account of the elections, this is the end of Livy's narrative on the year 460 BCE, and it ends on a grim note indeed. The consul and *patres* have successfully used terror (Livy's precise word) in the form of threats to cause plebs and tribunes bodily harm outside of the city boundaries, as well as to take over the government through an officially sanctioned dictator-ship, to coerce elements problematic to the "state." The language of national security blends with that of medicine in justifying such extreme tactics: *non ita civitatem aegram esse ut consuetis remediis sisti possit*, "the state was so sick that the usual remedies could not help it" (3.20.8). Yet the formulation only highlights the abstract nature of "the state," and the way in which one interest group (the ruling class) has taken over the discourse, and thus pre-tends to have the authority to evaluate and speak for the state (any deviation from this norm is figured by "sickness," which must presumably be purged). Meanwhile, those elements that have been stripped of their normal protec-tions and citizen rights, having no court of appeal beyond that which itself legislated away their security, are left with no choice but to surrender to the state or be treated as common enemies. Livy *Ab Urbe Condita* book 3 thus shows how a particular category of outlaw (one analogous to our category "terrorist") functions within the state. Furthermore, by problematizing the use of a terrorist event in this way, Livy's text highlights the degree to which signifiers such as "terrorist," "outlaw," or "conspirator" are arbitrary con-structions subject to (ab)use by any who are strong enough to take control of the discourse, and that neither can such constructed categories be used in a nonartificial, that is, apolitical or disengaged manner, since they are in no way "natural," but a result of human activity within the context of a state.

Yet the foregoing analysis would not be complete without pushing the text's insights to their logical limits—if the category of "terrorism," or anal-ogous categories such as those deployed by the Roman state in Livy's nar-rative, are truly constructs dominated by discourse, then they are, to put it crudely, empty of content (since they are receptacles to be filled with dissidents and other inconvenient parties); not solidly and naturally defined or defin-able (strict definition would make them less flexible tools), but a blank space whose outlines are given form by the surrounding social structure. Form, not content, is their predominant characteristic. As such, it is not surprising that the meanings of terms such as "terrorism" have changed so much over time, been put to so many uses, and indeed even now resist any and all attempts to define them. This is their secret and their strength, and they mislead those who would essentialize them, including scholars. For, if terrorism et alia qua things are red herrings in politics, they are also red herrings in history.

Historians who go looking for them guided only by the current definition (as set into play by contemporary political events) will, in "finding" what they seek, merely retroject the current category, just as Livy projects Catiline back into the fifth century in constructing Herdonius as a member of the category "conspirator." It is not for nothing that the term "repetition" comes from the Latin *repeto*, to seek again. Such (re)constructions of history are unable to add to our existing knowledge, since they merely reproduce it, and they only seem to be genuine engagements with comparative and transhistorical material, when in fact they twist that material to serve current, mainstream categories. What these circular arguments lose in epistemological validity they more than make up for in their ability to legitimize the political status quo by giving the illusion that its artificial categories accurately represent real, recurring threats; this in turn helps to foster fear, the essential driver of state counterterrorist activity. Incidentally, this process also flattens and falsifies historical and cultural difference, much as in Livy's account archaic Rome becomes late Republican Rome, to our eternal detriment.[16] It is a classic case of the structures of knowledge being perverted to serve state power.

The alternative is to avoid mistaking hollow labels such as "terrorism," *coniuratio*, and all their ilk for substantive reflections of reality, and falling into the intellectually sterile trap of anachronistically detecting them everywhere. If the reality of these categories is that they are largely formal constructs, then the only viable approach left us is to study their socially determined shape and function, and not their content. From such a functionalist perspective, our object of study becomes the set of categories whereby groups are marginalized by making them the objects of fear, and by which extralegal actions against them and others are justified on the grounds of imminent threat and unofficial status. This is to say, it is precisely this *form* of manipulation of discourse which defines such categories; the labels, the content hardly matters. The added advantage of a formal/functionalist approach is that it preserves genuine possibilities for cross-cultural and diachronic comparative material, without limiting access to exempla that match the content checklist of a narrow cultural and historical category (such as "terrorism"). This comparative material is absolutely crucial because it offers almost the only opportunity for a "reality check," without which structures of knowledge can unwittingly become circular and self-reinforcing. Livy is a prime example of the aid such other voices can provide in helping us think creatively and productively about contemporary concerns. By exposing the workings of state counterterror both within the narrative (by showing the dynamics of fear and manipulation at play in the Roman state response, and blatantly minimizing the importance of the actual attack) and across narratives (by alluding to themes of historical recurrence and typology across time periods and historical texts such as Sallust's), Livy's text points modern historians toward the problems inherent in attempting to trace the workings of categories such as terror. Perhaps it also offers one avenue to a solution.

NOTES

1.   All translations are my own.

2.   Livy's concise description runs *sedabant tumultus, sedando interdum movebant*, "they attempted to pacify the uproar, but their attempts at times only roused it further" (3.15.7).

3.   There is debate about how to translate and understand the title *patres* in its early Republican context; it is often taken as meaning "senators"; but it can also mean simply the men of the leading families, whether they had any such official title or not at the time, for it is unclear how old the formal institution of the Senate might be; cf. T. J. Cornell, *The Beginnings of Rome: Italy and Rome from the Bronze Age to the Punic Wars* (c. 1000–264 BC) (London: Routledge, 1995), 245–51; B. G. Niebuhr, *The History of Rome* (London, 1837), 1.338ff; A. Momigliano, *Terzo contributo alla storia degli studi classici* (e del mondo antico) (Rome: Edizioni di Storie e Letteratura, 1966), 591n93; Jean-Claude Richard, *Les origines de la plèbe romaine* (Paris: École française, 1978), 233–34; Robert E. A. Palmer, *The Archaic Community of the Romans* (New York: Cambridge University Press, 1970), 197–99. In the text I have simply chosen to leave the title in its original Latin.

4.   Bruce Hoffman, *Inside Terrorism* (New York: Columbia University Press, 2006), 1–42, provides an excellent discussion on the history and difficulties involved in defining the term "terrorism." He ends by eschewing definition in favor of a substrate of common characteristics, an approach that seems eminently sensible in view of the inability of bodies such as the United Nations to agree on a working definition, even after convening a panel of experts. According to Robert Adolph's

keynote address at the "Re-Visioning Terrorism" conference, the panel came up with no less than 109 different possible definitions; Mr. Adolph is chief of the Middle East and North Africa Desk for the United Nations' Department of Safety and Security.

5.   Bottiglieri, "Il caso di Appio Erdonio," *Atti dell'Accademia di Scienze Morali e Politiche* 88 (1977): 7–20, sees this account of evidence for ethnic conflict based on his reading of Dionysios' version of the story; but even there it is clear that Herdonius is acting in no official capacity. Peruzzi, "Le coup de main d'Appius Herdonius," *La parola del passato* 62 (1987): 440–49, has a slightly different take on the Sabine character of Herdonius' attack.

6.   And, since the attackers know that they cannot possibly take over Rome on their own, their seizure of the Capitol is much more the assumption of a public platform than of an attack position.

7.   R. M. Ogilvie, ed., *A Commentary on Livy* (New York: Oxford University Press, 1965), 423–24, and *ad* 3.15.5, 7; 3.16.2-4; and 3.17.1. In his note to 3.16.1, Ogilvie also sees a possible allusion to Cicero's speech *in Catilinam*, and so the references may extend beyond Sallust, though he is certainly the primary model. On the other hand Noè, unlike Ogilvie, sees Catilinarian elements in Dionysios' account as well, which if true might point to a common source for this aspect of Livy's reading.

8.   Incidentally, he also raises the important theme of the literariness of history and the recurrence of types and events, as well as the question of the nature of the relationship between the two. The ramifications of this dimension will be discussed in the paper's conclusion.

9.   E.g., Cic. *Cat.* 4.10.20; Sall. *C.* 52.17 and 52.24; and Suet. *Caes.* 17.

10.   In his preface alone, for instance, Livy writes that other peoples must accept Rome's version of events with the same equanimity that they accept their rule, even when they claim such seeming absurdities as their descent from Mars (*A Commentary on Livy*, 7); and that he is much mistaken unless *nulla umquam res publica nec maior nec sanctior nec bonis exemplis ditior fuit*, "there has never been a state greater nor more religiously observant nor richer in good examples" than Rome (11).

11.   Walters, "Invading the Roman Body: Manliness and Impenetrability in Roman Thought," in *Roman Sexualities*, edited by J. P. Hallett and M. B. Skinner (Princeton: Princeton University Press, 1997), 38–39. Succinctly and with further bibliography: "The status of being a respectable, freeborn Roman citizen was thus marked, at least in theory, on the corporeal level by bodily inviolability. Roman citizens, however low their social status, were not to be beaten, raped, or otherwise assaulted."

12.   The story is recounted in 3.11–14. Ogilvie, *A Commentary on Livy*, 416–18 believes that it is almost certainly a fabrication meant to explain the tradition that Cincinnatus was called to the dictatorship as he was plowing, an improbable state of economic affairs for such a prominent figure; cf. Cornell, *Beginnings*, 249n27.

13.   The situation is complex, but I can offer a brief overview. Certain magistrates, among them the consuls, but not the tribunes of the people, were endowed with imperium, a broad, vaguely defined executive and judicial power. Over time this power was increasingly defined by the creation of new laws, and especially a set of laws allowing for appeal, which fall under the rubric of *provocatio*, from the "calling forth" of the citizen assembly. In particular, the *leges Porciae* of the second century BCE included a provision that "extended *provocatio* to citizens in the military sphere (i.e., outside the city of Rome)" (*OCD s.v. "provocatio"*). This formulation reveals a basic dichotomy in Roman thinking about imperium, namely, that it mattered whether one was within the sacred precinct of the city (called the pomerium), in which case civilian law applied; or outside of it, in which case the default assumption was that one was on campaign, so martial law applied. Although *provocatio* was anachronistic for the fifth century, Livy assumes it is in force, but in a form predating the *leges Porciae*; and so in his reconstruction, a meeting outside the city would have meant that the consul's judgments and actions would have carried absolute authority, and been completely beyond appeal.

14.   As seen in the foregoing discussion of 3.17.7–9, for instance, and in the language of 3.20.8 and following, with which I deal in depth immediately below. It might not be inapposite to add the testimony that surfaces in the trial of Cincinnatus's son Caeso Quinctius at 3.11.6–13.10 which, while not directly relating to Herdonius's attack, demonstrates the continuing pattern of state violence and intimidation used to suppress the Lex Terentilia.

15.   The antecedent is somewhat obscure; the majority of the previous sentence deals with the thought process of the tribunes; yet the following sentence tells that *tribune cum perturbata plebe veniunt*, "the tribunes, along with the worried plebs, came [to the Senate]" (3.21.1) in order to request a reprieve from this threatening extramural levy, as well as enforcement of the law preventing the same men (i.e., Cincinnatus) from holding the same magistracy more than once every ten years. Thus it seems fairly clear that both the people and the tribunes are opposed to Cincinnatus's plan.

16.   The most glaring example, of course, is the retrojection of the late Republican villain Catiline, his political means, and his agenda into archaic Rome; yet without getting into excessive detail, much of Livy's description of the political institutions

of the archaic Roman period is anachronistic, as when he pretends the powers of the tribunes were constitutionally well defined, as they were later (Ogilvie *ad* 3.20.8); that certain offences such as criminal *vadimonium* already existed in the fifth century (Ogilvie, *A Commentary on Livy*, 417); the law on *provocatio* (252); and many others. In particular, his characters' (invented) speeches often refer to ideas and concerns current in late Republican and early Imperial Rome.

WORKS CITED

Bottiglieri, Anna. "Il caso di Appio Erdonio." *Atti dell'Accademia di Scienze Morali e Politiche* 88 (1977): 7–20.

Capozza, Maria. *Movimenti servili nel mondo romano in età repubblicana.* Rome: L'Erma di Bretschneider, 1966.

Cornell, Tim J. *The Beginnings of Rome: Italy and Rome from the Bronze Age to the Punic Wars (c. 1000–264 BC).* London: Routledge, 1995.

———. "Rome and Latium to 390 BCE." *Cambridge Ancient History, Volume II.* Cambridge: Cambridge University Press, 1989.

Hallett, Judith P., and Marilyn B. Skinner, eds. *Roman Sexualities.* Princeton: Princeton University Press, 1997.

Hoffman, Bruce. *Inside Terrorism.* New York: Columbia University Press, 2006.

Hornblower, Simon, and Antony Spawforth, eds. *The Oxford Classical Dictionary.* 3rd ed. Oxford: Oxford University Press, 2005.

Lintott, Andrew W. *Violence in Republican Rome.* Oxford: Oxford University Press, 1968.

Momigliano, Arnaldo. *Terzo contributo alla storia degli studi classici (e del mondo antico).* Rome: Edizioni di Storie e Letteratura, 1966.

Niebuhr, Barthold G. *The History of Rome.* 3 vols. 3rd ed. Translated by J. C. Hare and C. Thirlwall. London, 1837.

Noè, Eralda. "Il tentativo di Appio Erdonio nella narrazione di Dionigi." *Rendiconti della Reale Accademia dei Lincei* 32 (1977): 641–65.

Ogilvie, Robert M., ed. *A Commentary on Livy.* Books 1–5. New York: Oxford University Press, 1965.

Palmer, Robert E. A. *The Archaic Community of the Romans.* New York: Cambridge University Press, 1970.

Peruzzi, Emilio. "Le coup de main d'Appius Herdonius." *La parola del passato* 62 (1987): 440–49.

Richard, Jean-Claude. *Les origines de la plèbe romaine*. Paris: École française, 1978.

Walters, Jonathan. "Invading the Roman Body: Manliness and Impenetrability in Roman Thought." In *Roman Sexualities*, edited by J. P. Hallett and M. B. Skinner, 29–43. Princeton: Princeton University Press, 1997.

7

Terror in the Old French Crusade Cycle: From Splendid Cavalry to Cannibalism

SARAH-GRACE HELLER

It is worth examining memories of the Crusades in discussions of terrorism in history as well as the current political situation, particularly since the term "crusaders" has been used synonymously with "Americans," for instance, in the main piece of propaganda that linked Osama Bin Laden to the 9/11 attacks. The fatwa, whose title is translated as the "World Islamic Front Statement Urging Jihad Against Jews and Crusaders," issued in February 1998, proclaimed:

> The Arabian Peninsula has never—since Allah made it flat, created its desert, and encircled it with seas—been stormed by any forces like the crusader armies spreading in it like locusts, eating its riches and wiping out its plantations. All this is happening at a time in which nations are attacking Muslims like people fighting over a plate of food.[1]

Bin Laden, along with four other leaders of Jihad movements in Egypt, Pakistan, and Bangladesh, issued this "ruling to kill the Americans and their allies" as a reaction to the American presence in Muslim holy places and the destruction and massacres brought on Iraq by the "crusader-Zionist alliance," viewing these actions as a "war on Allah." This text presents "crusaders" as ravenous, indiscriminate, and land hungry.

Al Qaeda's damning use of the term "crusader" belies the word's ubiquity and indeed benignity in common American parlance. Dozens of university and high school sports teams are nicknamed "Crusaders,"[2] waging their annual athletic battles against Tigers, Trojans, and the like. The evangelical preacher Billy Graham brought a triumphal and celebratory tone to the word beginning in 1947, with over 400 touring revivals he termed "Crusades," huge spectacles that invited people to "turn to Christ" from lives of sin or godlessness. Similarly, the "Campus Crusade for Christ," one of the largest evangelical organizations in the United States and 190 other countries, founded in 1951, uses the logo, "a caring community passionate about connecting people to Jesus Christ."[3] The word is also frequently used simply to express any type of compassionate fight against injustice or perceived social wrong, a "remedial enterprise undertaken with zeal and enthusiasm."[4] President George W. Bush's call for a "crusade" on September 16, 2001 proved more controversial worldwide than many Americans accustomed to the word's banality might have expected (Ford).

More in line with the Al Qaeda use of the term, Old French retellings of the first Crusade vaunt the use of terror-inspiring techniques by Westerners, including the catapulting of recognizable corpses and heads into besieged cities by noble crusade leaders, cannibalism of Muslim cadavers, and rape of women by a group called the Tafurs ("a horde of dispossessed and unmounted combatants loosely associated with the organized effort of the crusade" in Nelson, 851). It would be useful for Westerners to be better acquainted with what it popularly meant to be a "crusader." The Middle Ages, and indeed most any period or event prior to the past two centuries (or even the past five decades), are lacunae in the history of terrorism,[5] and deserve inclusion to broaden the understanding of fear tactics that have proven effective in different cultures. Terrorism works when it is unexpected; expanding the range of our expectations diminishes its potential impact.

THE OLD FRENCH CRUSADE CYCLE

One place to study representations of the crusades popular from the late twelfth into the sixteenth century is in the works of the Old French Crusade Cycle, which recount the First Crusade (1095–1099). The cycle has been one of the more obscure works in modern scholarship of medieval French literature, yet was quite popular in its day. Indeed, its obscurity in recent centuries may be due in part to shame at the use of what could be termed "terrorist" techniques by certain members of the Frankish host, which were not consonant with the rules of organized warfare developed by treaties and conventions over the centuries. The *Song of Antioch* and *Song of Jerusalem* represent terror-inducing acts ambivalently, with both jocular humor and discomfort at the acts involved; the narrator does not offer the reader moral guidance for interpreting them. This study examines representations of fear inspired by battle tactics: when do the Franks (as the crusaders are called in the text) imagine they have terrified the Saracens (as Muslims were frequently called in Old French literature)? I will begin with some background to situate these relatively little-known texts, and then proceed to consider some passages featuring fear-inspiring deeds through the lens of "terrorism."

The central nucleus of the Old French Crusade Cycle was composed between the third quarter of the twelfth century and the beginning of the thirteenth. It was in circulation in the period of the Third (1188–1190) and Fourth (1204) Crusades and in the wake of the fall of Jerusalem to Saladin (1187) (Nelson, 27–29; Cook, 205–06). My examples are primarily from the oldest episode (or "branch") of the cycle, the *Chanson d'Antioche* (*Song of Antioch*).[6] The Antioch narrative has attracted interest for its significant degree of corroboration of historical accounts (Duparc-Quioc, *Le cycle*; Hatem; Heller; Paris "Nouvelles études," 1877, 1878), its claim to originally having an eyewitness author (Beer; Cahen; Duparc-Quioc, *Le cycle*), and more recently for its depiction of cannibalism (Buchanan; Janet; Rubenstein). I will also draw on its continuation, the *Chanson de Jérusalem* (Thorp).

The Crusade Cycle's influence may be observed from the surviving texts; all or parts of fifteen different branches (separate but related stories) are extant in a total of sixteen known manuscripts and fragments, copied from the thirteenth to the fifteenth centuries. The *Chanson d'Antioche* exists in complete form in nine extant manuscripts as well as in two fragments and a prose version; the *Jérusalem* is found with it in eight cyclical manuscripts, three fragments, and the prose. Further circulation is suggested by library inventories such as those of King Charles V of France and Duke Philip the Good of Burgundy, which list volumes whose incipits indicate they contained all or parts of the cycle, now lost (Myers, xiii–lxxxviii; Thorp, 10–13). These numbers are significantly larger than many single-manuscript medieval works that have received far more scholarly attention, such as a good number of the chansons de geste. A 700-line fragment of a Provençal version of the *Song of Antioch* exists (Meyer; Paris, " La Chanson d'Antioche," 1888, 1890, 1893; Sweetenham and Paterson). A Spanish translation, the *Gran Conquista de Ultramar*, was made sometime between 1293 and 1312, and an edition was printed in the sixteenth century (Cooper). In short, interest in the crusade cycle saw frequent renewal across Europe over at least four centuries, long beyond the actual period of crusading. It survived in noble and royal libraries as well as in popular memory, and was more influential than might be supposed given its current status (it has only recently been fully edited, and many branches remain untranslated).[7]

MEDIEVAL "TERRORISM"?

How anachronistic is it to speak of terrorism and the First Crusade? The Oxford English Dictionary traces the term "terrorism" back to 1795 when it appeared in the *Annual Register* to describe the uses of terror by the French Revolutionary governments of 1789 to 1794.[8] Such words are often born old. "Crusade," for example, appears several generations after the crusades began ("croisement" around 1195, "crozata" at the beginning of the thirteenth century in Occitan with regard to the Albigensian crusade, in the fifteenth century for the French "croisade").[9] At the time, the people sewing crosses to their garments called themselves "pilgrims," the knights *milites christi.*" Their general aim was to defend access to the holy sites in Jerusalem and Palestine, although different groups—the pope, clerical intellectuals, land-owning barons, and the heterogeneous groups of men, women, and children who set off on crusades—certainly each held their own aims and ideals of the project (Riley-Smith).

Studying historical models such as crusade narratives to understand terrorism is supported by the work of the US National War College advisor Audrey Cronin, who notes that "groups that use terrorism are as different as the charismatic leaders that typically lead them." Examining how diverse leaders have used fear and the reactions they elicited can shed light on so-called "unlawful" tactics that succeed precisely because they are experienced as baffling. She notes that terrorism is a strategy focusing on perception, shifting with the perceptions of its audience (12). The Crusade Cycle rewrites events to emphasize the fear that certain strategies inspired in the Muslims who witnessed them, provoking them to surrender, flee, or convert. The texts stage Syrian fear for the pleasure of European audiences, promoting terrifying strategies as effective.

Sociolinguist Steven Pinker defines large-scale terrorist plots as "novel, undetectable, catastrophic, and inequitable;" they "maximize both unfathomability and dread" ("Terrorism"). I will not argue that what happened on the First Crusade was a "plot." It was not a secret, and it was not terribly well organized. On the contrary, much of what happened was improvised. Given space limitations, excluded from this study will be instances of standard battle tactics that aroused terror (e.g., splitting a man in two from horseback or other types of prowess typical of the Old French epic tradition). Instead, drawing on Pinker's qualifiers, I will focus on some instances that exhibit qualities of novelty, unfathomability, and which induced dread.

FRIGHTENING DEEDS

The *Chanson d'Antioche's* version of the First Crusade takes up its narrative as Peter the Hermit embarks as a pilgrim to Rome, then visits the Holy Sepulchre in Jerusalem, which he finds has been turned into a stable (Nelson, laisse 15).[10] Peter is told in a dream to organize a rescue. He convinces the pope to raise an army, and takes this group as far as Civetot, near Nicaea, where after some initial success (the Turks flee as heads go flying; laisses 16–23), they are slaughtered by the men of Corbaran, the Seljuk Turk commander of the Persian army controlling Syria at the time, who is in town to receive tribute owed to the Sultan of Persia by the Turks in that area. The

Turks attack during the celebration of the mass and decapitate the priest, whose headless body miraculously remains standing until the end of the mass, when it finally falls. The narrator represents this as a miracle, and shows the Turks interpreting it as a sign that the wrath of God will be upon them (laisse 25). The battle of Civetot rages three days. The Christians are slaughtered; Peter escapes and reports his defeat to pope Urban II, who preaches the crusade at Clermont, raising a powerful army of Frankish barons, joined by the Normans Bohemond and Tancred of Sicily and southern Italy, among others (laisses 35–44). They make it to Civetot and the fortified city of Nicaea, which the crusaders attack without success. Soliman of Nicaea sends his interpretor, a Burgundian (l. 1585), disguised as a crusader (literally "faus pelerins," false pilgrim, l. 1605) through the siege positions for reconnaissance. The Normans Bohemond and Tancred catch on: they capture the interpretor, learn of Soliman's plans, and then bind his hands and legs and catapult him into the walled city (laisse 65). I would argue that this is a first instance of terror strategy. The Frankish host is suffering from bad conditions, lack of supplies, and an inferior position. The song represents this act as sending a clear message about spies: "Pour çou l'ont fait François que c'est honte et viutés" (Thus the Franks showed them it was shameful and vile; l. 1629). The text then imagines the reaction from the city:

> Quant par miliu de Nike fu la nouviele oïe,
> N'i a Turc ne Persant qui durement ne crie:
> "Ahi! Mahomet, sire, a cest[u]i fai aïe!
> Se li cors en est mors, l'arme ne soit perie!
> Li Diu[s] u li Franc c[r]oient, que il ne l'emport mie!"

> (When the news was heard throughout Nicaea,
> There was not a Turk or a Persian who did not cry out woefully,
> "Alas! Mohammed, lord, help that man!
> If his body is dead, may his soul not be lost!
> May the God in whom the Franks believe not carry it away!" (ll. 1630–1634)

In contrast with battle scenes focused on the clash of two armies, here it is the calculated tactic of staging the dramatic death of a single man that puts an entire city in an uproar. The text emphasizes the effect on the entire population: every Turk and Persian sends up the woeful cry of "ahi!," the powerless lament of those who do not know what to do, in unison. The traitor is punished in the French imagination by the infidel prayers bidding his soul not be taken by the Christian God, but rather by Mohammed, understood by the Christian audience as effective damnation.

Pinker remarked that "the effects of terrorism depend completely on the psychology of the audience. Terrorists are communicators, seeking publicity and attention, which they manufacture through fear" (B5). Bohemond and Tancred succeed at communicating here; anyone who dares defy them will meet a gruesome end. Catapulting the translator destroys the tranquility of the city, and advertises the ferocity of the Frankish host. The Normans' startling reversal of their inferior position through the manipulation of fear effectively jettisons the need for the interpreter, literally: the bold and savage act of catapulting the turncoat Burgundian communicates a clear message. Old French texts reliving the crusade recognize and deny by turns the language barrier between Muslims and Christians. At times translators are mentioned, as here, but likewise there are times when the narrator puts comprehensible words into the mouths of Turks, Persians, or Arabs directly, presenting them as if they were transparent to all, fabricating dialogue for narrative effect. This scene ultimately demonstrates that it does not matter what exact words the Turks uttered. Tancred and Bohemond managed to push them visibly to their knees: they orchestrated perception, for both the crusade army and the city's citizens. Through terror-inducing shows of prowess such as this, reinforced by the appearance of the crusade host around the city ("Ne vous mervilliés mie s'il i ot d'esbahis"; You won't be surprised that some among them were terrified; l. 1668) and later battle, the Franks eventually manage to get the leaders of the Nicea to flee and achieve a surrender (laisses 64–84).

Siege warfare is highly theatrical: managing perception is essential. Rather than parallel clashes of warriors on the battlefield, it consists of surrounding the inhabitants of a walled city, cutting off their supply and communication lines, and waiting until they surrender, starve, or succumb to disease. It can take a long time. There are good sight lines; the two groups watch one another at all times.

Terrorist actions breed dread. Once the Normans begin to send such messages, there are several instances in the cycle when the Franks scare the Saracens simply by their appearance. After the battles at Civetot and Nicaea, the crusaders set out for Tarsus through a sand storm, and many die. They ride four days without finding food or pasture. Their horses are exhausted, and the squires are wearing the halberks (coats of mail) for the barons, who are dragging along behind. Their boots are worn through, their soles split open, their feet hurt, they are fainting from the pain (Nelson, ll. 2804–11). When they look ahead, the barons think they see Muslims and prepare for battle by putting on the halberks, but the host they saw turns out to be Tancred's men. However, when the Turks in Tarsus see the men in shining armor embracing joyfully at this unexpected reunion, the reality of the starving and exhausted state is erased: the Turks see only a confident host. They are filled with fear, and eventually will surrender the city, feeling betrayed and inadequately protected by their ruler Soliman. The narrator emphasizes their fear: "Quant ce voient li Turc, si sont espoenté/ Et dist li .i. a l'autre: 'Mal somes engané!'" (When the Turks see this, they were terrified, and said to each other, "we are in trouble!" [ll. 2823–24]). While this episode was more luck than tactic, the narrator stresses how it was the appearance of Frankish battle-readiness that decided the outcome. At another point, just seeing the normally starving Franks eating well is enough to terrify the Turkish citizens to the point of surrender (ll. 2938–39).

Speaking of food, we progress to what the modern reader may consider the most appalling examples. The crusaders march on the city of Antioch and organize a siege. There is a fortified iron bridge at the main gate, and attempts to take it using standard battle tactics and siege engines fail, with great bloodshed. Disgruntled, the Frankish leaders decide to construct a fortress on the site of a mosque outside the city. As they excavate the foundations, they dig up the adjacent cemetary, finding buried weapons, silver, fine Asian fabrics, and Almerían silks. They share the wealth with their poor, an observation that implies justification of the deeds as consonant with a pious undertaking. They also unearth Muslim corpses. The desecration enrages the locals, who attack. The Franks kill them, and catapult their heads along with "twenty-five times twenty" cadaver skulls over the polished stone walls of Antioch (Nelson, laisse 164). The representation of Antioch's reaction emphasizes the chagrin as the corpses are recognized, personalizing the horror:

Quant paien l'ont veü, grant i fu l'estormie:
Et li pere et la mere, lor serors, lor amie
Qui connurent les tiestes, cescus en brait et brie
Et maudient la tiere u no jens fu norie!
Et dist li .I. a l'autre: "N'i porons garir mie
Quant il les mors destierent—çou est grans diablie—
Et les vis nos ocient par lor grant felounie!
Mahons, vengiés nos ent que cascuns vous en prie!
Perdu avons l'isçue devers cele partie
Se nous de l'amiral n'e[n] avoumes aïe,
Tout seroumes destruit et livré a hascié."
Este vous la cité de grant doel raemplie!

(When the pagans saw this, great was the outcry:
And fathers and mothers, their sisters, their beloveds,
Whoever recognized their heads, every one of them laments and cries
And curses the land where our race was raised!
And each says to the other: "We will not recover easily
When they ravage our walls—this is great devilry—
They massacre our faces with their evil crimes!
Mohammed, avenge us all, we who pray to you!
We will have lost the access on this side
If the emir does not bring us aid,
We shall all be destroyed and hacked to pieces."
Here is the city filled with great woe! (ll. 3989–4000)

The text follows the literary convention that makes Muslims pagans and idolators (Bancourt, 1.387–417; Daniel, 9–10). The pagans express their horror to what the French reader would see as a mute and impotent god. (It is worth remarking that the 1998 World Islamic Front fatwa likewise calls "crusaders" pagans). The narrator represents the Turks as labeling this behavior "diablie," the work of the devil, and "felony," a word used commonly to describe the most uncourtly behavior possible. But given that these words come from the purported mouths of Turks, would the French reader agree, or assume the contrary and delight triumphantly in the Muslim dismay? The narrator himself does not comment directly, but does present the deeds as effective.

The situation in Antioch got worse before it improved. Everyone was starving, eating the pack animals, buying two beans at a week's wages, the war horses eating their harnesses. Peter the Hermit speaks to the "King of the Tafurs," a group on foot, also termed "ribauds:" literally rogues, scoundrels, depraved ones.[11] The text clearly distinguishes between the well-dressed noble crusaders ("barons") and this impoverished group, yet treats them together as essential to the Christian project. The Tafur king instructs his fellows to take the dead Turks in the valley and eat them. They sort the fresh from the rotten, skin them, roast them, and eat them at the base of the walls of the city, a perfect place to stage the terrifying meal:

> Quant paien l'ont veü des murs de la cité,
> S'en furent esmaié et forment esfraé.
> Pour le flair de la car sont au mur aceuré;
> De .XXX.M. paiens sont Ribaut esgardé
> Que n'i ait .I. tout seul ki n'a des jous ploré,
> De la jent qu'il manjuent ont grant doel demené.

> (When the pagans saw this from the walls of the city,
> They were terrified and horribly afraid.
> The smell of meat drew them to the wall;
> The Ribauts were watched by 30,000 pagans,
> Not a single one with cheeks dry of tears.
> There was great mourning for the people they were eating. (Nelson, ll. 4956–61)

There follow some forty lines of laments to Mohammed and Apollin, details of cuts of meat and uses of cutlery, comments on how it "tastes better than pork or venison," and defecating afterwards on the tombs of the cemetary (ll. 4962–5014). The poem gives ample attention to this moment, dwelling on the reactions of the populace through the device of prayers to their supposedly false gods. The great knights are listed, which is a standard epic trope in recounting a battle, but in this case the narrator says they laughed, asking the King of the Tafurs if he was full. When Garcion, the governor of Antioch, approaches Bohemond about it, Bohemond disavows responsibility, saying "this was not by our command or our will;" the Tafurs are strange and not like us (ll. 5036–51). This tactic of anthropophagy is corroborated in Latin chronicles, with reactions varying from shame ("pudor," Ralph of Caan) to horror ("horribile dictu," Robert the Monk and Albert of Aachen) to doubt (Guibert of Nogent, the only one to mention the Tafurs by name, but who says they faked the cannibalism to frighten the enemy) to no commentary (the *Gesta Francorum* author, Peter Tudebode), among others (Janet, 181; Rubenstein, 530–37). Rubenstein notes that the chronicles disagree about the relative secrecy of the acts, as well as the response of the leaders (533). These acts of cannibalism have been treated extensively in several studies, and had precedents in many earlier and contemporary cultures (Rubenstein, 543–47; Tattersall). Here, I would emphasize that for the Old French Crusade Cycle audiences, cannibalism was one of a variety of fear-inducing acts represented as part of the successes of the First Crusade, acts repeated and amplified in later times when subsequent crusades had failed and were failing. The "terrorists" were Christian, but also not; from the lands of the Franks, but not really of their race (*gens*). Their psychological victory over the inhabitants of Antioch, as well as over their own hunger and misery, is a marvel. The *Antioche* narrator does not rehearse the French audience's reaction. The episodes are presented with full moral ambiguity. There were no suicide bombers on the crusade, strictu sensu, but if suicide bombing is analogous to breaking a taboo and violating oneself in the interest of communicating a strategic message, the Tafurs welcomed opportunities for self-violation with the goal of intimidating others, and earned a certain respect for their boldness.

The Frankish catapulting of massacred bodies is repeated in the *Chanson de Jérusalem* (Thorp, laisse 85), in this instance by the Tafurs. This branch of the cycle is derivative of the *Antioche* branch, repeating and adapting many of the deeds and tropes of the earlier text. The repetition of the catapulting of cadavers suggests the theme's success with readers more than historical accuracy. The Tafurs take on a much larger role in the *Jérusalem* text, helping Godfrey of Bouillon take and hold the city when many of the other crusaders return home.[12]

The Tafurs also grew famous for other acts that might now be labeled "terrorism"[13] such as raping women and carrying off their clothing, represented as causing great weeping and screams among the Saracen women (Thorp, ll. 4871–77). Again, communication is shown as key for the tactic: fear is disseminated audibly through the victims' cries and visually through their nakedness. This particular act, unlike the abuse of corpses, is condemned as grievous to Jesus ("De cel pesa Jhesu le fil sainte Marie"; l. 4878). Looting is similarly condemned (as "vilonie"; l. 4857), associated with the sin of covetousness, which often brings misfortune on the battlefield. Later in the *Jérusalem,* as the Frankish victors themselves become the besieged, the Tafurs are shown taking the worst punishment from the Turks, (laisse 195), who speak of fearing them as devilish cannibals (ll. 7072–76, 7312–15). The Tafurs are literally roasted by the Turks, and they roast them in turn. Their king reminds them how God feeds the birds ("Soviegne vos de Diu qui fist oisel volage"; l. 8796). The text does not make cannibalism or desecration of corpses one of their crimes, but rather credits the terror it inspired with the victory that liberated the holy places.

CONCLUSION

These episodes, largely forgotten in the West, give considerable insight into the above-mentioned fatwa's reference to "crusader armies spreading in it like locusts, eating its riches." The notion of "attacking Muslims like people fighting over a plate of food" is not strictly figurative, as most Western readers would assume. In the 1980s Amin Maalouf called attention to a tradition of Arab popular poetry remembering the cannibals of Ma'arra (as the area outside Antioch is called in Arabic), which associates the term "crusade" with anthropophagy and desecration (Maalouf, 36–55). Although no Arabic chronicle records the cannibalism, Occidental vernacular poems and Latin chronicles did (Rubenstein, 527). President Bush's speech writers were perhaps thinking of Eisenhower's book on D-Day when they put "crusade" in his speech,[14] or the many aforementioned American uses of the term. If Americans are first cousins to the Europeans, and decide to use terms such as "crusade," there is an argument for knowing how "unlawful" and shocking tactics were used on the original campaign and then celebrated for many centuries.

In Cronin's analysis, "terrorism's strategic logic is to draw enough power from the nation-state so as to enable a weaker, nonstate actor to accomplish its political aim" (11). This model fits the situation of the crusades, in which a very heterogeneous group from afar descend upon well-established, fortified merchant cities that had been minding their own business. The First Crusade is the only completely successful one of the nine numbered crusades, and this is why: the citizens of these cities were not expecting them. Terror worked on the First Crusade because it was unexpected; the actions of the crusaders can be described as terrorism because they were nonstate actors confronting states. Catapulting cadaver heads offers, as Pinker puts it, "a large psychological payoff for a small investment in damage" (B5). It could be compared to using box cutters to hijack a plane: the crusaders employed simple, found resources and desperate attitudes to send a message to a complacent populace from a vastly inferior position.

Cronin's key argument for ending terrorism is to understand that all terrorist movements come to an end, usually regardless of efforts to combat them. This was true on crusades. They won Jerusalem, but no one wanted to be king. Godfrey, a bastard son from the Lorraine, accepted the crown after many others refused. The *Chanson de Jérusalem* emphasizes that Godefrey had to ally with the Tafurs to win and hold Jerusalem. He soon died, and the next century saw many succession crises. The states in the Levant were much more prepared for subsequent crusades, which were all failures to varying degrees. The Tafurs get written out: on later crusades, proclamations limited the "rabble" allowed to embark. The deluxe noble and royal codices, which preserve the Crusade Cycle, include illuminated miniatures of great knights on horseback, city walls, and threatened city governors fleeing, but none celebrate or even depict the Tafurs.[15] The Tafurs are strange, as Bohemond says, and ultimately marginalized. We should, however, remember them, and use the word "crusade" with care.

NOTES

1.   World Islamic Front, "Jihad Against Jews and Crusaders, World Islamic Front Statement," *Federation of American Scientists (FAS)*, February 23, 1988, http://www.fas

.org/irp/world/para/docs/980223-fatwa.htm. The original statement was published in the Arabic newspaper *Al-Quds al-Arabi* (London), February 23, 1998, 3.

2.   A few collegiate examples include Valparaiso University in Indiana, Holy Cross in Massachusetts, Capital University in Ohio, the University of Dallas and Mary Hardin-Baylor University in Texas, North Greenville University in South Carolina, Clarke University in Iowa, Alvernia University in Pennsylvania, Madonna University in Michigan, and Northwest Nazarene University in Idaho.

3.   "Cru," *Campus Crusade for Christ*, http://www.cru.org/index.htm. The organization was founded in 1951, and in 2011 changed its name to "cru," partly in sensitivity to negative connotations of the term "crusade." A number of donors withdrew their support in response. See Lillian Kwon, "Campus Crusade for Christ Loses Donors Over Name Change," *The Christian Post*, August 4, 2011, http://www.christianpost.com /news/campus-crusade-for-christ-loses-donors-over-name-change-53394/.

4.   "Crusade," Entry 2, *Merriam-Webster Online Dictionary*, http://www.merriam -webster.com/dictionary/crusade.

5.   For instance, one "Chronology of Modern International Terrorism" begins with the Muslim Assassins (8th–14th centuries), the Jewish Zealots (1st century C.E.), jumps to the French Revolution (1789–1799), then chronicles a series of events beginning in 1968; Stephen Sloan, *Terrorism: The Present Threat in Context* (Oxford: Berg, 2006), 5–18. Cronin traces events from the last quarter of the nineteenth century; see Audrey Kurth Cronin, *Ending Terrorism: Lessons for Defeating al-Qaeda*, Adelphi Paper 394 (London: Routledge, 2008).

6.   Jan A. Nelson, *The Old French Crusade Cycle, Vol. IV. La Chanson d'Antioche* (Tuscaloosa: University of Alabama Press, 2003); Suzanne Duparc-Quioc, *Le cycle de la croisade* (Pais: Champion, 1955); Guidot Bernard, ed. and trans., *La Chanson d'Antioche: Chanson de geste du dernier quart du XIIe siècle* (Paris: Champion, 2011). I am using Nelson's edition and consulting the editions of Duparc-Quioc and Guidot. Translations are my own.

7.   A ten-volume edition of the Old French Crusade Cycle was published by various editors by the University of Alabama Press beginning in 1981 and ending in 2003; most branches have still not been translated. Guidot's complete edition and modern French translation of the *Chanson d'Antioche* appeared in 2011. Previously only abridged translations of the two historical pieces, *The Song of Antioch* and *The Song of Jerusalem* were available; Danielle Régnier-Bohler, ed., *Croisades et pélérinages: Récits, chroniques et voyages en terre sainte, XIIe–XVIe siècle* (Paris:

Robert Laffont, 1997). English translations of a few passages of *The Song of Antioch* appeared in Alfred Foulet, "The Epic Cycle of the Crusades," in A History of the Crusades, edited by Kenneth M. Setton, Harry W. Hazard, and Norman P. Zacour (Madison: University of Wisconsin Press, 1989), before Susan B. Edgington and Carol Sweetenham's complete translation in 2011: *The Chanson d'Antioche: An Old-French Account of the First Crusade* (Burlington, VT: Ashgate, 2011). For summaries of the works of the cycle, see Karl-Heinz Bender, "La Geste d'Outremer ou les épopées françaises des croisades," in *La Croisade: Réalités et fictions. Actes du colloque d'Amiens, 18-22 mars 1987*, edited by Danielle Buschinger (Göppingen: Kümmerle, 1989).

8.   "terrorism, n." *OED Online, Oxford University Press*, http://www.oed.com /view/Entry/199608?redirectedFrom=terrorism.

9.   "croisade, étymol. et hist." Centre Nationale des Ressources Textuelles et Lexicales (CNRTL), http://www.cnrtl.fr/etymologie/croisade.

10.   The text is versified in monorhyme "laisses," that is, stanzas of unequal length which narrate a particular topic or moment. I am using Nelson's edition (*The Old French Crusade Cycle*). Translations are my own.

11.   On the Tafurs, see Lewis A. M. Sumberg, "The 'Tafurs' and the First Crusade," *Medieval Studies* 21 (1959): 224–46, who notes that despite some attention in the nineteenth century, the major mid-twentieth-century crusade histories fail to mention them. He treats them as a Flemish fringe group. The origins of the name have been debated, inconclusively (226–27); Alexander Haggerty Krappe says it is Armenian for "vagabond" in "L'Anthropophagie des Thafurs," *Neophilologus* 15, no. 1 (1930): 274n2). Only the Crusade Cycle and the chronicle of Guibert de Nogent mention them in the crusade context; the cannibalism is discussed in many sources, thoroughly surveyed in Rubenstein and Janet. The *Jérusalem* describes them in terms of their poverty (e.g., ragged, non-noble dress; Thorpe, ll. 1815–18, 1830–36), physical suffering (wounds, sunburn, broken legs, flesh burnt in sieges, ll. 1819–22, 2249–50, 3017–21) which is presented at times as virtuous (e.g., ll. 6410–11). They are depicted using non-noble, improvised weapons such as clubs, sticks, hoes, pickaxes, pilgrim's staffs, lead-weighted maces; the Tafur king carried a scythe (ll. 1823–26, 3010–15, 3022). The Bishop of Martirano blesses them (ll. 3033–39). Godefroy of Bouillon frequently consults them (laisses 106, 133).

12.   In the *Chanson de Jérusalem*, the Tafur king is given the honor of making the first assault, laisse 78, and leading attacks at other points, laisse 107; the nobleman

Thomas of Marle does homage to their "king" to be able to participate in their attack, laisse 136. Godfrey is crowned king of Jerusalem with a crown of leaves by the Tafur king, laisses 156–57. When most of the crusaders leave, the Tafurs parade in front of Saracen messengers ten times wearing different clothes (laisse 184 and again, 204).

13.   Rape has been labeled terrorism by numerous commentators for its use in the Democratic Republic of Congo. See, for instance, Marc Sommers and Kathryn Birch, "Combat the Terror of Rape in Congo," *Christian Science Monitor*, January 27, 2009, http://www.csmonitor.com/Commentary/Opinion/2009/0127/p09s02-coop.html.

14.   "Tenth Crusade," *Wikipedia*, http://en.wikipedia.org/wiki/Tenth_Crusade.

15.   See Myers, "The Manuscripts of the Cycle," xxiv–xlviii, for descriptions of illustrations in the manuscripts. Several manuscripts (BnF français 786, 795, 12258) are digitalized and available throught the Bibliothèque nationale de France website, http://mandragore.bnf.fr.

WORKS CITED

Primary Sources

Edgington, Susan B., and Carol Sweetenham, trans. *The Chanson d'Antioche: An Old-French Account of the First Crusade*. Burlington, VT: Ashgate, 2011.

Guidot, Bernard, ed. and trans. *La Chanson d'Antioche: Chanson de geste du dernier quart du XIIe siècle*. Paris: Champion, 2011.

Nelson, Jan A., ed. *The Old French Crusade Cycle, vol. IV. La Chanson d'Antioche*. Tuscaloosa: University of Alabama Press, 2003.

Thorp, Nigel R., ed. *The Old French Crusade Cycle, vol. VI: La Chanson de Jérusalem*. Tuscaloosa: University of Alabama Press, 1992.

Secondary Sources

Bancourt, Paul. *Les Musulmans dans les chansons de geste du cycle du roi*. 2 vols. Aix-en-Provence: Publications Universitaires de Provence/ Marseille, 1982.

Beer, Jeanette. "Heroic Language and the Eyewitness: The *Gesta Francorum* and *La Chanson d'Antioche*," In *Echoes of the Epic*, edited by David

Schenck, Mary Jane Schenck, and William Calin, 1–16. Birmingham, AL: Summa, 1998.

Bender, Karl-Heinz. "La Geste d'Outremer ou les épopées françaises des croisades." In *La Croisade: Réalités et fictions. Actes du colloque d'Amiens, 18–22 mars 1987*, edited by Danielle Buschinger, 19–30. Göppingen: Kümmerle, 1989.

Buchanan, Sarah. "A Nascent National Identity in the *Chanson d'Antioch*." *The French Review* 76, no. 5 (2003): 918–32.

Cahen, Claude. "A propos d'Albert d'Aix et de Richard le Pèlerin." *Le Moyen Age: Revue d'Histoire et de Philologie* 96, no. 1 (1990): 31–33.

Cook, Robert Francis. Review of *Le Premier Cycle de la Croisade. De Godefroy à Saladin: Entre la chronique et le conte de fees*, by Karl-Heinz Bender et Hermann Kleber. *Olifant* 14, no. 3–4 (1989): 198–208.

Cooper, Louis, ed. *La gran conquista de Ultramar*. 4 vols. Bogotá: Instituto Caro y Cuervo, 1979.

Cronin, Audrey Kurth. *Ending Terrorism: Lessons for Defeating al-Qaeda*. Adelphi Paper 394. London: Routledge, 2008.

Daniel, Norman. *Heroes and Saracens: An Interpretation of the Chansons de Geste*. Edinburgh: Edinburgh University Press, 1984.

Duparc-Quioc, Suzanne. *Le cycle de la croisade*. Paris: Champion, 1955.

———. *La Chanson d'Antioche: Étude critique*. 2 vols. Paris: Geuthner, 1978.

Eisenhower, Dwight D. *Crusade in Europe*. New York: Doubleday, 1948.

Ford, Peter. "Europe Cringes at Bush's 'Crusade' Against Terror." *The Christian Science Monitor*. September 19, 2001. http://www.csmonitor.com/2001/0919/p12s2-woeu.html.

Foulet, Alfred. "The Epic Cycle of the Crusades." In *A History of the Crusades*, edited by Kenneth M. Setton, Harry W. Hazard, and Norman P. Zacour, 98–115. Madison: University of Wisconsin Press, 1989.

Hatem, Anouar. *Les poèmes épiques des croisades: Genèse—historicité—localisation. Essai sur l'activité littéraire dans les colonies franques de Syrie au Moyen Age*. Paris: Librairie Orientaliste Paul Geuthner, 1932.

Heller, Sarah-Grace. "Surprisingly Historical Women in the Old French Crusade Cycle." In *Women and Medieval Epic: Gender, Genre, and the Limits of Epic Masculinity*, edited by Jana Schulman and Sally Poor, 41–66. New York: Palgrave Macmillan, 2007.

Janet, Magali. "Les scènes de cannibalisme aux abords d'Antioche dans les récits de la première croisade: des chroniques à la chanson de croisade." In *Histoire du roman: Actes du colloque du Centre d'études médi*évales *et dialectales de Lille. Bien dire et bien aprandre* 22, edited by Catherine Croizy-Niquet and Philippe Logié, 179–91. Lille: Centre d'Etudes médiévales et dialectales, 2004.

Krappe, Alexander Haggerty. "L'Anthropophagie des Thafurs." *Neophilologus* 15, no. 1 (1930): 274–78. http://dx.doi.org/10.1007/BF01510218.

Maalouf, Amin. *The Crusade Through Arab Eyes*. Translated by Jon Rothschild. New York: Schocken, 1984.

Meyer, Paul. "Fragment d'une Chanson d'Antioche en provençal." *Archives de l'Orient latin* 2 (1884): 467–509.

Mickel, Emanuel J., and Jan A. Nelson, eds. *The Old French Crusade Cycle. Vol. I. La Naissance du Chevalier au Cygne. Elioxe. Beatrix.* Tuscaloosa: University of Alabama Press, 1977.

Myers, Geoffrey M. "The Manuscripts of the Cycle." In *The Old French Crusade Cycle. Vol. I,* edited by Jan A. Nelson and E. J. Mickel, xiii–lxxxviii. Tuscaloosa: University of Alabama Press, 1977.

Paris, Gaston. "La Chanson d'Antioche provençale et la Gran Conquista de Ultramar." *Romania* 17 (1888): 513–41.

———. "La Chanson d'Antioche provençale et la Gran Conquista de Ultramar." *Romania* 19 (1890): 562–91.

———. 1893. "La Chanson d'Antioche provençale et la Gran Conquista de Ultramar." *Romania* 22: 345–63.

Paris, Paulin. "Nouvelles études sur la Chanson d'Antioche." *Bulletin du Bibliophile et du Bibliothécaire* (1877).

———. "Nouvelles études sur la Chanson d'Antioche." *Bulletin du Bibliophile et du Bibliothécaire* (1878).

Pinker, Steven. "Terrorism." *The Chronicle Review.* August 12, 2011, B5.

Régnier-Bohler, Danielle, ed. *Croisades et pélérinages: Récits, chroniques et voyages en terre sainte, XIIe–XVIe siècle.* Paris: Robert Laffont, 1997.

Riley-Smith, Jonathan. *The First Crusade and the Idea of Crusading.* Philadelphia: University of Pennsylvania Press, 1986.

Rubenstein, Jay. "Cannibals and Crusaders." *French Historical Studies* 31, no. 4 (2008): 525–52. http://dx.doi.org/10.1215/00161071-2008-005.

Sloan, Stephen. *Terrorism: The Present Threat in Context*. Oxford: Berg, 2006.

Sumberg, Lewis A. M. "The 'Tafurs' and the First Crusade." *Medieval Studies* 21 (1959): 224–46.

Sweetenham, Carol. "How History Became Epic but Lost Its Identity on the Way: The Half-Life of First Crusade Epic in Romance Literature." *Olifant* 25, no. 1–2 (2006): 435–52.

Sweetenham, Carol and Linda M. Paterson. *The Canso d'Antioca: An Occitan Epic Chronicle of the First Crusade*. Aldershot, UK: Ashgate, 2003.

Tattersall, Jill. "Anthropophagy and Eaters of Raw Flesh in French Literature of the Crusade Period: Myth, Tradition, and Reality." *Medium Aevum* 57, no. 2 (1988): 240–53.

8

The Invention of Modern State Terrorism During the French Revolution

GUILLAUME ANSART

ORIGINALITY OF THE TERROR

Terror, of course, has been used throughout history by despots and tyrants of every kind. Even under what Montesquieu, in *The Spirit of the Laws* (1748), called "moderate" governments (e.g., ancient republics or modern monarchies), the notion that times of crisis and exceptional circumstances, when the very survival of the body politic is at stake, may sometimes require the suspension of normal legal guarantees, was commonly accepted. Ancient Rome could and did rely many times on the institution of the dictatorship; Renaissance Italy developed the theory of *ragione di stato*; and French absolutism also used the concept of *raison d'état*.[1] However, the Terror in revolutionary France (September 1793–July 1794) did inaugurate something new. It marks the first time a government attempted to institute a "despotism of freedom," that is, to base a regime of terror on the universal values of liberty and equality.

THE INSTITUTIONS OF THE TERROR

The Terror would not have been possible without the power vacuum created by the fall of the monarchy in August 1792. For the next three years, France was left without a constitution, without a separate executive power, and with only a single assembly of elected representatives: the National Convention. All legal political power would have to emanate from the Convention. During the winter and spring of 1793, a first constitution (the *Girondine*) was presented to the Convention, but was rejected; then a second, Jacobin constitution was adopted, but immediately set aside because of the institution of the revolutionary government.

The revolutionary government, responsible for the implementation of the Terror, took shape gradually over the course of 1793. Power became concentrated in two committees of the Convention: (1) the Committee of General Security, overseeing justice, the police, and surveillance in general, and (2) above all the Committee of Public Safety (created in April), invested with extensive executive and other powers. In Paris, a special revolutionary tribunal, under the direct control of the Convention and the two committees, was established in March to judge expeditiously those suspected of counterrevolutionary activities or sympathies. Outside of Paris, the Convention appointed representatives to local administrations and the armies with almost unlimited powers to organize repression in conjunction with local surveillance committees. Such were the main institutions of the Terror, which the Convention declared "the order of the day" on September 5. The revolutionary government itself was officially proclaimed on October 10 and further codified on December 4. Two of the most famous, or infamous, laws from this period were the Law of Suspects (September 17, 1793), which called for the arrest of all "those who, by their conduct, associations, comments, or writings have shown themselves partisans of tyranny or federalism and enemies of liberty," and the law of 22 Prairial Year II (June 10, 1794), marking the culmination of the Terror, which broadened the notion of "enemy of the people" to such an extent that every citizen critical of the government could potentially be included in that category, and which radically streamlined the already summary procedures of the Revolutionary Tribunal, eliminating the preliminary examination of the accused and the right to a defense counsel.

THE THEORY OF TERROR

One of the most common interpretations of the Terror, especially among left-leaning historians, has been to explain it as a response to external circumstances.[2] Indeed, 1793 was a grim year for the French Republic: the threat of foreign invasion, counterrevolutionary activity in the provinces—particularly the civil war in *Vendée*[3]—and serious economic difficulties, all contributed to a sense that the Revolution was in danger and that exceptional measures were needed to save it. Another factor often invoked is the increasing pressure exercised on the Convention by the Parisian *peuple* and the *sans-culotte* activists. Here, the role of spontaneous popular violence is brought to the fore.

Without denying the importance of these factors, other, for the most part, more recent interpreters of the Revolution have insisted on the inner logic of the Terror.[4] From a theoretical standpoint, the Terror rests on a few basic assumptions regarding the people and its sovereignty. The *peuple* is inherently good. It is at one with itself and knows no internal divisions (Manin, "Saint-Just," 190–201). Therefore, the collective will of the people, the only legitimate source of political power, is also one and indivisible. Moreover, the Jacobins conceived the axiom of the sovereignty of the people in absolute terms, on the model of Rousseau's *Social Contract* (1762). But the principle of the unity and absolute sovereignty of the people had to be reconciled with the necessity, in a large modern nation, of political representation. Essentially, the Jacobins attempted to solve this basic contradiction between representation and direct democracy with a political fantasy: the Convention did not simply represent the people; it *was* the people (Manin, "Saint-Just," 171–78).[5] Thus, Robespierre, for instance, established his position of power as the voice of the people through a series of sweeping identifications: his power emanated from the Committee of Public Safety, which was itself an emanation of the Convention, whose power he, Robespierre, identified with the will of the people; consequently, his voice was none other than the people's voice (Lefort, 64). "It is the inevitable paradox of direct democracy that it replaces electoral representation with a system of abstract equivalences in which the people's will always coincides with power and in which political action is exactly identical with its legitimacy" (Furet, *Interpreting*, 48).

Again, for the advocates of Terror, there could be no divisions within the people; the only dividing line was between the people and its enemies. But since it did not exist in reality, the unity of the people had to be constantly created or recreated by eliminating dissenting groups, which, by their very dissent, had placed themselves outside of the people. Hence the successive attacks against real or imagined factions and conspiracies: Louis XVI and the royalists, the *Girondins*, the *Hébertistes*, the *Dantonistes*.[6] Every purge was meant to restore the fiction of the unity of the people: "The image of a society which is at one with itself and which has been delivered from its divisions can only be grasped during the administration of the purge, or, better still, during the work of extermination" (Lefort, 84).[7]

To this fiction of perfect unity—within the people and the Convention, as well as between the two—must be added another, that of transparent immediacy. Because they could act as screens between the Convention and the people, administrations were to be continually monitored and purged (Manin "Saint-Just," 178–90). Similarly, revolutionary justice had to be almost instantaneous, requiring only the short time it takes for virtue to distinguish between friend and foe. As Robespierre famously said, "Terror is nothing but prompt, severe, inflexible justice; it is therefore an emanation of virtue; it is not so much a specific principle as a consequence of the general principle of democracy applied to the homeland's most pressing needs" (Robespierre *Virtue and Terror*, 115; speech of February 5, 1794); or as Georges Couthon, another member of the Committee of Public Safety, put it, "The time prescribed for punishing the enemies of the Fatherland must be reduced to the time it takes to recognize them; it is a matter of annihilating them rather than of punishing them" (qtd. in Lefort, 82). The law of 22 Prairial left only two options to the jury of the Revolutionary Tribunal, acquittal or death.

All this leads us to one of the most important conceptual categories of the theory of Terror, that of *enemy of the people*. It emerged in Robespierre's and Saint-Just's speeches on the trial of Louis XVI in late 1792 (Edelstein, 146–58, 249–53; Manin, "Saint-Just," 206–08). The King, they argued, had severed the bond that united him to the nation. He could not claim the protection of positive law because he had put himself outside of civil society. In relation to each other, the nation and the King found themselves back in the state of Nature, so the monarch should be treated according to the Law of Nations [*droit des gens*] or Natural Law. The King was not a citizen to be judged but an enemy to be destroyed. Saint-Just told the Convention that "Louis XVI must be judged as a foreign enemy" (Saint-Just, 82; speech of November 13, 1792);[8] and Robespierre agreed: "Citizens, be careful; you are being misled here by false notions. You are confusing the rules of civil and positive law with the principles of the law of nations; you are confusing relations between citizens with those between a nation and an enemy conspiring against it" (Robespierre *Virtue and Terror*, 58; speech of December 3, 1792; translation slightly amended).

Once established, the category of enemy of the people could easily be extended. Saint-Just emphasized with great lucidity the importance of the King's trial for the future of the Revolution: "The spirit with which the king will be judged will be the same as that with which the Republic will be founded" (Saint-Just, 81; speech of November 13, 1792). The spirit Saint-Just hoped would prevail during the King's trial, and which did to some extent, clearly foreshadows the logic of revolutionary justice: "Tribunals are established only for the members of the city," "at the moment a man is guilty, he steps outside of the body politic" (Saint-Just, 80, 81; speech of November 13, 1792). Robespierre will offer the same argument at the height of the Terror: "Social protection is due only to peaceful citizens; there are no citizens but republicans in the Republic. Royalists and conspirators are foreign to it, or rather they are enemies" (Robespierre, *Virtue and Terror*, 115; speech of February 5, 1794). Dissent could only be the instrument of factions which conspire to divide the people and undermine the unity of the Republic in order to destroy it. So the Terror always formulated the threats posed by the enemies of the Republic in terms of aristocratic/foreign conspiracies (Furet, *Interpreting*, 53–56).

The regime of Terror is thus a state of war, which makes revolutionary government quite different from normal constitutional government: "Revolution is the war of liberty against its enemies: the constitution is the system of liberty victorious and at peace. . . . Revolutionary government owes good citizens full national protection; to enemies of the people it owes nothing but death" (Robespierre *Virtue and Terror*, 99; speech of December 25, 1793). A war to the death, then, between good and evil, virtue and vice, the will of the people and aristocratic conspiracies, Natural Right and the enemies of Nature.[9]

THE LANGUAGE OF TERROR

More than just a political theory and a simple set of institutions to put it into practice, the Terror was also a performative language, a language which embodied terror by aiming to silence all debate. In this sense, the language of Terror was Terror itself (Lefort, 60).

As we have seen, the Terror assimilated dissent to treason, to conspiracies hatched by counterrevolutionary elements and foreign powers bent on dividing the people to weaken the Republic. In fact, no one was safe from the accusation of conspiracy. On the right, those who asked for a pause in the Terror were charged with *modérantisme* and pro-aristocratic leanings; on the left, those who preached atheism and even more radical purges were denounced for *exagération* and a secret desire to discredit the Revolution by their excesses. But no one could tell precisely where the truth between *modérantisme* and *exagération* lay: "What will trace the line of demarcation between all the contradictory excesses? Love of the homeland and truth," Robespierre answered rather tautologically (Robespierre, *Virtue and Terror*, 101; speech of December 25, 1793). As for Saint-Just, he understood better than anybody the paralyzing effect of intimidation produced by this constantly shifting rhetorical battleground, but he shrewdly blamed the enemies of the Revolution for this perverted state of affairs. In his next to last speech to the Convention, he told the deputies: "Attacked by every faction, you fought against *modérantisme*: you were called domineering; you fought against counterrevolutionary extremism: you were accused of *modérantisme*. Whatever you do, you will never be able to satisfy the enemies of the people" (Saint-Just, 260; speech of April 15, 1794).

The vagueness or indeterminacy of the language of Terror was essential to its efficacy. It terrorized because no one could know for certain what it took to be considered part of the people or one of its enemies. At the same time, it helped sustain the fantasy of the unity of the people, for any attempt to give precise definitions of such categories as "the people" or "the enemies of the people" would have instantly revealed the real divisions these categories masked (Manin, "Saint-Just," 204–06, 208–09). What did all the alleged enemies of the people, the royalists, the *Girondins*, the *Hébertistes*, the *Dantonistes*, have in common? Very little. But the language of Terror could silence competing discourses by reducing them all to their "objective" identical result, undermining the Revolution. "Judge them, not by the difference of language, but by the sameness of the results" (Robespierre, *Virtue and Terror*, 119; speech of February 5, 1794).

Finally, the language of Terror reveals a tendency toward the sublime or the inhuman (Žižek, x–xix). The sublime cannot be represented, contained or fully grasped. As defined by Kant in the *Critique of Judgment* (1790), it transcends the senses and is experienced as a feeling of awe and admiration, for instance when considering the spectacle of the immensity of Nature. The Revolution offers a similar spectacle. The Revolution is sublime because it released energies beyond the merely human and on a par with the great phenomena of Nature—the world emerging from chaos, the birth of a new life: "Liberty has been established; it emerged in the midst of storms: it has this origin in common with the world, which emerged from chaos, and with man, who cries while being born" (Saint-Just, 258; speech of April 15, 1794).[10] The birth of the Republic is thus likened to the mystery of an act of pure creation. Conversely, the Terror celebrated a cult of death and martyrdom. Revolutionaries, to be pure, must not be afraid to die. In a speech delivered to the Convention on 11 Germinal Year II (March 31, 1794),[11] the day after the arrest of Danton and Camille Desmoulins, Robespierre exclaimed: "I say that anyone who trembles at this moment is guilty" (qtd. in Lefort, 64). To be afraid is to be guilty, not just because fear might constitute a sign of some specific guilt, but because, more essentially, it is a crime to fear the people and the Revolution. Fear *is* guilt, for it betrays a lack of commitment to the Revolution (Lefort, 64–67; Žižek, xvi–xvii). In the words of Saint-Just: "You must punish not only traitors, but even those indifferent to the Revolution; you must punish whoever remains passive within the Republic and does nothing for it" (Saint-Just, 169; speech of October 10, 1793). Robespierre, for his part, knew no fear and could still say, the day before his execution: "What can they hold against one who wants to speak the truth and consents to die for it?" (Robespierre, *Virtue and Terror*, 140; speech of July 26, 1794). In the end, for the discourse of Terror, "the ultimate, perhaps the only, referent of truth is death itself" (Huet, 54): "I promised some time ago to leave a testament that would be redoubtable to oppressors of the people. I am going to proclaim it now with the independence appropriate to the situation I am in:

I bequeath them the terrible truth and death" (Robespierre, *Virtue and Terror*, 134; speech of July 26, 1794; translation slightly amended).

NOTES

1.   For a classic book on the doctrine of *ragione di stato/raison d'état*, see Friedrich Meinecke, *Machiavellism: The Doctrine of Raison d'État and its Place in Modern History*, translated by Douglas Scott (New Haven: Yale University Press, 1957).

2.   See the classic works of the great French Marxist or neo-Marxist historians of the Revolution: Albert Soboul, *The Sans-Culottes: The Popular Movement and Revolutionary Government, 1793–1794*, translated by Rémy Inglis Hall (Garden City, NY: Doubleday, 1972) and *Précis d'histoire de la Révolution française* (Paris: Éditions sociales, 1962); Georges Lefebvre, *La Révolution française* (Paris: Presses universitaires de France, 1930); Albert Mathiez, *La vie chère et le mouvement social sous la Terreur* (Paris: Payot, 1927) and *La Révolution française*, 3 vols. (Paris: Armand Colin, 1922–1927).

3.   The very rural and conservative province of *Vendée*, on the Atlantic coast just south of Brittany, was the scene of the most intense rebellion against the Revolution. It erupted early in 1793 with the formation of the "Catholic and Royal Army." While the rebels enjoyed some initial successes, by the end of the year they had essentially been defeated by the revolutionary forces.

4.   See especially François Furet, *Interpreting the Revolution*, translated by Elborg Forster (Cambridge: Cambridge University Press, 1981) and "Terror," in *A Critical Dictionary of the French Revolution*, edited by François Furet and Mona Ozouf, translated by Arthur Goldhammer (Cambridge, MA: Harvard University Press, 1989), 137–50; Keith M. Baker, "Political Languages of the French Revolution," in *The Cambridge History of Eighteenth-Century Political Thought*, edited by Mark Goldie and Robert Wokler (Cambridge: Cambridge University Press, 2006), 626–59; Bernard Manin, "Saint-Just, la logique de la terreur," in *Libre: Politique, anthropologie, philosophie* 6 (Paris: Payot, 1979), 165–231; and Dan Edelstein, *The Terror of Natural Right: Republicanism, the Cult of Nature, and the French Revolution* (Chicago: University of Chicago Press, 2009).

5.   With this fantasy, the Jacobins could endorse the practical imperative of political representation without abandoning Rousseau, who had explicitly rejected

representation in book 3, chapter 15 of *The Social Contract*, where he states that laws, to be valid, have to be ratified by the people as a whole. On the complex question of Rousseau's influence on the Revolution, see Bernard Manin, "Rousseau," in *A Critical Dictionary of the French Revolution*, edited by François Furet and Mona Ozouf, translated by Arthur Goldhammer (Cambridge, MA: Harvard University Press, 1989), 829–43; and Marie-Hélène Huet, "The Revolutionary Sublime," *Eighteenth-Century Studies* 28, no. 1 (1994), 51–64. For Manin, this influence has traditionally been overstated. Huet, on the other hand, argues that Robespierre in particular, in his reluctance to embrace representation, remained essentially faithful to Rousseau.

6.   *Girondins*: the more moderate faction among the Jacobins (as opposed to the *Montagnards*, whose ranks included Robespierre and Saint-Just). The *Girondin* leaders were executed in October 1793. *Hébertistes*: followers of the radical journalist and pamphleteer Jacques-René Hébert, who called for an intensification of the Terror. Hébert and his supporters were guillotined in March 1794. *Dantonistes*: followers of the *Montagnard* leader Georges Danton, who favored easing the Terror. Danton and his friends were guillotined in April 1794.

7.   See also Manin, "Saint-Just," 202–10; Furet, "Terror," 149.

8.   Translations of this and other Saint-Just speeches below are my own.

9.   On the importance of Natural Right in revolutionary ideology, see Edelstein, *The Terror of Natural Right*, who traced a long tradition of "natural republicanism" in French political thought, a tradition that culminated with the Republic of Nature envisioned by the *Montagnards* during the Terror. The concept of a republic based on Natural Law (as opposed to a régime relying on a constitution and positive law) made it possible to brand enemies of the republic as enemies of Nature, thereby justifying the swift and implacable form of justice used against them.

10.   Mary Ashburn Miller, in *A Natural History of Revolution: Violence and Nature in the French Revolutionary Imagination, 1789–1794* (Ithaca: Cornell University Press, 2011), has shown how the rhetoric of the Jacobins often borrowed its images and symbols from natural history. The Enlightenment had produced a rich body of literature on natural disasters. Eighteenth-century naturalists, philosophers, or observers of contemporary events had given increasing currency to the idea that catastrophic phenomena, such as earthquakes, volcanic eruptions, and violent storms, should not be understood simply as destructive freak accidents, but rather as inevitable, indeed, necessary occurrences in the normal process through which Nature

regenerates itself. The Revolution could easily be interpreted and legitimized in similar terms: it was to the political realm what volcanic eruptions or earthquakes were to the natural world; its violence was as inevitable, necessary and regenerative as that of Nature itself.

11. This speech is analyzed in Claude Lefort, "The Revolutionary Terror," in *Democracy and Political Theory*, translated by David Macey (Minneapolis: University of Minnesota Press, 1988), 59–69; and Slavoj Žižek, "Robespierre, or, the 'Divine Violence' of Terror," introduction to *Virtue and Terror*, by Maximilien Robespierre, edited by Jean Ducange, translated by John Howe (London: Verso, 2007), xv–xvii.

WORKS CITED

Baker, Keith M. "Political Languages of the French Revolution." In *The Cambridge History of Eighteenth-Century Political Thought*, edited by Mark Goldie and Robert Wokler, 626–59. Cambridge: Cambridge University Press, 2006.

Edelstein, Dan. *The Terror of Natural Right: Republicanism, the Cult of Nature, and the French Revolution*. Chicago: University of Chicago Press, 2009.

Furet, François. *Interpreting the French Revolution*. Translated by Elborg Forster. Cambridge: Cambridge University Press, 1981.

———. "Terror." In *A Critical Dictionary of the French Revolution*, edited by François Furet and Mona Ozouf, translated by Arthur Goldhammer, 137–50. Cambridge, MA: Harvard University Press, 1989.

Huet, Marie-Hélène. "The Revolutionary Sublime." *Eighteenth-Century Studies* 28, no. 1 (1994): 51–64.

Lefebvre, Georges. *La Révolution française*. Paris: Presses universitaires de France, 1930.

Lefort, Claude. "The Revolutionary Terror." In *Democracy and Political Theory*, translated by David Macey, 59–88. Minneapolis: University of Minnesota Press, 1988.

Manin, Bernard. "Saint-Just, la logique de la terreur." In *Libre: Politique, anthropologie, philosophie* 6, 165–231. Paris: Payot, 1979.

————. "Rousseau." In *A Critical Dictionary of the French Revolution*, edited by François Furet and Mona Ozouf, translated by Arthur Goldhammer, 829–43. Cambridge, MA: Harvard University Press, 1989.

Mathiez, Albert. *La Révolution française*. 3 vols. Paris: Armand Colin, 1922–1927.

————. *La vie chère et le mouvement social sous la Terreur*. Paris: Payot, 1927.

Meinecke, Friedrich. *Machiavellism: The Doctrine of Raison d'État and its Place in Modern History*. Translated by Douglas Scott. New Haven: Yale University Press, 1957.

Miller, Mary Ashburn. *A Natural History of Revolution: Violence and Nature in the French Revolutionary Imagination, 1789–1794*. Ithaca: Cornell University Press, 2011.

Robespierre, Maximilien. *Textes choisis*. 3 vols. Edited by Jean Poperen. Paris: Éditions sociales, 1956–1958.

————. *Virtue and Terror*. Edited by Jean Ducange. Translated by John Howe. London: Verso, 2007.

Saint-Just, Louis-Antoine de. *Œuvres choisies*. Edited by Dionys Mascolo. Paris: Gallimard, 1968.

Soboul, Albert. *Précis d'histoire de la Révolution française*. Paris: Éditions sociales, 1962.

————. *The Sans-Culottes: The Popular Movement and Revolutionary Government, 1793–1794*. Translated by Rémy Inglis Hall. Garden City, NY: Doubleday, 1972.

Žižek, Slavoj. "Robespierre, or, the 'Divine Violence' of Terror." Introduction to *Virtue and Terror*, by Maximilien Robespierre, vii–xxxix. Edited by Jean Ducange. Translated by John Howe. London: Verso, 2007.

PART 3

America and the War on Terror

9

Fictions of Counterinsurgency

LOUISE BARNETT

Some contextualizing of the post-9/11 world we live in may be in order before arriving at my subject. The apparatus of counterterrorism now seems to be everywhere in our national life, spreading a pall of secrecy over many areas. At least two and a half million people hold confidential, secret, or top-secret clearances (Mayer, 48), and there are literally millions of classified documents. At the forefront of transforming the United States into a surveillance state is the massive bureaucracy of the National Security Agency (NSA) in which warrantless wiretapping of American citizens at home has been quietly—and many would say unconstitutionally—added to the original announced goal of wiretapping foreign communications. Surely this runaway operation should have given us pause, even before it reeled in the head of the CIA for the noncrime of having a consensual affair.

Other dark sites are American airports, where another huge bureaucracy routinely inflicts indignities on the traveling public. This domestic front will not be my topic although it deploys many fictions: one example we have all had to deal with, annoyingly, is restricting our carry-on liquids to no more than three ounces each, as if this is an explosion-proof amount. It isn't. Then what purpose does this practice serve? If it does not guarantee safety, then it is undoubtedly intended to create the illusion of safety through a performance of "security theater." There is also the fiction that all classes of people are equally likely to be terrorists, including great-grandmothers, double amputees, cancer patients, and toddlers. It's no small irony that as our political system has less and less meaningful democracy, to use Noam Chomsky's term, we have a kind of nonsensical democracy in a place where it doesn't belong. I'll leave the parsing of such policies to others.

And I don't even know where to put the knowledge that Guantanamo detainees are being urged to read Stephen Covey's *The Seven Habits of Effective People* (Frank, 9–11). Today there's really too much stuff out there that you can't make up.

My topic will be, rather, the fictions of counterinsurgency, a form of unconventional warfare designed to defeat an insurgency—that is, irregular enemy forces—by winning over the civilian population that supports them. Counterinsurgency as a war tactic has a long history: as a strategy, it has been an important mode of American military action in the twenty-first century, yet, it is basically and irremediably flawed because of a simple truth—we cannot win the hearts and minds of a populace that is simultaneously being slaughtered by our soldiers. In Afghanistan, we found out, we could not even convince many of these soldiers that their job was community outreach as opposed to killing enemies. The rules of engagement make the killing of both enemy combatants and civilians inevitable and frequent. Armies will always be better at destruction, which they are trained to do, than at nation building.

The politicians who authorize this kind of war give the military an impossible mission. The generals tasked with providing positive results then tell the politicians what they want to hear because that is how they advance their careers (both the politicians and the generals). As Thomas E. Ricks described official military pronouncements in the early years of the Iraq War, "For more than three years, they had told the American public that they were making progress when they were not" (Ricks, 441). Those who speak truth to power suffer the consequences, witness the forced retirements of Generals Eric Shinseki and Antonio Taguba.[1] The men who do the actual killing are focused on returning home alive. These are the "facts on the ground," and they transcend the accident of whichever political party happens to hold power and whether there is an antiwar movement or not. Under both Democratic and Republican presidents, a huge antiwar movement could not prevent 58,000 American deaths in Vietnam in a losing cause, but it was convenient to blame civilian disloyalty for the defeat. In spite of the almost total absence of an antiwar movement over the past eleven years, our military has not been able to win in Afghanistan as it did not in Iraq. As long as the military is guided by and promulgates fictions of counterinsurgency, success is out of the question—regardless of public opinion back home.

Here, just as in holding up the three-ounce rule to examination, it is easy enough to simply open at random the *Counterinsurgency Field Manual*, the one created in 2006 under the impetus of General David Petraeus to reflect the most current military practice. We can read what we find there and compare it to the reality of our hot war of the moment, Afghanistan. The fictions begin immediately. Generals Petraeus and James Amos, representing the Army and the Marine Corps, state in the forward to this manual: "A counterinsurgency campaign is . . . a mix of offensive, defensive, and stability operations conducted along multiple lines of operations" (Petraeus, Amos, and Nagl, xlv). One can envision the PowerPoint pie chart in which each activity receives its precise percentage of the whole. This mix of operations sounds quite reassuring; it seems to cover all bases, while the "multiple lines of operations" is similarly suggestive of forethought, control, and comprehensiveness. "Forethought, control, and comprehensiveness": it's so easy to imitate military-speak, and we're so used to empty abstractions like this that suggest mastery without resorting to facts.

The forward continues by defining the task of actually conducting a counterinsurgency campaign: it will comprise "activities that soldiers and Marines have not been trained to do" (Petraeus, Amos, and Nagl, xlvi). That's hardly promising in a world that has more and more come to depend upon specialization and expertise. The generals go on to say that these fighting men and women "are expected to be nation builders as well as warriors" (xlvi). Could this be contradictory on some level? No, the generals describe it as merely challenging, daunting, and difficult—words that in the past would have characterized many a straightforward military mission.

Lieutenant Colonel John Nagl, an enthusiastic proponent of counterinsurgency, says the same thing as the counterinsurgency manual, in his own way: "We need the ability to kill people and break things with our Army, absolutely. But we also need, in this modern era . . . an Army that can protect people and build things. And what we're doing is looking for the right balance between those two" (qtd. in Vlahos). Critics such as West Point Professor Lt. Col. Gian Gentile argue—convincingly, in my opinion—that there can be no balance between these two antipodal activities ("Misreading").[2] Conventional wars did the killing and breaking first; constructive activities followed. Counterinsurgency requires both at the same time, a key reason for its failures in Vietnam, Iraq, and Afghanistan.

Furthermore, in conventional warfare, the soldier or Marine would be prepared for the enemy to greet him with a hand grenade or other weapon, while in the counterinsurgency situation described in the *Field Manual*, troops must be prepared to be greeted with a hand grenade or a handshake. Is this a task for a high school dropout who gets into the infantry on a moral waiver?

We might pause here and contemplate the dilemma of the polar opposites of handshake and hand grenade. One represents enmity and death, the other friendship, mutual effort, positive action. If we take this example literally, it describes the impossible. If it is intended simply to counsel caution, it still invokes a context in which even great vigilance may not be enough. There have been numerous instances in Afghanistan where men in Afghan Army uniforms have suddenly fired on American soldiers working with them, standing next to them, in fact.[3] This illustrates the familiar problem in a counterinsurgency situation of being unable to count on the military we have trained to fight on our side.

Just as in Vietnam before we withdrew, American officials in Afghanistan speak of a competent Afghan military as an essential ingredient in our plans, and describe progress optimistically. The view on the ground, as usual, suggests otherwise. In a firefight on October 3, 2009, one of the deadliest battles of the war, Afghan troops performed badly in every respect (Lardner). Rather than throwing themselves into the fight that broke out when 300 insurgents attacked an isolated combat outpost, they cowered in their rooms. Worse, under cover of the chaos that ensued, they stole digital cameras and other personal belongings of Americans engaged in fighting. Of the 36 Afghans at the base, 15 deserted. Well, that was 2009.

A year later, C. J. Chivers reported on the Afghan Army in *The New York Times* that at

the small-unit level, Western troops and journalists have documented their corruption, drug use, mediocre or poor fighting skills, and patterns of lackluster commitment—including an unwillingness to patrol regularly and in sizable numbers, or to stand watch in remote outposts. At the higher levels, Western military officers often describe patronage, favoritism, and an absence of managerial acumen, rooted in part in the pervasive culture of corruption and in widespread illiteracy. Now, 14 percent of the combined force can read or write—at the third-grade level. (Chivers)

In July, 2011, as General Petraeus bid farewell to his position as commander in Afghanistan, he characterized the Afghan army and police as "increasingly credible" forces (Bennhold). Yet, out of 160 Afghan battalions, only one was considered able to function without US assistance. *That's* "increasingly credible?" We went into Afghanistan in 2001. After *ten years*, their army was only "increasingly credible?"

It is indisputable that the Afghan people have a long, proud history as warriors, so could it be that, like the South Vietnamese troops of the past, they feel no enthusiasm for their corrupt central government and no allegiance to the rich Americans who could not help but communicate their sense of superiority to the troops they were training? Even before we get to the possession of such items as digital cameras, size and appearance alone convey American superiority. In the documentary *Restrepo*, big, healthy Americans are juxtaposed with physically slight village elders with scraggly beards and bad teeth. Prematurely aged by malnutrition and poor health care, some are probably much younger than they look. They know that our priorities are not their priorities. As Tobias Wolff wrote in his Vietnam War memoir *In Pharaoh's Army*, the Tet attack proved to the Vietnamese that "for all our talk of partnership and brotherhood we disliked and mistrusted them, and that we would kill every last one of them to save our own skins" (Wolff, 140).

Our caring about problematically friendly foreigners is always limited by so many factors: our own safety, money, time, other commitments, and—finally—will. They know, and we know, that our concern for these "friendlies," however friendly they may be, can never be as great as our concern for ourselves. Whatever our official fiction, we may give them up at any time, and we *will* give them up at some point. We announced a firm departure date for Afghanistan well in advance. Even if our ultimate departure was negotiable, the knowledge that we would leave at some point was unlikely to inspire Afghan loyalty. As a contemporary gloss on this point, consider our shameful lack of help for those Iraqis who worked for us during the Iraq war and consequently are at risk in today's Iraq. While we drag our feet about letting them into this country, a number have already been murdered.

A word now about the role of military acronyms and euphemisms in creating enabling fictions for counterinsurgency operations. Many military abbreviations are innocuous shortcuts—MOS for military occupation specialty, for instance—but some also substitute an abstraction for a potentially unpleasant reality, *collateral damage* being one of the foremost examples. Just recently, in a conference on our nineteenth-century Indian Wars, a participant remarked about a well-known massacre of noncombatants that "women and children were victimized by Army bullets."[4] The reference to Army bullets is a little too vivid to be out-and-out military speak, but the passive construction and the attribution of agency to bullets rather than shooters makes this utterance a hybrid construction, halfway to "collateral damage."

The deviation of language from reality into fiction performs an essential function in the military. William Calley, the officer held responsible for the My Lai massacre of March 16, 1968, describes a conversation he had with the colonel he reported to when, after the massacre but before it became public knowledge, he received a promotion and served as a community aid officer in a Vietnamese village: "Sir, I'm causing dissension here," Calley began. The colonel asked him, "Do you know how to solve it?" Calley replied sincerely: "No sir." The colonel: "Do you know my philosophy?" Calley: "Yes sir." Colonel: "And it is—?" Calley: "Solve it." In other words, Calley tells the reader, "The Colonel couldn't worry about it. Division didn't care. . . . it wanted statistics, but it would never ask him, 'How much dissension now?' Dissension looked bad" (Sack, 143). So the only data quantified was positive, which naturally gave a somewhat skewed impression of the war that was actually being fought.

No one would be against solving problems: it just happened to be impossible in the situation Calley was in, which is why he had consulted his commanding officer. Similarly, when General Petraeus was the man of the moment in Iraq, he ended every day by inquiring of his staff, "How have we helped the Iraqi people today?" (Petraeus, Amos, and Nagl, xv). No doubt he genuinely hoped that the Iraqi people had been helped, and no doubt his subordinates gave him the answers he was looking for or got their behinds kicked. This is the man who said, "I don't do optimism or pessimism. I do realism" (Harnden). Perhaps we need an asterisk here to indicate realism as defined in the military.

Do people involved in a war understand the fictions that they themselves participate in? One might assume that they could not help but know and therefore accept the need for obscuring the truth. More likely, for many, the necessity of pleasing superiors and following prescribed procedures takes priority over thinking too much about such fictions. An air force pilot in Vietnam knew that his bombing mission had destroyed a number of peasant huts rather than military structures, but his after-action report had no category for civilian buildings destroyed—only military targets—so it was inevitable that whatever structures were destroyed would be counted as military (Schell, 179–80). Further up the chain of command, there is an even stronger personal investment in going along: promotion and long-term career prospects depend on treating such fictions as truths.

Counterinsurgency theoreticians, on the other hand, probably believe their fictions more wholeheartedly because their ideas are never checked against facts, even when, as in the following example, facts are brought up. A recent book defending the war in Afghanistan begins with a series of acknowledged negatives: the war's long duration and lack of progress; its apt comparison to the Vietnam War. "In fact," the authors admit, "after all the mistakes that have been made to date, after all the years and lives and dollars that have been squandered, the Afghanistan war may turn out to be unwinnable." And now comes the leap of faith: "But it is too soon to be fatalistic" (O'Hanlon, 61). Optimistic predictions follow, depending entirely upon President Karzai morphing into George Washington.[5]

Similar pronouncements abound in the *Counterinsurgency Field Manual*. It describes counterinsurgency as "manpower intensive," meaning that a minimum requirement of force density should be twenty counterinsurgents for every thousand civilians. This number can include the host nation's military—in this case, Afghan soldiers—and its police. Most reliable sources place the population of Afghanistan at close to thirty million, which would require a counterinsurgent force of one million, five hundred thousand. The United States has 90,000 troops in Afghanistan, and the 47 other countries that have joined us have little more than 33,000 combined. Some of these allies have well under 100 boots on the ground; Austria, for example, has three, while our stalwart ally, Tonga, has sent 55. The Afghan army and police, as of 2010, comprised 256,000, with the usual promise that another 50,000 would be added by the end of 2011. The grand total is less than a third of what the *Field Manual* regards as necessary. Moreover, someone has pointed out that if the Afghan Army increased to the size of its ultimate goal, 400,000, this would mean recruiting every literate male in Afghanistan.

The more significant number comes out of another formula, not the ratio of counterinsurgents to inhabitants, but that of terrorists killed to terrorists created. The *Field Manual* asserts that an operation is a failure if it kills five terrorists but creates fifty more (Petraeus, Amos, and Nagl, 45). That observation is commonsensical, but operations where civilians are collateral damage happen all the time, leaving a legacy of bitterness that can be exploited by the insurgents. Further, the enemy is rarely a static entity. Various sources have stated that there are few Al Qaeda operatives left in Afghanistan, possibly as few as a couple hundred. The military mindset is to think in terms of neutralizing that number, but if others take the place of the two hundred eliminated, no progress occurs. This was the pattern in Vietnam. North Vietnam had a large reservoir of draft-age people to replace whatever losses they sustained. And we knew this at the time. What we did not know was another strategy to substitute for killing the enemy.

Since the Afghan Taliban is fed by jihadists from a Muslim population of more than a billion people, part of the coalition strategy has been to win some over to our side. When individual Afghan fighters have renounced the Taliban, however, interviews have determined that it has been because they objected to killing fellow Afghans. Their hatred of Americans remained constant (Flintoff). It might seem to be self-evident that when you want people to like you, you should not be "victimizing them with bullets." If we regarded Afghans as people whose feelings are like our own, we would realize that this policy generates ill will of the sort that no amount of good intentions will overcome.

And yet, if a choice must be made, the military will default to killing. There is the huge fiction that an American infantryman of average intelligence who has been dropped into a country where everyone not in his unit is, as far as he's concerned, a hostile alien, and in any case he can't tell which one is offering the handshake and which one has the hand grenade—that this young soldier can win the hearts and minds of these dark-skinned folks of a radically different culture and language by being as adept at nation-building as he is at killing people and breaking things. Even Jimmy Carter might have a problem in such a context, but this is an undereducated young person, often with a troubled history, who has had eight weeks of basic training and eight weeks of advanced infantry. That he says "Fuck this nice guy shit," as a soldier told Rajiv Chandrasekaran in Afghanistan, seems more realistic (Chandrasekaran, 277).

When the war is waged by remote control, as is the case of ever more frequent drone attacks, resentment is likely to be particularly strong. Any number of civilians have been mistakenly targeted or killed accidentally, but every so often we succeed in hitting an Al Qaeda target. For our war machine, the military objective outweighs the civilian cost. Afghans are likely to feel differently. The American public might be surprised to learn how much is tolerated under the rubric of collateral damage. The success of a mission, or even the goal of a mission, whether successful or not, almost always justifies to the military way of thinking whatever collateral damage takes place.

This principle has been consistently upheld by military courts. It includes, as was widespread in Vietnam, the execution of civilians who are in the path of a mission. In Iraq, such an incident occurred when a civilian wandered into an area where Americans were setting up a sniper position. The sergeant in charge ordered a soldier to kill the unlucky Iraqi, planted a weapon on the body, and radioed his superior that the position had been attacked.[6]

To my civilian mentality, execution has a kind of culpability that differs from the panicked killing by frightened, trigger-happy soldiers who believe, however foolishly, that they are under enemy attack—the kind of response that tragically killed Pat Tillman in Afghanistan. Why couldn't the snipers in Iraq have restrained and gagged the civilian until their operation was over? Surely he would have preferred it. Certainly his family would have. They testified eloquently at the court-martial about the loss of this husband and father of four—to no avail. The sergeant who gave the order was exonerated, although—inconsistently—the sniper triggerman who obeyed the order was convicted. It wasn't reassuring to be told by a defense witness at the court-martial of the triggerman that if the actions of every combat serviceman in Iraq were subjected to the same scrutiny as the defendant's, "we would have thousands" of cases.

This man stated that the shooting "was a result of Iraq's violent environment and the often difficult and confusing choices that servicemen make daily." This isn't inaccurate. The counterinsurgency world, where handshakes and hand grenades may be ambiguously proffered, is a dangerous one, but the choice made in this particular killing does not seem to be difficult or confusing so much as convenient and wrong. Had it been according to the rules of engagement, as the snipers claimed, there would have been no need to pretend that they had been attacked by planting a weapon on the body.

We should not cherish the illusion that civilian public relations or good works will ever be the military's first choice. In a very clear-cut example of choosing between winning hearts and minds and killing, the senior American civilian adviser in Quang Nam Province, Vietnam wrote on March 18, 1968 to the commander of American troops in Vietnam, General William Westmoreland, to beg that Korean troops be removed from the province: "The Vietnamese peasants are, of course, deathly afraid of the Koreans. Many say that they prefer the VC to the Koreans. . . . [This] may actually be causing an increase in VC sympathizers throughout the Korean TAOR [tactical area of operations]" (Greiner, 190). Even the South Vietnamese officials of the province, usually so indifferent to the concerns of their own people and compliant toward the American military—even these officials—asked that the South Koreans be sent elsewhere.

Yet, Westmoreland refused to remove either the marauding South Koreans or rogue American troops. Fighting a losing war, he wanted and needed their aggressive edge. That such a victory would be built on the bodies of apolitical rural villagers was an aspect of the situation best ignored. This military mindset may not be shouted in the public square, but it still dominates.

So we might say that one of the problems of counterinsurgency is that micro and macro are inevitably as out of sync as theory and practice. For the overall effort to succeed, we need the support of the people. But in the microcosm of military action, where quantifiable data is the major measurement of progress, we need to do things that will create hostility among the very people we want to get on our side. That macro and micro can function smoothly together is one of the most salient fictions of counterinsurgency.

This brings up a significant aspect of our way of waging war today. Our military effort not only depends on huge numbers of foreign contract workers to staff American bases, it depends on money to substitute for other kinds of effort. Money has its limitations in counterinsurgency. In 2007, General Petraeus paid leaders in the Sunni Triangle of Iraq to join our effort. Their repudiation of Al Qaeda became known as the Anbar Awakening, a change of allegiance that combined with the troop surge of that year to alter the dynamic of the war. Desperate for some good news, American media awarded success to the surge and its proponents, General Petraeus and President Bush. "Could the surge have worked without the Awakening?" Dexter Filkins asks in a recent article, and answers, "Almost certainly not" (Filkins, 80).

Several other facts support his conclusion. First, the surge coincided with the Shiite militia leader Muqtada al-Sadr announcing a six-month ceasefire and standing down his attacks against Iraqi Sunnis and coalition forces; then, he extended the cease-fire for another six months. Second, Iraqi Sunnis were already disenchanted with Al Qaeda, which mostly consisted of non-Iraqis enforcing a harshly austere form of Islam on them. The Sunnis were receptive to the American overture of money because they were ready to throw off Al Qaeda: "Absent those two necessary conditions, there would have been no let up in the level of violence despite the surge" (Gentile).

Moreover, the money wasn't going to be paid forever. If you buy some-one's allegiance with money, be prepared for the allegiance to disappear when the payments end. And in the triumphalist narrative about the success of the surge, everyone seems to have forgotten that the point of the surge was to tamp down the violence enough to move the political process along. Four years down the road after the surge, the news was still more negative than not. A *New York Times* headline of August 16, 2011 read: "A series of attacks sent the message to Iraq and the United States that after tens of thousands of lives lost and hundreds of billions of dollars spent, insurgents remain a threat" (Schmidt). Such terrorist bombings still occur with depressing fre-quency—the two politicians who were supposed to share power in the first post-occupation government did not speak to each other. Consequently, the government of Iraq became almost as dysfunctional as our own. On almost every key issue, no progress has been made, and the reappearance of Muqtada al-Sadr with a plan to gain political power is an ominous development—and not merely because he hates the United States.

Not that American interests fared well under the Maliki government. The two countries failed to achieve an accord much desired by the United States government: a status of force agreement that would have left a small American military contingent in Iraq after the end of the occupation in 2011. American influence in Iraq has continued to dwindle, as illustrated in November of 2012 by the Iraqi release from prison of Ali Musa Daqduq over strong American protest. A "prominent Iraqi" quoted in a *New York Times* story on the release commented that it "'underscores how little influence Washington holds over Baghdad's government since American troops left the country last December'" (Gordon).

The evening of May 1, 2011, during a tense Phillies-Mets game, fans began chanting "USA, USA." Given the omnipresence of Blackberries and iPads these days, they knew before the announcers did what had happened. The players on the field, unlike most people in our society at all times, were out of reach of the internet, so they were the last to know: Osama Bin Laden was dead. Such moments inspire patriotic outbursts, especially among members of a like-minded group like a stadium of baseball fans. Americans were bound to rejoice in the death of a man who, for a decade, had personified terrorism for them.

As a historian, I reflected on a story I had read that very morning that illustrates the profound disconnect between the thinking of officials at the top of the hierarchy and some of those in the field.[7] The story reports on the trial of two young soldiers in the 5th Stryker Brigade, who, along with some like-minded unit members, murdered three random civilians in Afghanistan in 2010 and attempted to disguise each killing as a combat incident. Until it became impossible to ignore, the sergeant's immediate superiors had followed a time-honored military policy of overlooking suspicious circumstances and accepting the explanation that the Americans had been attacked. Locals knew better: the first victim was a fifteen-year-old farmer who had been working in his family's field until called over by the soon-to-be murderers. The other two Afghans killed were known to be peaceful men unacquainted with weapons, the least likely villagers to suddenly attack a group of heavily armed American soldiers.

While the commander of American troops in Afghanistan was an enthusiastic proponent of counterinsurgency, the 5th Stryker Brigade had a combat culture that resisted the official philosophy. As one officer told State Department officials, "'We're just here to rack 'em and stack 'em'" (Chandrasekaran, 159). The investigation that followed the exposure of the civilian murders determined that the general in charge of the brigade had no direct blame. But, the report concluded, "had he still been on the job, he should have been relieved of command . . . in part because of 'his failure to follow instructions and intent'" (Chandrasekaran, 161).

Only four weeks before the killings began, the chairman of the Joint Chiefs of Staff, Admiral Mike Mullen, paid a heavily publicized visit to the area. The military's strategy of counterinsurgency, he reminded members of the 5th Stryker Brigade, required them to win hearts and minds by protecting the population. "If we're killing local civilians," he cautioned, "we're going to strategically lose." In contrast, Corporal Jeremy Morelock, one of the soldiers involved in the killings, told Army investigators, "None of us in the platoon—the platoon leader, the platoon sergeant—no one gives a fuck about these people." While Morelock and his buddies were committing the murders, documenting their actions with photographs of themselves smiling over the corpses and taking severed fingers as trophies—photos reminiscent of Abu Ghraib—in the parallel universe of counterinsurgency strategy, their commanding officer was meeting with Afghan village officials to ensure them of the beneficent intentions of the United States.

The year 2012 saw the quiet disappearance of counterinsurgency strategies in Afghanistan and references to them in Washington and in the media. Statistics were grim: the 2,000 mark in deaths of American soldiers in Afghanistan was reached on September 30, 2012. By the end of the year, another 174 had been added. As of November 2012, 52 NATO personnel had been killed by Afghan soldiers they were training.[8] Robert Bales, an American sergeant who seems to have run amok, has now been tried for having killed on March 11, 2012, sixteen Afghan civilians—men, women, and children—in a village near his base. The cultivation of opium poppies continues to flourish, and, as long as he remained in office, President Karzai remained ineffective and uncooperative. Perhaps most significant, the promise of withdrawing troops, deemed necessary to appease the war-weary American public, can only have a negative effect on Afghanistan. It might be right for Afghans to assume responsibility for the security of their country, but few experts believed they would be able to do so by our target departure date of 2014.[9]

Rajiv Chandrasekaran's recent book on Afghanistan lays the blame for the failure of the war at Washington's door. He asserts that the military never fully embraced counterinsurgency. Few were motivated to learn an Afghan language. They stayed in their comfortable bases, enjoying the lattes, deluxe ice creams, and flat-screen TVs that have become standard, rather than mingling with the people and winning these often hostile or unfriendly folk to our side. For all the talk of training Afghan troops to take over, American commanders never allocated enough men to serve as trainers. Worst of all, in Chandrasekaran's account, was the lack of coordination among the initiatives pursued by different parts of the American war and redevelopment effort. In an all-too-familiar situation, rivalry within the American military vitiated the war effort: the Marines were over-deployed in a nonstrategic area while the important city of Kandahar needed more troops. Projects to supply badly needed electricity foundered. Farmers were not helped. And the embassy and military, responding to their policy makers in Foggy Bottom and the Pentagon, pursued, often ineptly, different visions of what to do.

As for counterinsurgency, it suffered serious blows when its enthusiastic proponent, General Stanley McChrystal, was removed from command almost immediately, and his successor, General David Petraeus, the man who wrote the book on counterinsurgency, left the field after only a year in order to head the CIA. For the rank and file military men in Afghanistan, the choice of a handshake or a hand grenade was no choice. Preferring to concentrate on the possibility of the hand grenade, they performed their time-honored functions of killing and breaking.

The results have been predictable. An article in *The New York Times* summarizing the year 2012 reports that "insider attacks, by Afghan security forces on their Western allies, became 'the signature violence of 2012,' in the words of one former American official. The surge in attacks has provided the clearest sign yet that Afghan resentment of foreigners is becoming unmanageable, and American officials have expressed worries about its disruptive effects on the training mission that is the core of the American withdrawal plan for 2014" (Rosenberg). The restrained journalese language seems blander than the situation requires. Surely, Afghan resentment could do more than "disrupt": it could create catastrophe, derailing the American exit strategy. The syntax, with its string of phrases, tends to obfuscate this stark message. For the people of Afghanistan, the outlook is even grimmer. When American troops depart, their country will be contested by a corrupt government too weak to protect them and a harsh, ideologically driven force of extremists.

In reality, there are no good options. An editorial in *The New York Times* titled "Choices in Afghanistan," confined itself to considering how many American troops would remain in the country *after* our withdrawal. It mentioned that we have spent 39 billion dollars training and equipping the Afghan army and police—with a notable lack of positive results ("Choices").

For the two twenty-first century wars against insurgencies, whatever large American aims existed at the beginning were eventually supplanted by the mission of extricating the United States from an embarrassing situation—if not an out-and-out defeat, something closely akin to it. In these unconventional wars, neither conventional warfare nor counterinsurgency has produced the desired results.[10]

To say that counterinsurgency failed profoundly in both Iraq and Afghanistan, and to predict that it would fail just as spectacularly in any similar war of choice the United States has the poor judgment to embark upon, expresses an important but only a partial truth. The greater truth is that counterinsurgency as envisioned in the *Field Manual* is like so many idealistic plans of action—rational and even admirable in theory, but impossible in practice. Even assuming a situation of full resources properly coordinated—a huge cadre of expert nation builders fluent in the languages and cultures of the occupied land—we could still find that the country's population preferred the brutality of the indigenous enemy to foreign sympathy and largesse. Ultimately, whatever our good intentions, we can never truthfully affirm that we have no self-interest on the table and that this self-interest will not, in the long run, be determinative. The underlying premise of counterinsurgency that a foreign population can be brought to embrace our goals as their own is the greatest fiction of them all.

NOTES

1. General Shinseki, chairman of the Joint Chiefs of Staff, publicly indicated that the approaching Iraq War would require far more troops than Secretary of Defense Rumsfeld believed; General Taguba was given the unenviable task of producing a report on the Abu Ghraib scandal. A critic of present-day generalship, Colonel Paul Yingling, was denied admission to the Army War College, an important credential in an Army career, "even though his own writings were being studied there"; he, too, retired. See Thomas E. Ricks, *The Generals: American Military Command From World War II to Today* (New York: Penguin, 2012), 444.

2. Gian P. Gentile, "Misreading the Surge Threatens U.S. Army's Conventional Capabilities," *World Politics Review*, March 4, 2008, http://www.worldpoliticsreview.com/articles/1715/misreading-the-surge-threatens-u-s-armys-conventional-capabilities.

3. Alissa J. Rubin and Sangar Rahimi, "Afghan Military Officer Kills 8 U.S. Service Members," *NYTimes.com*, April 28, 2011, http://www.nytimes.com/2011/04/28/world/asia/28afghanistan.html; Alissa J. Rubin, "Afghan Who Killed 6 G.I.'s Was Trusted Officer," *NYTimes.com*, November 30, 2010, http://www.nytimes.com/2010/12/01/world/asia/01afghan.html; Rod Nordland, "Afghan Officer Turns Against U.S. Soldiers, Killing 2," *NYTimes.com*, April 5, 2011, http://www.nytimes.com/2011/04/05/world/asia/05afghanistan.html.

4. Audience participant, Little Big Horn Associates annual symposium, Oklahoma City, OK, June 18, 2011.

5. He didn't.

6. All information on this case, including citations, has been taken from Solomon Moore, "G.I. Gets 10-Year Sentence in Killing of Unarmed Iraqi," *NYTimes.com*, February 11, 2008, http://www.nytimes.com/2008/02/11/world/middleeast/11sniper.html.

7. Details of this event and quotations are taken from Mark Boal, "The Kill Team: How U.S. Soldiers in Afghanistan Murdered Innocent Civilians," *Rolling Stone*, March 27, 2011, http://www.rollingstone.com/politics/news/the-kill-team-20110327.

8. These figures are widely available, on websites such as icasualties.org and, for American casualties only, www.defenselink.mil/news/casualty.pdf.

9. The official timetable called for American withdrawal in 2014, regardless of how the war effort stood at the time.

10.   The rise of the Islamic State in the years since 2012 has profoundly altered the situation in Iraq for the worse in terms of the government's control of territory and ability to function effectively. Afghanistan now represents an earlier stage of that same process, as an article in the *New York Times* recently indicated. See The Associated Press, "Islamic State Group Loyalists Eye a Presence in Afghanistan," *NYTimes*, September 8, 2015, http://www.nytimes.com/aponline/2015/09/08/world/asia/ap-as-afghanistan-islamic-state.html.

WORKS CITED

Bennhold, Katrin. "Afghanistan War 'Fragile' but Doable, General Says." *NYTimes.com*. July 20, 2011. http://www.nytimes.com/2011/07/21/world/asia/21iht-military21.html.

Boal, Mark. "The Kill Team: How U.S. Soldiers in Afghanistan Murdered Innocent Civilians." *Rolling Stone*. March 27, 2011. http://www.rollingstone.com/politics/news/the-kill-team-20110327.

Chandrasekaran, Rajiv. *Little America: The War Within the War for Afghanistan*. New York: Knopf, 2012.

Chivers, C. J. "Gains in Afghan Training but Struggles in War." *NYTimes.com*. October 12, 2010. http://www.nytimes.com/2010/10/13/world/asia/13kabul.html.

"Choices on Afghanistan." Editorial. *NYTimes.com*. January 6, 2013. http://www.nytimes.com/2013/01/07/opinion/choices-on-afghanistan.html.

Filkins, Dexter. "General Principles: How Good Was David Petraeus?" *The New Yorker*, December 17, 2012, 76–81.

Flintoff, Corey. "Former Taliban Reconcile with Afghan Government." Morning Edition. *National Public Radio*. March 30, 2011. http://www.npr.org/2011/03/30/134733852/former-taliban-reconcile-with-afghan-government.

Frank, Thomas. "Easy Chair: Required Reading." *Harper's*. June 2011, 9–11.

Gentile, Gian P. "Misreading the Surge Threatens U.S. Army's Conventional Capabilities." *World Politics Review*. March 4, 2008. http://www.worldpoliticsreview.com/articles/1715/misreading-the-surge-threatens-u-s-armys-conventional-capabilities.

Gordon, Michael R. "Iraq Said to Release Ali Musa Daqduq, a Hezbollah Operative." *NYTimes.com*. November 16, 2012. http://www.nytimes.com/2012/11/17/world/middleeast/iraq-said-to-release-hezbollah-operative.html.

Greiner, Bernd. *War Without Fronts: The USA in Vietnam*. Translated by Anne Wyburd and Victoria Fern. New Haven: Yale University Press, 2009.

Harnden, Toby. "Afghanistan: Gen Petraeus says U.S. forces will remain until end of 2014." *Telegraph*. June 25, 2011. http://www.telegraph.co.uk/news/worldnews/asia/afghanistan/8187965/Afghanistan-Gen-Petraeus-says-US-forces-will-remain-until-end-of-2014.html.

Hetherington, Tim, and Sebastian Junger, dirs. *Restrepo: One Platoon, One Valley, One Year*. San Francisco: Outpost Studios, 2010.

Lardner, Richard. "Afghan Soldiers Ran, Hid During Attack." *Deseret News*. June 10, 2011. http://www.deseretnews.com/article/700143338/Afghan-troops-ran-hid-during-deadly-attack.html.

Mayer, Jane. "The Secret Sharer: Is Thomas Drake an Enemy of the State?" *The New Yorker*. May 23, 2011, 48.

Moore, Solomon. "G.I. Gets 10-Year Sentence in Killing of Unarmed Iraqi." *NYTimes.com*. February 11, 2008. http://www.nytimes.com/2008/02/11/world/middleeast/11sniper.html.

Nordland, Rod. "Afghan Officer Turns Against U.S. Soldiers, Killing 2." *NYTimes.com*. April 5, 2011. http://www.nytimes.com/2011/04/05/world/asia/05afghanistan.html.

O'Hanlon, Michael E. and Hassina Sherjan. *Toughing It Out in Afghanistan*. Washington, DC: Brookings Institution, 2010.

Petraeus, David H., James F. Amos, and John A. Nagl. *The U. S. Army/Marine Corps Counterinsurgency Field Manual*. Chicago: University of Chicago Press, 2007.

Ricks, Thomas E. *The Generals: American Military Command from World War II to Today*. New York: Penguin Press, 2012.

Rosenberg, Matthew. "Afghan Soldier's Journey from Friend to Killer of Americans." *NYTimes.com*. January 4, 2013. http://www.nytimes.com/2013/01/04/world/asia/afghan-soldiers-journey-from-friend-to-killer-of-americans.html.

Rubin, Alissa. "Afghan Who Killed 6 G.I.'s Was Trusted Officer." *NYTimes.com.* November 30, 2010. http://www.nytimes.com/2010/12/01/world/asia /01afghan.html.

Rubin, Alissa J. and Sangar Rahimi. "Afghan Military Officer Kills 8 U.S. Service Members." *NYTimes.com.* April 28, 2011. http://www.nytimes .com/2011/04/28/world/asia/28afghanistan.html.

Sack, John. *Lieutenant Calley: His Own Story.* New York: Viking, 1970.

Schell, Jonathan. *The Military Half: An Account of the Destruction in Quang Ngai and Quang Tin.* New York: Knopf, 1968.

Schmidt, Michael S. "U.S. Report Finds Security Deteriorating in Iraq." *NYTimes.com.* July 31, 2011. http://www.nytimes.com/2011/07/31/world /middleeast/31iraq.html.

Vlahos, Kelley B. "Gian Gentile: Exposing Counterfeit Coin." *Antiwar.com.* May 7, 2009. http://original.antiwar.com/vlahos/2009/05/06/gian-gentile -exposing-counterfeit-coin/.

Wolff, Tobias. *In Pharaoh's Army: Memories of the Lost War.* New York: Viking, 1994.

10

The Cultural Politics of WMD Terrorism in Post-Cold War America

HAROLD WILLIFORD

After the terrorist attacks of September 11, 2001, a perception developed that the events were a shock to the American political consciousness. One author asserted, for example, "most Americans had no narrative with which to anticipate, and in that sense psychologically prepare for, what actually took place" (Lifton, 160). In response, Audrey Kurth Cronin critiqued "the ahistorical and amnesiac approach to global terrorism that prevailed in the post-9/11 era" and Judith Butler decried the attitude that "there is no relevant prehistory to the events of September 11th" (Cronin, 134; Butler, 6). They refer to, respectively, the international political conditions and history of imperialism that provide context for the rise of Al Qaeda. While valuable, such arguments address only the international half of the historical framing of September 11. Jean Baudrillard saw complementary continuities with popular American disaster and war films and (in)famously claimed, "we can say they did it, but we wished for it" (Baudrillard, 5). While it would be difficult to access the full sweep of his claim about cultural fantasy and desire, his observation still demands an inquiry into the historical interplay of American culture and counterterrorism. This paper juxtaposes close readings of policy analyses of terrorism with popular fiction from the period between the Cold War and the

"War on Terror." This begins as opposite poles of "fact" and "fiction," but texts from both domains exhibit an overwrought fascination with terrorism long before 2001. The ensemble of cultural texts indicates that rather than experiencing a sudden shift, America was predisposed and poised to respond to September 11 with the War on Terror and its extralegal practices.

Popular fictional works from the 1990s confirm Baudrillard's core claim that the destruction of the Twin Towers resembles a preexisting set of cultural images. The 1996 blockbuster movie *Independence Day* depicts the fiery collapse of the Empire State Building and other skyscrapers at the hands of alien invaders. Tom Clancy treated America to the image of a Japanese pilot crashing an airplane into the U.S. Capitol Building in his 1994 novel *Debt of Honor*. But where *Debt of Honor* evoked World War II *kamikaze* pilots, another of Clancy's novels, the 1998 bestseller *Rainbow Six*, looked forward. It recounts a tale of terrorists with apocalyptic aspirations. *Rainbow Six* functions as a nexus of counterterrorism and American culture in the 1990s that sutures diverse issues, from capitalism and multinational corporations to reproduction and gender politics, with terrorism. Examination of how military and cultural questions unfold and interact in this elaborately plotted, lengthy "techno-thriller" reveals that a shift in counterterrorist culture occurred before September 11.

The ahistoricity of American policy analysts' representation of post-Cold War terrorism indicates that this shift happened with the fall of the Berlin Wall. Clare Sterling portrayed terrorist groups as Soviet surrogates in a web controlled by Moscow in *The Terror Network* (1981). Despite its dubious credibility and propagandistic nature, Sterling's book definitively shaped how the Reagan administration understood "terrorism" (Gibson, 270). After the collapse of the Soviet Union, however, national security analysts trumpeted the development of "new" terrorism (Cameron, 162; Deutch, 11; Laqueur, 32). Without Moscow to restrain them, terrorists were supposedly now "less predictable" and, according to these commentators, more likely to use nuclear, chemical, or biological weapons, collectively known as "weapons of mass destruction," or "WMD" (Rose, 134). Jan Lodal, for example, confidently claimed, "some day, someone will use a nuclear bomb" and "millions will be killed" (Lodal, 132). In testimony before a Senate subcommittee, an expert asserted, "the threat of terrorist use of [WMD] has never been greater; and at the same time, it is never going to be less than it is right now" (Cameron, 2). Gavin Cameron concluded a book on nuclear terrorism with the claim that "the current psycho-dynamics of terrorist groups" and "the nature of terrorism in the 1990s" had suddenly increased the threat of WMD terrorism (162). Spending on WMD counterterrorism increased from negligible amounts to $1.5 billion during this period (Falkenrath, 147). American counterterrorists appear to have forgotten these developments once the War on Terror began.

That forgetfulness forms only one part of a pattern of American cultural amnesia where terrorism is concerned. The portrayal of the "new" post-Cold War WMD terrorism does not reflect historical reality. In 1946, a Jewish extremist group attempted to poison thousands of German prisoners of war at Nuremburg with arsenic, a chemical weapon, and aspired to use WMD to kill up to six million more former Nazis (Sprinzak and Sprinzak, 17). The Rajneeshees, an Oregonian religious cult without connection to Moscow, committed the only "successful" bioterrorist attack in 1984 when they contaminated salad bars at ten local restaurants with salmonella and infected hundreds, but caused no fatalities (Carus, 115). Around the same time, a Christian millenarian group stockpiled cyanide in Arkansas with outlandish plans to poison the water supply of an undetermined major city (Hamm, 151). Many members of the loose network of American right wing militant groups were radicalized by fears of communism, not by Soviet loyalties (Flynn and Gerhardt, 14). In the world of fiction, *The Turner Diaries*, a white supremacist novel written by William Luther Pierce in 1978, concludes with a suicide bomber crashing a plane loaded with a nuclear weapon into the Pentagon. WMD and diverse ideological objectives were far from "new" elements of terrorism. If history contradicts the "new" terrorism narrative, analyzing its contemporaneous cultural and political roots might provide an explanation for how WMD terrorism became a new focus of the national security complex and the significance of the choice to portray it in that manner.

Terrorism, as a word, lacks a stable definition. Meanings are often attributed to it based on the speaker's agenda (Hoffman, 23). Meanwhile, those described as terrorists often reject the label and seek to apply it to their opponents. Definitions of terrorism have differed amongst government agencies within America alone (39). While functionally problematic, that discord reveals the cultural and political forces that gather loosely related concepts under the umbrella of the many meanings of "terrorism." Counterterrorist identity is fragmented—the inevitable result of the instability inherent in "terrorism." As the counterterrorist defines and delegitimizes the terrorist, he simultaneously defines and legitimizes his own identity. Counterterrorist representations of terrorism operate in this dynamic, where even as they may fail to describe actual nonstate militants, they ultimately reveal the counterterrorist's own priorities and anxieties.

Political theorist Michael Rogin's model of countersubversive psychology provides a framework for understanding the relationship between counterterrorist subject and his—constructed— terrorist opponent. In 1987, at the end of the Cold War, Rogin analyzed the history of American responses to perceived "threats" to the United States, including Native Americans, organized labor, and Communists. Rogin explored the incongruity between reality and the hysterical representation of these groups as "demons" in American politics. He found that those representations performed essential functions in the justification of growing American power in their respective eras. For example, threat of invasion by "savage" Native Americans in the nineteenth century became reason for westward expansion—invading and displacing the land's original inhabitants, who had been figured as undeserving heathens, to prevent an imagined invasion by the "savages." Rogin provocatively posits that a countersubversive subject attributes characteristics to his "subversive" opponent to rationalize engagement in forbidden behaviors, fulfilling a repressed desire to mirror the subversive (Rogin, *Ronald Reagan*, 10).

The Cold War is replete with examples of this dynamic. In texts created by twentieth-century American countersubversives, "frenzied doubling . . . reveal[s] the connections" to the subversive that countersubversives tried to conceal (Rogin, *Ronald Reagan*, 10). The threat of Soviet nuclear missiles became a justification for Americans to maintain tens of thousands of nuclear warheads (Franklin, 52). A perceived need to preserve American freedom from Communist oppression permitted the rapid expansion of government surveillance of Americans (Rogin, *Ronald Reagan*, 258). The Communist "demon," rather than the reality of the Soviet threat, both shaped and was shaped by American countersubversives' desire to accumulate particular forms of power.

The collapse of the Soviet Union left the United States without a clear opponent to motivate countersubversive politics. Americans had been able to "cast themselves as the righteous heroes of a morality play performed on world history's stage" by seeing their Soviet opponents as "literal incarnations of human evil (the devil)" (Gibson, 289). The fall of the Berlin Wall, however, ended the ease of the Capitalist-Communist and American-Soviet moral binaries. Instead, a world of multipolar politics developed where America's role and moral credibility were less clear (Gibson, 289; Sherry, 438). The grandiose and global threat of WMD terrorism had the potential to fill that post-Cold War "demon gap." The mutable meaning of terrorism rendered it particularly suitable for this function.

Rogin claimed in 1987 that the "theory of international terrorism encapsulates and brings up to date the entire history of American countersubversion" (Rogin, *Ronald Reagan*, 80). Analysis of how terrorism interacted with capitalism, national identity, family, and personal identity—four elements about which American countersubversives have been historically anxious (Rogin, *Ronald Reagan*, 68)—illustrates how the WMD-wielding terrorist began to function as a "demon" right after the Cold War. The element of mirroring in Rogin's theory further provides a framework for understanding particularly eerie similarities between "terrorist" and American "counterterrorist" practices. I argue that the 1990s theory of "international terrorism" not only brought American countersubversion "up to date," but then pushed it in a new direction, from the Cold War surveillance state to broader dreams of slipping off institutional—and territorial—constraints on countersubversive power. Counterterrorists' exaggerated figuration of terrorism as threatening global destruction and their responses reveal a desire to enter an extralegal, nonstate environment where they wield rogue sovereign power.

Counterterrorist discourse from the 1990s indicates that capitalism's "victory" in the Cold War rendered private ownership and the free market problematic for national security. During the Cold War, the American military had led technological development from which the private sector benefited. In the 1990s, this "spinoff" reversed and the military began to rely on private contractors for new technology (Sherry, 403). Meanwhile, high salaries in private sectors appeared to draw highly qualified individuals away from government jobs, as the end of the Cold War removed a normative imperative toward public service (Oehler, 143). Abroad, the chaotic politics of post-Soviet Russia struck Americans as the perfect storm for a black market for nuclear weapons, in which free market incentives would drive ex-Soviet scientists to sell "loose nukes" to terrorists (Cameron, 4). A passage in Clancy's *Rainbow Six* reflects this shift. A fictional expert describes a "good terrorist" as a "businessman whose business is killing people to make a political point . . . almost like advertising" (87). The incongruity of this image of a terrorist as a calculating "businessman" with the 1990s panic about destructive ideological madmen illustrates that terrorism functioned not simply as a concept in national security policy, but also as an object upon which Americans could work through myriad, more abstract political concerns and cultural anxieties.

As Clancy weaves conjectured threats posed by the free market into an apocalyptic fantasy in *Rainbow Six*, a general anxiety about nonstate organizations, including but not limited to terrorists, emerges in his narrative. The central villain of *Rainbow Six* is a biotechnology firm, run by environmental extremists. These extremists genetically modify the Ebola virus to render it an unimaginably potent biological weapon and plan to spread it at the Olympic Games. They intend to exterminate the human species, save themselves. Confronted with this threat, one of Clancy's counterterrorists meditates on how "the changing technological world" has "given immense power to relatively small organizations" (860). Confronted with nonstate "foreign policy," the hero wonders, "when did *they* [corporations] begin to think they could play games at this level [that of the nation-state]?" (860). Most disturbing for the hero, while "governments were selected, by and large, , by their citizens," corporations "answered—if they did so at all—to their shareholders" (860). Clancy's fictional corporation replaces Sterling's exaggeratedly powerful Moscow as the American countersubversive's archenemy, positioned at the center of a web of terrorist groups to carry out its diabolical plan. Clancy further stages the anxieties about the free market expressed in the policy world with the inclusion of a former FBI agent turned private consultant as a key terrorist mastermind. Nonstate threats, epitomized by Clancy's blending of terrorism and corporation, stepped into the Soviet demon's shoes.

In Clancy's fiction, the "new" terrorist provides the foundation for enactment of a counterterrorist fantasy of mirroring nonstate threats. His American heroes lead an interstate counterterrorist team, which includes French, German, British, and Israeli members alongside a large contingent of Americans, transcending nation-state borders and identities. The American leader believes that if "people realize what a bio-tech company can do if it wants," the result would be "global panic," which matches another hero's conclusion that "in this New World Order things had little in the way of controls at all, and that was something somebody should think about" (Clancy, 858, 860). The resulting strategy, however, is to toss aside transparent governance to avoid publicity (858). Already a "blacker than black" operation, known only to a handful of elite officials, the counterterrorists pursue a range of extralegal strategies, including entering Brazilian airspace in violation of international law (explicitly noted in the narrative), entering America without getting their passport stamped (a violation of America's own borders), and extrajudicial punishment (850, 800, 894). The counterterrorist team is based in England, because of the "very cordial relationship" between UK Special Forces and British Airways, a blending of corporation and counterterrorists that permits the heroes to fly unnoticed on civilian airplanes—emulating the tactics of modern terrorists (27). Employment of private organizations came to fruition in the War on Terror, exemplified by Blackwater's provision of private security in Afghanistan and Iraq and the use of private air transport in the CIA extraordinary rendition program. Lack of democratic accountability and absence of oversight is as much of an element of counterterrorist organization as the theorized nonstate enemy.

The importance of mobility, another key factor in counterterrorist politics, reveals the deterritorialization of internationalism that came with the shift to nonstate and extralegal countersubversive aspirations. Clancy's counterterrorists' ability to respond to terrorist attacks anywhere in the world reflects proposals for global surgical counterstrike ability as a core counterterrorist national security policy (Rosenbaum, 159). Such mobility responds to concerns expressed by then-National Security Advisor Sandy Berger in 2000 that "the transnational network of terror groups" is particularly troubling because "they are loosely connected" and "cannot be extinguished with one stroke" (36–37). Meanwhile, the "large number of vulnerable U.S. targets abroad allows terrorists to achieve dramatic results without having to penetrate America's borders" (Simon, 109). The "pervasive force" of globalization brought multinational corporations and easy international transit, making borders increasingly meaningless.

The departure from physical geography changed the ontology of conflict. Adriana Cavarero draws on Carl Schmitt's *Theory of the Partisan* to explain how the "partisan who has abandoned the tellurian dimension," moving from territorial armed conflict focused on borders to attacks in any location imaginable, introduces "a new type of war in which the global space of combat is characterized by 'pure means of destruction,' in other words 'weapons of absolute annihilation [that] require an absolute enemy lest they should be absolutely inhuman'" (Cavarero, 69). The abandonment of earthbound warfare by modern "partisans" arguably begins with airplanes, which ultimately facilitated the prospect of the total destruction of a nation with nuclear weapons—without an army ever setting foot on the country's soil.[1] The disappearance of the Soviet Union and subsequent focus on terrorism removed the last semblance of geography. American analysts conjectured that terrorists, without territory against which retaliation could be effected, would not be dissuaded from using WMD by the logic of mutually assured destruction, which had been the stabilizing force in the Cold War nuclear standoff between two territorial powers (Tucker, 267). The constructed threat of nonterritorial WMD actors has now led to a "global space" of counterterrorist combat, with covert American operations occurring around the globe with scant regard to other states' sovereignty.

WMD terrorism intervened as the image of a force so transgressive that it provided a context in which post-Cold War American impulses toward nonstate actions seemed—relatively—acceptable. Terrorism is already labeled "unconventional" violence, but WMD terrorism breaks another "taboo"—that against the use of WMD.[2] The second transgression puts terrorists on the scale of Schmitt's "absolute enemy," which "makes it possible to dehumanize [them] and see [them] as . . . morally abject criminal[s]" so that "those who annihilate [them] 'are [not] themselves criminal and inhuman'" (Cavarero, 69). Understanding WMD terrorism as a specific manifestation of the dehumanized, absolutely destructive, non-tellurian partisan reveals the connections between *Rainbow Six* and the 1996 alien-invasion blockbuster *Independence Day*. Where *Rainbow Six* only raises the threat of terrorist violence on a global scale, *Independence Day* fully depicts "nontellurian" warfare "characterized by 'pure means of destruction'" through images of worldwide destruction inflicted by UFOs that never land on the earth's surface.

Read together, *Independence Day* and *Rainbow Six* reveal how concerns about American national identity interacted with the image of WMD terrorism. As both alien and terrorist are disconnected from geography, their similar functions as nonstate threats are summarized by how the semantics of "extraterrestrial" and "extraterritorial" collapse into "nontellurian." In addition to wielding WMD and being highly mobile, the aliens further share the key characteristic of randomness with terrorists. The aliens in *Independence Day* do not specifically target humanity, but merely intend to exploit Earth's resources and then move on. While their nomadic, parasitic civilization underscores the prominence of nonstatism, their unexpected invasion on a sunny summer day presages September 11. Cavarero explains that randomness provides the essential horrifying element of contemporary terrorism because it negates the individual identity of its victim (Cavarero, 75–76). Terrorism, as understood in countersubversive discourse, kills a small number of people, but chooses victims indiscriminately to send the message that it could happen to anyone. Terrorism therefore commits ontological violence as it turns a *someone* into an "interchangeable and exemplary" *anyone* (Cavarero, 76). To acknowledge the terrorist threat is to accept having been "degraded . . . from singular being to random being" (76). Where Cold War binarism reinforced American exceptionalism, random terrorism can undermine the specificity of American identity.

WMD terrorism, portrayed as threatening worldwide destruction, enabled the American counterterrorist to reinterpret the individualized ontological violence of terrorism into a communal threat to reestablish American exceptionalism. Both *Rainbow Six* and *Independence Day* stage threats of extinction, which facilitates the enactment of a fantasy of uniting humanity against the dehumanized enemy, respectively, environmental extremists who hate their own species and unfeeling aliens. Ever since the constructed black-and-white morality of World War II produced a euphoric, but transient, unity in America, American culture has exhibited a desire to reproduce that unity (Sherry, 88, 498). Counterterrorist politics, however, has the more ambitious desire of achieving global unity in the abstract political space opened by the decreasing importance of geographical borders. Clinton administration officials and neoconservatives alike argued for the inclusion of China and Russia in comprehensive international coalitions in the context of counterterrorism, precisely because they thought the United States would retain its sway over those coalitions

(Berger, 27). Politicians celebrated the number of participants in the Gulf War coalition (Sherry, 471). *Rainbow Six* picks up this theme with its international team, but *Independence Day* truly carries out the fantasy as the Americans not only include Russia and Japan in their counterattack against the aliens, but, in this movie made shortly after the Gulf War, the Israelis and Iraqis also come together under Anglo-American leadership. This replay of colonial power structures hints at the nature of the unity. Rather than the reduction of a random victim into *anyone*, the theoretically massive scale of WMD terrorism could motivate "countersubversive" alignment of *everyone* against the "subversive" terrorists—and the assertion of American dominance over everyone.

The unity envisioned by counterterrorist politics commits the same onto-logical crime against individual identity as terrorism. In 1988, Ronald Reagan mused in an interview that in case of a threat from "another planet," humans might "find that we didn't have any differences between us at all, we were all human beings, citizens of the world, and wouldn't we come together to fight that particular threat?" (Rogin, *Independence Day*, 8). *Independence Day* stages this exact fantasy as the victorious final counterattack, and develops the theme in the Hollywood President's climactic speech. Channeling Reagan, the fictional president enacts the real one's dream, announcing, "we can't be consumed by our petty differences anymore." The ultimate counterterrorist goal is the same ontological crime as terrorism: the obliteration of differ-ence and reduction of individuals to mere members of the human species. The achievement of this goal then permits inscription of American identity on the newly blank slate of humanity.

American nationalism transcended state borders in the 1990s. International institution building became valuable because the United States could act as a "gatekeeper," forcing other nations to conform to its values (Berger, 24, 27). In the realm of fiction, *Rainbow Six* focused on U.S. leadership of an inter-state group, the other members of which are measured against standards set by the Americans. It is *Independence Day*, however, that carries the fantasy to completion. The counterattack takes place on July 4th, which allows the Hollywood President to proclaim:

> should we win the day, the 4th of July will no longer be known as an
> American holiday, but as the day when the world declared in one voice,

we will not go quietly into the night, we will not vanish without a fight. We're going to live on, we're going to survive. Today we celebrate our independence day!

Forgetting "petty differences" becomes an imposition of American identity on the world, celebrated with missiles turning into a patriotic display of fireworks as the credits roll. The opportunity for remaking the world in America's image only comes about, however, through the deaths of billions in a WMD holocaust perpetrated by the aliens on the world's metropolises. The tone of unmitigated triumph at the conclusion of the movie is only possible because those victims, stripped of their individuality like victims of terrorism, are perfectly interchangeable with the survivors. They are easily forgotten because humanity is saved by the survival of some reproducing population—anointed with an American identity by the globalization of July 4.

The Hollywood President attempts to cast the battle against the aliens as the inheritor of the American Revolution with the claim that they "will once again be fighting for freedom." The parallel breaks down, however, as he elaborates, "not from tyranny, oppression or persecution, but from annihilation." Annihilation, as used in the film, refers to an event, not a political condition. The connection between nationalism and reproduction explains the reduction of counterterrorist politics to survivalism. Jacqueline Stevens argues that birthright membership societies, such as nation-states that grant citizenship to those born to its citizens (or on its territory), are a form of reproduction. They assuage masculine "womb envy," born of the male body's inability to give birth, through "political practices that assume the same ontological status as maternity" (Stevens, 161). Birthright citizenship becomes a way to perpetuate national identity.

The importance of perpetuation of the human species (always within the framework of American identity) that defines WMD counterterrorism reveals an aspiration to global control over political identity beyond the normal order of national birthright citizenship. Counterterrorist fantasy perpetuates its version of American national identity outside the structures of the territorial state and legal institutions of citizenship through self-appointment as guardians of all humanity. During the War on Terror, this fantasy became very real for those in other nation-states on the receiving end of misadventures in "democratization" and "winning hearts and minds." Interventions in Afghanistan and Iraq, the latter expressly premised on an imagined WMD threat, went beyond political goals to the "export[ation] of American progress" at the expense of other cultures (Butler, 142). The unifying and controlling force of American national identity became a tool of power unconstrained by the state's territorial limits and institutional checks. Counterterrorist reproductive politics explains how the counterterrorist seeks to sever the hyphen between nation and state while retaining the power afforded by birthright citizenship.

In pre-September 11 counterterrorist fiction and post-September 11 political tropes, marriage and reproductive politics recreate patriarchal dominance in this global space. *Rainbow Six* foregrounds reproduction with the character of Patsy Chavez, wife of one of the counterterrorist heroes and daughter of their leader. Pregnant for nearly the entire novel, whenever she appears, Clancy notes her pregnancy in some fashion. In general, the (always) male counterterrorists consider it their "self-assigned job" to ensure that their wives do not fear for their safety (Clancy, 7). This patriarchal protection is put into action when a group of terrorists attempt to hold Patsy and her mother, the counterterrorist leader's wife, hostage at a hospital and the counterterrorists heroically rescue them from the "baby-killer[s]" or "woman killer[s]" (662). During this scene, the group's emotions reveal that the counterterrorist team has replaced the state. The two women are "family for all of them" and lives that "belong" to the male counterterrorists drawn from across state boundaries (603). The reproductive community transcends territory but remains imbued with the identity of the American leadership.

Independence Day also stages a patriarchal pageant when a pilot marries a single mother, who works as an exotic dancer before the alien invasion, resolving the tension created by female sexuality and independent maternity. The departure of men for Europe in World War II created an opening for female empowerment, as represented by "Rosie the Riveter" (May, 215). This change in gender politics gave rise to Cold War masculine anxieties encapsulated in fears of smothering mothers, as exemplified by Angela Lansbury's "Mrs. Iselin" in *The Manchurian Candidate*. As the War on Terror takes place both at home and abroad, the implosion of geography permits men to function simultaneously as warrior and as patriarch in the counterterrorist fantasy of globally reproducing American national identity.

The resuscitation of patriarchy is borne out in *Independence Day*, which gruesomely punishes female attempts at autonomy (Rogin, *Independence Day*). For example, the First Lady stays in Los Angeles under the shadow of a UFO to imitate the bravery of her husband, who remains in the White House with an alien ship poised overhead. She ultimately dies after sustaining injuries when her helicopter crashes during the aliens' WMD attack. She admits on her deathbed that she should have listened to her husband's command that she evacuate sooner. The antifeminism of the moment overwhelms since the President did not evacuate any sooner, with flames chasing Air Force One down the runway—and he had their daughter with him. Susan Faludi has described how this brand of patriarchal politics surged in popularity following September 11, from the predictions of a post-9/11 baby boom to the portrayal of Jessica Lynch as a damsel in distress.

The shift in gender politics indicates the deep connections between counterterrorist politics and the so-called "culture wars." Michael Sherry proposed in the mid-1990s that militarist rhetoric's shift in focus from Communists to domestic advocacy groups indicated an inward turn from the international Cold War to domestic politics (502). Recognition of counterterrorist gender politics leads to an alternative explanation: any remnants of a sharp domestic-foreign distinction fell with the Berlin Wall. The threat of terrorist attacks originating in the "homeland" justified proposals for increased military presence in domestic civil society. Those threats, however, were inextricably tied to images of international terrorism, as implied in a remark by Lewis "Scooter" Libby about attacks of "ambiguous" origin (Libby, 307). Rather than an inward turn, the culture wars developed during the fusion of domestic and foreign politics. In the context of the culture wars, the counterterrorist response to feminism came with the incorporation of earlier conservative heteronormative repugnance to LGBT advocacy.

The ability of LGBT individuals to serve openly in the U.S. military became a crucial issue in the culture wars in the early 1990s. Military service has been an effective way to claim equal rights. The racial civil rights movement capitalized on African Americans' history of military service to demand their rightful place in the American polity. LGBT individuals, unable to serve openly, could not rely on their military service to advocate for equal rights (Sherry, 490). In the fictional realm, *Independence Day* purified its polity, killing off the human characters who have been coded as gay to leave a cohort of hypermasculine warriors to fight the sexually ambiguous aliens. Unsurprisingly, the only gay character in *Rainbow Six* is a German terrorist, and the terrorists tend to be nonreproductive, sexually promiscuous individuals—contrasted with the monogamous, family-oriented counterterrorists. After September 11, this anxiety played out in what Jasbir Puar describes as the "queering" of the Islamic or Arab "terrorist." As counterterrorist discourse focused on Islam, cultural conservatives have begun to deploy images of Islamic extremism and Shari'a law in discussions of gay rights.[3]

Examination of a shift in negative stereotypes of gay men reveals how deeper anxieties raised by the body's vulnerability to physical harm in a world of permeable geographical borders underlie countersubversives' association of LGBT individuals with terrorists. During the "Lavender Scare" of the McCarthy era, homosexuals were depicted as vulnerable to Soviet corruption, particularly as their taboo sexuality rendered them susceptible to blackmail. They were the weak link in the national chain—a potential hole in the national border for the entrance of foreign Soviet influence. During the "Don't Ask, Don't Tell" debates in the early 1990s, however, the male homosexual came to embody the threat of penetration instead of passivity. Opponents of allowing lesbians and gays to serve openly in the military panicked about straight soldiers having to shower under the so-called penetrating gaze of gay men (Sherry, 488). Clancy, meanwhile, anxiously gestures at anal penetration when he notes with surprising detail that his fictional terrorists weaponize the Ebola virus by adding colon cancer genes (Clancy, 125–26). The redefinition of the negative stereotype of the homosexual male from passive to penetrating reflects how the rise of nonstatism moved the locus of conflict from national borders to the social space within the nation and between individual bodies, each of which is a potential vector for the countersubversive's positive national identity or association with the negative subversive. The gay rights movement coincided with heightened penetration anxieties of individuals who sensed the vulnerability of their skin in a world where weakened territorial borders no longer functioned as a buffer between an individual body and the feared possibilities of contagion and violence of the "foreign" world. These antigay politics were reified when "Don't Ask, Don't Tell" and the militaristically entitled "Defense of Marriage Act" drew a non-geographical border of unequal citizenship through American society. The latter law drives home that LGBT individuals, coded as non-reproductive, were to be excluded from citizenship in the nonstate, patriarchal counterterrorist society organized around "traditional" families that carried on wholesome American values.

The counterterrorist brand of homophobia, premised on phobias of anal penetration, draws attention to the counterterrorist's sadistic practices against bodies that are not part of its global enterprise. In one disturbing scene in *Rainbow Six* that works through race and sexuality, the two lead counterterrorist heroes, John Clark and Domingo Chavez, torture a terrorist, Timmy. The interaction revolves around Chavez's threat to sever Timmy's penis (661–63). Chavez's race plays a key role because his Latino background makes him inscrutable and unpredictable for an Irish terrorist, so the latter believes the threat might come true. Meanwhile, Chavez invokes transsexuality by terming phallic amputation a "sex-change operation." He justifies this punishment by reminding himself that this terrorist kidnapped his pregnant wife. The terrorist misappropriation of phallic power, represented in the specter of rape, becomes the basis for a sexualized talionic justice. In the preceding scene, the counterterrorists take advantage of a terrorist in a post-anesthesia "suggestive state" to penetrate his mind for information, explicitly acknowledging that this information is legally useless (659–60). These scenes of terrorist vulnerability before counterterrorist power display the dynamics of extralegal practices.

The escape from legal strictures into nonstate spaces is the heart of counterterrorist fantasy. Judith Butler describes the War on Terror, particularly extralegal detention practices, as a situation in which "petty sovereigns abound . . . delegated with the power to render unilateral decisions, accountable to no law and without any legitimate authority" (56). *Independence Day* stages the destruction of American political institutions, reducing the government to the pure executive power of the president—situated at the ultimate black site, Area 51. Butler's focus on Guantanamo Bay, a stateless netherworld similar to the apocryphal Area 51, indicates how nonstate spaces allow for extralegal responses to terrorism, where the counterterrorist mirrors the terrorist's arrogation of the decision of who lives and who dies. Perhaps an exchange from *Rainbow Six* best sums up counterterrorist mirroring. Two of the "good guys" are discussing a fictional hijacking that occurred on an Ethiopian Airlines flight. After the hijackers had been restrained, the security forces slit their throats. The counterterrorists approve of the "simple, but effective" action because "*nobody* had messed with that airline since" (Clancy, 21). The violence served no safety purpose, but was intended to send a message.

Clancy's extralegal counterterrorist fantasy and *Independence Day*'s exuberant destruction of civil society did not exist in a vacuum in the 1990s. In a 1998 article, three prominent neoconservatives directly linked Clancy's fiction to their concerns about WMD terrorism, writing, "long part of the Hollywood and Tom Clancy repertory of nightmarish scenarios, catastrophic terrorism has moved from far-fetched horror to a contingency that could happen next month" (Carter, Deutch, and Zelikow, 80). They predicted that "an act of catastrophic terrorism would be a watershed event in American history," which, "like Pearl Harbor . . . would divide our past and future into a before and after" (80). Just two years later, the Project for the New American Century published its report, *Rebuilding America's Defenses*, in which the authors contemplate how "the process of transformation" of the military in the fashion favored by neoconservatives "is likely to be a long one, absent some catastrophic and catalyzing event—like a new Pearl Harbor" (Donnelly, 51). American analysts had not only fantasized about extralegal counterterrorist practices, they even anticipated the before-and-after dichotomization of history around an event of catastrophic terrorism. They appear to have shoehorned September 11, which, although not a WMD terrorist attack, was dramatized to serve as one, into a preexisting narrative. Recognition of the American cultural and political prehistory of the War on Terror points to the disturbing possibility that the acceptance of extralegal tactics was not a decision taken under duress, but the enactment of longstanding counterterrorist fantasies by a culture poised to respond to the events of September 11 in this specific, problematic fashion.

ACKNOWLEDGMENTS

This chapter is based on my undergraduate thesis, which Northwestern University awarded the Kenneth Janda Prize for Best Undergraduate Honors Thesis in Political Science in 2010. I would like to thank Professor Bonnie Honig, my thesis advisor, for her guidance.

NOTES

1.   See H. Bruce Franklin, *War Stars: The Superweapon and the American Imagination*, Rev. and exp. ed. (Amherst: University of Massachusetts Press, 2008), for a discussion of how technology changed the geographical ontology of warfare.

2.   As epitomized in the title of Brad Roberts's article, "Terrorism and Weapons of Mass Destruction: Has the Taboo Been Broken?" *Politics and the Life Sciences* 15, no. 2 (1996): 216–17.

3.   Conservative commentator Robert P. George claimed, for example, that the 2011 New York gay marriage law "will impose a form of liberal *dhimmitude* on faithful Catholics, Evangelical Protestants, Eastern Orthodox Christians, Mormons, Orthodox Jews, and devout Muslims" (NRO Symposium, *National Review Online*, July 23, 2011, http://www.nationalreview.com/article/272527/can-marriage-be-saved -nro-symposium.).

WORKS CITED

Baudrillard, Jean. *The Spirit of Terrorism*. New revised edition. London: Verso, 2003.

Berger, Sandy R. "A Foreign Policy for the Global Age." *Foreign Affairs* 79, no. 6 (2000): 22–39.

Burleigh, Michael. *Blood and Rage: A Cultural History of Terrorism*. London: Harper, 2008.

Butler, Judith. *Precarious Life: The Powers of Mourning and Violence*. London: Verso, 2006.

Cameron, Gavin. *Nuclear Terrorism: A Threat Assessment for the 21st Century*. New York: St. Martin's, 1999.

Carter, Andrew, John Deutch, and Philip Zelikow. "Catastrophic Terrorism— Tackling the New Danger." *Foreign Affairs* 77, no. 6 (1998): 80–94.

Carus, W. Seth. "The Rajneeshees (1984)." In *Toxic Terror: Assessing Terrorist Use of Chemical and Biological Weapons*, edited by Jonathan B. Tucker, 115–37. Belfer Center Studies in International Security. Cambridge, MA: MIT Press, 2000.

Cavarero, Adriana. *Horrorism: Naming Contemporary Violence*. New Directions in Critical Theory. New York: Columbia University Press, 2009.

Clancy, Tom. *Rainbow Six*. New York: Berkley Books, 1998.

Cronin, Audrey Kurth. "What is Really Changing? Change and Continuity in Global Terrorism." In *The Changing Character of War*, edited by Hew Strachan and Sibylle Scheipers. New York: Oxford University Press, 2011.

Deutch, John. "Terrorism." *Foreign Policy* 108 (1997): 10–22.

Donnelly, Thomas, Donald Kagan, and Gary Schmitt. *Rebuilding America's Defenses: Strategy, Forces and Resources for a New Century*. Washington, DC: Project for the New American Century, 2000. http://www.information clearinghouse.info/pdf/RebuildingAmericasDefenses.pdf.

Emmerich, Roland, and Dean Devlin. *Independence Day*. Directed by Roland Emmerich. MPEG-4 video file, 2 hr 24 min. Los Angeles: Twentieth Century Fox, 1996.

Falkenrath, Richard A. "Problems of Preparedness—US Readiness for a Domestic Terrorist Attack." *International Security* 25, no. 4 (2001): 147–86.

Faludi, Susan. *The Terror Dream: Fear and Fantasy in Post-9/11 America*. New York: Metropolitan Books, 2007.

Flynn, Kevin and Gary Gerhardt. *The Silent Brotherhood: Inside America's Racist Underground*. New York: Free Press, 1989.

Franklin, H. Bruce. *War Stars: The Superweapon and the American Imagination*. Revised and expanded edition. Amherst: University of Massachusetts Press, 2008.

Gibson, James William. *Warrior Dreams: Paramilitary Culture in Post-Vietnam America*. New York: Hill and Wang, 1994.

Hamm, Mark S. *Terrorism as Crime: From Oklahoma City to Al-Qaeda and Beyond*. New York: New York University Press, 2007.

Hoffman, Bruce. *Inside Terrorism*. Revised and expanded edition. New York: Columbia University Press, 2006.

Johnson, David K. *The Lavender Scare: The Cold War Persecution of Gays and Lesbians in the Federal Government*. Chicago: University of Chicago Press, 2004.

Kaplan, David E. "Aum Shinrikyo (1995)." In *Toxic Terror: Assessing Terrorist Use of Chemical and Biological Weapons*, edited by Jonathan B. Tucker, 207–26. Belfer Center Studies in International Security. Cambridge, MA: MIT Press, 2000.

Laqueur, Walter. "Postmodern Terrorism." *Foreign Affairs* 75, no. 5 (1996): 24–36.

Libby, Lewis. "Legal Authority for a Domestic Military Role in Homeland Defense." In *The New Terror: Facing the Threat of Biological and Chemical Weapons*, edited by Sidney D. Drell, Abraham D. Sofaer, and George D. Wilson, 305–27. Hoover National Security Forum Series. Stanford: Hoover Institution Press, 1999.

Lifton, Robert Jay. *Superpower Syndrome: America's Apocalyptic Confrontation with the World*. New York: Nation Books, 2003.

Lodal, Jan. *The Price of Dominance: The New Weapons of Mass Destruction and Their Challenge to American Leadership*. New York: Council on Foreign Relations Press, 2001.

Macdonald, Andrew [William L. Pierce]. *The Turner Diaries*. Arlington, VA: National Vanguard Books, 1980. First published in 1978.

May, Elaine Tyler. *Homeward Bound: American Families in the Cold War Era*. Fully revised and updated 20th anniversary edition. New York: Basic Books.

NRO Symposium. "Can Marriage Be Saved?" *National Review Online*. July 23, 2011. http://www.nationalreview.com/article/272527/can-marriage-be-saved-nro-symposium.

Oehler, Gordon C. "Warning and Detection." In *The New Terror: Facing the Threat of Biological and Chemical Weapons*, edited by Sidney D. Drell, Abraham D. Sofaer, and George D. Wilson, 138–54. Hoover National Security Forum Series. Stanford: Hoover Institution Press, 1999.

Puar, Jasbir K. *Terrorist Assemblages: Homonationalism in Queer Times*. Next Wave. Durham: Duke University Press, 2007.

Roberts, Brad. "Terrorism and Weapons of Mass Destruction: Has the Taboo Been Broken?" *Politics and the Life Sciences* 15, no. 2 (1996): 216–17.

Rogin, Michael. *Independence Day*. BFI Modern Classics. London: British Film Institute, 1998.

————. *Ronald Reagan, the Movie: And Other Episodes in Political Demonology*. Berkeley: University of California Press, 1987.

Rose, Gideon. "Review: It Could Happen Here: Facing the New Terrorism." *Foreign Affairs* 78, no. 2 (1999): 131–37.

Rosenbaum, David M. "Nuclear Terror." *International Security* 1, no. 3 (1977): 140–61.

Sherry, Michael S. *In the Shadow of War: The United States since the 1930s*. New Haven: Yale University Press, 1995.

Simon, Jeffrey D. "Misunderstanding Terrorism." *Foreign Policy* 67 (1987): 104–20.

Sprinzak, Ehud and Idith Zertal Sprinzak. "Avenging Israel's Blood (1946)." In *Toxic Terror: Assessing Terrorist Use of Chemical and Biological Weapons*, edited by Jonathan B Tucker, 17–41. Befer Center Studies in International Security. Cambridge, MA: MIT Press, 2000.

Stevens, Jacqueline. *Reproducing the State*. Princeton: Princeton University Press, 1999.

Tucker, Jonathan B. "Lessons from the Case Studies." In *Toxic Terror: Assessing Terrorist Use of Chemical and Biological Weapons*, edited by Jonathan B. Tucker, 249–69. Belfer Center Studies in International Security. Cambridge, MA: MIT Press, 2000.

11

Historicizing the Present in 9/11 Fiction

TODD KUCHTA

Near the end of Ian McEwan's *Saturday*, Henry Perowne sits in a London traffic jam caused by the historic 2003 protest against the impending invasion of Iraq. As the narrator tells us, Perowne "tries to see [this moment], or feel it, in historical terms. . . . But he can't quite trick himself into it. He can't feel his way past the iron weight of the actual. . . . He doesn't have the lyric gift to see beyond it" (168). Like Perowne, the novels inspired by 9/11 and the global "war on terror" repeatedly attempt to view the present with a perspective Fredric Jameson calls *historicity*. More than mere historical context, historicity involves "a perception of the present as history . . . a relationship to the present which somehow defamiliarizes it and allows us that distance from immediacy which is at length characterized as a historical perspective" (*Postmodernism*, 284). Jameson's hypothesis is that today, such a perspective is more difficult to achieve than in the heyday of the historical novel, "when contemplation of the past seemed able to renew our sense of our own reading present" (*Postmodernism*, 284–85). If all postmodern narrative struggles to historicize the present, I want to suggest that the first generation of 9/11 fiction by McEwan, Jonathan Safran Foer, Don DeLillo, and Mohsin Hamid does so in ways that challenge Jameson's notion of historicity. Rather than looking back on the past to elucidate the present, a hallmark of both the traditional historical novel and its postmodern variant, 9/11 novels feature characters engaged, like Perowne, in a hyperconscious effort to situate themselves in a present they perceive as a new historical reality. While such fiction may reproduce the widespread sense that "everything changed on 9/11," it also seeks to provide an orientation toward the present that theorists of classic postmodernism like Jameson and Linda Hutcheon are ill disposed to recognize. In what follows, I consider the limits of their approaches to historicizing the present and suggest how Slavoj Žižek and Michel Foucault may offer more fruitful ways to read the struggle for historicity in 9/11 fiction.

For some early commentators, 9/11 heralded the end of postmodernism—or a caricature of postmodern moral relativism and ironic detachment.[1] Yet the attacks and their aftermath also intensified postmodernity's "nanosecond culture" (Heise, 2) and its association with a "perpetual present" (Jameson, *Postmodernism,* 170). Minute increments of time mediated our experience of the attacks, attuning us ever more intensely to the momentary and the instantaneous. Cable news "tickers" began to crawl along our TV screens just hours into the coverage, feeding us a constant stream of information (Poniewozik). As if to control the chaos, we marshaled as much temporal and numerical precision as possible to describe the events, which we abbreviated to "9/11" and centered at "ground zero." The attacks and their aftermath spawned an entire culture of microtemporality, in which the passing moment's impending dangers and missed opportunities became a dominant structural device or thematic motif. The brief span of 102 minutes—the duration between the first plane crash and the second twin tower collapse—took on epic proportions, lending memorable titles to a *New York Times* bestseller and a TV documentary, while *The 9/11 Commission Report* devoted nearly as many pages to its own minute-by-minute account.[2] The seven minutes George Bush spent in a Florida classroom before responding to news of the second attack also gained agonizing magnitude, particularly in Michael Moore's *Fahrenheit 9/11.* Meanwhile, ticking time bomb scenarios began to dominate newscasts and policy debates, and to organize fictions like TV's *24* and Frédéric Beigbeder's novel *Windows on the World.*[3] Though perhaps less overtly, the works by McEwan, Foer, and DeLillo connote this altered temporality in their very titles—the diurnal precision of *Saturday,* the affective intensity of *Extremely Loud and Incredibly Close*, the impending doom of *Falling Man*.

But 9/11 fiction is not unique in its fascination with the present, which Ursula Heise identifies as a hallmark of postmodern narrative since Beckett, Borges, and the *nouveau roman* (31–32, 64–65). For Heise, the distinguishing feature of time in postmodern fiction is a "focus on the moment or the narrative present at the expense of larger temporal developments" (64). Invoking Jameson's notion of historicity, Heise concedes that while such gestures defamiliarize the present, they fail to muster "anything like a historical perspective" (74). Linda Hutcheon's notion of historiographic metafiction, which has become the paradigmatic genre of postmodern literature and the dominant category for discussing it, would appear more useful for tracing the relations between fiction, history, and the present. And yet, while works of historiographic metafiction sometimes incorporate the present into their narrative frame, Hutcheon's own approach often subordinates that present to history. Though she claims postmodernism "refuses to recuperate or dissolve either side of the dichotomy" between past and present (Hutcheon, 106), the past remains her privileged term. In describing postmodernism, she frequently invokes architect Paolo Portoghesi's phrase "the presence of the past," which lends its two key terms equal weight, implying that the past shapes the present just as the present colors our view of the past. But rather than emphasizing a historical perspective trained on the here and now, Hutcheon repeatedly imagines the present as turned toward history. She claims that postmodernism "articulate[s] the present in terms of the 'presentness' of the past" (34), imposing on the current moment a backward glance that recalls Walter Benjamin's angel of history. As Hutcheon affirms near her conclusion, "postmodernism's orientation toward 'the presence of the past'" aims "to make us look to the past from the acknowledged distance of the present" (230). Absent is any sense that our admittedly partial knowledge of the past might dwell more fully on our current moment.[4] Rather than historicizing the present, then, Hutcheon's postmodernism historicizes from a vantage that is self-consciously *of* the present, even as it empties that present of any historical significance other than shaping our view of the past.

Likewise, Jameson's notion of historicity is not without its limitations. His critique of postmodernism's impoverished historicity—its inability to historicize its own present—draws on Georg Lukács's reading of the nineteenth-century historical novel. That genre's significance, according to Lukács, lay not in depicting the past faithfully, nor in "alluding to contemporary events . . . but in bringing the past to life as the prehistory of the present, in giving poetic life to those historical, social and human forces which, in the course of a long evolution, have made our present-day life what it is and as we experience it" (53).[5] Eschewing direct representation of the contemporary moment, the traditional historical novel still managed to engage the present by endowing readers with a kind of peripheral vision. The subtitle of Sir Walter Scott's *Waverly*—'*Tis Sixty Years Since*—captures something of the effect, indirectly alluding to the present as both linked to and distinct from the past. But in postmodernity, Jameson argues, we have lost this capacity "to renew our sense of our own reading present" through "a contemplation of the past," although the rise of science fiction has helped to compensate for this loss.[6] As his praise of both the traditional historical novel and the genre of science fiction suggests, Jameson's notion of historicity requires some artificial means of closing off the present, bracketing it from the flow of time, and creating a "distance from immediacy" through "a process of reification" that disrupts "our immersion in the here and now" and lets us "grasp [the present] as a kind of thing" (*Postmodernism*, 284). If the traditional historical novel grasps the present by examining its prehistory, science fiction does so by imagining a possible future. In either case, Jameson's historical present appears unable to sustain direct fictional scrutiny, and can at best be thrown into relief by a sidelong glance toward some distinct past or future. His present can emerge only as the shadowy afterimage of that past or future, rather than a fictional subject in its own right.

While Jameson and Hutcheon differ on the relation between postmodern fiction, history, and the present, their views fail to accommodate the distinct situation of 9/11 novels, which struggle to construct a historical perspective in a present that refuses either to subordinate itself to the past or to be cordoned off and reified into "a kind of thing" (Jameson, *Postmodernism*, 284). If Hutcheon's "presence of the past" (230) cedes the contemporary moment to history, and Jameson's historicity demands a leap beyond the present, 9/11 fiction attempts to historicize the present from within the present itself, as it unfolds. It is not simply that 9/11 novels are not historical novels, whether in the traditional or postmodern sense (though they certainly view 9/11 in light of the past—as with the references to Dresden and Hiroshima in Foer, Baader-Meinhof in DeLillo, and the Enlightenment in McEwan). It is rather that 9/11 novels refuse to subordinate the present to history or to foreclose the present as a means of contemplating it.

Take the first U.S. novel to center on 9/11, Jonathan Safran Foer's *Extremely Loud and Incredibly Close*.[7] The novel recounts the quest of precocious nine-year-old Oskar Schell to unlock the secret of a key left behind by his father, who died in the World Trade Center. Drawing on a number of postmodern elements, the novel harnesses multiple narrators, integrates an array of diverse texts and images, celebrates *petits récits*, and embraces contingency. Oskar's father responds to his son's questions about the meaning of life with an incredulity toward metanarratives—"there doesn't have to be a reason. . . . We exist because we exist" (13)—while the novel also recalls historiographic metafiction by emphasizing the textuality of past events like the bombings of Hiroshima and Dresden.[8] Yet Oskar remains focused primarily on a present that continues to unfold. When he returns home from school on the morning of September 11, he discovers that the telephone answering machine has recorded and precisely timed five of his father's messages from inside the south tower. Oskar seeks to recapture the last moments before his father died—the irony being that Oskar is actually present for but unable to answer the last call his father makes just moments before the second tower collapses around him.

In his quest to compensate for his traumatic inaction, Oskar comes into contact with two characters who, like him, try to articulate the present while perceiving its fluid motion and larger trajectory. His grandfather, who suffers aphasia and communicates through a series of written notes and journals, compares his own writing to "a loaf of black bread that I left out one night." He later sees an "outline of the mouse that had eaten through it" and then "cut[s] the loaf into slices and s[ees] the mouse at each moment" (113). Though looking retrospectively on a past event, Oskar's grandfather strives to capture its perpetual unfolding as it moves toward the present. Oskar's grandmother offers a slightly different means of historicizing the present. Engaged in an autobiography whose "conclusion" appears to succeed where Tristram Shandy's failed, she eventually brings her past up to speed with the present: "I just made it up to the present moment," she declares upon finishing. "Just now. I'm all caught up with myself" (120). More than mere historical records, these are attempts to historicize the present as it continues to unfold. Like his grandfather, Oskar views the passage of time in relation to distinct moments, particularly those final messages his father left on the answering machine. But like his grandmother, Oskar wants to catch up with his present, in this case to compensate for the traumatic inaction that keeps him mired in the past.

And yet, for all its emphasis on the present as a process, Foer's novel falls back on a fundamentally nostalgic vision of history, a desire to retrieve a pre-traumatic past imagined as innocent or whole. This desire is reflected in the way that characters ultimately fetishize frozen moments, whether his grandfather's slices of time or his grandmother's belief that her life is now complete. In some ways, Oskar appears more equipped than his elders to view the present as history. Near the end of the novel, looking out over New York City from atop the Empire State Building, he declares "you can see what it's really like, instead of how it feels when you're in the middle of it" (245). But such a perspective is short lived, as the novel's closing lines and famed flip-book confirm. For all its reputed hokeyness, the flip-book of the falling man in reverse may come closer than anything else in the novel to historicizing the present by coordinating individual moments with the passage of time in order to satisfy a demand in the present. But the result is a mere reversal of history, a return to an impossible time when, as Oskar puts it in the novel's closing words, "we would have been safe" (326).

If Foer's attempt to historicize the present ultimately yields to a frozen or inverted past, the very title of Don DeLillo's *Falling Man* insists on the movement of the present, in this case its "unavoidable downward motion" (Versluys, 35). The novel begins with Keith Neudecker fleeing the north tower on 9/11 and unintentionally returning to his former home, where his estranged wife and son still reside. DeLillo captures Keith's initial response to the attacks with an avalanche of uncoordinated conjunctions: "It was not a street anymore but a world, a time and a space, of falling ash and near night. He was walking north though rubble and mud and there were people running past. . . . There was glass in his hair and face, marbled bolls of blood and light" (*Falling Man*, 3). Besides reflecting the chaos of 9/11, DeLillo's opening captures everyday objects in alarming new contexts: people with "shoes in their hands" "taking shelter under cars"; "standard sheets" of office paper falling from the sky; "runners who'd stopped" or "were walking backwards" (3–4). Whereas Jameson requires us to defamiliarize our present to perceive it historically, DeLillo reveals that 9/11 *imposes* such defamiliarization upon immediacy—and does so without recourse to a distinct past or future. DeLillo's characters constantly try to situate themselves in this new immediacy, often to account for what appears directly before them. Unaware that one of the twin towers has fallen, Keith assumes "one tower was blocking his view of the other tower, or the smoke was. . . . One tower made no sense" (21). His wife Lianne captures her own sense of defamiliarization and absence by adapting the first and third lines of a Bashō haiku: "*Even in New York—I long for New York*" (34). And days after the attacks, Keith stands next to a man at the perimeter of the twin tower rubble who simply repeats "I'm standing here" into his cell phone, a vain and incomplete attempt to capture the passing moment. Keith echoes the phrase when he returns to his own apartment the first time after the attacks (25, 27).[9]

As this last example suggests, DeLillo's characters often draw on repetition to comprehend the unfamiliarity of the present. It is a distinct form of repetition we can approach via Slavoj Žižek's account of what Lacan called the two deaths. For Lacan, any death or traumatic event must occur twice to be historicized. The second death is necessary for the initial, inexplicable trauma—the first death—to register itself meaningfully in the existing symbolic network. "When an event erupts for the first time," Žižek explains, "it is experienced as a contingent trauma, as an intrusion of a certain non-symbolized Real." This initial trauma Žižek calls a "non-historical place," one "which cannot be symbolized" until it is "retroactively produced" through repetition (*The Sublime*, 150). It is only through repetition that the event "finds its place in the symbolic network" (64–65). In doing so, the second death makes possible a historical interpretation of the initial, hitherto unrepresentable trauma. Žižek and others have drawn on Lacan's notion of two deaths to read 9/11 as a symbolic repetition of the fall of the Berlin Wall, which enabled us to begin historicizing the post-Cold War era that Francis Fukuyama prophesied as "the end of history." As Phillip Wegner explains, "it [was] only with the fall of the twin towers that the destruction of the symbolic universe of the Cold War [was] finally accomplished . . . in ways not possible in the immediate, uncertain aftermath of the Cold War" (9).[10] More recently, Žižek has described the 2008 financial crisis as an economic repetition of 9/11's political trauma, "since the collapse of the liberal-democratic political utopia on 9/11 did not affect the economic utopia of global market capitalism." In this account, the financial crisis finds its "historical meaning" as "the end of the economic face of Fukuyama's dream," whose first death took place on 9/11 (*First as Tragedy*, 5).

Falling Man enacts the pattern of Lacan's two deaths, even as DeLillo's characters struggle to extract historical significance from the symbolic repetition of traumatic events. Consider a crucial scene when Keith and Lianne watch a video replay of the planes striking the towers. "It still looks like an accident, the first one," Keith says. "I'm standing here thinking it's an accident." "Because it has to be," Lianne replies. "The way the camera sort of shows surprise." "But only the first one," they repeat to each other. "By the time the second plane appears," Keith adds, "we're all a little older and wiser" (*Falling Man*, 135). Note the variety of repetitions here: the newly reunited couple replaying the attack, the second plane following the first into the twin towers, Lianne re-experiencing Keith's apparent death, and the couple repeating their words to each other. These repetitions reinforce what Keith and Lianne and the camera itself seem to intuit—that the second crash has created a space within the new symbolic order to assimilate the trauma of the first crash. At the same time, this moment fails to initiate the historicizing process of the second death. Keith's repetition of the man on the cell phone when he says "*I'm standing here* thinking it's an accident" precisely captures this dilemma, grounding Keith in a definitive time and space even as it reveals his faulty perception of what he sees (emphasis added). Likewise, while the second plane crash makes Keith and Lianne "a little older and wiser," the contingent trauma of the first plane lingers, overshadowing the historical perspective that the second plane, or the couple's reunion, or their replaying of the attacks, or their repeated words to each other, should impart. Engaged in a series of repetitions that should historicize the present, Keith and Lianne experience a disorienting profusion of symbolic second deaths that seem to prolong rather than terminate the "non-historical" *durée* of a traumatic present (Žižek, *The Sublime,* 150). Keith's wayward reunion with Lianne, his extramarital affair, and his descent into gambling only reinforce his difficulty in processing that trauma.

In contrast, Lianne appears better able to historicize the present after witnessing the titular falling man, performance artist David Janiak, who surprises unsuspecting bystanders by diving unannounced from buildings and bridges with the aid of a hidden safety harness. Lianne happens upon two of Janiak's "performances" within thirty-six days of 9/11 (DeLillo, *Falling Man*, 170); three years later she comes across his obituary—he has died, ironically, of natural causes. Lianne learns that just as Janiak relied on the most basic safety gear, avoiding bungee cords or pulleys that would "absorb the shock of longer falls" (220), he seemed intent on shocking his viewers rather than cushioning the traumatic blow of his apparent death. Janiak refused to disclose anything that would elucidate his purpose: none of his falls were "announced in advance," none were "designed to be recorded by a photographer," and Janiak denied all opportunities to discuss his intentions (220, 222). If anything, he seemed bent on reappropriating the media monopoly over 9/11, and Lianne wonders whether his goal was for viewers to "spread the word" about his actions "intimately, as in the towers and in the hijacked planes" (165).

But to what end? While critics interpret Janiak's performances in a variety of ways, I'm aware of none who pursue his links to the avant-garde. Yet these links may shed light on Janiak's attempts to historicize the present by symbolically repeating the deaths of those who fell from the twin towers. Lianne not only discovers that Janiak trained in the avant-garde theatrical methods of Meyerhold, Grotowski, and Vakhtangov, but she also discovers an anecdote of Janiak "as a Brechtian dwarf, assault[ing] another actor, seemingly trying to rip the man's tongue out" (DeLillo, *Falling Man*, 223). While this anecdote calls to mind Janiak's own refusal to announce or explain his performances, the reference to Brecht suggests that Janiak may stage his falls as a form of *Verfremdungseffekt*, the alienation effect Brecht developed to estrange theatre audiences from the seemingly natural qualities of realistic drama, with the goal of demystifying what appeared eternal and inevitable in bourgeois society. Janiak does not perform behind the fourth wall of the proscenium, of course, but his tactics recall the motives Brecht himself articulated for the alienation effect: "to historicize the incidents portrayed" and to "keep their impermanence always before our eyes, so that our own period can be seen to be impermanent too" (96, 190). In this context, it is crucial that when Lianne first sees the falling man, New York is adjusting to the new normal after 9/11. Amid familiar sites at Grand Central—"tourists taking pictures" and "commuters in running flurries"—Lianne also notices "troopers in tight clusters or guardsmen with dogs." Despite her cognitive dissonance at these signs of heightened security, she thinks "this is routine and always will be" (32). It is precisely at this moment that Janiak appears, estranging a dangerous new present that risks congealing into normalcy. In doing so, Janiak is not so much repeating or re-presenting 9/11 as using its imagery to provoke contemplation in the present. As John Duvall puts it, Janiak's act "bypasses representation and functions as a form of witness" (167). "Rather than simply represent what happened when people jumped from the World Trade Center, Janiak's art extends the moment of 9/11 into the present" (161). Though Janiak's provocations elicit anger from spectators and the mayor alike, Lianne responds in ways that, unlike Keith, suggest a reckoning with her own post-9/11 present. What strikes Lianne upon seeing the falling man's first performance—perhaps her first symbolic repetition of 9/11—is "the awful openness of it" (33). But a second viewing inspires her to end her work with Alzheimer's patients, a painful decision that nonetheless marks her movement beyond her own immediate post-9/11 coping mechanism (170). This is reinforced when Lianne sees Janiak's obituary: having concluding her research on the falling man after his death, she appears ready to end her desultory relationship with Keith, going "to sleep finally on her husband's side of the bed" (224). Ironically, then, it is Janiak's actual death that seems to inspire in Lianne the kind of contemplation intended by his symbolic repetition of 9/11 deaths.

Ian McEwan's *Saturday* is likewise preoccupied with an attempt to historicize the present as it unfolds. Set on February 15, 2003, the day of the largest political demonstration in London's history, the novel centers on Henry Perowne, a neurosurgeon and "an habitual observer of his own moods" (5), whose hyperconscious attention to temporal and spatial situatedness recalls DeLillo's characters in *Falling Man*. Indeed, McEwan devotes lengthy and extensively detailed passages to the series of events that make up Perowne's day, from his early morning view of a fiery jetliner crossing London's skyline to a series of parallel "crashes"—a collision with a colleague on the squash court and, more significantly, a fender bender that results in a domestic break-in and threats of violence against his family. To some extent, these symbolic repetitions recall the multiple second deaths of *Falling Man*. Yet in discussing *Saturday*, I want to suggest that Michel Foucault's view of the present tells us more about the limits of this novel's historical perspective.

Foucault's inspired phrase "history of the present" derives from *Discipline and Punish* (31), but his most sustained thoughts on this idea come in his late work on Immanuel Kant. Foucault claims that Kant's brief essay "What is Enlightenment?" invents a new orientation toward the present: unlike the Cartesian question "Who am I?" that applies to anyone at any time, Kant asks "What are we? in a very precise moment of history" (*The Essential Foucault*, 133–34). Moreover, whereas earlier philosophers viewed the present as a distinct era (Plato), a herald of the future (Augustine), or a transition (Vico), Kant imagined the present "in an almost entirely negative way, as an *Ausgang*, an 'exit,' a 'way out' . . . He is not seeking to understand the present on the basis of a totality or of a future achievement. He is looking for a difference: What difference does today introduce with respect to yesterday?" (*The Essential Foucault*, 44–45). Refusing to make the present a totality or *telos* as does Jameson, this "negative" view of the present as an exit or difference chimes with the defamiliarizing strategies of Foucauldian genealogy, the historical approach that unravels the seeming inevitability of the present by looking for alternate lines of development or emergence in our past.[11] Foucault also discovers in Kant a crucial ethos toward the present. Updating the Enlightenment's self-imposed task—"Dare to know"—Foucault derives from Kant the need for "a critical ontology of ourselves," an obligation to view ourselves as historically distinct rather than as some timeless or eternal version of humanity. The ontology of ourselves requires "an attitude, an ethos . . . in which the critique of what we are is at one and the same time an analysis of the limits imposed on us and an experiment with the possibility of going beyond them" (*The Essential Foucault*, 56). This ethos involves challenging the historical forces that have made us. Its purpose is "not to discover what we are but to refuse what we are" (134). Such a refusal is crucial to Foucault's history of the present, marking our capacity both to recognize the forces that shape our current selves and to release us from their grasp. In this sense, Foucault would historicize the present by neither bracketing it off like Jameson, nor symbolically repeating it like Žižek, but by refusing it, rejecting it, escaping it.

Saturday evokes and in some ways aspires to a Foucaltian view of the present. Perowne is a disciple of the Enlightenment who praises freedom of thought, reason, and self-determination. He counts Newton and Bach among his heroes and even lives in a Regency-era home. More specifically, Perowne's thoughts are reminiscent of Foucault's desire to historicize the present by specifying its difference with respect to yesterday.[12] "And now, what days are these?" Perowne asks himself early in the novel (4), keeping his finger on the pulse of this new moment when "airliners look different in the sky" and "misunderstanding is general all over the world" (16, 39). He also diagnoses the changes in himself. Awaiting the latest word on the crashed jetliner, he notices that "his nerves, like tautened strings, vibrate obediently with each news 'release'" (181). "It's part of the new order," he thinks, "this narrowing of mental freedom, of his right to roam. Not so long ago his thoughts ranged more unpredictably, over a longer list of subjects" (180). Despite his ability to recognize these restricting forces, Perowne falters in his self-imposed task to imagine the present as an exit from them. Indeed, while consciously admitting to the shortcomings of "the new order," he just as often reverts to an idyllic view of the present as a bourgeois utopia: "if the present dispensation is wiped out now," he thinks, "the future will look back on us as gods . . . blessed by supermarket cornucopias, torrents of accessible information, warm clothes that weigh nothing, extended life-spans, wondrous machines" (77). Such moments, which the narrator calls Perowne's "aggressive celebration of the times" (78), ultimately outweigh his desire to transcend the historical limits of the present—limits he justifiably sees as imposed by the global "war on terror."

In a scene that underscores his unfulfilled desire for illumination and transcendence, for an enlightened exit from the confines of the present, Perowne sits in a late-afternoon traffic jam:

> He tries to see it, or feel it, in historical terms, this moment . . . when the unprecedented wealth of masses at serious play in the unforgiving modern city makes for a sight that no previous age can have imagined. Ordinary people! Rivers of light! He wants to make himself see it as Newton might,

or his contemporaries Boyle, Hooke, Wren, Willis—those clever, curious
men of the English Enlightenment. . . . Mentally he shows it off to them
. . . . All this teeming illumination would be wondrous if only he could see
it through their eyes. But he can't quite trick himself into it. . . . He doesn't
have the lyric gift to see beyond it. (168)

Attempting to historicize the present from the perspective of his
Enlightenment heroes, Perowne is either unconvinced by his own paeans to
the present or lacking the "lyric gift" of his daughter and father-in-law, poets
both. But his dissatisfaction turns toward yet another "aggressive celebration
of the times" when Perowne's dyspeptic father-in-law, John Grammaticus,
arrives for a family gathering. Perowne finds him looking at the nearby British
Telecom Tower and wondering how Robert Adam, the neoclassical architect who designed Perowne's square, would see it. Perowne responds with
unqualified optimism: "All that glass, and the unsupported height, would have
amazed him. So would the electric light." But Grammaticus is having none
of it: "Adam would have been stunned by the ugliness of that glass thing. No
human scale. Top heavy. No grace, no warmth. It would have put fear in his
heart. If that's going to be our religion, he'd've said to himself, then we're
truly fucked" (197).

This face-off reveals the limits of *Saturday*'s attempts to historicize the
present. While Perowne and Grammaticus both attempt to defamiliarize
the present through the eyes of the Enlightenment, McEwan can broker no
compromise between Perowne's "rivers of light" and Grammaticus's "we're
truly fucked." In this sense, both characters exhibit what Foucault considers
"one of the most harmful habits . . . in modern thought," namely, a view of
the present as an exceptional rupture, whether as a high point or low point
in history. Arguing that "the time we live in is not *the* unique or fundamental
or irruptive point in history," Foucault refuses "the facile, rather theatrical
declaration" that our present moment is one of either "total perdition, in the
abyss of darkness, or a triumphal daybreak." As Foucault puts it, we must
view the present as both "a time like any other" and "a time that is never quite
like any other" (*The Essential Foucault*, 93–94).

If *Saturday* ultimately founders as a Foucauldian history of the present, I
want to close with a work whose own conclusion resonates powerfully with

Foucault's view of the present as both an exit and an obligation to refuse what we are. Mohsin Hamid's 2007 novel *The Reluctant Fundamentalist* is narrated by Changez, a Pakistani immigrant who wins a scholarship to Princeton, then lands a job with a prestigious U.S. financial firm, but grows increasingly resentful toward America following 9/11. Eventually returning to Lahore, Changez becomes a university lecturer and admits to vague connections with jihadist students. Changez narrates his tale in the second person to an American male, an undercover agent or government assassin, over a long evening meal. Though Changez offers himself as a courteous host and appears intent on demonstrating the good will of Pakistanis, his tale of disillusionment with the United States casts a shadow over the novel. Having safely escorted the American to his hotel in the novel's closing pages, Changez attempts to shake his hand, but a sinister figure—a surly waiter from earlier that evening—approaches. As the American reaches into his jacket, Changez attempts to disrupt the exchange of gunfire that seems inevitable, politely reminding the American of their "shared intimacy," and hoping that the "glint of metal" he sees is merely "the holder of your business cards" (Hamid, 184).

In a powerful act of historicizing the present, Hamid closes the novel before gunfire breaks out. As Changez tells the American before the other man closes in, "you should not imagine that we Pakistanis are all potential terrorists, just as we should not imagine that you Americans are all undercover assassins" (183). Despite this caveat, it's clear that Changez *is* in some way involved with potentially dangerous militants and the American *is* a government agent. At the same time, Hamid suggests that we might refuse the positions we inhabit and play our hands differently. Given what our histories have made us, Hamid asks, how do we now respond? Like a Foucauldian history of the present, *The Reluctant Fundamentalist* compels us to grasp our current moment as an opportunity for an exit—not a refusal to engage with the present, but what Foucault calls "an analysis of the limits imposed on us and an experiment with the possibility of going beyond them" (*The Essential Foucault*, 56). The novel does not attempt, like Foer, to freeze or rewind history to capture some lost, illusory innocence. Nor does it require DeLillo's symbolic repetition of an originating trauma, or McEwan's recourse to an idealized or demonized view of the present in relation to the past. Rather,

Hamid reminds us of the historical potential of the present—and of our own ability to alter that history before it's too late.

NOTES

1.   Though I hesitate to use "9/11" to designate the events of 11 September 2001, I retain it here for brevity. For early responses to 9/11 as the end of postmodernism, see Roger Rosenblatt, "The Age of Irony Comes to an End," *Time*, September 24, 2001, http://content.time.com/time/magazine/article/0,9171,1000893,00.html; and Edward Rothstein, "Attacks on U.S. Challenge Postmodern True Believers," *NYTimes.com*, September 22, 2001, http://www.nytimes.com/2001/09/22/arts/22CONN.html.

2.   The full title of Jim Dwyer and Kevin Flynn's book is *102 Minutes: The Untold Story of the Fight to Survive inside the Twin Towers* (2005). The unrelated History Channel documentary, *102 Minutes that Changed America* (2008), which uses amateur footage to recreate events in nearly real time, also runs to 102 minutes. For the 9/11 commission's chronological account, see the National Commission on Terrorist Attacks Upon the United States, *The 9/11 Commission Report* (New York: Norton, 2004), 1–46 and 285–323.

3.   Like *102 Minutes that Changed America*, *24* is organized around a "real-time" sequence of events, while each chapter of *Windows on the World* reflects a single minute between 8:30 and 10:29 am on 9/11.

4.   Also see Mark Currie, *About Time: Narrative, Fiction, and the Philosophy of Time* (Edinburgh: Edinburgh University Press, 2007), who claims that the category of historiographic metafiction both "distort[s]" our sense of contemporary literature and diminishes the richness of the narrative present by relegating it to "a place from which we continuously revise stories about the past" (26, 6).

5.   Georg Lukács, *The Historical Novel*, translated by Hannah and Stanley Mitchell (Lincoln: University of Nebraska Press, 1983). Lukács denies that the historical novel should seek to depict the past with "historical fidelity," insisting that "the more remote an historical period . . . the more the action must concern itself with bringing these conditions plastically before us, so that we should . . . re-experience them as a phase of mankind's development which concerns and moves us" (42). At the same time, Lukács notes that "[Sir Walter] Scott very seldom speaks

of the present" (32) and that doing so was "a practice which Pushkin cruelly ridiculed in the work of Scott's incompetent imitators" (53).

6.   Fredric Jameson, *Archaeologies of the Future: The Desire Called Utopia and Other Science Fictions* (London: Verso, 2005). Jameson links the decline of the historical novel with the rise of science fiction, which "registers some nascent sense of the future . . . in the space on which a sense of the past had once been inscribed" (286). If the historical novel allowed readers to historicize their present through an indirect comparison with the past, science fiction affords a similar thought experiment, "transforming our own present into the determinate past of something yet to come" (288). By projecting us forward in time, science fiction alters our reading present into the past history of a fully realized if fictional future. Also see Fredric Jameson, *Postmodernism, or, the Cultural Logic of Late Capitalism* (Durham: Duke University Press, 1991), 284–85.

7.   Jonathan Safran Foer's *Extremely Loud and Incredibly Close* (Boston: Houghton Mifflin, 2005) and Ian McEwan's *Saturday* (London: Vintage, 2006) were both released in the U.S. in April 2005, though *Saturday* first appeared in the UK in January of that year.

8.   Indeed, Foer's account of Dresden appears to make unacknowledged use of sources available online. See Kristiaan Versluys, *Out of the Blue: September 11 and the Novel* (New York: Columbia University Press, 2009), 94, 199n7.

9.   DeLillo claims he stood next to a man repeating that phrase when he visited the rubble of the twin towers ten days after 9/11. See Don DeLillio, "In the Ruins of the Future: Reflections on Terror and Loss in the Shadow of September," *Harper's Magazine* (December 2001): 38.

10.   Phillip E. Wegner, *Life Between Two Deaths, 1989–2001: U.S. Culture in the Long Nineties* (Durham: Duke University Press, 2009); Slavoj Žižek, *Iraq: The Borrowed Kettle* (London: Verso, 2004). Wegner builds on Žižek's claim that 9/11 brought an end to Fukuyama's "end of history" thesis, which replaced communism's failed utopian project with a "utopia of global capitalist liberal democracy." Žižek argues that "the 'end of utopia' repeated itself in a self-reflexive gesture: the ultimate utopia was the very notion that, after the end of utopias, we were at the 'end of history'" (*Iraq*, 122–23).

11.   Gary Gutting, "Michael Foucault: A User's Manual," in *The Cambridge Companion to Foucault*, edited by Gary Gutting (Cambridge: Cambridge University Press, 1994), 1–27. As Gutting suggests, Foucault's "genealogical method can be understood in terms of his desire to write histories of the present" (12). "Whereas

much traditional history tries to show that where we are is inevitable, given the historical causes revealed by its account, Foucault's histories aim to show the contingency—and hence surpassability—of what history has given us. Intolerable practices and institutions present themselves as having no alternative. . . . Foucault's histories aim to remove this air of necessity by showing that the past ordered things quite differently and that the processes leading to our present practices and institutions were by no means inevitable" (10).

12. This, despite McEwan's underhanded allusions to Foucault: Perowne recalls his daughter at Oxford being convinced "that madness was a social construct" (*Saturday*, 92), and on the same page, Perowne is down the street from a pub named after Panopticon designer Jeremy Bentham.

WORKS CITED

Brecht, Bertolt. *Brecht on Theatre: The Development of an Aesthetic*. Edited and translated by John Willett. New York: Hill and Wang, 1997.

Currie, Mark. *About Time: Narrative, Fiction, and the Philosophy of Time*. Edinburgh: Edinburgh University Press, 2007.

DeLillo, Don. *Falling Man*. New York: Scribner, 2007.

———. "In the Ruins of the Future: Reflections on Terror and Loss in the Shadow of September." *Harper's Magazine*. December 2001, 33–40.

Duvall, John N. "Witnessing Trauma: *Falling Man* and Performance Art." In *Don DeLillo: Mao II, Underworld, Falling Man*, edited by Stacey Olster, 152–68. London: Continuum, 2011.

Foer, Jonathan Safran. *Extremely Loud and Incredibly Close*. Boston: Houghton Mifflin, 2005.

Foucault, Michel. *Discipline and Punish: The Birth of the Prison*. Translated by Alan Sheridan. New York: Vintage, 1979.

———. *The Essential Foucault: Selections from Essential Works of Foucault, 1954–1984*. Edited by Paul Rabinow and Nikolas Rose. New York: New Press, 2003.

Gutting, Gary. "Michel Foucault: A User's Manual." In *The Cambridge Companion to Foucault*, edited by Gary Gutting, 1–27. Cambridge: Cambridge University Press, 1994.

Hamid, Mohsin. *The Reluctant Fundamentalist*. Orlando: Harcourt, 2007.

Heise, Ursula. *Chronoschisms: Time, Narrative, and Postmodernism*. Cambridge: Cambridge University Press, 1997.

Hutcheon, Linda. *A Poetics of Postmodernism: History, Theory, Fiction*. New York: Routledge, 1988.

Jameson, Fredric. *Archaeologies of the Future: The Desire Called Utopia and Other Science Fictions.* London: Verso, 2005.

———. *Postmodernism, or, the Cultural Logic of Late Capitalism*. Durham: Duke University Press, 1991.

Lukács, Georg. *The Historical Novel*. Translated by Hannah and Stanley Mitchell. Lincoln: University of Nebraska Press, 1983.

McEwan, Ian. *Saturday*. 2005. London: Vintage, 2006.

National Commission on Terrorist Attacks Upon the United States. *The 9/11 Commission Report: Final Report of the National Commission on Terrorist Attacks Upon the United States*. New York: Norton, 2004.

Poniewozik, James. "The Tick, Tick, Tick of the Times." *Time*. November 24, 2010. http://content.time.com/time/specials/packages/article/0,28804,2032304_2032745_2032850,00.html.

Rosenblatt, Roger. "The Age of Irony Comes to an End." *Time*. September 24, 2001. http://content.time.com/time/magazine/article/0,9171,1000893,00.html.

Rothstein, Edward. "Attacks on U.S. Challenge Postmodern True Believers." *NYTimes.com*. September 22, 2001. http://www.nytimes.com/2001/09/22/arts/22CONN.html.

Versluys, Kristiaan. *Out of the Blue: September 11 and the Novel*. New York: Columbia University Press, 2009.

Wegner, Phillip E. *Life Between Two Deaths, 1989–2001: U.S. Culture in the Long Nineties*. Durham: Duke University Press, 2009.

Žižek, Slavoj. *First as Tragedy, Then as Farce*. London: Verso, 2009.

———. *Iraq: The Borrowed Kettle*. London: Verso, 2004.

———. *The Sublime Object of Ideology*. London: Verso, 1989.

12

Reading 9/11 Through the Holocaust in Philip Roth's *The Plot Against America* and Art Spiegelman's *In the Shadow of No Towers*

STELLA SETKA

Much of the literature published in the decade following 9/11 has attempted to define, identify, or explain the terrorist figure. In Jess Walters' *The Zero*, for example, a former police officer named Brian Remy sifts through the fragments of papers that litter the streets of New York in the aftermath of 9/11, in the service of a shadow intelligence agency known only as the Department of Documentation, in an effort to uncover an elusive terror cell at large in the city. Mohsin Hamid's *The Reluctant Fundamentalist* asks readers to consider the perspective of the Muslim Other by asking us to view the post-9/11 landscape through the eyes of an American-educated Pakistani man named Changez, whose exposure to the tide of racism in America following 9/11 leads him to sympathize with the terrorists. Similarly, John Updike's *Terrorist* invites readers into the mind of eighteen-year-old Ahmad Ashmawy Mulloy, a half-Irish, half-Egyptian boy who decides to become a terrorist when he feels his Islamic faith threatened by the hedonism and materialism of mainstream American culture. Although these novels approach terrorism from different angles, they are all concerned with driving factors—such as globalization and American exceptionalism—that contribute to the making of terrorists.

Two notable exceptions to this rule are Philip Roths' *The Plot Against America* and Art Spiegelman's *In the Shadow of No Towers,* both of which are marked by the relative absence of an external terrorist threat. In these texts, what terrorizes is not external, but is rather a threat that comes from within. These works open up new spaces for reading the trauma of 9/11 not simply as the tragic story of a single day in 2001, but as a traumatic event that shares referents with other catastrophes in history, most notably the state-sanctioned, systematic destruction of Europe's Jews. This connection becomes more apparent when we remember that the Holocaust began with the implementation of laws that denied Jews their civil liberties and human rights. Similarly, the works of both Roth and Spiegelman identify the repression of civil liberties in America following 9/11 as the source of their terror. In a sense, the authors of these works are infinitely more concerned with the politicization of 9/11 than they are with the terrorist attacks themselves.

As Margaret Scanlan notes in her essay, "Strange Times to be a Jew: Alternative History after 9/11," the patriotic narrative of the War on Terror that was constructed in the immediate aftermath of 9/11 "overwhelmed subtler or more critical accounts of September 11," thus potentially making it problematic for writers who, like Roth and Spiegelman, wished to explore the ramifications of mobilizing military and political forces under the banner of patriotism (503). Spiegelman himself speaks to this in his preface to his book, where he says that unlike the "distinguished newspapers and magazines" of Europe, mainstream American publications—which "had actively solicited work" from him prior to 9/11—"fled" when he sought to publish excerpts from his text (preface). Roth, on the other hand, preempted any such expression of mainstream disapproval by publishing an essay, entitled "The Story Behind *The Plot Against America*," in the *New York Times Book Review* just prior to his novel's release. There, Roth describes the genesis of his novel, and explains that, contrary to the assumptions of reviewers who asserted that the book was written as a critique of the Bush Administration, his book was instead an "exercise in historical imagination" that asks why a Holocaust didn't happen in America when it could have. Most significant for my analysis is Roth's insistence that *The Plot Against America* is not a "roman à clef to the present moment," but a strict reconstruction of the early 1940s as they would have been with Charles Lindbergh as president ("Story"). However, his conclusion that the election of George W. Bush "reaffirmed" his understanding of history as radically unpredictable seems to only reinforce the reading of this text as, if not a novel dedicated to the memory of 9/11, a novel that is instead profoundly influenced by the aftermath of the event. Roth writes within the frame of a realist narrative, but rather than directly challenging the mainstream desire for a grand narrative of 9/11, he engages in subterfuge by representing post-9/11 America as seen through the lens of the 1940s—albeit through an alternate history in which Lindbergh wins the 1940 election and fans the flames of fascism in the US. These events are conveyed in retrospect by a fictional Philip Roth, who recounts the fear and uncertainty he felt as a child growing up under the anti-Semitic Lindbergh Administration.

However, it must be noted that *The Plot Against America* does not present direct one-to-one allegorical representations of present-day figures or situations. Unlike Bush, who relentlessly pursued war, Lindbergh wins the approval of America's Greatest Generation by running on an isolationist platform and, as a result, delays America's entry into World War II. The Other under attack in the novel is not Muslim, but Jewish, and the plot against America is not a terrorist plot concocted in the Middle East, but the "infiltration of inferior blood" of war-mongering, "loudmouthed Jews" whose presumed goal is to take over the God-fearing, Christian United States (*The Plot*, 14). I want to emphasize that the text is not as interested in faithfully mirroring the present as it is in revealing the equally constructed and contingent nature of both history and fiction. Roth explains in both his novel and his essay that "Turned wrong way round, the relentless unforeseen was what we schoolchildren studied as 'History,' harmless history, where everything unexpected in its own time was chronicled on the page as inevitable. The terror of the unforeseen is what the science of history hides, turning a disaster into an epic" (*The Plot*, 113–14). Here, Roth asks his readers to unlearn what they know about history so that they can imagine the events of the past as they unfold, and therefore empathize with the dreadful sense of "uncertainty" felt by the narrator and his family, an uncertainty that parallels what readers themselves experience as they confront the unknowns of the post-9/11 landscape (*The Plot*, 84). To underscore this idea, Roth makes calculated use of the word "terror," which calls to mind Bush's declaration of the War on Terror, and the way that the narrative of this "war" began with an act of storytelling that reached epic proportions leading up to the invasion of Iraq. Further, as Dan Shiffman argues, "it is hard to read Roth's statement about the tendency to turn disaster into an epic without thinking of former President Bush, a man Roth describes as 'unfit to run a hardware store let alone a nation'. . . who envisioned the nation's response to the terrorist attacks as a crusade of good against evil" (62). I suggest that Roth's narrative does not rewrite history simply to imagine what would have happened if America had adopted a pro-Nazi stance at the outset of WWII; indeed, revising history in this way would do little more than glorify the perceived righteousness of America's Greatest Generation by contrast, and would either be read as a nostalgic yearning for the good old days, or worse, an implicit endorsement of America's foreign policy post-9/11. Rather, it is in the text's selective alteration of historical references that Roth's critique of post-9/11 America and, in particular, the Bush Administration, is laid bare.

The most notable example of Roth's historical revisions pertains to Lindbergh's "Who are the War Agitators?" radio speech, delivered at an America First rally in Des Moines, Iowa on September 11, 1941. In this speech, Lindbergh excoriates those who strive, "for reasons which are not American" (*The Plot*, 371), to influence American foreign policy, thus reminding the conscious reader of Bush's repeated use of the term "un-American" to refer to those who protested the Iraq War. In Roth's rewriting of this event, Lindbergh delivers the speech a year earlier, in 1940, as the kickoff to his presidential campaign. Roth does not note the date of the event—September 11—in the diegetic narrative, but instead relegates this fact to the extradiegetic postscript. Roth's positioning of this date in his novel's postscript—which acts as something of an encyclopedia for the events and historical figures described in the novel—underscores the intertextuality of the novel with both the past and the present. Indeed, the postscript's self-declared "true chronology" prompts the reader to call into question what we can truly "know" about history, and reminds us of the way that history, like narrative itself, is constructed (363).

Further, as Hans Bertens suggests, our recognition of Roth's manipulation of history, and "the subsequent breaking of the illusion of reality," depends on our "familiarity with history," which calls into question what we can really know about the present (56). By manipulating the facts, Roth reveals just how useful alternative history—the achronic—is for producing historical thinking. Indeed, alternative history is a productive medium for prompting us to consider the ways in which we remember, forget, and even refashion the past, and Roth pushes the boundaries of this narrative mode with his novel, in effect not only asking us to imagine a fictive past that holds us in fear and suspense because its events are as yet unknown to us, but also to consider that past in relation to the present moment. Drawing on the early 1940s, Roth evokes "an undercurrent of Holocaust-born terror and [the] trauma beneath it all" to provide a foundation for the "perpetual fear" that pervades both his text and the post-9/11 landscape (De Cusatis, 706). In this way, Roth cleverly melds the fictional past with the present, creating an allegorical reading of the Bush Administration that challenges Republican-generated interpretations of the "facts" of 9/11 and the resulting political and military actions, all set against a backdrop that draws on our cultural knowledge of the Holocaust as a lens through which to interpret post-9/11 America. By distancing us from the present and challenging the means by which history is crafted, Roth creates a critical space from which to respond to traumas engendered by the gradual decay of civil liberties following the events of September 11.

Like *The Plot Against America,* Spiegelman's *In the Shadow of No Towers* suggests that the true trauma of 9/11 is what happened in its wake. As with his earlier graphic novel, *Maus,* Spiegelman's project here is "to produce the traumatic event as an object of knowledge and to program and thus transform its readers so that they are forced to acknowledge their relationship to posttraumatic culture" (Rothberg, 103). The challenge that Spiegelman undertakes in rendering the trauma of 9/11 is not simply a matter of recounting the isolated events of that day, but rather one that requires him to confront readers with the much larger trauma inflicted on the American public by the hijacking of US international and domestic policy by the Bush Administration.

For many readers, the connection between *In the Shadow of No Towers* and *Maus* is obvious, for it is through the conceptual lens of the Holocaust that Spiegelman initially experiences 9/11. In his preface to the text, "The Sky is

Falling!," Spiegelman himself invites the connection between these two graphic novels by explaining the relationship between the Holocaust and 9/11: "Before 9/11 my traumas were all more or less self-inflicted, but out-running the toxic cloud that had moments before been the north tower of the World Trade Center left me reeling on that faultline where World History and Personal History collide—the intersection my parents, Auschwitz survivors, had warned me about when they taught me to always keep my bags packed" (preface). As a child of survivors and a secondhand witness to their trauma, Spiegelman has been conditioned to view the world and his own life through the "conceptual screen" of that experience (Versluys, 50). As a primary witness to 9/11 and its traumatic aftermath— indeed, his preface describes not only the burning towers, whose destruction he witnessed, but the fact that the Bush Administration "immediately instrumentalized the attack for [its] own agenda"—Spiegelman returns to some of the visual motifs he employed in his earlier work as a means of articulating the burden of his "still-fresh wounds" (preface). This is most notable in his inclusion of the mouse figure.

Spiegelman vividly illustrates the imbrication of his secondary Holocaust trauma with his primary 9/11 trauma on the left panel of the second full page of his manuscript. In this section, we see two hulking figures hovering menacingly over a sleeping mouse-man who is slouched over a drafting table. Featured to the right of these figures is a series of stacked boxes that, taken together, resemble a smaller replica of the tower that he witnessed crumbling. Each of the four descending boxes contains a rendering of Spiegelman, who is struggling to recognize himself in a hand mirror. The self-proclaimed "heart-broken narcissist" seems to be drowning in his unfamiliar reflection (2). His trauma has so disoriented him that he is no longer able to recognize himself in the context of the traumatic landscape in which he lives. Read this way, we can interpret the evolution depicted in this series of frames as resulting from the traumatic aftermath of 9/11. He is "clean-shaven" prior to 9/11, and then, paralyzed by the Bush Administration's war-mongering appropriation of the event, grows a beard "while Afghans were shaving off theirs" (2). In the third box down, we see again a clean-cut Spiegelman, who confesses that he has removed his beard after receiving some "bad reviews," likely referring to his experience of being shunned by the more prominent print media outlets for his unpatriotic views. The final box, in which Spiegelman appears with the head of a mouse, invites readers to recall *Maus*—in which Jews are depicted as mice and the Nazis as cats—and therefore suggests that he interprets his rejections as the result of a violation of his civil liberties, a violation that for him, as for Roth, recalls the oppressive policies of the Nazi regime.

The transition between the third and final boxes is particularly significant. In the third box, Spiegelman has attempted to amend his response to traumatic events to suit prevailing social attitudes that would interpret his questioning of American geopolitical strategy as unpatriotic, an act which ultimately leaves its own little wound. Rather than curbing his anxiety, however, this act of self-censorship ultimately causes him to reassume the guise of a mouse. Just as the mouse image signifies the victimized and suffering Jews in *Maus*, in Spiegelman's more recent text it represents his sense of powerlessness in the face of forces greater than he. When asked why he reassumed the mouse mask, Spiegelman explains, "I felt I'd really lost a personal sense of self in a way. . . . And there were certain sequences where that *Maus* mask was very convenient to have in place again" (Gross). The helplessness that Spiegelman describes here helps to explain why his mouselike doppelganger is slumped unconsciously over his drafting table in the frame to the left of the minitower. He is overwhelmed by the ominous figures flanking him on either side: to the right is a rather feline-looking Bush pointing a pistol at a mouselike depiction of Osama Bin Laden, who, in turn, wields a bloody scimitar. And although Spiegelman is "equally terrorized by Al-Qaeda and by his own government" (Versluys, 2), I argue that his decision to render Bin Laden as a mouselike character suggests, perhaps, that the Arab terrorists have been equally terrorized by the American government. In this sense, Spiegelman's rhetorical strategy mirrors Roth's substitution of the Muslim Other with a Jewish Other; that is, the text asks readers to remember that just as Jews were singled out by fascist propaganda machines as political scapegoats, so too have Muslims been singled out by the American government as insidious and dangerous enemies of the state.

The return of the mouse in this graphic novel represents the displaced return of history, marking the moment where the trauma of 9/11 recalls the earlier traumas represented by the "twin towers of Auschwitz and Hiroshima," from which America learned nothing and is thus destined to repeat in the course of its "same old deadly business as usual" (Spiegelman, 8). Indeed, the historical connection between Auschwitz and 9/11 is so pervasive for Spiegelman that he can literally smell it. "I remember my father trying to describe what Auschwitz smelled like," he muses. "The closest he got," Spiegelman continues, "was telling me it was . . . 'indescribable' . . . . That's exactly what the air in Lower Manhattan smelled like after September 11!" (8). For Spiegelman, the direct experience of trauma during and after 9/11 recalls the Holocaust trauma of his parents. While it is ethically problematic to equate the smoke arising from Ground Zero with the human ash filtering down from the smokestacks of Auschwitz, the traumatic associations that Spiegelman makes indicate the potential of history to haunt us and to compound the effect of current and future traumas.

In *The Terror Dream*, Susan Faludi argues that the post-9/11 world finds us "rummaging through the past to make sense of the disaster, as if the trauma of 9/11 had stirred some distant memory, reminded us of something disturbingly familiar. As if we had been here before, after all" (3). Both *The Plot Against America* and *In the Shadow of No Towers* engage the transhistorical by merging "fact and fiction, factuality and invention, historicity and imagination" as a means of testifying to a traumatic event that recalls, for the narrators of these texts, previous historical traumas (Palacios, 82). Roth and Spiegelman not only communicate their experience of trauma, but move beyond their personal experiences to consider the events of September 11 against the larger backdrop of traumatic history and cultural wounds. Thus, unlike many other mainstream writers who, as Ruth Franklin observes, "continue stubbornly to insist on turning their gaze inward, bizarrely searching for the answer to the question of 9/11 in America," rather than viewing it as "the product . . . of historical, religious, and political forces," Roth and Spiegelman turn their gazes outward, to the past, to find a paradigm through which to consider the "unreal" reality of the post-9/11 condition (Žižek, 19). Prescriptive demands to the contrary—namely, that successful 9/11 literature should act as a site of healing and working through—seem to overlook the important function that works like *The Plot Against America* and *In the Shadow of No Towers* serve, which is not only to testify to their readers the experience of trauma, but to resist the notion that widespread cultural traumas can be so easily resolved. For Roth and Spiegelman, the impetus to enact such swift healing makes the possibility of forgetting and thus repeating history all the more possible.

WORKS CITED

Bertens, Hans. "Postmodern U.S. Fiction." In *A Companion to Twentieth-Century United States Fiction*, edited by David Seed, 48–59. Malden, MA: Blackwell, 2009.

De Cusatis, Felice. "The Plot *of* 'America'; A Reading of Philip Roth's *The Plot Against America*." Paper presented at the 20th AISNA Conference, University of Torino, Torino, Italy. September 24–26, 2009.

Faludi, Susan. *The Terror Dream: Fear and Fantasy in Post-9/11 America*. New York: Metropolitan Books, 2007.

Franklin, Ruth. "The Stubborn, Inward Gaze of the Post-9/11 Novel." *New Republic*. August 24, 2011. http://www.newrepublic.com/article/books/magazine/94180/september-11-the-novel-turns-inward.

Gross, Terry. "Art Spiegelman and 'The Shadow of No Towers.'" *Fresh Air.* National Public Radio. September 16, 2004. http://www.npr.org/templates/story/story.php?storyId=3921871.

Palacios, José Antonio Gurpegui. *Alejandro Morales: Fiction Past, Present, Future Perfect*. Tempe: Bilingual Review, 1996.

Roth, Philip. *The Plot Against America*. New York: Houghton Mifflin, 2004.

———. "The Story Behind *The Plot Against America*." *NYTimes.com*. September 19, 2004. http://www.nytimes.com/2004/09/19/books/review/19ROTHL.html.

Rothberg, Michael. *Traumatic Realism: The Demands of Holocaust Representation*. Minneapolis: University of Minnesota Press, 2000.

Scanlan, Margaret. "Strange Times to Be a Jew: Alternative History after 9/11." *Modern Fiction Studies* 57, no. 3 (2011): 505–31. http://dx.doi.org/10.1353/mfs.2011.0067.

Shiffman, Dan. "*The Plot Against America* and History Post-9/11." *Philip Roth Studies* 5, no. 1 (Spring 2009): 61–73. http://muse.jhu.edu/journals/philip_roth_studies/v005/5.1.shiffman.html.

Spiegelman, Art. *In the Shadow of No Towers*. New York: Pantheon, 2004.

Versluys, Kristiaan. "Art Spiegelman's *In the Shadow of No Towers:* The Politics of Trauma." *Out of the Blue: September 11 and the Novel.* New York: Columbia University Press, 2009. 49–77.

Žižek, Slavoj. *Welcome to the Desert of the Real.* London: Verso, 2002.

PART 4

Narrative, Cinematic, and Visual Case Studies

13

Regarding Terror: The German Autumn and Contemporary Art

FABIAN WINKLER

The *Rote Armee Fraktion*, RAF (Red Army Faction, or often publically referred to as the Baader-Meinhof Gang), was a terrorist organization in Germany that radicalized the left-wing ideas of the 1968 German Student movement. Some argue that it was the only revolution—albeit belated—from within German society against the Third Reich. To further their ideological and political agenda, the RAF soon employed violent means of increasingly gruesome proportions, which put the democratic system of the still young Federal Republic of Germany under a severe stress test. The group officially disbanded in 1998. However, their crimes, specifically those culminating in the tragic events of the German Autumn in 1977 and their representation in German culture (literature, film, and the arts) continue to spark controversial debates. Apart from its violent actions of domestic terrorism, the RAF has also deeply split German society as only few other post-WWII radical organizations have. While this can be certainly attributed to the fact that these events are part of more recent German history, it can be also argued that it is because of a lack of the RAF's historic documentation and public debate outside of mass media representations.[1] In his essay *Zwischen Popkultur, Politik und Zeitgeschichte—Von der Schwierigkeit, die RAF zu historisieren* (Between Pop Culture, Politics and

History—About the Difficulty of Historicizing the RAF),[2] German historian Wolfgang Kraushaar talks about the lack of a historic discussion of the RAF as "white spots in the history of German terrorism."

Although recent film productions such as Uli Edel's 2008 movie *The Baader Meinhof Complex* probably paint the picture of this era best known to an international audience, many German visual artists have, since the early 1970s, responded quite differently in their work to the *Rote Armee Fraktion's* ideologies and their acts of domestic terrorism. In an interview with Jörg Heiser in the *Süddeutsche Zeitung*, German theoretician and philosopher Felix Ensslin described the approach of many artists' dealing with the RAF in their works as an attempt at separation or individualization (*Vereinzelung*) of images rather than their duplication (*Verdoppelung*).

The ambitious exhibition project *Zur Vorstellung des Terrors: Die RAF-Ausstellung* (*Regarding Terror: The RAF-Exhibition*, curated by Klaus Biesenbach, Ellen Blumenstein, and Felix Ensslin) at the Berlin Kunst-Werke (KW) in 2005 attempted to "research and, for the first time, present together the media echo of the Red Army Faction and artistic positions directly or indirectly addressing the history of the RAF," according to the exhibition website of the KW Institute for Contemporary Art ("Regarding Terror: The RAF-Exhibition").

Rather than discussing the success or failure of this project to shine a new light on the history of the RAF, I am more interested in investigating strategies and positions in contemporary art that have been at the center of many debates surrounding the RAF Exhibition. These strategies and positions are by no means only related to an exclusively German context or one that only deals with sociopolitical trauma, such as the one created by the violent crimes of the RAF—in fact my own art practice deals with neither RAF nor sociopolitical trauma. They are part of a larger discussion of contemporary art, one that addresses its function and its role in a society. By introducing concrete and controversial examples in the context of the RAF exhibition and providing possible frameworks for their discussion, I intend to offer starting points for the constructive discussion of challenging contemporary works of art in a more general sense. In the context of the "Re-Visioning Terrorism" conference at Purdue University (September 8–10, 2011), the interesting question is how can contemporary art respond to and—with a deliberately idealistic and utopian intention—make a contribution to the prevention of sociopolitical trauma caused by acts of terrorism? I argue that with a more subtle understanding of some of the positions and strategies of contemporary art dealing with the complex issues of terrorism, audience members can better reevaluate their own responses to acts of terrorism. They are able to shape more individual perspectives and find ways to critique the often favored black and white stereotypes so ubiquitous in mass media representations.

In doing so, I also try to address one main point of criticism that was brought forward about the RAF Exhibition in Berlin: the alleged failure of presenting the audience with a more contemporary context beyond the 30-year history of the RAF in Germany. During the exhibition's press conference, this concern was specifically raised by the question: Can we use this exhibition as a model for dealing with other terrorist movements such as the ETA or IRA?[3]

ZUR VORSTELLUNG DES TERRORS: DIE RAF-AUSSTELLUNG (REGARDING TERROR: THE RAF-EXHIBITION)

Zur Vorstellung des Terrors: Die RAF-Ausstellung was an exhibition at the KW Institute for Contemporary Art in Berlin from January 30 to May 5, 2005. It was organized by a curatorial trio consisting of Klaus Biesenbach (founding and artistic director of the KW Institute for Contemporary Art Berlin); Ellen Blumenstein (independent curator, from 1998–2005 curator for the KW Institute for Contemporary Art); and Felix Ensslin (curator, theatre director, and since 2009 a professor of critical theory on the Faculty of Aesthetics at the Art Academy in Stuttgart). Felix Ensslin is also the son of Gudrun Ensslin, one of the founders and core members of the RAF. The exhibition focused on artistic responses to the massive amount of media and mediated images about the RAF. The curatorial principle did not allow the commissioning of new work specifically for the exhibition, but rather intended to show what had already been created—for the first time in one space. The artistic positions featured in the exhibition were contextualized by an archival collection of news coverage about the RAF and their terrorist acts in print and TV media.

The show found a massive and powerful opposition in the families of RAF victims and high-ranking German politicians. Public opposition ranged from claims of glorification of terrorism to lacking scientific rigor in the representation of history.

Rather than going into the details of the public reception of the exhibition, I would like to focus on some remarks the curators made about their understanding of contemporary art. More specifically, the focus will be on remarks about approaches to contemporary art that allow exhibition visitors new insights into this controversial part of German history, not through mechanisms of identification or emotional occupation, but by creating a distance that leaves room for individual interpretation.

An art exhibition is not a historical exhibition. This becomes clear in the curators' definition of *Vorstellung* (imagination) in the German exhibition title, which they define as the in-between space and interface between history and art.[4]

Ellen Blumenstein explains in her introductory essay to the exhibition catalog:

Denn die Kunst übernimmt in einer Gesellschaft häufig die Vorreiterrolle bei der Berarbeitung gesamtgesellschaftlicher Traumata. Die nächstliegende Form dieser (politisch/kritisch engagierten) Kunst ist die des Aufzeigens dieser Traumata, deren sich die Gesellschaft oft nichteinmal bewusst ist. Dabei geht es explizit nicht darum, mit Hilfe der Kunst Zeitgeschichte aufzuarbeiten, oder die Kunst in einen politischen Kontext zu stellen. Sondern es geht darum, dass der Künstler sich eines Themas annimmt, von dessen Bedeutung (für sich selbst und die Öffentlichkeit) er überzeugt ist, es filtert und transformiert in ein Kunstwerk, dass dem Betrachter eigene und neue Möglichkeiten der individuellen Reflexion eröffnet. (Biesenbach, Blumenstein, and Ensslin, 17)

(In a society art is often at the cutting-edge of handling social trauma. The nearest form of this politically/critically engaged art is the depiction of these traumata, which society is often not even aware of. Explicitly, art neither helps illustrate history nor should it be put into a political context. What matters is that the artist chooses a theme of importance to herself/himself and society, s/he filters it and transforms it into a work of art which opens up new possibilities for individual reflection to the audience.)

Interviewed by Jörg Heiser, Ensslin adds: "Aufgrund ihrer Brechungen wirft die Kunst jeden einzelnen Betrachter auf sich selbst und seinen eigenen Blickwinkel zurück, anstatt ihn an die wissenschaftliche Untersuchung der Fakten zu verweisen." (Visitors are not presented with a scientific approach to the representation of history which is based on facts but they see artworks that refract and mirror events and reflect them back onto the audience.) This echoes Canadian new media artist David Rokeby's metaphor of the mirror in interactive new media artworks. His text "Transforming Mirrors: Subjectivity and Control in Interactive Media" is based on the idea that (new media) artworks provide us with mirrors in which we see ourselves. What both Ensslin and Rokeby are alluding to is the fact that by "seeing ourselves" we also see parts of the outside world that have defined our image of self: our social, political, and cultural environment. This becomes part of the complex process of looking at art, and it provides a filter through which we see the events or themes it portrays. Most importantly, it results in individualized readings for each audience member that no longer only engage them on an emotional level (expressed by audience responses such as like, dislike, sad, happy, boring, etc.).

DÜRER, ICH FÜHRE BAADER UND MEINHOF ÜBER DIE DOCUMENTA V (DÜRER, I'LL GUIDE BAADER AND MEINHOF THROUGH DOCUMENTA V PERSONALLY)

Joseph Beuys's *Dürer, ich führe Baader und Meinhof über die Documenta V* (1972) was one of the more prominent works of the 2005 RAF exhibition in Berlin. Two yellow signs attached to posts rest on the back ends of two felt slippers filled with margarine and rose stems. In large, hand-painted black letters the first sign reads: "Dürer, ich führe persönlich Baader +" ("Dürer, I'll personally guide Baader +") and the second one continues: "+ Meinhof durch die Dokumenta V J. Beuys" ("+ Meinhof through Documenta V J. Beuys"). It is a work which too easily could be (and has been) looked at as an artistic affirmation of RAF ideals—after all, it places the names of Andreas Baader and Gudrun Ensslin, two of the RAF's founders and core members, in the same sentence as Albrecht Dürer's, one of Germany's greatest artists of the Renaissance. However, rather than promoting RAF ideals, it actually tries to achieve the opposite. Beuys created it as a humane gesture against the inhumane acts of the Baader-Meinhof gang. For a better understanding of the work it is important to know about the process of its creation. The year of 1972 was the height of the police pursuit of the first generation terrorists of the RAF. It was also the year of Documenta V at which the Fluxus artist Thomas Peiter did performances in the exhibition spaces of the Kassel Fridericianum disguised as Albrecht Dürer. He visited Joseph Beuys in his exhibition space, too, which was turned into a *Büro für Direkte Demokratie* (Office for Direct Democracy). One day, when Beuys saw Peiter in his Dürer costume, he exclaimed: *"Dürer, ich führe Baader und Meinhof über die Documenta V, dann sind sie resozialisiert!"* (Dürer, I'll guide Baader and Meinhof through Documenta V, then they will be rehabilitated) (Bisenbach, Blumenstein, and Ensslin, 38).

Joseph Beuys's art had the goal to change and transform. In this case, he proposed that art's power to transform human beings is so strong it can even rehabilitate terrorists. Beuys's often-quoted concept of social sculpture emphasizes this unique quality of art to change individuals. Social sculpture is based on the idea that every human being has the ability to be creative— as Beuys believed it to be one of mankind's defining skills, at the center of artistic production but also the foundation for every aspect of our political, scientific, humanistic, and so forth systems. If every human being is creative, that is, has the power to create (thus the famous Beuys quote: *"Jeder Mensch ist ein Künstler"*—"every human being is an artist"), then humans can use this creative force to shape social processes and achievements. Humans become creators rather than remaining consumers. Social sculpture is ultimately a process of sculpting society through actions derived from creative ideas; it is participatory and bottom-up rather than top-down. Beuys tried to promote this principle from an ideologically neutral position. As his former student and former CEO of the Free International University (FIU) Johannes Stüttgen writes:

> [Joseph Beuys war] direkt gegen das Prinzip "Ideologie" selbst angetreten, da er in ihm das Grundübel der gegenwärtigen Zeit- und Bewusstseinslage erkannt hatte. . . . Ideologien—so seine Diagnose—blendeten genau diese

Eigenbestimmung, die nämlich im Ich des Menschen zum Bewusstsein kommt, aus. Sie schieben in das [Welt]Gefüge eine Fremdbestimmung hinein, die dieses zersetzt und das 'Ich' ausschaltet. Beuys' Intention galt der Erstarkung dieser Ich-Instanz in der Welt, der Zurechtrückung ihrer im Weltgefüge vorgesehenen, zentralen Leitfunktion. (Biesenbach, Blumestein, and Ensslin, 36–37)

(Joseph Beuys personally opposed the principle of "ideology," he recognized in it the basic problem of the contemporary state of awareness. . . . Ideologies, so he diagnosed, disengage self-determination, which is located in the human ego. Ideologies introduce heteronomy to the world's structure, which will eventually destroy the ego. Beuys's goal was to strengthen the ego, and to return it to its central guiding function in the world structure.)

The following, second work sample from the 2005 RAF exhibition explores the idea of art's quality to exist in an ideologically neutral territory from a related but slightly different angle.

GERHARD RICHTER, OCTOBER 18, 1977

This work from 1988 consists of 15 oil paintings[5] depicting newspaper photographs, some of which are visually transformed and blurred by Richter's distinctive squeegee method. This group of paintings loosely follows a narrative starting with the portrait of one of the RAF founders, Ulrike Meinhof, as a youth, the arrest of members of the group in 1972, representation of the gang member's life in prison to the point of the death of four of them, Ulrike Meinhof in 1976 and Andreas Baader, Gudrun Ensslin, and Jan-Carl Raspe in the night of October 18, 1977 (an event referred to as Stammheim Prison's Death Night) at the height of the German Autumn. The paintings' narrative structure concludes with Baader, Ensslin, and Raspe's funeral on October 27, 1977. Again, it would be easy to see this work as an artistic chronicle of moments in the lives and deaths of Baader, Ensslin, Meinhof, and Raspe. Also, critics, not only of Richter's cycle but generally of controversial works of art engaging in a political or critical discourse, often argue that by choosing a topic, it becomes the object of the artist's admiration, thus giving way to the presumption of glorification. This argument infers that art exclusively revolves around the topoi of truth and beauty in which the artist identifies herself/himself strongly with the subject s/he chooses. I would argue against this rather simplistic notion of art. Rather, the artist, according to Joseph Beuys, has the opportunity to operate in an ideologically unoccupied space—a requirement for the artist not to be used as a tool for propaganda. If s/he doesn't, art merely becomes illustration and loses its sovereignty. Put differently, instead of taking sides, the artist creates a discourse, a tool for public debate that itself can become part of the artwork. This is an idea that Grant Kester, Chair of the Visual Arts Department at UCSD, explores in greater depth in his book *Conversation Pieces: Community and Communication in Modern Art*. And as Felix Ensslin puts it when asked by Jörg Heiser: "So erreicht Kunst eigentlich gerade das Gegenteil von Aufwertung oder Identifikation, nämlich eine reflexive Distanz" ("Art then achieves exactly the opposite of valorization/glorification or identification with its subject, which is a reflexive distance).

In the case of Richter's *October 18, 1977* cycle, his intention with these paintings goes well beyond that of creating an artistic chronicle of moments in the lives and deaths of prominent German terrorists. As Robert Storr, former curator in the Department of Painting and Sculpture at the Museum of Modern Art and Dean of the Yale School of Art writes about *October 18, 1977*:

> So far as the explicit but obscured subject is concerned, it is as if an all but unbearable truth had suddenly been brought forward into the light, only to be screened by shadows in a condition where the impossibility of seeing is both frustrating and a kind of a reprieve. Thus each canvas is an insistent reminder of what one may have forgotten or heretofore successfully avoided paying attention to. (Storr, Richter, and Museum of Modern Art, 28)

Ambiguity and in-between spaces are more complicated than clear-cut gestures of affirmation or negation. Yet they clearly yield many opportunities for a more nuanced and fruitful discourse. However, they are also a source of confusion. A concrete example of falsely reading an artist's engagement

Figure 1. Daniel Sauter and Fabian Winkler's *In the Line of Sight* at Ars Electronica 2009, OK Center for Contemporary Art, Linz Austria (Daniel Sauter).

with a topic as an affirmative illustration of the topic rather than a critical or discursive contribution was a relatively recent response to one of my own works, which I will turn to now.

IN THE LINE OF SIGHT

In the Line of Sight (see figure 1) is a new media artwork that I created collaboratively with Daniel Sauter, a new media artist and an associate professor at the University of Illinois at Chicago (UIC), in 2009. It is an art installation that uses 100 computer-controlled tactical flashlights to project low-resolution video footage of suspicious human motion. Each flashlight shines a light spot on the wall. All flashlights combined create a ten-by-ten matrix representation of the source footage, featured on a video monitor in an adjacent part of the gallery.

The flashlight matrix projects images that are difficult to decipher, deliberately vague, making the audience wonder what exactly the person is doing.

Pictures taken by law enforcement and national intelligence under difficult circumstances, (e.g., at night, from a distance, at low resolution, in passing) are constantly subject to analysis, debate, and scrutiny. Misinterpretations can lead to severe consequences.

With this project the artists enter into a controversial debate about a range of security issues including semiautomated decision making based on surveillance footage and the elusiveness of visual representation and pattern recognition in a digital post-9/11 world.

Smith & Wesson, the brand of the flashlights chosen for this installation, is best known for its product line of firearms. Conceptually, this fact references the violent dimension of light, from searchlights in WWII to tracer ammunition and propaganda architectures made of light. By walking between the light source and the projected images, the role of the visitors changes from observer to subject—with 100 flashlights pointed at them.

The comment a YouTube user made about an explanatory video of this project simply read: "It's not art, it's the first stages of a system of control." While this person clearly understood the context in which the artwork was created, s/he was not able to take the second step and engage in a critical discourse that the work wished to generate, respectively to overcome the idea that an artwork does not always have to positively embrace the topic it represents.

I strongly believe that the solution to this problem is not to make these works of art less intellectually challenging, but instead to create more of them and give audiences additional opportunities to encounter them. Works that require a more active participation of visitors in the process of meaning creation ultimately help audience members to form a more critical and self-reflexive view of the world around them.

HANS HAACKE NEW YORK POSTERS

Half a year after the attacks of 9/11, the New York public art program Creative Time commissioned conceptual artist Hans Haacke to create a series of posters commemorating the terrorist attacks on the World Trade Center. Unlike the spectacle of *Tribute in Light*,[6] the other Creative Time funded art project dealing with the trauma of 9/11, Hans Haacke's *Untitled*[7] successfully created a visual metaphor for the way that this tragic event has become a lens through which everyday realities are viewed and understood. Haacke's idea for this poster series was simple. The design consisted of a completely white sheet of paper from which only the silhouettes of the World Trade Center's twin towers were cut out. The final appearance of the posters in public space only varied by the different content of other placards (advertising for music events, commercial products, movies, etc.) showing through the architectural cutouts.

Hans Haacke's posters for New York allowed the audience to individually reflect on the loss caused by a traumatic event such as 9/11 (the cutout shape), but even more so to look at what is still there: the larger cultural context, the many different facets that make up a society (the posters showing through the die cuts of the twin towers). These facets often do not add up to a uniform picture of a society but rather highlight all of its complex elements. Haacke's poster project thus presents the audience member with a mirror in which to see herself/himself and their culture and offers a space for personal reflection on possible responses to the tragic events. Similar to the previously introduced examples, this work also demonstrates that contemporary art does not have the function of doing the work of interpretation for the audience. However, this and other works of contemporary art do help the audience to engage in an act of creation.

Being exposed to works of art such as the ones described above gives viewers the opportunity to create responses that are likely more varied, more meaningful, and ultimately more helpful in the prevention of future acts of terrorism than any response influenced by popular media images that often turn the public into ideologically controlled consumers. These works give audience members the opportunity to reevaluate their responses to acts of terrorism and help shape more nuanced and individual perspectives, which can put dominant interpretations in question.

NOTES

1.   *Zeitgeschichte-online*, a collaboration between the Zentrum für Zeithistorische Forschung (ZZF) the Staatsbibliothek zu Berlin—Preußischer Kulturbesitz (SBB) is one of the few comprehensive resources that offers texts and materials about the history of the RAF online. http://www.zeitgeschichte-online.de/thema/raf-zeitgeschichte-und-gegenwart.

2. All translations mine unless otherwise indicated.

3. Thomas W. Eller, "Ästhetischer Vampirismus," *artnet.de*, 2005. See Eller's comments in his exhibition review:

> Man kann die Ausstellung als Versuch einer kulturellen Entspannungspolitik betrachten. Alles, was einmal etwas bedeutete, wird entleert. Die RAF wird in die sentimentale Ecke abgeschoben. Sprachlos waren denn auch die Kuratoren auf die Frage eines spanischen Gastes, ob die Ausstellung als Modell des Umgangs mit anderen terroristischen Bewegungen wie der ETA oder der IRA dienen könne. Der größte Fehler der Ausstellung offenbarte sich in diesem Moment: Die Aktualität des Terrors wird insgesamt ignoriert. Ein Projekt, das sich das Thema RAF setzt, kann nur erfolgreich sein, wenn es das Wagnis eingeht zu fragen, was die wirklichen Schubkräfte waren. Weshalb haben die Menschen für ihre Ideen gemordet? Wir wollen doch für den Umgang mit Gefahr und Terror heute lernen.

> (One could look at this exhibition as an attempt at a cultural policy of détente. Everything which once had meaning now seems empty. The RAF is put into a sentimental context. And so the curators were speechless when a Spanish guest asked whether this exhibition could be used as a model for dealing with other terrorist movements, such as the ETA or the IRA. The greatest mistake of this exhibition became obvious in this moment: the timeliness of terror is ignored altogether. A project with the RAF as topic can only be successful if it risks asking what the real motivations were. Why did people commit murders for their ideas? After all we would like to learn how to deal with danger and terror today.)

4. *Vorstellung: der Zwischenraum und die Schnittstelle zwischen Historie und Kunst* (Klaus Biesenbach, Ellen Blumenstein, and Felix Ensslin, eds., *Zur Vorstellung des Terrors: die RAF Ausstellung. Band2* [Göttingen: Steidl, 2005], 13).

5. The titles of the paintings in the October 18, 1977 installation are:

Youth Portrait (Jugendbildnis); *Arrest 1* (Festnahme 1); *Arrest 2* (Festnahme 2); *Confrontation 1* (Gegenüberstellung 1); *Confrontation 2* (Gegenüberstellung 2); *Confrontation 3* (Gegenüberstellung 3); *Hanged* (Erhängte); *Cell* (Zelle); *Record Player* (Plattenspieler); *Man Shot Down 1* (Erschossener 1); *Man Shot Down 2* (Erschossener 2); *Dead 1* (Tote 1); *Dead 2* (Tote 2); *Dead 3* (Tote 3); *Funeral* (Beerdigung).

6. *Tribute in Light*, n.d., http://www.tributeinlight.com.

7. Hans Haacke: Untitled, *Creative Time*, n.d., http://creativetime.org/programs/archive/2002/HansHaacke/haacke.

WORKS CITED

Bisenbach, Klaus, Blumenstein, Ellen, and Ensslin, Felix, eds. *Zur Vorstellung des Terrors: die RAF Ausstellung. Band2.* Göttingen: Steidl, 2005.

Eller, Thomas W. "Ästhetischer Vampirismus." *artnet.de*. 2005.

Heiser, Jörg. "RAF-Ausstellung Der lange Marsch durch die Individuationen." *Süddeutsche Zeitung*. January 19, 2005. http://www.sueddeutsche.de /kultur/raf-ausstellung-der-lange-marsch-durch-die-individuationen -1.247575.

Kester, Grant H. *Conversation Pieces: Community and Communication in Modern Art*. Berkeley: University of California Press, 2004.

Kraushaar, Wolfgang. "Zwischen Popkultur, Politik und Zeitgeschichte. Von der Schwierigkeit, die RAF zu historisieren." *Zeithistorische Forschungen/Studies in Contemporary History* 1, no. 2 (2004). http:// www.zeithistorische-forschungen.de/16126041-Kraushaar-2-2004.

KW Institute for Contemporary Art. "Regarding Terror: The RAF-Exhibition." Accessed October 29, 2011. http://www.kw-berlin.de/en/exhibitions /regarding_terror_the_raf_exhibition_113.

Rokeby, David. "Transforming Mirrors: Subjectivity and Control in Interactive Media." In *Critical Issues in Electronic Media*, edited by Simon Penny, 133–58. Albany: State University of New York Press, 1995.

Storr, Robert, Gerhard Richter, and Museum of Modern Art. *Gerhard Richter: October 18, 1977*. New York: Harry N. Abrams, 2000.

.

14

Forms of (In)visibility in Recent Spanish Films on Basque Terrorism

JAUME MARTÍ-OLIVELLA

FRAMING THE ISSUE: THE CURRENT CONTEXT

Are We All Invited? The Place of the Citizen as Spectator in Spain Today

Todos estamos invitados (Everyone Is Invited, 2008) is the significant title chosen by Manuel Gutiérrez Aragón for his 2008 film portraying an amnesiac Euskadi Ta Askatasuna (ETA) patient, his female caretaker, and a university professor threatened by ETA for his critical statements regarding the political situation in the Basque Country. The significance of Gutiérrez Aragón's title is double edged. It suggests that all of us may become targets of terrorism, that is, that we all share in the potential of becoming victims while ironically stating that, in fact, not all of us are truly invited to be part of a (Basque) community that is portrayed as being constituted both by fear and by exclusion. And yet, there seems to be little room for choice in the subject position we take in Spain's current battle over victimhood and political legitimacy. "Are we all (still) Miguel Angel Blanco?" is the leading question posed by Justin Crumbaugh in his groundbreaking essay where he revisits the public impact of ETA's kidnap and murder of the young Popular Party councilman from Ermua, whose fate became a media phenomenon in Spain. Crumbaugh's question both echoes and undermines the one implied in *Everyone Is Invited* since it reiterates the continued potential to become a victim while, at the same time, exposing the symbolic fixation upon victimhood as the only political discourse available. In short, we, the Spanish citizens, are not invited but forced to become spectators of the symbolic battle inside Spain's body politic. In Crumbaugh's own words: "A striking development in Spain since the late 1990s . . . is the extent to which the victims of political violence have increasingly become more of a media spectacle than the terrorist themselves. . . . Since Blanco's assassination, victims of ETA constitute a kind of ideal ego of a new, seemingly incontrovertible model of democratic statesmanship" (378). That is why, I believe, Jaime Rosales's *Bat Buruan/Tiro en la cabeza* (*Bullet in the Head*, 2008), the film that will be my focus in this article, becomes such a powerful and unsettling representation of the current situation. Indeed, Rosales's film forces the spectator to occupy a rather paradoxical voyeuristic position where there is practically no choice for either identification or scopic gratification. As viewers, from the beginning, we are stuck as outsiders looking in without ever being privy to a word or a thought of the terrorist subject whose daily routine, together with Rosales's camera, we ceaselessly scrutinize throughout most of the film.

ETA's Recent Cinematic Representations as Forms of (In)visibility

Rosales's paradoxical portrayal of the terrorist subject relies nevertheless on the most common topos associated with it: its invisibility. I would be hard-pressed to find any Spaniard of my generation who has failed to see images of ETA press conferences with its masked members surrounding the ax and snake emblem of the group. Rosales's film removes that concealment to show us that the true mask, that is, the true invisibility of the terrorist subject, is precisely the mask of his/her normalcy. There are, nevertheless, other forms of visible invisibility in Rosales's film. More important among them is the spectral presence of the history of ETA's cinematic representations that have, more often than not, been ignored by most of the film reviewers. Indeed, Rosales's film is punctuated by recurrent references to many previous cinematic traces which bespeak his own belief in historical memory as the only space where the Basque conflict may overcome its current and systemic reduction to an "either/or" scheme. None of the other films dealing directly or indirectly with this topic produced outside Euskadi in the last decade completely escapes this reductionism. All those I know, despite their ideological and aesthetic differences, may be seen as portraying different forms of (in)visibility of a terrorist subject that is always constructed as either voiceless, spectral, or literally invisible. Such invisibility will be highly paradoxical in Jaime Rosales's *Bat Buruan/Tiro en la cabeza* (*Bullet in the Head*, 2008), since Rosales's kidnapped viewer and his/her fixed contemplation of the daily routine of the terrorist subject does not ultimately render him more visible, that is, more understandable, but keeps him always at both a literal and a symbolic narrative distance that ultimately forces us to interrogate our own positionality as viewers and as potential victims (or accomplices) of terrorism. The concept of invisibility is thus central to the three films briefly analyzed in this section.

Carlos Martín Ferrera's *Zulo* (*Hole*, 2005) is certainly the most abstract formulation of the subject of invisibility since it takes us literally with Miguel, the film's protagonist, inside the "zulo" of the title, a deep dug hole shaped as a circular well. There, he will be kept by two masked men who will never tell him why he is there or what will happen to him. The film offers no clue as to its connection with Basque terrorism. The only one is the known reality that ETA has used many similar spaces to hide both kidnapped men and weaponry. The other hint is the protagonist's name: Miguel, a name that echoes that of Miguel Angel Blanco, the well-known ETA victim from Ermua mentioned above. Shot almost entirely within the narrow space of the well, Martín Ferrera's film focuses on the relentless and undignified process of self-destruction suffered by the trapped man until we are shown his final "liberation" while the voiceover narration tells us and him that it is perhaps too late for any true liberation.

Miguel Courtois's *GAL. En el punto de mira* (*GAL. On Target*, 2006) is a very strong indictment of the Spanish government's direct sponsorship of the GAL (Grupos Antiterroristas de Liberación) in the 1980s, when

Felipe González was Spain's prime minister as leader of the PSOE (Spanish Socialist Party). And yet, the film's political clout is lost by its own partisanship. Positioned between the genres of docudrama and political thriller, Courtois's film becomes too often a prisoner to its own lack of restraint, mainly, by falling into an almost gratuitous spectacularization of violence and by turning Ariza, the tough contact man in real life, into an almost ridiculous womanizer and drug abuser in the film. The fact that Melchor Miralles, the real-life journalist who uncovered the GAL scandal, and *El Mundo*, the conservative newspaper where he still works today, are an essential part of the production team of the film does indeed add credibility to its contents, although it also contributes to the above mentioned partisan view. Despite its artistic flaws, this film is an important document since it sheds light on an obscure case of state-sponsored terrorism in Spain.

From the perspective of this essay, however, it becomes another instance of invisibility inasmuch as the ETA terrorists are here portrayed mainly as the anonymous victims of the GAL activities.[1] Manuel Gutiérrez Aragón's *Todos estamos invitados* (*Everyone Is Invited*, 2008), as stated earlier, becomes a clear illustration of the general predicament that such an invitation involves us all, that is, that we are all potential targets of terrorist violence. In its portrayal of the specificities of the Basque political conflict, however, the film restricts the scope of its central metaphor to mean that we are not all truly invited to attend the functions of the "sociedades gastronómicas," the exclusive and exclusively male Basque dining clubs that Gutiérrez Aragón singles out as symbols of the entire Basque society. It is in one of those that Xabier, the lead character played by José Coronado, finds that his presence is no longer welcome as it had been before due to his constant critical statements regarding the use of violence in Euskadi. The fear, and in some cases the resentment, of some of his peers will lead to further violence and exclusion. Shot also under the conventions of a political thriller, the film never quite manages to provide enough political background to sustain its historical claims. And, once again, when it comes to the direct representation of the terrorist subject, embodied here by the character of Josu Jon played by Oscar Jaenada, the director chooses to render him an amnesiac as a result of head injuries suffered when he was escaping a police chase. Amnesia, thus, becomes the film's second large metaphor. As such, it allows the director to inscribe not only the issue of historical memory but also the question of who will be able to claim the right narrative once the fight is over.

JAIME ROSALES'S *BAT BURUAN/TIRO EN LA CABEZA* IN CINEMATIC AND THEORETICAL CONTEXT

Between Hitchcock's *Rear Window* and Ford Coppola's *The Conversation*

A lot has been written about the controversy surrounding Rosales's film. Very little has been said, however, regarding the film's cinematic intertextuality and its theoretical implications. Although Rosales's filmmaking is more generally credited as being influenced by Robert Bresson's understatement and by Yasujiro Ozu's stillness, the two essential intertextual references here come from Hollywood, as Núria Vidal's review already suggests:

> The first sequences of *Tiro en la cabeza* send us directly to the beginning of Francis Ford Copola's *The Conversation* (1974). We see, but we can't hear. We know who the camera follows but we don't know why. We have an intuition of what is said by means of the facial expressions, but we can't find out who is behind the characters and compels them to behave as they do. When the action shifts to the interior of the houses, the referent changes. Here we are inside the domain of Hitchcock's 1954 *Rear Window*. People behave in their houses with a naturalness that makes you think nobody is watching. Unlike James Stewart's neighbors, whom we see as if acting in small theaters, Rosales positions himself with his framing technique and proposes each shot as a frame within a frame, (or a picture within a picture), both fragmented and determined by a doorframe, a window frame or the railing of a balcony. If, at the beginning, we felt like spies, now we have become voyeurs of an absolutely banal intimacy that we witness in real time, which in the film translates into a lengthening of cinematic time. (Vidal, 44; my translation)

There is, I should add, an important difference between Rosales's film and these two major Hollywood references, and that has to do with the spectator's positionality. Thus, if we as viewers soon fall for Stewart's voyeurism and end up as his accomplices in *Rear Window*, or if we feel truly intrigued and thus willingly become spies in *The Conversation*, it is almost impossible to say the same about Rosales's film, where we feel literally trapped, almost kidnapped, into being both spies and voyeurs. Both subject positions are however subverted in Rosales's film since the voyeur is not the protagonist but the spectator, while the protagonist is the object of the scopic intrusion, while, as spies, our prying into the character's private life always fails because we are never allowed to hear his conversations. Neither true policeman nor true voyeur, the viewer is forced to remain at the same time intimately close and quite remote from its intruded subject, just as we, ordinary people, are forced into constant contemplation and practical silence amidst the "conversation" between the terrorist subject and the State, its invisible enemy. Technically, moreover, the radical distance imposed by Rosales's telephoto lens acts as a Brechtian device that short-circuits any possible identification. At best, we remain intimate strangers—a proposition that seems to betray Rosales's own view not only of our fragmented society, but also of the human condition at large.

There is, on the other hand, a significant political coincidence between Rosales's and Ford Coppola's proposition. Thus, if Coppola's film, despite the director's disclaimers, was read as a direct critique of the illegal surveillance devices used by the Nixon administration to spy on their political foes, Rosales's film was released in the context of a number of political scandals surrounding corruption and illegal wiretaps in Spain. Concerning the film's voyeurism, it may be necessary to go back briefly to Freud's own definition of the term, which he always related to that of scopophilia: "But my research into the early years of normal people, as well as of neurotic patients, force me to the conclusion that scopophilia can also appear in children as a spontaneous manifestation. . . . Children of this kind turn into voyeurs, *eager spectators* of the processes of micturition and defaecation" (Freud, 269; emphasis added).

There are at least three aspects in the portrayal of voyeurism in Rosales's film that I find worth mentioning in relationship with Freud's definition. First, as I have already suggested and due to Rosales's closed scopic regime, we, as viewers, are not "eager" but forced spectators of the terrorist's private life. Second, again due to Rosales's constant juxtaposition of viewing obstacles, such as the windows and doors themselves but also such as the number of garbage containers that often block the view of the protagonist, we can only obtain partial and fragmented visions of the (undesired) subject of our contemplation. More importantly, Rosales seems to imply a direct albeit dramatically ironic reference to Freud's definition with his frequent images of garbage containers as blocking devices because, unlike the eager children exploring other people's genitalia and their basic functions, what Rosales inscribes here is the inevitable encounter with our own garbage, both in quite literal and metaphorical terms. In doing so, the director not only echoes one of the central metaphors in the representation of ETA terrorism within Basque (and Spanish) cinema, but also hints at the persistence, if not at the hegemony, of the "excremental" over the "sacramental" in our daily lives.[2]

Spectral Traces of Basque Cinema's Historical Representation of ETA

As mentioned earlier, the recurrent presence of the garbage metaphor directly connects Rosales's film with many previous cinematic renderings of ETA on screen, both in Euskadi and in the rest of Spain. More interesting than that almost conventional marker, there are quite a number of subtle references to crucial Basque films on the subject that are almost always tangentially inscribed in Rosales's narrative. To my knowledge, none of these references have been critically discussed, a fact, I believe, that is due in large part to the almost nonexistence of studies that deal with Basque cinema as an autonomous entity.

One of the most interesting of those visual traces alluding to previous Basque cinema is the emphasis on the back, and, more specifically, on the nape of the protagonist. The first occurrence of this in Rosales's film happens precisely in conjunction with the garbage metaphor. I am referring to the first daytime sequence when we see the backpack and the nape of the protagonist as he moves about the newspaper kiosk while being partially blocked from our view by what looks like a small garbage container placed between the camera and the character. From then on, we will see Jon Arretxe's back and nape repeatedly while he is telephoning, getting money from an ATM machine, or listening to a record within a music shop. More significantly, we will also see only his bare back and nape in the sequence where he is kissing and embracing his girlfriend. It is here where Rosales alludes to Helena Taberna's landmark film *Yoyes* (2000), which repeatedly used the visual emphasis on the protagonist's nape to inscribe a sense of vulnerability and foreboding.[3]

The intertextual connection between Rosales's and Taberna's films has, moreover, another important element, which acts both as framing device and as narrative metaphor: the constant use of windows framing the characters and our vision of them. In her film on María Dolores González Katarain, alias Yoyes, arguably ETA's most visible female member, Helena Taberna paid special attention to her lead character's both central and liminal position within the command structure of ETA. Yoyes's final rejection of the group's violent methods ultimately was paid with the sacrifice of her own life. Besides stressing Yoyes's victimhood status, Taberna's film uses her posthumously published diary, *Desde mi ventana* (*From My Window*, 1988) as a constant frame of reference, which the director visually inscribes in a series of shots through and from several of the windows appearing in the film.[4] Needless to say, both Taberna and Rosales seem to rely on the rich ambiguity of the very notion of framing and being framed, that is, fragmenting and being trapped, which both their real and symbolic window framing strongly illustrate.

Besides the references to Ana Díez's *Ander eta Yul* (*Andrew and Yul*, 1988), which was the first film structured by the sacramental/excremental tension that is at the core of the garbage metaphor, and to that of Helena Taberna's *Yoyes*, Rosales's film also includes traces of the work of Imanol Uribe and Julio Medem, whose *El proceso de Burgos* (*The Burgos Trial*, 1979) and *La pelota vasca. La piel contra la piedra* (*Basque Ball. Skin Against Stone*, 2003) constitute the two most important documentary films on the Basque political scene to date. Both films are invoked in almost non-diegetic ways in Rosales's *Bat Buruan/Tiro en la cabeza*. Thus, the Burgos plates of the car that the terrorists use in their trip to France inevitably bring to mind that city as both the location of Franco's first government and of the collective trial of the ETA members that also took place there during the 70s.[5] The initial sound and vision of the sea followed by noises of a Basque ball court in the background, used by Rosales in the beginning of his film, also force us to think of a similar, although much more clearly pronounced, initial sequence in Julio Medem's epochal documentary. Rosales himself has often cited Medem's work in interviews. What seems partly uncanny here is the fact that Rosales cast Jon Arretxe for the lead role, apparently without knowing about Arretxe's past, specifically, his having been arrested and tortured by the Guardia Civil as a result of unproven charges of belonging to ETA when he was only twenty-one years old. Doubtlessly, Rosales must have been conscious of Imanol Uribe's own gesture of casting five real life ex-prisoners of ETA, including Patxi Bisquert, future icon of the Basque cinematic screen, and Angel Amigo, coscreenwriter and producer of *La fuga de Segovia* (*Escape From Segovia*, 1981), the film that chronicled the historical and partly tragic escape from the Segovia prison. What the inclusion of these historical and cinematic traces adds to Jaime Rosales's film directly points to his own conviction that it will be only by acknowledging the importance of historical memory that we will be able to find a middle or common ground where the necessary dialogue may take place in and about the Basque Country if Euskadi is to reach any political normalcy.

Rosales's *Bullet in the Head* and Agamben's "Threshold of Indistinction"

Giorgio Agamben's crucial notions of "bare life," "*homo sacer*," and "state of exception" have been adopted in substantive ways in recent essays on Basque terrorism.[6] That is why I will limit myself here to suggest a possible linkage between Agamben's theoretical work and Rosales's *Bat Buruan/Tiro en la cabeza*. For that, I want to recall here the Italian thinker's notion of a "threshold of indistinction":

> What had to remain in the collective unconscious as a monstrous hybrid of human and animal, divided between the forest and the city—the werewolf—is, therefore, in its origin the figure of the man who has been banned from the city. . . . The life of the bandit, like that of the sacred man, is not a piece of animal nature without any relation to law and the city. It is, rather, a *threshold of indistinction* and a passage between animal and man, *physis* and *nomos*, exclusion and inclusion: the life of the bandit is the life of the *loup garrou*, the werewolf, who is precisely *neither man nor beast*, and who dwells paradoxically within both while belonging to neither. (Agamben, 105; first emphasis added; translated by Daniel Heller-Roazen)

If we substitute the word bandit with the word terrorist in Agamben's previous proposition, we can see how Rosales's film may be perceived as a visual reenactment of the werewolf predicament today. Specifically, the film takes us from the semidarkness of the terrorist city dwelling into the emptiness of the forest trail where we see him for the last time. Rosales thus marks the two symbolic points placed at the extreme of Agamben's "threshold of indistinction" and makes us aware, once again in Agamben's own words: "[that] it is not so much a war of all against all as, more precisely, a condition in which everyone is bare life and a *homo sacer* for everyone else" (Agamben, 106). Like Agamben's reasoning, Rosales's film is also based on the figure of the paradox. Indeed, with his relentless scrutiny of the Basque terrorist daily routine before showing his wolf-like metamorphosis, Rosales manages to depict both and at the same time the terrorist subject's "bare life"—the simplicity and banality of his "state of nature" existence—and his embodiment of the *homo sacer* position as the inhabitant of that indistinct area between human and animal, whose monstrous transformation marks the limits of human civility and forces us to revisit the question of the sacredness of human life itself.

JAIME ROSALES'S *BULLET IN THE HEAD*: FROM "THE TERRORIST SUBJECT" TO "THE SUBJECT OF TERRORISM"

Rosales' Portable Panoptikon and the "Bare Life" of the Terrorist Subject

It should be quite obvious by now that Jaime Rosales's *Bullet in the Head* is aimed at challenging the regular expectations of most filmgoers. The director himself has plainly stated it: "I am a quiet and moderate man but my cinema is not. It portrays violence. I do violence against conventional cinema" (qtd. in Vidiella, 18; my translation.). First and foremost in Rosales's violence of representation is, of course, his choice to leave the terrorist subject speechless or, at least, inaudible. And, paradoxically enough, this radical gesture obeys the director's ethical claim that we need to listen to the other if any solution is to be found. This silent representation of the terrorist's bare life, he suggests, forces the viewer to reconsider his/her own position in the face of political violence.[7] Needless to say, such decision is viewed by some as truly senseless since it replicates the very silence that the terrorists want to impose. A silence that Fernando Savater claims was always present during the San Sebastián Film Festival, which, according to him, had never uttered any public message of rejection against the violence of ETA until 2008, the very year of Rosales's film opening there. It is interesting to hear the philosopher's own words:

> Agobios de la cobardía, antes daba miedo hablar pero hoy, en un clima diferente y con *el ojo público* sobre lo que allí ocurre, lo peligroso es callar. (Savater, 37; emphasis added; my translation)

> (The stifling sensation of cowardice, before one was afraid to talk but today, in a different climate and with *the public eye* set on what happens there, the dangerous thing is to remain silent.)

Fernando Savater is one of the most prominent examples of what Joseba Gabilondo, following Gramsci's formulation, calls "organic intellectuals." Moreover, he has been extremely vocal in support of the constitutionalist front in the Basque Country, and his opposition to any political rapprochement with the Basque radical left has often been articulated in several national media. I have emphasized the expression "the public eye" in Savater's words because I believe it is at the heart of the issue here. Indeed, what area of our private lives is not subject "to the public eye" in our world? We are all, in fact, subjected to the State's surveillance systems or to the not so private eyes of the paperazzi's cameras. One could almost say that the Foucaldian panoptikon has metamorphosed itself into a portable telephoto lens that all of us are invited (forced) to use. In other words, we have become everybody else's "public eye." That might explain, to return to the specificity of Rosales's film, the second violent gesture of his proposal, namely, to compel us, the viewers, to look through such a reductive device. A device that, as Alex Gorina reminds us, "eliminates the depth of field and all the contours and creates a succession of frames where human figures coexist at the same distance and with identical dimensions" (Gorina, 92; my translation). This is true, although not entirely. The framing distance is certainly not always the same during the long and silent portrayal of the protagonist's bare life, and his figure is never blurred by "coexisting" with other human figures. From the long shot of the initial nocturnal window framing to the first medium shot of his nape in the newspaper kiosk sequence, we, the viewers, will be compelled to see Jon Arretxe at different distances. Thus, we will see him in profile, again at a medium-range distance, in the open space of a children's playground speaking to a woman and child, who, in fact, are his real-life sister and nephew. Then, back to a long-distance shot, we will see him inside a coffee shop speaking with a friend, both of them again in profile and framed by the window. Next, through another long-distance shot, we will find him in an open, and for the first time, clearly recognizable space, in the Amara railroad station in Donostia, where we see the EuskoTren arriving. The party he attends that night will again be portrayed as framed by windows and from the same initial distance.

Besides showing us the banal aspect of the protagonist's bare life, what many of these silent shots share is a similar image of Arretxe's back and nape, which, as mentioned when discussing such an emphasis in Helena Taberna's film *Yoyes*, suggests that Rosales is using a peculiar form of dramatic irony in stressing the vulnerability of his object of scrutiny, especially when most viewers know that he will be the one shooting at somebody else's head. Even during the seduction sequence, we will see only the protagonist's naked back in the foreground of the frame, once again reframed by the window at night. Ultimately, Rosales seems to be saying, despite the viewer's forced voyeurism, that the object of our public eye does not end up completely reified. In fact, the opposite seems to happen since it is his human vulnerability that gets stressed. This also explains why, after that seduction scene, we will see again the protagonist in an almost uninterrupted series of shots from the back, first near an ATM teller, next making a phone call from a public telephone box, and then inside a music shop where he is listening to a record with the ear phones on, while the camera focuses on the significant name of a pop band: the Sex Pistols.

This long scrutiny of the terrorist's bare life will reach closure with the repetition of the initial nocturnal shot, where we now see the protagonist having supper, framed and profiled by the lit window shining in the dark. The sequence ends, though, on a different register, when Rosales's panning stops on a bottle of oil outlined against the window frame in what constitutes a quasi "still life" that encapsulates the director's own aesthetic vision while suggesting what Hannah Arendt called "the banality of evil."[8] Thus, at the heart of Rosales's film we encounter the figure of the paradox. Elsewhere, I have studied at length the central place that the figure of paradox has in Basque culture in general and in Basque cinema in particular.[9] Here, I would like to consider how Rosales incorporates it as both a structuring principle and a social commentary. As a structural technique, it is used by employing a documentary, quasi non-narrative cinematic register to portray the fiction of the terrorist subject as "everyman." Then, when the film moves on and starts the recreation of a historical fact—the murder by ETA of two young Spanish civil guards in Cap Breton, France, in December 2007—Rosales shifts into a fictional, almost traditional narrative format in order to carry out such a reconstruction. Taken almost at face value, when thinking of the title of this essay, Rosales's paradoxical performance renders the silent/silenced terrorist subject almost invisible or incomprehensible due precisely to his very excessive "visibility."

The Return of the Gaze: The Cyclop's Eye

Most critics agree that the best sequence in the entire film occurs inside the coffee shop by the French freeway where the encounter between the terrorists and the Spanish civil guards takes place.[10] Before reaching that point, I want to briefly retrace our steps to focus on the moment of the second literal repetition of the film. This happens when we see the protagonist speaking with the same bearded friend we first saw during the sequence in the Amara railroad station. Now we will see them getting into a red car, which, driven by a young woman, will be soon reaching the French border, as the close-up shot of the "Frantzia 1 Km." road sign illustrates. Then, Rosales's camera will spend a few seconds portraying a pile of scrap by the road and the crane that is removing it, in another clear reminder of the garbage metaphor that, as I mentioned earlier, crisscrosses the entire film.

As if needing a visual correlative to underline that he is taking us for the ride, Rosales includes a series of on-the-road shots that take us from the expressway into a local road flanked by tall plane and leafless trees until we reach a small chalet in the French village where the terrorists will spend the night. Then, for a moment, Rosales returns to the distant framing gaze to portray the terrorists again through a lit window as they now sit and smile while having dinner during what looks like a very pleasant evening. The sequence will end with a beautiful shot of a bowl of fruit sitting at the angle of the window that inscribes the second almost painterly "still life" in Rosales's film. This distant stillness will be immediately changed by the background noise and the establishing shots of the sequence in the coffee shop. Soon, the camera will pan onto the table where the three terrorists are having breakfast, and, in passing over their figures in profile, we will distinguish a small ring on the girl's nose together with her Palestinian-like scarf, a fact that clearly marks her in generational terms, as if anticipating the final sequence where she will be marked in more specific gender terms when Rosales shows her almost compassionate look at the young French woman they have just tied to the tree in the forest.

Back in the coffee shop, we now see the young faces of the two civil guards who, despite not wearing their regular uniforms, are easily recognizable by their strong Spanish features. They are next seen paying the cashier while the camera moves in a manner that seems to stress the randomness of their presence together with that of the three terrorists in the same space of this self-service French coffee shop by the freeway. Interestingly enough, unlike what happened with the protagonist himself, the two civil guards appear facing the camera the first time we see them. At this moment of heightened tension, Rosales will resort to an almost traditional reverse shot format to construct the quick metamorphosis of the protagonist, a moment that has been referred to, following the director's own allusion, as the cyclop's eye scene. Indeed, a few seconds after one of the civil guards is left alone while his companion goes to the rest room, we see his eyes moving away from the menu and, in a quick almost freeze frame, finding and recognizing the table with the three terrorists.

Almost immediately, just after the next reverse shot registers the sudden nervousness of the civil guard, the camera will show us the back of one of the terrorists that blocks part of the protagonist's face and thus lets us only see one of his eyes. And then, it happens, in another almost magnetic quasi freeze frame, we see the moment of final recognition and, thus, the beginning of the metamorphosis when that single eye becomes the cyclop's eye that fiercely returns our gaze and that of the young civil guard. What follows is a concise and, at the same time, brutal rendering of a cold-blooded killing, the conclusion of a foretold death, and we are the horrified witnesses of that bullet in the head anticipated in the film's title. Before the brutal shots, moreover, we are given the opportunity to hear the only clearly audible words in the film: "Txakurra, txakurra!" (Dogs, dogs!),[11] as if Rosales needed to add a verbal layer to stress that passage between human and animal, which performs the "threshold of indistinction" described by Giorgio Agamben.

EPILOGUE: ROSALES'S DOUBLE CRITICISM AND OPEN-ENDED FINAL QUESTION

Rosales's collective implication will be reinforced by the film's finale. In this protracted last sequence, we accompany the terrorists and their kidnapped victim until they leave the main road for a rural path where, after leaving the car, they start walking through the forest with their victim, whom they finally leave blindfolded and tied to a tree. The slow tracking shot of the back of the shaking young woman tied and abandoned in the middle of the forest forcefully interpolates the viewer, thus reinforcing this idea of a collective victimization. This time, however, Rosales has showed us the face of the young terrorist girl trying to comfort and reassure the other woman, whose crying we cannot hear. Again, as in passing, Rosales offers us a gender-specific moment of hope, a further touch of humanity in the realm of the werewolf.

The open-endedness of the film is visually underlined by the long shot where we see the empty rural path after the car with the two terrorists has left the screen. This sequence recalls the ending of *The Hours of a Day*, Rosales's first feature film, where the quiet taxi driver also abandons his would-be victim in the midst of a rural path. The sequence also seems to quote Luis Buñuel's *The Discreet Charm of the Bourgeoisie* (1972) and those absurd and memorable random walks on empty roads. Here, however, the "randomness" is presented in paradoxical terms, which, as I mentioned earlier, may be interpreted as a visual embodiment of the *homo sacer* predicament described by Girogio Agamben, always already marking the limits of the city and the citizen.

In the context of this essay, the viewers' final identification with the anonymous young woman tied to the tree seems to suggest an identical message to the one plainly stated in the title of Gutiérrez Aragón's film: *Everyone Is Invited*. Indeed, we are all invited as potential victims of terrorism and/or of random violence. And yet, Rosales's film does not end on this almost disarming and common sense notion. Just as his voyeuristic camera is contradicted by his anti-spectacular presentation of the terrorist subject, his final sequence stresses the film's double critique or, at least, its testimony to a double silencing, that of the terrorist and that of the victim, both voices subsumed (or erased) by the very violence of terrorism and by the state's appropriation of the discourse on terrorist violence. Ultimately, Rosales leaves us with a silent, and yet resounding, open-ended question: Who can (freely) talk about the subject of terrorism?

NOTES

1.   This film is almost a sequel to Courtois' previous *El Lobo* (*The Wolf*, 2004), where he portrayed, also very forcefully but with a much higher level of dramatic restraint, the real-life infiltration of ETA by Mikel Lejarza, a Spanish State agent who managed to thwart almost a quarter of the group's terrorist activities between 1973 and 1975 before he was forced to assume a false identity and disappear for good.

2.   See my essay, "Invisible Otherness: From Migrant Subjects to the Subject of Immigration in Basque Cinema," where I first discuss the presence in Ana Díez's film *Ander eta Yul* (*Andrew and Yul*, 1988) of garbage as an extended metaphor for terrorism and her conflation of the excremental and sacramental narratives as they are symbolized in the confrontation between the lead characters amidst the ruins of the old seminary of their youth. For a thorough analysis of the dramatic convergence of the excremental/sacramental dialectics in Basque culture, see Joseba Zulaika, *Basque Violence: Metaphor and Sacrament* (Reno: University of Nevada Press, 1988).

3.   Helena Taberna herself pointed out the significance of these shots in her interview with María Camí-Vela. See Camí-Vela, "Entrevista con Helena Taberna," in *Mujeres detrás de la cámara. Entrevistas con cineastas españolas de la década de los 90* (Donostia/San Sebastián: Euskadiko Filmategia/Filmoteca Vasca, 1994).

4.   I have studied these shots in some detail in "(En)Gendering ETA and/in Basque Politics," an essay included as chapter four in my unpublished "Basque Cinema: The Shining Paradox."

5.   The historical significance of that trial, where sixteen ETA members were condemned to death by the already ailing Franco regime, is emphasized in Uribe's film, which becomes in itself a truly remarkable historical document by bringing together all

the voices of those tried in Burgos ten years later, when, as the director explains, they had already experienced a series of bitter political divisions. For Imanol Uribe's own account of the making of *El proceso de Burgos*, see Jesús Angulo, Carlos F. Heredero, and José Luis Rebordinos, *Entre el documental y la ficción. El cine de Imanol Uribe* (Donostia/San Sebastián: Euskadiko Filmategia/Filmoteca Vasca, 1994).

6.   See, for instance, Justin Crumbaugh, "Are We All (Still) Miguel Angel Blanco? Victimhood, the Media Afterlife, and the Challenge for Historical Memory," *Hispanic Review* 75, no. 4 (2007): 365–84; or Joseba Gabilondo, "Terrorism, State Terror, and the Historical State of Exception. For a Postnational History of Violence in Spain and the Basque Country," paper presented at the "Re-Visioning Terrorism" conference, September 8–10, West Lafayette, Indiana.

7.   See, for instance, these words by the director in the same interview with Rafa Vidiella: "I have a deep respect towards the victims from both sides, but, grounded on freedom and ethics, I want to offer a vision without stereotypes that makes possible to demystify terrorism. The terrorist is not a hero but he is not a psycopath either. He may be somebody to recover. If we all moderate ourselves, he might be the one giving up the arms, although to achieve that we need politicians with good solutions" (qtd. in Vidiella, 18; my translation).

8.   Sergi Sánchez, "Tiro en la cabeza. Un drama sin palabras," *La Razón*, October 3, 2008, 65. Sánchez writes: "It is not a question of humanizing the terrorist and much less of justifying him. It is rather the fact of understanding our position as 'voyeurs' and, more than anything else, of learning what it means the banality of evil that Hannah Arendt referred to" (my translation). Giorgio Agamben also refers to Arendt's work several times throughout his *Homo Sacer. Sovereign Power and Bare Life*, and, especially in his chapter on "Biopolitics and the Rights of Man" (126–35).

9.   I am referring to *Basque Cinema: An Introduction*, and to my manuscript "Basque Cinema: The Shining Paradox," where I elaborate on the "ez//bai" polarity at the heart of Basque culture and on the fact of the visible invisibility of a cinematic corpus that, more often than not, goes unnoticed as an autonomous cultural entity and is absorbed in the Spanish logic of the self-same.

10.   See, for instance, the already mentioned review by Alex Gorina, entitled precisely, "La mirada del cíclop," or the special emphasis and analysis given to that sequence in E. Rodríguez Marchante's review of the film for the *ABC* Madrid daily, or, finally, Imma Merino's review also entitled "L'ull del cíclop" that was published in *El Punt*.

11. The word "txakurra" does indeed mean dog in Euskara (Basque) although in political jargon it implies the meaning of "Spanish policeman."

WORKS CITED

Agamben, Giorgio. *Homo Sacer. Sovereign Power and Bare Life.* Translated by Daniel Heller-Roazen. Stanford: Stanford University Press, 1998.

Ander eta Yul. Directed by Ana Díez. Donostia/San Sebastián: Igeldo Zine Produkzioak, 1988. DVD.

Angulo, Jesús, Carlos F. Heredero, and José Luis Rebordinos. *Entre el documental y la ficción. El cine de Imanol Uribe.* Donostia/San Sebastián: Euskadiko Filmategia/Filmoteca Vasca, 1994.

Bat Buruan/Tiro en la cabeza. Directed by Jaime Rosales. Barcelona: Cameo, 2008. DVD.

Camí-Vela, María. "Entrevista con Helena Taberna." In *Mujeres detrás de la cámara. Entrevistas con cineastas españolas de la década de los 90,* 165–75. Madrid: SGAE/Ocho y Medio, 2001.

Crumbaugh, Justin. "Are We All (Still) Miguel Ángel Blanco? Victimhood, the Media Afterlife, and the Challenge for Historical Memory?" *Hispanic Review* 75, no. 4 (2007): 365–84.

El proceso de Burgos. Directed by Imanol Uribe. Donostia/San Sebastián: Cobra Films/Irrintzi Zinema/Severino, 1979. DVD.

Freud, Sigmund. "Three Essays on the Theory of Sexuality." In *The Freud Reader,* edited by Peter Gray, 239–93. Edited by Peter Gray. New York: Norton, 1989.

Gabilondo, Joseba. "Terrorism, State Terror, and the Historical State of Exception: For a Postnational History of Violence in Spain and the Basque Country." Paper presented at the Re-Visioning Terrorism Conference. West Lafayette, Indiana, September 8–10, 2011.

GAL. En el punto de mira. Directed by Miguel Courtois. Madrid: Aurum Producciones, 2006. DVD.

González, Katarain María Dolores. *Desde mi ventana.* Pamplona: Pamiela, 1988.

Gorina, Alex. "La mirada del cíclop." *El Temps:* 92. September 30, 2008.

La fuga de Segovia. Directed by Imanol Uribe. Donostia/San Sebastián: Frontera Films, 1981. DVD.

La pelota vasca: la piel contra la piedra. Directed by Julio Medem. Madrid: Alicia Produce, 2003. DVD.

Martí-Olivella, Jaume. "Invisible Otherness: From Migrant Subjects to the Subject of Immigration in Basque Cinema." In *Basque Cultural Studies*, edited by William A. Douglass, Carmelo Urza, Linda White, and Joseba Zulaika, 205–26. Reno: University of Nevada Press, 1999.

———. *Basque Cinema: An Introduction*. Reno: Center for Basque Studies, University of Nevada, 2003.

———. "Basque Cinema: The Shining Paradox." Unpublished manuscript, last modified 2014.

Merino, Imma. "L'ull del cíclop." *El Punt (Barcelona)*. October 13, 2008, 33.

Mucha, Martín. "Jaime Rosales: 'Ya he hecho la película del nuevo atentado.'" *El Mundo (Crónica)*. September 28, 2008, 9.

Rodríguez Marchante, E. "La transformación del hombre-lobo en pleno día y en un café de Capbreton." *ABC*. October 3, 2008, 99.

Sánchez, Sergi. "Tiro en la cabeza. Un drama sin palabras." *La Razón*. October 3, 2008, 65.

Savater, Fernando. "¡Allá películas!" *El País*. September 30, 2008, 37.

Todos estamos invitados. Directed by Manuel Gutiérrez Aragón. Culver City, CA: Sony Pictures, 2008. DVD.

Vidal, Núria. "L'estrena de la setmana: *Tiro en la cabeza*." *Time Out (Barcelona)*. October 3, 2008, 44.

Vidiella, Rafa. "Jaime Rosales: 'Yo soy tranquilo y moderado, pero mi cine no.'" *20 Minutos (Barcelona)*. September 24, 2008, 18.

Yoyes. Directed by Helena Taberna. Burbank: Buena Vista Home Entertainment, 2000. DVD.

Zulaika, Joseba. *Basque Violence: Metaphor and Sacrament*. Reno: University of Nevada Press, 1988.

Zulo. Directed by Carlos Martín Ferrera. Madrid: Vértice Cine, 2005. DVD.

15

Writing Victims: Post-Terrorist Fiction(s) in the Basque Country and Spain

ROLAND VAZQUEZ

INTRODUCTION

I headed to Euskadi, or the Basque Country, in Spain, in 2009–2010 for a year of research, convinced of the novelty of my project.[1] I was to study the discourse and infrastructure related to the movement of the victims of the terrorism of ETA (Euskadi 'ta Askatasuna, or Basque Homeland and Freedom). ETA had been an important parapolitical and even political actor in Euskadi and Spain since the 1960s. The group's continued violence after the Spanish transition to democracy in the late 1970s was indicative of suspicions among a sector of the Basque populace regarding the legitimacy of the transition, questioning Euskadi's belonging in Spain altogether (Linz, Gómez-Reino, Orizo, and Vila, 1986). Indeed, during ethnographic fieldwork I had conducted in the mid-1990s, Basque nationalism represented the dominant political discourse in Euskadi, and support for the extreme incarnation of radical Basque nationalism,[2] although far from the majority position, was well entrenched, and represented the squeaky wheel of Basque politics.

In 2009, words such as "peace" and "dialogue" were disappearing from the panorama. The late Mario Onaindia seemed correct in his assessment of the meaning of the watershed moment of the mass demonstrations following the summary 1997 kidnapping and killing of the Ermua Popular Party City Councilperson Miguel Ángel Blanco: that the Basque people were no longer asking for peace, but rather demanding freedom (Onaindia). And even this last word struck me in its stark denotative shift. In my earlier research, the dominant meaning of "freedom" was collective, referencing independence from Spain, whether invoked by supporters or critics. In contrast, in 2009, the term was nearly exclusively an individual-based concept, holding ETA's violent actions as the antithesis. In her historical analysis on the issue, in an implicit engagement with Adam Smith, Lynn Hunt (210) writes of the long-term and even partly counterintuitive success of conscience trumping the "soft power" of humanity to solidify the discourse of individual human rights, with their requisite responsibilities. Although I wish to take care not to overstate, it appeared to me that, in my absence, the concept of the Basque citizen, accepting the rule of law as sine qua non, had been born.

Local, regional, and global events had rendered the use of violence for political ends illegitimate. The attacks of September 11, 2001 drove this home, as did the March 11, 2004 al- Qaeda Madrid train bombings, which served as a shocking public mirror of horror in both method and scale. With respect to ETA in particular, a variety of ideas and actions discredited the group. The December 2006 bombing at Madrid's Barajas Airport without prior warning in the midst of a so-called "ceasefire" only served to further demonstrate ETA's madness to Basque public opinion.[3] The group still existed to the extent that it was, quoting Joseba Zulaika, the "ashes" of its former self (*Polvo*). In short, ETA was discredited to the point that it had been reduced to a straw man in societal understanding and became an easy target in political rhetoric.

Such a discourse was accompanied by mobilizing realities. Within the public sector, in 2001, under the aegis of the Basque Ministry of the Interior, the Department for Attention to Victims of Terrorism was established, under a Basque-nationalist-led coalition government, but in no small part the result of pressure from nongovernmental groups. The theme of the remainder of this paper brackets the better part of the institutional infrastructure, civic organizations, and other related initiatives to focus on the realm of literary fiction.

One genre that shares strong thematic and formal elements is the burgeoning victim testimonial literature (e.g., Arteta; Pagazaurtundua, *Los Pagaza*; San Sebastián; Villa); it will not be discussed further here because it explicitly stakes a claim to narrating reality as such. In looking at fiction, I elide questions of whether some or even most of this production is in fact "Basque." The attempt to answer this cultural and linguistic question is engulfed by the very political field that it purports to study, and is perhaps an essentialist will to classificatory power.[4] I am also at pains to make it clear that I am not claiming that the literature I am focusing upon has been the only important strand of fiction in and about Euskadi dealing with politics and violence. At least since the publication of Ramon Saizarbitoria's *A Hundred Meters* in 1976, some of the most important literature, especially in the Basque language, has focused on such violence (Arruti, 122; as exemplars see Atxaga; Saizarbitoria, *Hamaika*), and it has done so from a perspective centered on ETA. Indeed, to cite one example, the Spanish translator of Saizarbitoria's 1995 *The Uncountable Steps*, Jon Juaristi, called that work "the great Basque novel of my generation" (Blas, Saizarbitoria, and Juaristi, 118–19). Nevertheless, the literature described below is grounded in a distinctive vision. And it has experienced a meteoric ascent in production and acceptance alike.

LITERARY PRECURSOR

In an interview conducted shortly after having received Spain's National Prize of Letters in 2006, Raúl Guerra Garrido, the author based in San Sebastián for over half a century, expressed his opinions about the Basque political situation and the relationship of the trajectory of his work to it. According to Guerra Garrido, one of his ambitions was to write the post-terrorist Basque novel. His desire, he admitted, was political rather than literary, and he stated that such a work would be "a very tiresome love story, about two young people who are completely foolish and infatuated with each other," adding that it would be so "because that's what we need, a decent period of boredom and peace of mind" (Marín).[5] In the same interview, Guerra Garrido also claimed that, literarily speaking, he had nothing further to write about the Basque political situation, suggesting that there was nothing more to be said in the political climate of the day. He had a long trajectory of writing about social tension having its roots in his perception about the marginalization of Spanish immigrants, beginning with his 1969 novel *Cacereño* about an immigrant from western Spain who becomes a factory worker in an industrial Basque town.

Guerra Garrido's writing since 1969 has led him to be lauded as one of the leading practitioners of the "social realism" school of writing in Spain, making his work ultimately "something more than literature" (Ortiz, 12), and his Basque-theme fiction in particular has been praised to the point of canonization by those who argue that his literary trajectory represents a critical voice of the marginalization of the non-Basque Spanish immigrant in all respects. Regardless of one's ideological positioning vis-á-vis Guerra Garrido's writing, what is clear is that he was a forerunner. As Pedro Chacón notes, Guerra Garrido's novels were chronicling a distinctively immigrant point of view even before some of the classic Spanish-language social scientific literature appeared on identity politics in the Basque Country (71–73).

Within a year of that interview, he had published another novel centered upon the Basque situation. Its very publication would appear to suggest that Guerra Garrido's evaluation of his own creative flow was misplaced.[6] But, I would argue further that so, too, was his estimation of "post-terrorism." Speaking specifically of post-Marxism and postmodernism, Terry Eagleton has noted: "The term 'post,' if it has any meaning at all, means business as usual, only more so" (381). Taking Eagleton's formulation as a point of departure, of necessity, the "post-terrorist" novel is an important part of the literary landscape insofar as it represents an accentuation of the Basque "terrorist" novel of times past. Furthermore, if Joseba Zulaika (*Polvo*, 149) is correct in his assertion that any ETA activity after 2006 only guaranteed the defeat of that organization's national project, it would not seem a huge leap to assert that, even prior to ETA's apparent October 2011 dissolution, the reality in Spain and the Basque Country would have been more legitimately classifiable as post-terrorist rather than terrorist. But, then, what exactly does the "only more so" mean in this case? It is a quantitative leap in terms of the sheer number of works that have been produced and authors producing them. And it is qualitative in terms of the increased depiction of the ideological certainty of the story told about the civic project.

THE POST-TERRORIST LITERARY MOMENT

In more recent times, a critical result in the shift in focus is what types of characters become central in these literary works and, just as relevantly, which types are downplayed or excluded. One example of this trend comes from Luisa Etxenike's 2008 novel *The Blind Spot*. The work consists of two parts. The main character of the post-novel "Original Version" is the alleged author of the opus that appears first as "The Novel." *The Blind Spot* was awarded the 2009 prize for Basque Literature in Spanish, with the jury praising the novel's literary merits at length, but also lauding it "for dealing with a serene reflection and denunciation, from the point of view of the victims, of the irrational violence and its consequences" (Premios Euskadi de Literatura).

The novel's main character is Martín, an adolescent who is suddenly forced to grow up without his father, a bodyguard who dies in the line of fire protecting a politician targeted by ETA. The opus focuses on Martín's emotional distress in light of his father's death. It is clear that, if his father is a victim, then so is he. The introspection and interior life of the protagonist and his mother stand in marked contrast to the introduction of the antagonists as actual people, rather than uniquely as filtered through the emotional tribulations of the primary characters. In the entire book, the direct introduction of such characters occurs only once: when Martín enters a radical nationalist bar in San Sebastián. His intention is to hang postcards that he has just bought of places in the city, postcards that appear to remind him of his relationship with his father. His mementos stand in implicit opposition to the large signs of "Independence," "Prisoners Home," and other such proclamations. As he sits at the bar and begins to glue the postcards, his gesture meets with the opposition of the bartender and another worker in the bar, who tell him to take them off, with the bartender finally knocking them to the floor with a violent swing of his arm. They tell Martín to leave, with one bellowing, "Do you want me to beat the crap out of you?" (Etxenike, 35). In this scene, Martín and the bartenders, unnamed, occupy the same physical space. But it is for only an instant. Their respective moral spaces are distinguished by a chasm marked off by great ideological differences, but also by small details and gestures. As Etxenike notes twice (once for each bartender) so as to reiterate this subtle symbolic point, what separates Martín from them, "what distinguishes them from each other are the postcards, the reason and meaning of the postcards" (34, 35). Again, this is the only interaction that Martín has with people from that world; indeed, it is the only time that any such individuals appear in the novel—and they appear as unnamed, hostile individuals without life trajectories who utter single-sentence, aggressive comments where the possible escalation of violence is ever present. Before leaving the bar, Martín reflects on the attitudes and life possibilities separating him from them:

> This bar belongs to them—the ones who are not sorry about my father's death, the ones that are happy they have assassinated him. Surely they have offered a toast right here, at this bar counter, at these tables. Celebrating the assassination of at least a bodyguard right here, at least one of the two has fallen. Surely they have offered a toast.

> *Presoak etxera*, prisoners home, written on the walls. What is not written is that they are prisoners because they are criminals and, to what home? Because what is home for them . . . is not home for me anymore. Home is a place where people are not afraid, where you don't have to worry that someone will jump out of a corner or from the shadow and put a bullet in your head. (36)

These depictions of radical nationalists, especially their limited emotional character development, stand in marked contrast to the great degree of insight that we get into the characters from Martín's close circle. For example, he lists the things lost in death: "To die is to lose that smell of bread forever. And to lose everything else forever: fine sand, the pattern of San Sebastián's octagonal blue and white sidewalk tiles, the fishing boats surrounded by yachts and sailboats . . . the orange air at dusk" (27). Through some of these reflections, the reader is presented with victimization on a number of levels: Martín and his mother in life (as a result of their emotional distress from his father's death), Martín's father as a result of his own death, but, even earlier, Martín's father and mother in their shared life, as they strove to fight against the oppressive atmosphere by placing themselves in the "blind spot" of the rearview mirror (hence the book's title) where no antagonist could reach them (79–80). This set of descriptions ultimately points to a better understanding of a vivid emotional life and an implicit, didactic expansion of the circle of who might be considered a "victim," while at the same time marking those in that identity category off from those who, quite simply, could never be seen as such.

The book's first section is purportedly written by the main character of the post-novel, who at times feels guilty about what he qualifies as his less-than-dignified behavior, which he has attempted to write out of the novel. As he tells his mother about the book that he has written, "I need the novel to lie in order to rehearse some sort of dignity and decency in myself" (Etxenike, 177). Yet, although in its second register, Etxenike's work affirms a reality of human action that is in a certain sense less clear cut and less typological, frailty and self-doubt do not cloud the novel's moral geography; they ultimately reaffirm it, because what is represented is painted as even closer to real life. As the mother explains to her less-than-heroic son to assuage his bad feelings:

> The guilt is not ours. The guilt belongs to the assassins and their conspirators, and those that protect them one way or another: those that, though they could put the terrorists in their place by making it clear with every word that they are assassins and vile, do not do it, and allow confusion and ambiguity to spread. . . .
>
> The guilt is not ours. We are the victims, the threatened, the dead, the wounded in everyday happiness, in the foolish things that make happiness. (158–59)

In the midst of weakness and imperfection, moral high ground, the rule of law, and clear good versus evil are affirmed in both of the novel's registers, and, perhaps precisely because of its imperfections, in the post-novel that clarity has an even greater impact.

Etxenike's novel is not an isolated example of the relative exclusion of the antagonist's voice from the works of literature. One other is Pedro Mari Baglietto's 1999 *A Cry for Peace*. This novella is written as a stream of consciousness, internal first-person narrative of the main character on the last day of his life, prior to being assassinated. The work is meant to be historical fiction, a re-creation of the experience of Ramón Baglietto, the author's brother, who met this fate in 1980. Much of the novella deals with the life of the Baglietto family, including their emotional identification with and roots in the Basque Country. Although antagonists are frequently present in the mind of the protagonist, Ramón's killer "Basilio"[7] is the only one whose presence is narrated, and it is done twice. The first is in Ramón's retrospective thought about when he caught Basilio as a youth writing "You will die" near Ramón's house. Ramón did not give the incident much importance at the time, jokingly addressing him by saying, "You'll have to kill me very dead, Basilio" as the youth scampered off without saying anything (Baglietto, 33).

The second time is when Ramón's body is draped in his car on a mountain pass after a failed escape. The protagonist's narration at this moment is as follows:

> I do not know if it is due to the bullets or the violence of the crash, but I am completely unconscious. Nor do I know if I have died. But my attackers do not want to have any doubts. Their Renault 4 stops in back of my car and Basilio gets out carefully. His face is radiant. He seems to remember my words: "You'll have to kill me very dead!" His hand grips a locally made pistol: a Parabellum 9 millimeter. He walks with firm, confident steps. Finally, his name will be entered into the logbook of the heroes of the homeland. Finally, he will demonstrate that the formative work that the intellectuals of the Basque revolution have invested in him is going to yield its fruit. Basilio and his commando mates have decided that I will not return home tonight. Tonight or any other night. He points the barrel of his pistol coldly at my temple and fires with a gesture of pride. (Baglietto, 136)

These two moments, the only ones in which the antagonist appears physically, depict that presence as one-dimensional and in a light far from favorable.

To return to the work of Raúl Guerra Garrido, that author has observed that he cannot write from the perspective of a terrorist, just like he cannot write from the perspective of a woman, and he thus explains his failure to introduce this type of first-person perspective as rooted in the limits of his capacity for empathy (Cervantes TV). At the same time, however, there is a clear evolution in his work with respect to character inclusion. His 1976 novel, *A Very Unusual Reading of Das Kapital*, for which he won Spain's Nadal prize that year, is marked by ETA's kidnapping of a local industrialist. The kidnappers are in many ways parodied; for example, the five go by the names of Abel 1 through Abel 5, in a cross between fratricidal biblical parable and automaton revolutionary caricature, and their applications of Marxist doctrine are presented as misplaced and superficial. Nevertheless, they are characterized by two traits absent in the later Basque novels of Guerra Garrido: (1) the attempted use of logical argument to justify their political position and actions and (2) their very presence. Guerra Garrido's 1989 novel *The Letter*, about the chain of events unleashed by an extortion letter to a non-autochthonous business owner demanding the payment of a "revolutionary tax" to contribute to the project of Basque independence, stands in marked contrast. The author refers to this novel as "a radiography of fear" (Marín). What is striking in this Kafkaesque treatise with a Brechtian call to civic action (or observation of the complete lack of such action) is not only the lack of in-depth justification, but also the absence of the antagonists, despite their omnipresence in the minds and actions of the main characters. On only one occasion is the reader led to believe that the main character has come into contact with the violent elements of the radical Basque nationalist world, but it turns out to be a case of petty blackmail and mistaken identity.

Similarly, in Guerra Garrido's 2007 novel *The Solitude of the Guardian Angel*, the main character, the unnamed bodyguard (again, from outside of the Basque Country) of a retired and apparently harmless university professor who has been threatened by ETA, never comes in contact with the terrorists, to whom he refers (along with their overall human environment) as, quite simply, "the bad guys" (*los malos*). Although this social sphere is again omnipresent, the bodyguard's direct contact with it is extremely limited, and, as the novel progresses, the reader can be less sure of what s/he reads because of the main character's increasingly precarious mental state. On one occasion, the main character witnesses a radical nationalist street protest against the incarceration of certain ETA members; on the main avenue, he sees

> housewives, showing a photo on a small stick of one of their sons, apparently political prisoners for having assassinated at least one person. And it is not as though the photos were of the bad guys, but they were of the best killers from among those bad guys, and the mothers crying in grief that our sons are imprisoned in remote extermination prisons, and we can only go

to see them once a year on very dangerous, exhausting trips that are also of extermination. (Guerra Garrido, *La soledad*, 91)

Shortly thereafter, the protagonist tells of witnessing a woman who, out of hysteria, breaks the social "rule" of walking past in silence and briefly engages one of the mothers:

"You can go see your son once a year, but I can only see my husband in the cemetery. Do you know who that is in the photo you are carrying?"

"My son." . . . .

"No, that's nobody's son. It's my husband's assassin."

"Yeah? Go fuck yourself." (92)

Far later in the book, our unnamed protagonist tells of another direct encounter, his second and last with radical nationalists. The retired professor is to give a talk at his old university department, where he is of course accompanied by his bodyguards. There, he is met by a banner with a noose drawn on it, and the words, "For the old professor, fascist, liar, and traitor" (175). When the talk is about to get underway, it is preemptively interrupted by one of the professor's former colleagues, who states "I have only come to confirm that I agree neither with your conduct nor your ideology and so that you do not interpret my absence as being due to my inability to attend. Good night" (180). As this antagonist leaves, his eyes cross with those of the novel's protagonist, who thinks to himself, "he is without a doubt a first cousin of the bad guys. His gaze is despotic, metallic. He would love to knife me" (181).

In contrast to the (near) complete elimination of such voices noted above, other works offer more extensive depictions of radical Basque nationalist activity and violence. For example, the 2010 novel *Father Fatherland* by Vicente Carrión Arregui traces the evolution of Aitor Irastorza Sagarna from the age of 16 in 1995 until he is 21 in 2000. Much of the novel, especially its earlier part, deals with Aitor in the context of his social circle and family all of whom, with the exception of his mother, are implicated in radical nationalist activity in the bastion of this political persuasion. Perhaps the most important symbol for the main character is his father, an ETA member who was killed by right-wing Spanish paramilitaries shortly after Aitor's birth. Aitor is no different from those in his immediate circle, and is involved in this political world full-throttle, for example, preparing Molotov cocktails at the behest of his cousin Hodei (Carrión Arregui, 39–40). Aitor is also caught by the police while attempting to help Hodei use some of these incendiary devices against a local business that refuses to pay the "revolutionary tax" to further the cause of independence (65). With time, however, and under the influence of his girl-friend, his mother, and his father's diaries (given to him by his mother), Aitor grows to see the abstract concept of the homeland, especially as a fount for misplaced hatred and destruction, as paling in comparison to human relation-ships as they cross social strata and ideological difference. At a critical junc-ture in the novel, his father's diaries lead Aitor to reflect that "he has spent his entire life trying to hold together with patriotic glue those fragments of the child that broke apart after his father's killing, only to realize now that it was not worth the effort" (193). In a word, he evolves, and that evolution is most clear when the main character is held in relief compared to his former cronies. Hodei asks him in a subsequent late-night meeting, in an implicit test of loy-alty, to track the movements of the socialist Fernando Buesa, a nonfictional politician whose death in 2000 serves as a marker near the end of the novel.[8] Although the main character is not yet strong enough to categorically reject the request, in response to it, "Aitor tried to see something in the darkness that surrounded him. Inside and out" (287). He ultimately extricates himself from his previous social caste, with its hatred and penchant for destruction. So, although Father Fatherland is marked by a vivid presence of radical Basque nationalist characters, their presence ultimately serves as a foil to the emo-tional and civic growth of the main character.

Another work, whose very title suggests an empathetic chord, is Verónica Portell's 2006 collection, *And Nevertheless, I Understand You.* More than a set of short stories, this book is a mosaic surrounding a single event from multiple perspectives over the course of a very short period of time: the (fictional) kidnapping of the (fictional) city council-person Javier Ortigueira. This work is a thinly veiled allusion to Miguel Ángel Blanco, with the difference that Ortigueira is (surprisingly) res-cued. Although Portell's work attempts to be empathetic and inclusive, this perspective does not come without limitations. Perhaps emblematic of this is the last portrait, subsequent to Ortigueira's rescue. Called "Nobody Knows" (Portell, 173–77), it is a love story between an ETA member and a city councilwoman (both nameless) affiliated with a Spanish party. In spite of their mutual affection, his attempts to protect her from ETA, and their tenuous personal truce that mirrors the larger world's vacillation between the absence of hostility and its presence, the fact that he began observing her as a potential assassination target ultimately removes any apparent symmetry in their relationship and makes the two vastly different ethical registers clear.

CONNECTIONS AND REFLECTIONS

One trend regarding these works is the political connections and the experiences of many of the authors involved in such cultural production, with the former often serving as sources of inspiration and/or resulting from the latter. These elements cannot be separated from each other. One ethnographic moment that comes to mind involves an interview with Maite Pagazaurtundua, whose brother was a local policeman killed by ETA and who serves as the President of the Madrid-based Foundation for Victims of Terrorism. When I asked her about her short stories, she told me that her literary production was something completely separate from her civic duties. Nevertheless, given her stories, for example, about a man who returns after twenty-five years to his Basque hometown, where he had been mayor until he left following a failed attempt on his life, only to reminisce extensively with a friend of his failed assassin (Pagazaurtundua, *El viudo*, 83–89); and, about a woman who decides to choose her lovers from within the ranks of the bodyguards of potential ETA victims so as to minimize the possibility of extended romantic attachments (Pagazaurtundua, *El viudo*, 51–82), I am skeptical about this assertion. Similarly, Raúl Guerra Garrido was a member of the Ermua Forum in protest of Miguel Ángel Blanco's death, as well as being a foundational member of the Spanish UPD party; his family pharmacy was also burned to the ground as a result of targeted street violence (an event he recounts in his 2003 essay, "Secret Notebook"). Pedro Mari Baglietto is actively involved in government supported primary- and secondary-school victim awareness programs. Verónica Portell's father was a journalist killed by ETA. Mikel Azurmendi (*Melodías*; *Tango*), is a university professor who took an extended sabbatical from teaching in response to threats and has received Spain's Medal for the Order of Constitutional Merit for his anti-ETA activities and writings. Anjel Lerxtundi, whose 2001 novel *Perfect Happiness* (later made into a movie) is about the psychological effects of witnessing an ETA killing on a girl in her youth and later as an adult, was the first figure from the artistic community to speak at the introductory Victims of Terrorism commemoration organized by the Basque Department for Attention to Victims of Terrorism in 2007. Hence, the double entendre of "Writing Victims."

Many of these authors have received prizes and recognition for their literary creations. In addition to those noted, Fernando Aramburu's 2006 collection of short stories about victims and civic disengagement, *The Fish of Bitterness*, won the Mario Vargas Llosa NH Prize for Short Stories, perhaps the most important of such prizes in Spain, and Dulce Chacón Prize for Spanish Narrative in 2007, and the Royal Academy of the Spanish Language Prize in 2008; Anjel Lertxundi has won numerous prizes; Pedro Villora's play *Electra in Oma* (dedicated simply "to the victims"), which places the well-known Greek tragedy in the Oma forest in which Basque artist Agustin Ibarrola's painted trees were attacked by ETA supporters, thus displaying resistance, and in the ancient Greek spirit of art as civic education, won Spain's first ever Beckett Prize in 2005, and was a 2007 finalist for Spain's National Prize for Dramatic Literature.

In closing, in spite of the range in quality, generally speaking, post-terrorist fiction in the Basque Country and Spain provides vivid depictions of the interior lives of its protagonists, and has been written by a range of authors, including those who are highly esteemed. It reveals a strong connection to a political vision that has largely led to a distancing from certain character types, most notably including a marked shift from earlier work's revolutionary-oriented characters to ones heavily slanted toward victims. Although the political context in such cases is far from homologous, this leads me to reflect upon Transitional Justice Studies.

This is a field that, in recognition of its connections to on-the-ground political realities, appears to have been heading in the opposite direction, shifting its object of interest from those framed as victims to those framed as perpetrators—a change that has proven practical for conflict resolution (Merry). Looking at a global context having its roots in the Vietnam War and particularly international legal developments beginning in the 1980s, Caroline Eliacheff and Daniel Soulez even argue that the victim has replaced the hero as the fundamental archetype of our times, with ambivalent societal effects (see also Pascal Bruckner, 123–54). This ambivalence, with respect to a societal project that these authors depict, is in fact mirrored in the literature that I am describing here—the very important work of bringing the experience of victims to the fore. In spite of a great range in the literary qualities of these works, they frequently manage to wonderfully chronicle rich interior lives focusing on love, loss, displacement, and suffering, in a way that is absent for the most part in the social scientific literature.[9] At the same time, they tend do so from a position of great ideological certainty, and one that does not recognize that the fact that they are critical truths in no way implies that they are not partial. I am reminded of the former Spanish Minister of the Interior Jaime Mayor Oreja's controversial statement while in office that "the victims are always right." In her book *Precarious Life*, with respect to war and noting the differential allocation of grief across populations and individuals, Judith Butler underscores the critical importance of the question: "Who counts as human? Whose lives count as lives? And, finally, What *makes for a grievable life?* (20). The very existence of the literature examined here says at least as much about Basque and Spanish social and political dynamics as the situations it attempts to capture in terms of who is grieved and, ultimately, who is able to claim the limited good of victim status and the moral high ground that accompanies it. In attempting to put this literature into perspective, I am reminded that one charge of the "Re-Visioning Terrorism" conference was to see if it is possible to shed new light on the phenomenon of "terrorism." If I were to restrict myself to the material of the Basque-themed, post-terrorist fictions in striving to answer this question, the answer would seem to be "no"—by and large, it is indeed "business as usual, only more so."

NOTES

1.   This work was supported by the Program for Cultural Cooperation, University of Minnesota and Spain's Ministry of Culture under Grant 3773. I would like to thank organizers Ben Lawton and Elena Coda, as well as Patricia Hart, for the opportunity to participate in the "Re-Visioning Terrorism" conference, and two anonymous reviewers for their comments. This paper's origins lie in a comment made to me by Faustino López de Foronda during a 2010 interview. It is my hope that the "definitive cessation of armed activity," declared October 2011, contributes to rendering the prefix "post" true in all senses.

2.   Despite recognizing the ideological valence of the term "radical nationalist," I use it as a gloss for those accepting violence as a means to independence.

3.   See the Euskobarometro public opinion surveys from the University of the Basque Country regarding the plummeting support for ETA even prior to 2011 (www .ehu.es/euskobarometro).

4.   One relevant development was the August 2010 foundation of the Association of Writers of the Basque Country, an institutionally funded initiative promoting Basque writers in the Spanish language and in opposition to a more longstanding exclusively Basque-language homologue (see "Los escritores vascos;" Larrinaga). This opposition is reminiscent of the duplication and confrontation characteristic of so many facets of Basque society; see Roland Vazquez, *Politics, Culture, and Sociability in the Basque Nationalist Party* (Reno: University of Nevada Press, 2010), 64–66.

5.   This was not an isolated comment; Guerra Garrido had made similar statements since at least 1999 and he continued to do so in 2011; see, for example, Cervantes TV, "Entrevista a Raúl Guerra Garrido," April 27, 2011.

6.   Although the interview occurred prior to the Barajas bombing, which could have proven a creative impetus, Guerra Garrido repeated this assertion subsequently (e.g., Cervantes TV).

7.   "Basilio" is the only person referenced in the book whose real name is not used. He is really Candido Azpiazu Beristain, who was released from prison in 2004.

8.   The death of Buesa and his bodyguard, Jorge Díez in February 2000 at ETA's hands convulsed Basque society due to Buesa's antiauthoritarian pedigree and penchant for consensus building in the Basque Parliament.

9.   But see Begoña Aretxaga, *States of Terror* (Reno: Center for Basque Studies, 2005), 147–62, 231–39; and Joseba Zulaika, *Basque Violence* (Reno: University of Nevada Press, 1988), 74–101 as stunning exceptions.

WORKS CITED

Aramburu, Fernando. *Los peces de la amargura*. Barcelona: Tusquets, 2006.

Aretxaga, Begoña. *States of Terror*. Reno: Center for Basque Studies, 2005.

Arruti, Nerea. "On the Lightness of Being." In *Writers in Between Languages*, edited by Mari José Olaziregi, 115–30. Reno: Center for Basque Studies, 2009.

Arteta, Iñaki. *Olvidados*. Madrid: Adhera, 2008.

Atxaga, Bernardo. *Gizona bere bakardadean*. Iruña: Pamiela, 1993.

Azurmendi, Mikel. *Melodías vascas*. San Sebastián: Hiria, 2008.

———. *Tango de muerte*. Barcelona: El Cobre. 2011.

Baglietto, Pedro Mari. *Un grito de paz*. Madrid: Espasa Calpe, 1999.

Blas, Andrés, Ramón Saizarbitoria, and Jon Juaristi. "Debate sobre nacionalismo vasco." *Revista de Occidente* 200 (1998).

Bruckner, Pascal. *The Temptation of Innocence*. New York: Algora, 2000.

Butler, Judith. *Precarious Life*. London: Verso, 2004.

Carrión Arregui, Vicente. *Padre Patria*. San Sebastián: Hiria, 2010.

Chacón Delgado, Pedro José. *Perdí la identidad que nunca tuve*. Madrid: Sepha, 2010.

Cervantes TV. "Entrevista a Raúl Guerra Garrido." April 27, 2011.

Eagleton, Terry. *The Ideology of the Aesthetic*. Oxford: Basil Blackwell, 1990.

Eliacheff, Caroline and Daniel Soulez. *El tiempo de las víctimas*. Madrid: Akal, 2009.

Etxenike, Luisa. *El ángulo ciego*. Barcelona: Bruguera, 2008.

Guerra Garrido, Raúl. *Cacereño*. 1969. Madrid: Grupo Libro, 1994.

———. *Cuaderno secreto*. Barcelona: El Aleph, 2003.

———. *La carta*. 1989. Madrid: Alianza, 2007.

———. *La soledad del ángel de la guarda*. Madrid: Alianza, 2007.

———. *Lectura insólita de El Capital*. Madrid: Destino, 1977.

Hunt, Lynn. *Inventing Human Rights: A History*. New York: Norton, 2008.

Larrinaga, M. "Nace la Asociación de Escritores de Euskadi, abierta a 'todos' los idiomas." *Gara*. August 19, 2010. http://gara.naiz.eus/paperezkoa /20100819/216402/es/Nace-Asociacion-Escritores-Euskadi-abierta -todos-idiomas.

Lertxundi, Anjel. *Perfect Happiness*. Reno: Center for Basque Studies, 2007.

Linz, Juan J., Manuel Gómez-Reino, Francisco Andrés Orizo, and Darío Vila. *Conflicto en Euskadi*. Madrid: Espasa-Calpe, 1986.

"Los escritores vascos se unen para defender sus derechos." *El País*. August 19, 2010. http://elpais.com/diario/2010/08/19/paisvasco /1282246813_850215.html.

Marín, M. "Entrevista: Raúl Guerra Garrido, Premio Nacional de las Letras." *El País*. November 30, 2006. http://www.elpais.com/articulo/cultura /novela/posterrorismo/seria/relato/novios/enamorados/necios/elpepicul /20061130elpepicul_5/Tes.

Merry Engle, Sally. Discussant commentary, session on "The Category of Perpetrator in Human Rights Discourse." Joint meeting of SUNTA and AES, San Juan, PR, April 15, 2011.

Onaindia, Mario. *Guía para orientarse en el laberinto vasco*. Madrid: Temas de Hoy, 2000.

Ortiz Alfau, Ángel. *Raúl Guerra Garrido*. Madrid: Primitiva Casa Baroja, 1989.

Pagazaurtundua, Maite. *El viudo sensible y otros secretos*. Barcelona: Seix Barral, 2005.

———. *Los Pagaza. Historia de una familia vasca*. Madrid: Temas de Hoy, 2004.

Portell Torres, Verónica. *Y sin embargo, te entiendo*. San Sebastián: Hiria, 2006.

Premios Euskadi de Literatura. "Literatura en castellano." 2009. http://www .euskadi.eus/r33-2734/es/contenidos/informacion/euskadi_litera_2009 /es_literatu/cast.html.

Saizarbitoria, Ramón. *Ehun metro*. Donostia: Kriselu, 1976.

———. *Hamaika pauso*. Donostia: Erein, 1995.

San Sebastián, Isabel. *Los años de plomo*. Madrid: Temas de Hoy, 2003.

Vazquez, Roland. *Politics, Culture, and Sociability in the Basque Nationalist Party*. Reno: University of Nevada Press, 2010.

Villa, Irene. *Saber que se puede*. Madrid: Martínez Roca, 2004.

Villora, Pedro. *Electra en Oma*. 2006. Madrid: Fundamentos, 2008.

Zulaika, Joseba. *Basque Violence*. Reno: University of Nevada Press, 1988.

———. *Polvo de ETA*. Irun: Alberdania, 2007.

16

Knights of Justice?
Blockbuster Terrorism in *Code Geass: Lelouch of the Rebellion*

AARON CHOO AND WILSON KOH

The only ones who should kill are those who are prepared to be killed!
Wherever oppressors act to abuse their power by attacking the powerless,
we shall appear again! No matter how mighty, how formidable our foe
may be! Those of you with power—fear us! Those of you without it—rally
behind us! We, the Black Knights, shall be the ones who stand in judgment
of this world! (Taniguchi, n.p.)

This is the manifesto of the hero of *Code Geass: Lelouch of the Rebellion* (henceforth simply *Code Geass*, 2006–2008), an epic anime series that forms the centerpiece of a multimedia franchise. The hero, Lelouch, is a high school student in an alternate near-future Japan that has been conquered by the Holy Britannian Empire, a fictional imperialist analog of the British Empire. Lelouch leads a double life as the masked terrorist "Zero," fighting to liberate Japan through violent and spectacular attacks against the colonial authorities. Following its debut in 2006, *Code Geass* quickly gained international popularity and critical acclaim, with popular reviewers praising its apparently sophisticated philosophical conflict, where Lelouch and servants of the Britannian Empire are all shown to possess equally valid rationale for their actions. The series has been broadcast internationally, and was shown in the United States on Cartoon Network's Adult Swim channel. By November 2008, *Code Geass* had sold over one million anime DVDs and Blu-Rays in various countries, making it one of the world's most popular animated programs (Carothers). The series has spawned related stories and retellings in the form of manga (Japanese comics), novels, and video games, as well as a vast array of merchandise. A third season of the anime was announced in August 2011.

Why has *Code Geass*, with its central conceit of "terrorist as hero," been able to command this degree of popular and critical acclaim? What is it saying to its audiences about terrorism, and why is it taking this stance? To answer these questions, this paper provides a multipart answer. It first reads *Code Geass*'s fictional portrayal of terrorism in relation to post-9/11 scholarly perspectives on "new terrorism" and asymmetric warfare. Then, it further analyzes *Code Geass* against Jean-Francois Lyotard's theory of eclectic "little narratives," and finally as a cultural artifact within a global media market dominated by the ethos of the Hollywood blockbuster franchise. This paper finds that *Code Geass* intentionally rejects the present orthodoxy regarding terrorism and authority. Instead of portraying a frightening religious fanatic who defies rational understanding, *Code Geass* depicts a terrorist with sympathetic motives that audiences can comprehend, a comforting fantasy amidst a political climate dominated by constant risk and uncertainty. In addition, *Code Geass* presents a disenfranchised role model who is able to rise up successfully against a repressive state apparatus. This false and pleasing fantasy of individual empowerment defies status quo conceptions of the government as the only legitimate authority in society, satisfying consumers who are increasingly suspicious of such metanarratives. But despite such countercultural claims, *Code Geass* remains a commercial popular media franchise. *Code Geass* is a non-Western text and an episodic television series rather than a film, but it nonetheless follows the model of the postmillennial Hollywood blockbuster. This paper ultimately argues that *Code Geass*'s use of terrorism as a theme merely exploits the post-9/11 zeitgeist in order to make itself appear sophisticated and relevant, maximizing its appeal to audiences. *Code Geass* thus represents what this paper terms "blockbuster terrorism," symptomatic of how popular media oversimplifies the complex political issue of terrorism for profitable consumption across a wide spectrum of audiences.

ONLY A CERTAIN AMOUNT OF TERROR

According to Paul Virilio, terrorism and war are intrinsically acts of spectacle, the aim is "not so much to capture as to 'captivate' [the enemy], to instil the fear of death into him before he actually dies" (1). But Virilio subsequently notes that terrorism is the dark cousin of war, and a "psychic anaesthesia" (33) accordingly pervades acts of terror despite the proliferation of war-related media. "Man can only take a certain amount of terror," Virilio writes, describing how victims mentally block out realities that are too horrifying to them (33). James Chapman, accordingly, notes that war films are caught between a "desire to capture authentic images of the war and the tendency to aestheticize war through aspects of film form and style" (12). This tension gives rise to a "pleasure culture of war," where war is romantically represented as a *Boys' Own*-style adventure story of heroes and villains (Chapman, 4). In a roughly similar vein, the "war on terror" is also portrayed in a romanticized and aesthetically pleasing fashion in popular media. *V for Vendetta* (2006) features balletic "bullet-time" duels between a masked insurgent and the security forces of a totalitarian dystopia. *Gundam 00* (2007–2009) is an anime series with soap-opera-like personal revelations. Its hero, a former terrorist, dramatically discovers that he caused the death of a friend's family in one of his past attacks.

Yet, despite these similarities, postmillennial representations of the "war on terror" are nonetheless distinct from their closely linked antecedent of the war epic. Traditional war films ultimately looked back on history; the genre was "dominated, unsurprisingly, by films about the two World Wars" (Chapman, 248). Yet, where war films used to dwell on the past, more contemporary popular entertainment about terrorism—this includes films and television programs alike—looks at the present or future, reflecting real-life anxieties over when the next terrorist attack will inevitably occur. Thus, popular media portrayals of terrorism are inextricably products of an era overshadowed by the specter of 9/11.

ANOTHER MAN'S FREEDOM FIGHTER

In this context, it is significant that *Code Geass* portrays its hero as a romanticized revolutionary, a Che Guevara or Yasser Arafat figure rather than an Osama Bin Laden or Anders Behring Breivik. All these men have been referred to as terrorists, but individuals such as the former pair are generally viewed more favorably than the latter. Terrorism is a highly contested concept, and there is no universally agreed definition of what constitutes a terrorist (Byford, 34). But since 9/11, many theorists have drawn a distinction between "old terrorists" and the "new terrorists" that are said to exist today (Martin, 5–8). Old or traditional terrorists fit the maxim of one man's terrorist being another man's freedom fighter. In Ireland, terrorism "made heroes out of gunmen [and] policemen into villains" (Fromkin, 686–87). Similarly, Alan Dershowitz notes that "the very brutality and desperation" (31) of acts committed by the Palestinian people in the 1960s and 1970s gave them greater international legitimacy. Acts of violence committed by a clearly defined group with explicit grievances against the state are often viewed with some sympathy by observers outside the conflict zone, especially since such violence rarely spills beyond national borders (Martin, 5–8).

New terrorists are a different breed. Since 9/11, attention has been drawn to a vast and nebulous global network of belligerents willing to kill en masse for religious or politically vague motivations (Blakely, 12–13). Most disturbingly, their violence is not confined to a far-flung corner of the globe, but is everywhere and indiscriminate, seemingly aimed at the destruction of society and the elimination of large sections of the population (Weinberg, 47). However, *Code Geass* does not glorify a new terrorist. Instead, it situates its protagonist firmly within a traditional emancipatory context. Although he is referred to as a terrorist, Lelouch's terrorism is aimed at freeing a people from colonial domination. *Code Geass* thus fits within Virilio and Chapman's conceptions of aestheticized violence, evoking the trappings of terrorism, but presenting a terrorist that does not unsettle audiences.

A BAD KIND OF BODY LANGUAGE

This trend toward aestheticized violence is evident within the first few episodes of *Code Geass*. In Lelouch's debut appearance as the masked terrorist Zero, he threatens to release poison gas on a crowd of civilians. The sequence is intended to evoke the 1995 Aum Shinrikyo sarin gas attack in Tokyo, an especially powerful image for Japanese audiences. But Lelouch's gas turns out to be harmless colored smoke, a distraction so he can rescue a friend from military custody. Throughout the series, Lelouch takes pains to avoid harming noncombatants. The first time civilians die from his plots, Lelouch is struck by remorse. *Code Geass* belabors the point by making this a personal tragedy for Lelouch; the father of his love interest is among the victims. *Code Geass* thus presents a terrorist whose attitudes toward violence essentially mirror the contemporary liberal sensibilities of audiences. According to Christopher Coker, killing "is not only an action, but also a speech act. It involves signs, gestures, and expressions . . . a body language, if you like, aimed at other bodies" (115). A society's cultural norms and morals define how violence is conducted, giving rise to different "grammars of killing." In contemporary liberal society, the use of violence is constrained by moral imperatives to minimize suffering. Soldiers are expected to avoid civilian casualties and undue acts of cruelty (Coker, 14).

Terrorists have a different grammar of killing. It was once said that terrorists want "a lot of people watching, not a lot of people dead" (Weinberg, 47). But the past decade has proven that some terrorists are willing to perform indiscriminate slaughter in the name of religious authorities. Objectively, the number of deaths caused by even the largest terrorist attacks do not compare to deaths from natural disasters. But such incidents can be seen as random occurrences, while a terrorist attack is a deliberate act of malevolent agency and thus far more disturbing. Terrorist attacks are intended to create a sense of vulnerability and helplessness, causing both physical harm and long-term psychological trauma (Ditzler, 187–206). For instance, survivors of suicide bombings may develop bumps beneath their skin months after the attack, as DeLillo describes:

this is caused by . . . tiny fragments of the suicide bomber's body. The
bomber is blown to bits, literally bits and pieces, and fragments of flesh
and bone come flying outward with such force and velocity that they get
wedged . . . in the body of anyone who's in striking range. . . . They call
this organic shrapnel. (DeLillo, 6)

In Iraq, insurgents have created a new form of media spectacle, releas-
ing videos depicting grotesque beheadings of their captives. A beheading is
a humiliating mutilation of the body, showing it to be penetrable, reducing
it to a mass of abject and base effluvia. Contemporary information age culture values the sanctity of the individual, and perhaps, by extension, also the
inviolability of the body. Fitness, health, and physical well-being have become
prime foci of social concern. But actors living outside the contemporary liberal experience have very different opinions. It is likely that the perpetrators
of such acts are quite aware their target audiences would find such footage
unthinkably barbaric; they deliberately attack such sensibilities (Coker, 122).

Genuine terrorist attacks are therefore far removed from the sanitized
depictions of violence in *Code Geass.* While people die in *Code Geass,* most
victims are a faceless mass with no names or distinct identities, anonymous
to the viewer. The resulting corpses are also depicted as intact bodies without
any disfigurement, calculated to elicit tears as opposed to disgust. The only
indicator that the victims are dead is the copious presence of exaggeratedly
red blood on the surface of their image-bodies. These are deliberate stylistic
choices; the lack of gore in *Code Geass* is in line with the series' nature as
an entertainment property meant for mass distribution. Television requires
its own grammar of killing, an aesthetically pleasing violence that does not
disturb the viewer, but rather pleasantly captivates him with stylized imagery.

POST-HEROIC WARFARE

Much in the same way *Code Geass* gives an oversimplified view of bloodshed, it also conflates the full spectrum of political violence into a single
absurd narrative. Lelouch and his followers are initially a poorly armed rag-
tag group. But by the end of the series, the Black Knights are a uniformed

military force, able to challenge the state's armed forces on equal terms. This is a supremely unrealistic progression. In the real world, terrorism is not necessarily synonymous with revolutionary war or guerrilla warfare (Lacquer, 26; Martin, 21–31). There have been high-profile incidents where terrorist gunmen have engaged security forces directly, such as the 2008 Mumbai attacks. Yet even in Mumbai, the gunmen did not follow military rules of engagement, deliberately targeting civilians. Terrorists do not fight like soldiers. Most contemporary terrorist groups are organized as loose networks of cells, a structure intended to evade capture by state authorities. Terrorism is a weapon of the weak, a form of asymmetric combat used by those unable to challenge the state on its own terms (Gray, 5–14).

Small armed groups have historically been able to eject perceived foreign invaders or colonial occupiers from their territory, but such victories have generally not come due to strength of arms. In such cases, state authorities have typically given in to demands for autonomy only after a prolonged period, when the conflict became too drawn-out or costly to sustain. A protracted civil conflict erodes domestic support and damages morale within the state's armed forces, as was the case for the French in Algeria (Fromkin, 686–91). Arguably, insurgents in Iraq and Afghanistan are attempting to weaken the resolve of the US and its allies in a similar fashion (Cordesman, 2–6). However, this form of civil conflict is not the kind shown in *Code Geass*. When Lelouch and his followers vanquish their enemies, they do so in the most literal manner possible, defeating them decisively on the battlefield in honorable combat.

Although *Code Geass* refers to its hero as a terrorist, by the end of the series he effectively leads a conventional army. Throughout *Code Geass*, Lelouch and his allies emerge victorious against government forces not only through superior tactics, but also through superior technology, engaging in an arms race with their foes. The tendency to reduce victory in battle to a matter of relative technological capability is not exclusive to popular media. The 1990s saw a vast body of literature lauding the miracles of military technology in winning wars, the "Revolution in Military Affairs" (Rasmussen, 43–90). But scholars and practitioners today recognize that superior technology is not a panacea, especially when one's enemy is a nonstate actor rather than another military. Real-world terrorists rarely attack a state's armed forces directly, instead concentrating on civilian "soft targets." Terrorism renders the technological and operational advantages possessed by a state's military largely irrelevant (Gray, 5–14).

However, popular media depictions such as *Code Geass* remain rooted in the fetishism of military technology, portraying confrontations with terrorists as clashes on the battlefield. *G.I. Joe* (2009), for example, features gung-ho soldiers equipped with the latest guns, armor, and vehicles. Camera pans over these armaments—frequently just before use against the leaders of COBRA, an evil terrorist organization determined to rule the world—are a recurring feature of the movie. In the world of *Code Geass*, giant robots, or *mecha*, have become the dominant weapons of war, rendering tanks and infantry obsolete. These machines are called Knightmares, deliberately evoking the medieval adventure-romance. Lelouch pilots the Gawain Knightmare, and other named mecha include the Lancelot and the Siegfried. Most of the cast are Knightmare pilots, and characters resolve battles through heroic one-on-one duels. *Code Geass* manages to portray single combat in a manner that satisfies the contemporary aversion toward harm befalling the individual: Knightmare pilots in *Code Geass* are safely encased in the cockpits of their high-tech titans. There is little bloodshed, and pilots frequently eject upon defeat rather than being killed.

Such conventions are typical of the mecha genre, but the presence of mecha combat in a series purportedly about serious political themes is particularly problematic. In *Code Geass*, combat is a heroic act, but in the real world, glory on the battlefield is rapidly becoming an archaic concept. Edward Luttwak argues that contemporary society is in fact moving toward a form of post-heroic warfare, in line with how people in the postmodern context are averse to taking risks as individuals. Since the wars of the twentieth century, the claim of *dulce et decorum est pro patria mori* has been increasingly challenged. Soldiers who die in service to the state may still be honored as heroes, but they are increasingly seen as victims as well (Luttwak, 109–22). The family of a fallen soldier may well hail his personal sacrifice while simultaneously vilifying the government whose foreign policy sent him into battle. In an age where real-world soldiers may be less than convinced that their leaders have the legitimate authority to order them into battle, *Code Geass* paints a comforting caricature where combatants are either unwitting pawns of a literal evil empire, or righteous individualists fighting to overthrow an unjust state apparatus.

A NEW AGE OF HEROES

This skepticism toward government bodies and the concurrent celebration of the individual evokes Jean-Francois Lyotard's comment that the current post-modern age is one typified by "incredulity towards metanarratives" (xxiv). For Lyotard, "the old poles of attraction" represented by grand overarching stories—of church, of state, of heroes of contemporary history, of "truth"—are losing their appeal, and "it does not look as though they will be replaced, at least not on their former scale" (14). These metanarratives once functioned as a means through which a culture masked its own inherent contradictions and instabilities, thus reifying the social order. But the postmodern condi-tion is one of incredulity toward metanarratives. Instead, alternative "little narratives" are increasingly favored, "stories that explain small practices, local events, rather than large scale universal or global concepts . . . [little narratives are] situational, provisional, contingent, temporary and make no claim to universality, truth, reason or stability" (Klages, 169).

Daya Thussu claims news reports after 9/11 serve to circulate metanarra-tives about terrorism, in an attempt to legitimize the US-led "war on terror." Thussu argues news media has made audiences accept the image of the mad Muslim terrorist, "a turbaned, bearded . . . gun-wielding Osama bin Laden, fit[ting] the image of a villain in popular Western imagination" (10). Much in the way Muslims receive disproportionate attention, nonstate terrorist groups also receive maximum opprobrium, while state terrorism is ignored. Thussu further posits that the news media spreads the myth of American morality; that US conceptions of democracy and human rights should be adopted across the globe (12–13).

However, while Thussu believes such myths are fully accepted by con-sumers, Virilio suggests that the news media—which, since "the 1920s, long before the New Deal . . . [have] lost their neutrality as they fell under the con-trol of industrial-commercial interests bent upon economic warfare" (Virilio, 23)—have historically been viewed with a certain measure of skepticism by audiences. The 2012 iteration of a Gallup poll running since 1997, which asks a random sampling of 1,017 American adults, "How much trust and confidence do you have in the mass media—as newspapers, TV, and radio—when it comes to reporting the news fully, accurately, and fairly?" (Morales), supports Virilio's suggestion. A record 60% of respondents answered "Not very much/None at all" (Morales). Further, when the poll's result history is considered, one notes that the most trust in the mass media that was ever indicated was in 2005, where 55% of respondents answered that they trusted it a "Great deal/Fair amount," meaning that even then, 44% of respondents that year had answered "Not very much/None at all" (Morales). The ability of the news media to influence opinions, thus, may be greatly overestimated.

As a post-9/11 text, *Code Geass* works within this climate of popular skepticism, presenting a constant and explicit renunciation of conventional metanarratives regarding terrorism. It presents a little narrative of the terrorist as an appealingly understandable, avenging hero figure. Alternatively, considering how the medieval romance's ethic of chivalry is co-opted into Lelouch's Black Knights terrorist cell, and how the series provides a new, larger-than-life dichotomy of heroes and villains, *Code Geass* is simultaneously also readable as prefiguring a new metanarrative regarding terrorism. Lelouch is an individual with the ability to influence society and rival governments, able to control his own destiny by opposing state forces. He is not a bearded Arab, but instead a Caucasian youth drawn in the fashion of East Asian characters, appealing to ethnicities within the global marketplace of anime fans. Rather than religious or insane, he is prefigured as a rational chessmaster. Finally, the idea that moral authority lies only with the state is disavowed in *Code Geass*; the government uses massacres and nuclear weapons to put down resistance. The subsequent retaliatory attacks of Lelouch and his Black Knights are cast as heroic endeavors. As a result, *Code Geass* offers its audiences a potent locus around which their skepticism toward the news media can be symbolically validated and celebrated.

SOMETHING FOR EVERYONE

The "Massacre of the Elevens" major plot arc toward the end of *Code Geass*'s first season most strikingly epitomizes *Code Geass*'s disengagement from news media metanarratives. In Episode 22, a maddened Britannian princess orders the massacre of Japanese civilians. The princess's aide signals the on-site news crew to "cut the mics and cameras, NOW!" In response, Lelouch's Black Knights hijack the feed to show the atrocity over live television and the Internet, aware that the state will be able to "cut off the broadcast any minute now." As a result, riots break out all over Japan. The state's leaders are thus represented as untrustworthy and genocidal maniacs all too willing to censor unwelcome information, while conventional news outlets are represented as the state's running dogs. *Code Geass* thus posits that it is only through the valiant efforts of terrorists that the abuses of the state (and its apparatus) can be exposed, and justice properly served.

The visual grammar of the scene encourages *Code Geass*'s audiences to adopt this disengagement. Long shots drawn at crowd level align audiences with their on-screen counterparts—viewers across Japan—who are confused and aghast at the images of wholesale carnage. When the scene shifts to the site of the massacre proper, this alignment is made more immediate. Audiences see close shots of dying civilians looking up to the camera, pitifully beseeching Lelouch to help them, for he is not part of the abusive state apparatus. Rather, as a severely-wounded Japanese grandmother babbles, he is "the Messiah of Japan . . . [their] only hope."

Yet such disengagement belies the fact that *Code Geass* was prefigured as a markedly commercial product-franchise. *Code Geass*'s narratives feature stock characters from disparate popular anime genres. Its terrorist-hero exists alongside European witches, *samurai*, knights, short-skirted schoolgirls, and animal mascots. All of these characters further interact with one another in archetypical anime situations ranging from duels on war-torn battlefields to romantic comedies in a high school classroom. Additionally, in an industry where visual spectacle is a key locus of pleasure for audiences, it is telling that the artist group CLAMP was contracted to design *Code Geass*'s characters. CLAMP is known for titles that have cross-gender appeal, depicting handsome men drawn in the flowing, ethereal art style of *shojo* ("young women," intended for female audiences), engaging in the kind of violence associated with *shonen* ("young men") manga. That *Code Geass* is filled with slender, young men (e.g., Lelouch) and with female characters who are either buxom pinups or waifish Lolitas suggests that its producers are tapping on CLAMP's successful track record of cross-gender visual appeal to attract varied audiences. CLAMP artist Ageha Okawa acknowledges tha Lelouch was created to be a character that would appeal to "everyone," and that *Code Geass* likewise was envisioned as a "hit" show that would similarly appeal to "everyone" (Newtype, 46). These are ideologies of commodity fetishism and scopophilia, which, in the form of supplementary merchandise, the producers of *Code Geass* literally encourage their audiences to buy into. These ideologies are far removed from the values of countercultural rebellion that the anime's narratives espouse.

THE WHITE KNIGHT

At the same time, the manner in which *Code Geass*'s producers position the text within the larger intertextual network of anime is also significant. *Code Geass* is often compared to the influential *Gundam* franchise. The *Gundam* franchise has endured for over three decades, and is popular worldwide. Its eponymous mecha are iconic not only within the giant robot genre, but also within the larger sphere of Japanese pop culture. For most audiences of anime, the mecha in *Gundam* stand for a particular and complex regime of heroism. The series is widely hailed as one of the first anime franchises to address themes of war and violence, for its heroes and villains both wax poetic upon the regrettable nature of war. Thus the *Gundam* franchise essentially provides a metanarrative regarding heroism within anime. The presence of mecha in *Code Geass* draws immediate comparison to *Gundam*, especially since the Knightmare units in *Code Geass* evince a visual and presentational similarity to *Gundam* mecha.

The Lancelot Knightmare, for example, features a bright and predominantly white color scheme, exaggerated weapons and shoulder armor, and a toyetic capability for baroque upgrades, which it manifests in the form of glowing angel wings. This draws upon the visual design conventions of mecha piloted by the heroes of over twenty iterations of the *Gundam* franchise. Further, both the Lancelot and the Gundam are presented as objects of spectacle. Beyond the lengthy fight scenes these mecha engage in, even their prefight "power up" sequences fetishize them appealingly. A typical "power up" sequence in *Code Geass* features the predeployment Lancelot posing dramatically directly toward the camera. This camera then essays lavishly animated pans and zooms onto various parts of the Lancelot's body as it whirrs into operation. The "power up" sequence climaxes with an explosive display of the Lancelot's power. It either fires its gun, or unfurls its wings, or blasts its jets. All this is set to increasingly high-tempo heroic music, and a verbal countdown that anticipates the Lancelot operating at full power. The Lancelot's pilot, similarly, epitomizes the *Gundam* franchise's conception of a hero. He is brave, capable, and loyal, yet secretly troubled by a dark past.

All of these intertextual references—the visual and the presentational—are particularly powerful, when one considers that in *Code Geass* the Lancelot is an antagonist. It is a creation of the Britannian Empire, and its *Gundam* pilot analog is Lelouch's rival and dramatic foil. The *mecha* that Lelouch and his followers use are, in contrast, squat, dark, and comparatively primitive. Their vaguely sinister appearance evokes the disposable mass-produced generic, bad-guy *mecha* that the hero-pilots of *Gundam* effortlessly cut down by the hundreds. Thus, the Lancelot's spectacular deployment on the battlefield ups the dramatic tension of the scenes for audiences with even a passing familiarity with anime: it seemingly presents insurmountable odds for Lelouch to overcome. But Lelouch often manages to defeat the Lancelot, despite his disadvantaged position, through the use of cunning tactics and planning. The dominant markers of pleasure and identification in anime are thus deliberately relocated in *Code Geass*. The Lancelot/Gundam might be a weapon of unmatched physical power, but Lelouch is repeatedly able to play its pilot, a *Gundam* analogue, for a fool. This is rhetoric that positively differentiates *Code Geass* from the overarching *Gundam* metanarrative franchise and iconography that *Code Geass* operates within. If *Gundam* is supposed to be complex, *Code Geass* is apparently much more so.

BLOCKBUSTER TERRORISM

Lyotard would have found *Code Geass*'s sustained disengagement with conventional metanarratives familiar. For him, the deployment of pastiche and iconoclasm within a contemporary text affords its producers a financially profitable advantage:

> Eclecticism is the degree zero of contemporary general culture: one listens to reggae, watches a western, eats McDonald's food for lunch and local cuisine for dinner, wears Paris perfume in Tokyo and "retro" clothes in Hong Kong.

... It is easy to find a public for eclectic works. ... But this realism of the "anything goes" is in fact that of money. ... Such realism accommodates all tendencies, just as capital accommodates all "needs," providing that the tendencies and needs have purchasing power. (Lyotard, 76)

While Lyotard was writing in the late 1970s, his findings anticipate Thomas Schatz's research on the structural qualities of the postmillennial Hollywood blockbuster. Schatz finds that with each passing year since the 1990s, "[Hollywood's] compulsive pursuit of franchise-spawning blockbusters has become more acute, and more successful" (25). As such, in postmillennial Hollywood, the term "blockbuster" has become synonymous with a commercially successful film that is the center of a multimedia event designed to market a wide variety of thematically related products to widely different audiences. In a hyper-fragmented global media marketplace, blockbuster film franchises now push classical genre conventions to absurd lengths, overtly incorporating elements from other genres, targeting mass audiences as opposed to niche ones. These blockbusters are spectacular serial narratives about the adventures of an iconoclastic male hero-figure, invariably featuring stylized PG-13 action sequences. Their storyworlds sacrifice theoretical depth for narrative complexity, so much so that a single film cannot resolve all plot threads. Supporting characters, consequently, can be profitably deployed to appear in "spin-off" supplementary texts even after the iconoclast-hero fights his way to a "happy ending" (Schatz, 32–33).

While *Code Geass* is a Japanese anime, it nonetheless exemplifies these blockbuster franchise conventions, combining elements of comedy and teenage romance with ostensibly political themes and stylized violence. It further centers these themes around a "terrorist" hero. Its sequels and spin-offs also focus on fleshing out its world. Despite Lelouch's resounding victory at the anime's end, Lelouch's sister stars in an ongoing manga series. The upcoming third season of the anime will be set during the events of the previous one, introducing new characters who will have adventures on a different continent.

In conclusion, the post-9/11 era has seen the plot device of terrorism gaining newfound prominence as another narrative thread within the spectacular and generically hybrid narratives of popular media such as *Code Geass*.

This producer strategy thus tenuously links these texts with a regime of relevance and sophistication, with an apparently engaged treatment of pressing contemporary concerns, and often with the ethos of skepticism that characterize the age. The present era is one where the specter of terrorism dominates daily life, with the next terrorist attack ever-looming over the horizon. Yet paradoxically, at the same time, many living in this climate of perpetual terror do not have an informed understanding of terrorism. For those who do not engage with academic discourse or even the news media, popular entertainment media depictions may well shape opinions regarding terrorism and related political issues.

Code Geass is an example of a multimedia franchise often characterized by its audiences as complex and sophisticated in its handling of political themes. But the overriding intent of texts like *Code Geass* is still to entertain rather than inform, meaning that their treatment of terrorism is stereotypical and at best cursory. This oversimplification of the complex political issue of terrorism for profitable consumption across a wide spectrum of audiences is what can be termed "blockbuster terrorism"; texts which operate in this mode invoke the iconography and plot device of terrorism for calculatedly commercial purposes. They are visually spectacular, generically hybrid, and have an appealing veneer of irreverent sophistication about them. But for all their sound and fury, these texts ultimately end up saying nothing worthwhile about terrorism at all.

WORKS CITED

Blakeley, Ruth. "State Terrorism in the Social Sciences: Theories, Methods and Concepts." In *Contemporary State Terrorism: Theory and Practice*, edited by Richard Jackson, Eamon Murphy, and Scott Poynting, 12–27. Abingdon: Routledge, 2010.

Byford, Grenville. "The Wrong War." *Foreign Affairs* 81, no. 4 (2002): 34–43.

Carothers, Rachael. "Hai Fidelity: Code Geass R2." *Anime News Network*. November 18, 2008. http://www.animenewsnetwork.com/hai-fidelity /2008-11-18.

Chapman, James. *War and Film*. London: Reaktion, 2008.

Code Geass. Season 1 and 2. Directed by Goro Taniguchi. Aired October 2006–September 2008. Tokyo: MBS.

Coker, Christopher. *Ethics and War in the 21st Century.* London: Routledge, 2008.

Cordesman, Anthony H. *Terrorism, Asymmetric Warfare, and Weapons of Mass Destruction: Defending the U.S. Homeland.* Westport: Praeger, 2002.

DeLillo, Don. *Falling Man.* New York: Scribner, 2007.

Derschowitz, Alan. *Why Terrorism Works.* New Haven: Yale University Press, 2002.

Ditzler, Thomas F. "Malevolent Minds." In *Understanding Terrorism,* edited by Fathali M. Moghaddam and Anthony J. Marsella, 187–206. Washington, DC: American Psychological Association, 2004.

Fromkin, David. "The Strategy of Terrorism." *Foreign Affairs* 53, no. 4 (1975): 683–98.

Gray, Colin S. "Thinking Asymmetrically in Times of Terror." *Parameters* 32, no. 1 (2002): 5–14. http://strategicstudiesinstitute.army.mil/pubs /parameters/Articles/02spring/gray.htm.

G.I. Joe. Directed by Stephen Sommers. Hollywood: Paramount Pictures Home Video, 2009. DVD.

Gundam 00. Directed by Seiji Mizushima. Aired October 2007–March 2009. Tokyo: MBS.

Klages, Mary. *Literary Theory.* New York: Continuum, 2007.

Laqueur, Walter. "Postmodern Terrorism." *Foreign Affairs* 75, no. 5 (1996): 24–36.

Luttwak, Edward N. 1995. "Toward Post-Heroic Warfare." *Foreign Affairs* 74, no. 3 (1995): 109–22.

Lyotard, Jean-Francois. *The Postmodern Condition: A Report on Knowledge.* Minneapolis: University of Minnesota Press, 1984.

Martin, Gus. *Understanding Terrorism.* London: Sage, 2003.

Morales, Lymari. "U.S Distrust in Media Hits New High." *Gallup.* September 21, 2012. http://www.gallup.com/poll/157589/distrust-media-hits-new -high.aspx.Newtype.

"Interview with Goro Taniguchi and Ageha Okawa, Head Writer of CLAMP." *Newtype.* May 2007, 45–50.

Rasmussen, Mikkel Vedby. *The Risk Society at War.* Cambridge: Cambridge University Press, 2006.

Schatz, Thomas. "New Hollywood, New Millennium." In *Film Theory and Contemporary Hollywood Movies*, edited by Warren Buckland, 19–46. New York: Routledge, 2009.

Thussu, Daya. "Televising the 'War on Terrorism': The Myths of Morality." In *Media, Terrorism, and Theory*, edited by Anadam P. Kavoori and Todd Fraley, 3–18. Lanham, MD: Rowman & Littlefield, 2006.

V for Vendetta. Directed by James McTeigue. Burbank: Warner Home Video, 2006.

Virilio, Paul. *War and Cinema*. New York: Verso, 2009.

Weinberg, Leonard. *Global Terrorism*. Oxford: Oneworld Publications, 2005.

Contributors

Hatem N. Akil teaches English at Seminole State College in Florida. He also taught digital media at the School of Visual Arts and Design at the University of Central Florida, and film production at American Intercontinental University. His research centers on visual and cultural theory within the contexts of Islam and the West. He received his PhD in texts and technology from the University of Central Florida. He studied theater at UCLA and the Academy of Dramatic Arts, in Damascus, Syria, and English and world literature at the University of Damascus. He is also the author of *The Visual Divide*, "Cinematic Terrorism," and "Murder of the Image."

Guillaume Ansart is an associate professor of French at Indiana University, Bloomington. His recent research has focused on the political culture of late eighteenth-century France, especially Raynal and Diderot's *Histoire des deux Indes* and Condorcet, whose writings on the United States he has edited and translated (both books published in 2012).

Ricardo Apostol is an assistant professor of classics at Case Western Reserve University. His research interests lie in the areas of Augustan literature, literary theory, and reception studies. His current projects include a book theorizing genre through an investigation of *Aeneid* 8, as well as articles on Ovid, Petrarch, Livy, and Virgil.

Louise Barnett is a professor of American studies at Rutgers, the State University of New Jersey. Among her books are *Atrocity and American Military Justice in Southeast Asia* (2010), *Ungentlemanly Acts: The Army's Notorious Incest Trial* (2000), and *Touched by Fire: The Life, Death, and Mythic Afterlife of George Armstrong Custer* (1996/2006). Her current project is a book on the marriages of six prominent, nineteenth-century American couples.

Jonathan Beever is an assistant professor of ethics and digital culture in the Department of Philosophy and the texts and technology program at the University of Central Florida. He received his PhD in philosophy from Purdue University in 2012 and held a postdoctoral research appointment funded by the National Science Foundation in biomedical engineering at Purdue and was a postdocotoral scholar at Penn State University's Rock Ethics Institute. Beever works primarily at the intersections of ethics, science, and the environment, and has interests in contemporary continental philosophy and semiotics.

Aaron Choo is a researcher at the Singapore Institute of International Affairs (SIIA) in the institute's Future 50 program, which explores emerging trends that may affect Asia in the coming decades. His current research interests include Japan-Asia relations, Asian regional integration, and online activism.

Sarah-Grace Heller is an associate professor of medieval French at the Ohio State University. She is the author of *Fashion in Medieval France* (2007) and articles on the Crusade Cycle, the *Roman de la Rose*, semiotics, and consumption.

Timothy Howe is an associate professor of history and ancient studies at St. Olaf College in Northfield, Minnesota. He is the author of *Pastoral Politics: Animals, Agriculture and Society in Ancient Greece* (2008), *All Things Alexander the Great* (2016), and editor of *Greece, Macedon and Persia: Studies in Social and Military History in Honour of Waldemar Heckel* (2014), *Traders in the Ancient Mediterranean* (2014), and *Brill's Companion to Insurgency and Terrorism in the Ancient Mediterranean* (2015).

Wilson Koh is a PhD candidate at the University of Queensland's school of English, Media Studies, and Art History. His dissertation examines how long-running television programs have adapted to the postbroadcast era. His current research interests include celebrity culture, commercial nationalism, and postmillennial media franchising.

Todd Kuchta is an associate professor of English at Western Michigan University and the author of *Semi-Detached Empire: Suburbia and the Colonization of Britain, 1880 to the Present* (2010). He is currently working on a book about terrorism and representations of history in modern British, postcolonial, and contemporary U.S. fiction.

Kenneth E. Noe is an assistant professor of philosophy at Harris-Stowe State University in St. Louis, Missouri. He holds a PhD in philosophy from Southern Illinois University Carbondale. He completed his master's degree at Loyola Marymount University in Los Angeles, California. His research lies in contemporary continental philosophy, social and political philosophy, and aesthetics. He is currently revising a book manuscript on Deleuze's inheritance of transcendental philosophy and its critical rehabilitation of the roles of habit and affect in the formation of epistemic and practical norms.

Jaume Martí-Olivella teaches in the languages, literatures, and cultures department at the University of New Hampshire. He cofounded CINE-LIT in 1991. He is also cofounder and former president of the North American Catalan Society (NACS). He is the author of *Basque Cinema: An Introduction* (2003) and coeditor of the volume *Spain is (Still) Different: Tourism and Discourse in Spanish Identity*. (2008). He has also coedited five CINE-LIT Proceedings. Currently, he is completing a manuscript on *Contemporary Catalan Cinema: Catalonia's New Gaze.*

Stella Setka holds a PhD in English from Purdue University. Her scholarship on ethnic American literature and women's studies has been published in journals such as *MELUS, Mosaic, American Periodicals*, and *Jewish Film & New Media*, and she is currently at work on a monograph that examines the role of the supernatural in cultural trauma narratives by black, Jewish, and Native American authors. Setka is a lecturer in Jewish Studies and the director of National & International Scholarships at Loyola Marymount University.

Roland Vazquez is a professor of social science and anthropology at Upper Iowa University in Fayette, Iowa. His research interests include Basque and Spanish politics, especially the links between institutional realities and culture. His book, *Politics, Culture, and Sociability in the Basque Nationalist Party* (2010), is an ethnographic study of partisan competition. He is currently working on an ethnography focusing on the political culture of post-terrorism in Basque society based on a 2009–2010 research sabbatical.

Harold Williford received his JD from New York University School of Law in 2013 and his BA in political science and French from Northwestern University in 2010. After graduating from law school, he worked as an associate at White & Case LLP in New York. From 2015 to 2016, he is a law clerk to the Honorable Nancy F. Atlas. The views expressed in his chapter are solely his own and were not written during the course of his legal employment.

Fabian Winkler is an artist working with the potential of new media technologies to create critical, transformative and sometimes playful cultural artifacts. He received degrees from the Staatliche Hochschule für Gestaltung ZKM in Karlsruhe, Germany and UCLA, Department of Design Media Arts. He is currently an associate professor in the area of electronic and time-based art at Purdue University.

Index